Immersion in the Visual Arts and Media

Studies in Intermediality

Executive Editor

Walter Bernhart (*Graz*)

Series Editors

Lawrence Kramer (*New York*)
Hans Lund (*Lund*)
Ansgar Nünning (*Gießen*)
Werner Wolf (*Graz*)

VOLUME 9

The titles published in this series are listed at *brill.com/siim*

Immersion in the Visual Arts and Media

Edited by

Fabienne Liptay
Burcu Dogramaci

BRILL
RODOPI

LEIDEN | BOSTON

Assistance to the editors, index of names: Patricia Vidovic.
Copyediting: Hayley Blair Haupt, Jessica Hoffmann.
Proofreading: Jessica Hoffmann.
Translations from German to English: Hayley Blair Haupt (Bauer, von Brincken, Dogramaci, Elsaesser, Liptay, Prümm), Rachel King (Krüger).
Book layout: Studio K:100 / Dominik Schwarz, Max Edelberg, assistance: Teresa Schwarz.
Cover design: Studio K:100 / Max Edelberg.
Printing funded by:

VolkswagenStiftung

LMU LUDWIG-MAXIMILIANS-UNIVERSITÄT MÜNCHEN

SPONSORED BY THE Federal Ministry of Education and Research

DAAD Deutscher Akademischer Austausch Dienst German Academic Exchange Service

Library of Congress Control Number: 2015952864

ISSN 1871-8787
ISBN 978-90-04-30819-0 (hardback)
ISBN 978-90-04-30823-7 (e-book)

Printed by Printforce, the Netherlands

Contents

Introduction

Burcu Dogramaci & Fabienne Liptay
Immersion in the Visual Arts and Media 1

Part 1: Materials and Sensations of Immersion

Burcu Dogramaci
Water, Steam, Light:
Artistic Materials of Immersion 21

Robin Curtis
Immersion and Abstraction as Measures of Materiality 41

Katja Kwastek
Immersed in Reflection?
The Aesthetic Experience of Interactive Media Art 67

Fabienne Liptay
Neither Here nor There:
The Paradoxes of Immersion 87

Jörg von Brincken
Phantom-Drug-Death Ride:
The Psycho-sensory Dynamic of Immersion in Gaspar Noé's *Enter the Void* 111

Part 2: Archaeologies and Technologies of Immersion

Karl Prümm
From the Unchained to the Ubiquitous Motion-Picture Camera:
Camera Innovations and Immersive Effects 139

Gundolf S. Freyermuth
From Analog to Digital Image Space:
Toward a Historical Theory of Immersion 165

Martin Warnke
On the Spot:
The Double Immersion of Virtual Reality 205

Ursula Frohne
Expansion of the Immersion Zone:
Military Simulacra between Strategic Training and Trauma 215

Thomas Elsaesser
Immersion between Recursiveness and Reflexivity: *Avatar* 251

Part 3: Landscapes and Architectures of Immersion

Henry Keazor
Projection Rooms:
Film as an Immersive Medium in the Architecture of Jean Nouvel ... 281

Ole W. Fischer
"The Treachery of Images":
Architecture, Immersion, and the Digital Realm 301

Matthias Krüger
Painting Immersion:
Hans Thoma's Landscapes 321

Matthias Bauer
Immersive Exhibition Design:
Titanic Belfast and the Concept of Scenography 345

Notes on Contributors 383

Index of Names 389

Introduction
Immersion in the Visual Arts and Media

Burcu Dogramaci & Fabienne Liptay

1. Liquidity and Liquefaction

In his text, "Liquid Architectures in Cyberspace", the artist Marcos Novak describes a digital architecture free from the rules of perspective, the laws of gravity, and the logic of Euclidean geometry. It is an architecture that yields to the forces of poetic fantasy, an architecture that is dematerialized and variable, which in the process of becoming, transforms and incorporates the fourth dimension of time. Novak summarizes all of these metaphorically ambivalent facets in the characteristics of liquid, which in this context also serves as a code for the digital: "I use the term liquid to mean animistic, animated, metamorphic, as well as crossing categorical boundaries, applying the cognitively supercharged operations of poetic thinking" (1991: 250).

The idea of liquidity and liquefaction informs wide areas of recent cultural imagination, referring to a myriad of phenomena that relate to experiences of uncertainty and instability, of complexity and change. As such, it is addressed in Zygmunt Bauman's concept of a "liquid modernity" that characterizes the "software era" (2000: 121) of disembodied labor in late global capitalism and has frequently been linked to the advent of digital media and the universal flow of data (see Bauman/Lyon 2013). Accordingly, the word 'immersion' and its use in the context of current media studies seem to be almost institutionally associated with digital media technologies. At the same time, however, the term 'immersion' (derived from the Latin 'immersio') may refer to any act or experience of plunging into something, without necessarily applying to computer-generated virtual environments. Due to the term's wide variety of uses, especially in the English language, a baptismal font or a swimming pool, a chemical solution or a medicinal bath, the shadow of a planet or a foreign language can equally serve as immersive 'media'.

Among other aspects, we are interested in the historical typifications that prefigured today's distinctly media-oriented understanding of immersion. Considering the fact that the concept of 'liquid' spaces appeared long before the digital creation of augmented or virtual environments, we are particularly interested in the question of where this concept can be found throughout the history of the visual arts and media. This entails searching history for the "operations of poetic thinking" (Novak 1991: 250) within which immersive spaces formed even before the invention of cyberspace. We envision a double perspective on the concept of immersion: firstly as it has developed in the theories of the arts and media and secondly as it is produced and reflected by the artworks themselves. Painting and architecture, photography and film, video installation and new media art are all remarkably rich in metareferential images of immersion (see Wolf, ed. 2009; 2011) that often draw on motifs such as water, bodily fluids, data streams, and wetware – cybernetic images in which the technical and the organic converge. At the same time, processes of dissolution and liquefaction emerge as motifs, which also serve to transgress spatial borders and to break out of the boundaries of Cartesian coordinates. The liquid aggregate state, into which images entered even before digitization, competes with the dominant concepts of the image as a window or a mirror (see *Illustrations 1* and *2*)[1]. These concepts imply a separation of the image space from the viewer through a material surface or pane. The anticipation and construction of liquid spaces that invite the viewer to immerse him- or herself eliminate this barrier and replace the separation between viewer and image with sen-

Illustration 1:
Film still from Orphée
(dir. Jean Cocteau, France 1949).

1 For an elaborate account of transparency (window) and reflection (mirror) as concepts that designate different forms of media experience, see Bolter/Gromala 2003.

Illustration 2:
Film still from Orphée
(dir. Jean Cocteau, France 1949).

sory, full-body experiences of artworks (cf. Papenburg 2011: 117f.). Occasionally, the concept of immersion also serves as a display onto which these artworks project their own media-specific techniques and potentials of addressing recipients and users. An example of this is the frequent visual or narrative portrayal of immersive scenarios, such as entering into a picture or a virtual matrix, often accompanied by an exploration of the representational or simulated space and its confusion with 'reality'. At the center of these metareferential scenarios is the idea of a liquefaction of space, which makes the experiences of 'immersing', 'melting', or 'plunging' into a medium possible in the first place.

Against this background, the leap into the liquid mirror made by the poet (Enrique Rivero) in Jean Cocteau's *The Blood of a Poet* (*Le sang d'un poète*, France 1930) is almost emblematic: since the Renaissance, the mirror has been a central metaphor for the picture and a recurring motif of pictorial self-awareness (cf. Stoichita 1997: 184f.). Not only do the tableau and the mirror share in mimetically replicating the world, they are also similar in the rectangular format of their display surfaces[2]. By no means does the liquefying mirror glass in Cocteau's film, which allows the poet to completely immerse himself in this medium (see *Illustration 3*), represent merely the discovery of a simple trick or a visually interesting motif with which to stage the act of crossing over into another world beyond this one. Rather, the notion still prevalent today in the European tradition of the picture as

2 In this same context, Victor I. Stoichita also refers to "the consubstantiality between 'mirror' and 'painting'" (1997: 190) ("la consubstantialité entre 'miroir' et 'tableau'"; 1993: 207).

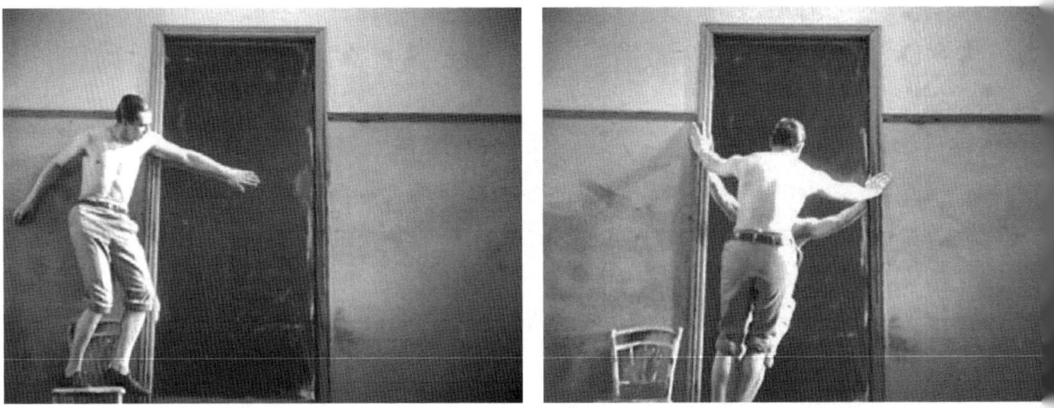

an impenetrable rectangular surface is put into question[3]. Even the poet believes that one cannot pass through a mirror before he tries and is shown otherwise[4]. In *Orpheus* (*Orphée*, France 1949), Cocteau once again varies the motif of the liquefying mirror, visualized by a vat of (poisonous) mercury into which Jean Marais dips his gloved hands (see *Illustration 4*)[5]. His reflection is visible in the surface of

3 See the legend of a Chinese painter who was so pleased with his painting that he disappeared into it. Béla Balázs writes, "such tales could never have been born in the minds of men brought up in European ideas of art. The European spectator feels the internal space of a picture as inaccessible, guarded by its own self-sufficient composition" (1952: 50).

4 See the comments in the screenplay as to the special effects used to achieve the mirror scene: "The mirror has been substituted by a tank of water, the setting is upside-down, the chair nailed on the left. This is all shot from above. The actor plunges. A quick cut back to the room as it was ends the illusion" (Cocteau 1970b: 21). ("On a substitute au miroir une cuve d'eau, fixé le décor dessus, cloué la chaise à gauche. L'appareil de prise de vues se trouve à pic sur le tout. L'acteur plonge. L'image redressée, vite coupée, terminera le trompe-l'œil"; 1957/1995: 1286).

5 In the screenplay, the scenes are described as follows: "She moves back with the young man just behind her. She goes quickly toward the mirror and passes through it with Cegestius. The mirror ripples like water" (Cocteau 1972: 117). ("La Princesse recule, le jeune home toujours à petite distance derrière elle. Elle avance très vite vers le miroir et y pénètre avec le jeune homme. Plan vu de l'intérieur du miroir qui ondule comme de l'eau"; 1950: n. p.). "Orpheus walks forward, his gloved hands extended toward the mirror. His hands touch the reflected hands in the mirror. [...] Orpheus walks through the mirror with his hands in front of him. The mirror shows the beginning of the Zone. Then the mirror reflects the room once more" (1972: 153). ("Orphée, les mains en avant, entre dans le miroir. Grand plan des mains qui pénètrant dans le miroir. [Fait dans une cuve de mercure.] On voit, dans le miroir, une ébauche de la zone où s'enfoncent Orphée et son guide. Puis l'image de la chambre s'y reforme"; 1950: n. p.).

Illustration 3:
Film stills from Le sang d'un poète
(dir. Jean Cocteau, France 1930).

the liquid metal before he immerses his fingertips. On the other side of the mirror, Orpheus finds a desolate landscape of ruins, a zone between life and death, haunted by the soul of a glass vendor, whom Cocteau, in his preface to the screenplay, describes as "the only one able to illustrate the saying that there is nothing so hard to break as the habit of one's job; since, although he died very young, he still persists in crying his wares in a region where windowpanes are meaningless" (1992: 157). In a figurative sense, however, the windowpane, like the mirror, can also be understood as an obsolete metaphor for the picture: as a relic of a world in which pictures were still impenetrable, framed surfaces (see *Illustration 3*)[6]. The association of the picture with the transparent but solid barrier of the window elaborately captures this idea of impenetrability even if linear perspective presupposes a spatial continuity that extends from the viewer's real space to the picture's representational space[7].

At the point where the mirror liquefies under the influence of "poetic thinking", a historical shift in the cultural imagination and con-

6 In his futuristic novel, *The Shape of Things to Come* (1933), on which the screenplay for the film *Things to Come* (dir. William Cameron Menzies, UK 1936) is based, H. G. Wells predicts that the "age of windows" would only last four centuries (qtd. Friedberg 2006: 133).

7 On the interplay of immersion and distance in the creation of aesthetic illusion, cf. Wolf 2013: 14f.

ceptualization of images is provoked[8]. It implies not only the dissolution of old classification systems, but also the invention and the establishment of new, previously unknown ones. Of course, it is only in retrospect that this shift may also be seen as an anticipation of virtual reality in which the surface of the picture transforms into an enterable space. In the words of Janet H. Murray, immersion, in this sense, not only relates to "the sensation of being surrounded by a completely other reality, as different as water is from air", but also entails "learning to swim" (1997: 99): to test the possibilities and limitations of media-based environments and to learn to master them. These are the kinds of digital 'swimming lessons' taken by the protagonist in the Wachowskis' film trilogy *The Matrix* (USA/Australia 1999–2003), Neo (Keanu Reeves), who lives within a simulated reality. In order to prove to him that the world he believes to be reality is actually nothing but a digital simulation, his mentor, Morpheus (Laurence Fishburne), liquefies a mirror. Here digital morphing enables the creation of the effect Cocteau was only able to achieve through the use of analog special effects. Transformed into a viscous

Illustration 4: Film still from Orphée *(dir. Jean Cocteau, France 1949).*

8 For Cocteau, the motifs of immersing and plunging are also metaphors for the 'sources' of artistic creativity: "In *The Blood of a Poet* I've tried to film poetry the way that the Williamson brothers filmed the bottom of the sea. It meant letting down the diver's bell deep inside me, like the diver's bell they let down deep into the sea. It meant capturing the poetic state" (1970a: 62). ("Dans *Le Sang d'un poète*, j'essaye de tourner la poésie, comme les frères Williamson tournent le fond de la mer. Il s'agissait de descendre en moi-même la cloche qu'ils descendent dans la mer, à de grandes profondeurs. Il s'agissait de surprendre l'état poétique"; 1932/1995: 1310). Further in the same text, Cocteau writes: "There is no film technique. There is the technique that each person discovers – you sink or swim. In the circumstances, you invent your own swimming style" (ibid.: 64). ("Il n'y a pas de technique du film. Il y a la technique que chacun se trouve. On se noie ou l'on nage. On invente par force son style de nageur"; ibid.: 1312).

state in-between the solid and the fluid[9], the mirror magnetically clings to Neo's hand as he touches it in disbelief. Upon touching it, his body also liquefies, melting into a liquid metal. Gradually Neo learns to see through the matrix, to perceive the numerical code as falling streams of green rain, and thereby to discover the limits once defined by frames and surfaces in the pre-digital age of pictures.

2. Unframing and Framing Aesthetic Experience

Most likely, there will never be a fully unframed cinematic image as Peter Weibel describes it in his vision of the "neurocinema" (1997; 2003): a 'technology of cerebral stimulation' ("Technologie der mentalen Stimulation"; 1997: 191)[10], in which the viewer constructs his or her own film, drawing from the variable data stored on a brain chip: "Instead of *trompe l'oeil*, the next step might be *trompe le cerveau* – the cinematographic apparatus will deceive the brain, not the eye, will steer and govern precisely pulsed neural networks with the help of molecular machines" (2003: 599). And yet these 'liquid visions' ("[l]iquide Visionen"; 1997: 194), as Weibel calls the pictures of the future, appear in the media discourse long before cybernetics pushes them toward what is technologically possible[11].

Peter Sloterdijk's remark that immersion "as a method unframes images and vistas, dissolving the boundaries with their environment" (2011: 105)[12] poses the question of how exactly this dissolving of boundaries manifests itself. The frame establishes a reassuring distance between the artwork and the viewer. In 1902, Georg Simmel wrote: "it [the frame] excludes all that surrounds it, and thus also the viewer as well, from the work of art, and thereby helps to place it at

9 In discussing this scene, Bettina Papenburg refers to Mary Douglas, who, in her study *Purity and Danger* (1966), pointed to the unsettling ambiguity of substances such as treacle that resist the classifications solid or liquid (cf. 2011: 121).

10 Unless otherwise indicated, all translations are ours.

11 Oliver Grau traces the history of immersion in art and media history back to antique murals such as the wall paintings in the Roman Villa dei Misteri near Pompeii, which eliminate the boundaries between the viewer's space and the illusory space of the painting (cf. 2003: 25).

12 "Immersion ist ein Entrahmungsverfahren für Bilder und Anblicke, die zur Umgebung entgrenzt werden" (Sloterdijk 2006: 58).

that distance from which alone it is aesthetically enjoyable" (1994: 11)[13]. The frame is, however, not only a kind of safety net preventing the viewer from confusing reality with the illusionism of the representation but also a "cognitive guide of interpretation" (Wolf 2006: 4) that provides historically and culturally shifting frames of reference. Despite cinema's continuing efforts to create enveloping experiences through large formats and wide screens, 3-D projection and digital surround sound[14] (see Recuber 2007), framings are still to be found in theater architecture, in the rectangular format of the screen that echoes the film's aspect ratio and the curtains and proscenium arch that mark the boundaries between screen and movie theater. As a representative of expanded cinema, Jeffrey Shaw even considers the correspondence between framed and frameless spaces as a constant within the history of cinema and its technological experiments. He sets the tendency to push the frame beyond the viewer's field of vision, to make it disappear in the expanded film spaces of CinemaScope, IMAX, or 3-D cinema, against the opposing tendency of accentuating the frame, which constantly throws the viewer back to the experience "that despite these expansive and sensational forms, such cinema remains what it was, a framed and contained space of removed experience" (2002: 269). In doing so, he does not understand the frame as merely the physical boundary of the image that separates it from its surroundings but as a tool to establish an aesthetic space of illusion, as is characteristic for classical and mainstream cinema. As opposed to the way it is commonly understood, 'immersion', in this context, does not appear as a sign of a particularly powerful aesthetic illusion (cf. Curtis 2008: 89) but as a keyword of the radical destruction of this illusion and with it the crossing of the boundaries of familiar visual experiences.

What is more interesting about Shaw's thoughts than the anti-Hollywood iconoclastic gestures of experimental film making is the circumstance that here, immersion is not understood as a form of enhancement but as the disruption of aesthetic illusion. Thus, it is about realigning the relationship between audience space and screen space in such a way "that the actuality of the viewing environment is thereby interpolated with the virtuality of the cinematic environment"

13 "Er [der Rahmen] schließt alle Umgebung und also auch den Betrachter vom Kunstwerk aus und hilft dadurch, es in die Distanz zu stellen, in der allein es ästhetisch genießbar wird" (Simmel 1902/1995: 101).

14 On the contribution of sound to the immersive experience, see Dyson 2009.

(Shaw 2002: 269). In this way, the viewer is challenged to relocate him- or herself in the spatial structure of the expanded cinema: "The goal is not the totalitarian spectacle that overwhelms and belittles the viewer, rather it is the sublime demonstration that affirms each viewer's unique position and critical relationship to the representation" (ibid.: 271). From here, unusual perspectives on the discussion of immersive art and media practices open up that allow the importance of the actual viewing environment to come into view. This occurs precisely at the point at which, with regard to definition, the maximal displacement of the surroundings from the viewer's field of perception is claimed and associated with a lessening of the viewer's ability to remain at a critical distance (see Grau 2001 and 2003; 2005)[15].

Rather than adhering to such cultural pessimism, which only reverses the narrative of technological progress by replacing it with that of an irreversible decline, we would like to propose an alternative approach that takes into consideration the variability and complexity of immersive experiences according to their specific contexts. For even if aesthetic experiences increasingly appear to be 'unframed', works of art are still 'framed' by the context of their reception, which positions viewers within a network of architectural and technological, institutional and economical, cultural and social determinants. For this reason, we would like to question the prevalent idea of a loss of critical distance in the confrontation with pictures that physically and emotionally involve the viewer. Pictures call upon our sense of responsibility and power of judgment at precisely the point at which we completely immerse ourselves in them and risk getting in touch with the object of our intellectual contemplation[16]. As surfers, divers, and swimmers, we may not – or rather no longer – maintain a proper distance from works of art and media, but we are still free to position ourselves in relation to them, to act within them, to actively participate in them, or to simply step out of them[17].

15 "Immersion can be an intellectually stimulating process; however, in the present as in the past, in most cases immersion is mentally absorbing and a process, a change, a passage from one mental state to another. It is characterized by diminishing critical distance to what is shown and increasing emotional involvement in what is happening" (Grau 2003: 13).

16 On the pre-discursive quality of immersion and the challenges and phantasmatic threats it poses for theoretical contemplation, see Grizelj/Jahraus/Prokić 2014.

17 On the role of participation in the context of immersion, cf. Sloterdijk 2007: 288–293.

3. Textual and Contextual Effects of Immersion

For this reason, it seems even more urgent to us to reconstruct the historical discourse of immersion along the media interfaces that regulate the real or imaginary practices of media use in dealing with "cultural data" (Manovich 2001: 80). This should by no means imply a focus on the technological and instrument-based factors that enable immersive experience. Rather, we understand immersion as the result of a complex framework of reception within which the interface functions as the actual site of historically shifting relations between media and users. On the assumption that the conflicting interpolation of the real and artificial environments is to be seen as being practically constitutive for the creation of immersive media offerings, this book focuses on an aspect that, in the research discourse, is marginal at best.

If one calls to mind, for example, the light rooms of Dan Flavin, Olafur Eliasson, or James Turrell, it becomes evident that, so far, predominantly phenomenological methods have been decisive in experiments. From here, one could certainly ask whether these rooms shaped and ultimately configured by light also have an intense immersive effect on visitors precisely because the viewers' destabilization and confusion, especially with regard to architectural concepts, are described as being characteristic of an immersive design (cf. Falkenhausen 2008: 136f.). As these examples show, the creation of immersive experiences is, to a considerable degree, dependent on the spatial parameters that can be inherent to the work itself or subsequently assigned to it. At the 2013 Berlinale, the participatory installations by the Brazilian artist Hélio Oiticica were shown in the Liquidrom, a wellness pool in which festival visitors in swimsuits could dive and listen to the sounds of John Cage underwater while the collaborative project created with Neville D'Almeida, *CC4 Nocagions* from the series *Block-Experiments in Cosmococa – program in progress* (Brazil/USA 1973), could be seen as a slide show projected in the dome. The organizers complied not only with the deceased artist's instructions, which stipulated that the viewers should see the projection from the pool (cf. Basualdo 2001: 114), but also with his concept, which falls under the term 'quasi-cinema', of sensorially expressing a melding of everyday experience and art (cf. Buchmann/Hinderer Cruz 2013: 46f.). In the digital age, this idea has been updated insofar as it allows for the present forms of a "relocation" (Casetti 2012) of film beyond cinema to be put in a historical perspective and the history of post-cinema to be written.

This book is part of a series entitled *Studies in Intermediality* (SIM), dedicated to the intermedia study of aesthetic phenomena. Its objective is to examine aesthetic concepts that maintain their relevance past the boundaries of various media. At the same time, these studies, in a particular way, demand that the media-related differences be acknowledged. In this context, the term 'immersion' presents a special challenge, because its almost inflationary use is accompanied by the problem of drawing the boundaries of its application with regard to its definition. In the broadest sense, 'immersion' describes a sensation that can equally arise while reading a book, watching a film, visiting an exhibition, or playing a computer game, namely, the impression of being placed in or surrounded by the space artificially created by the respective medium. This impression can be summoned by addressing both our perceptual apparatus as well as our imagination – two examples of entirely different modes of aesthetic experience[18]. The breadth of this spectrum is already suggested in the definition of 'immersion' in question, which Janet H. Murray expresses as a perceptual sensation "of being surrounded by a completely other reality" (1997: 98), while Marie-Laure Ryan understands it as a mental act by which "consciousness relocates itself to another world" (2001: 103). As an almost ubiquitous phenomenon (cf. Curtis/Voss 2008: 4), immersion can result from the various forms of psychological and perceptual relocation in the fictional or factual worlds created by the arts and media; it, thus, serves as a rather flexible term to address different experiences in different media environments. The argument that 'immersion' is more or less "an excessively vague, all-inclusive concept" (McMahan 2003: 67) also implicitly states the dilemma that a supposedly transmedia phenomenon must be transferable to the perceptual conditions of various media. The objective of this book is thus not to attempt to establish another definition of 'immersion' but to put the sustainability of the concept to the test in concrete case studies. In this collection of essays, immersion often proves to be less of a heuristic tool set than a vague horizon of universal fantasies about the melding of human and medium, from which every observation of historically

18 On the necessity to distinguish between perceptual and psychological immersion, cf. Thon 2008: 31.

concrete relationships has to differentially break away. In this sense, the concept of immersion can establish an experimental design that serves the exploration of a permanently shifting relationship between media and their users.

In the process, this book can also build upon the preliminary works that have appeared in the series *Studies of Intermediality*. In particular, it aims to draw on the volume *Immersion and Distance* (SIM 6), edited by Werner Wolf, Walter Bernhart, and Andreas Mahler. In this book, the aesthetic illusion is understood, in connection with Kendall L. Walton (cf. 1990: 273), as the result of an interaction between critical distance and complete immersion, as a reception attitude toward fictional and factual representations that oscillates between perception 'from without' and perception 'from within' (cf. Wolf 2013: 16f.)[19]. This attitude is the result of both textual as well as contextual factors that regulate the recipient's willing suspension or construction of disbelief (cf. ibid.: 23; with references to Coleridge 1817/1965: 169; and Gerrig 1993: 230). Especially with regard to the importance that is given to the configuration of these multifaceted factors, this book can profit from and contribute to the theoretical debate on aesthetic illusion. For while the success of aesthetic illusion is essentially linked to the creation of a "sense of probability and life-likeness" (Wolf 2013: 25) that accounts for the picture's or text's "reading in terms of natural objects" (Gombrich 1960/2000: 360), the discussion of concrete examples documented here has shown that, in the case of immersion, the representational dimensions are far less pivotal than the experiential dimensions: the matrix of textual and contextual effects that allows for an involvement with, participation in, or appropriation of the media or artwork[20]. Moreover, as to the question of the abilities of media to reflect their own potential, connections to the two volumes *Metareference across Media* (SIM 4) and *The Metareferential Turn in Contemporary Arts and Media* (SIM 5) have also arisen.

Taking an interdisciplinary approach, this book brings together contributions by representatives from different disciplinary fields for a multidimensional view on immersion in the visual arts and media. It is organized into three sections dealing with the aspects of "materials

19 For a general theory of aesthetic illusion, see Wolf 1993; Koch/Voss, eds. 2006.

20 For a differentiation between "*representational* realism" and "*experiential* realism" in the context of immersion, cf. Griffiths 2008: 285 [emphases in the original].

and sensations", "archaeologies and technologies", and "landscapes and architectures" of immersion. In looking into the history of immersive media technologies, the authors of this volume generally approach immersion as a "cultural topos" (Huhtamo 1995: 160f.; see also 2011) and trace the kinds of fears and desires hidden within its ideological manifestations. To rephrase a formula by Janet H. Murray, "the exploration of the border between the representational world and the actual world" (1997: 103) could be the motto for this volume's search for boundary crossings. What varying scenarios of thresholds and transitions exist? How do theses scenarios relate to the different media that are considered as particularly immersive? And what are the ideological and historical preconditions that allow for their re-emergence in different times and places?

The present volume documents and enlarges the discussions of an interdisciplinary conference on immersion that the editors organized in the summer of 2011 at the University of Munich. We would like to thank the authors for their contributions to this volume and their patience during the editing process. In addition, we would like to thank Hayley Blair Haupt for the thoughtful translation of the majority of the texts included in this volume, Jessica Hoffmann for the efficient and careful proofreading of the manuscript, and Patricia Vidovic for her enduring assistance in copyediting. The publication of this book would not have been possible without their invaluable support and professional work. Last but not least, sincere thanks are given to the editors of the series *Studies in Intermediality,* Werner Wolf and Walter Bernhart, who not only willingly accepted our manuscript for publication but also saw through all phases of the editing process in matters of formal presentation and scholarly content. The preparation of the publication was generously funded by the Volkswagen Foundation (VolkswagenStiftung) and the German Academic Ex-change Service (DAAD) from subsidies granted by the Federal Ministry of Education and Research (BMBF). For additional financial support we would like to thank the Faculty of History and the Arts, School of Arts (University of Munich), especially Regina Wohlfarth, who supported this interdisciplinary endeavor from its very beginnings.

This volume is dedicated to her.

References

Balázs, Béla (1948). *Filmkultúra: A film müvészetfilozófiája*. Budapest: Szikra.

— (1952). *Theory of the Film: Character and Growth of a New Art*. Transl. Edith Bone. London: Dobson.

Basualdo, Carlos (2001). *Hélio Oiticica: Quasi-Cinemas*. Exh. cat. Columbus, OH: Wexner Center for the Arts, 18 September – 30 December 2001. Ostfildern-Ruit: Hatje Cantz.

Bauman, Zygmunt (2000). *Liquid Modernity*. Cambridge/Malden, MA: Polity Press.

—, David Lyon (2013). *Liquid Surveillance: A Conversation*. Cambridge/Malden, MA: Polity Press.

Bolter, Jay David, Diane Gromala (2003). *Windows and Mirrors: Interaction Design, Digital Art, and the Myth of Transparency*. Cambridge, MA/London: MIT Press.

Buchmann, Sabeth, Max Jorge Hinderer Cruz (2013). *Hélio Oiticica and Neville D'Almeida: Block-Experiments in Cosmococa – program in progress*. London: Afterall Books.

Casetti, Francesco (2012: online). "The Relocation of Cinema". *Necsus*. http://www.necsus-ejms.org/the-relocation-of-cinema/. [26/09/2014].

Cocteau, Jean (1932/1995). "*Le sang d'un poète*: Postface". *Romans, poésies, œuvres diverses*. Paris: Le Livre de Poche. 1309–1315.

— (1950). *Orphée: Film*. Paris: Editions de La Parade.

— (1957/1995). "*Le sang d'un poète* (scénario)". *Romans, poésies, œuvres diverses*. Paris: Le Livre de Poche. 1277–1308.

— (1970a). "*The Blood of a Poet*: Postscript". *Two Screenplays: The Blood of a Poet. The Testament of Orpheus*. Transl. Carol Martin-Sperry. London/New York, NY: Calder & Boyars. 61–67.

— (1970b). "*The Blood of a Poet*: Screenplay". *Two Screenplays: The Blood of a Poet. The Testament of Orpheus*. Transl. Carol Martin-Sperry. London/New York, NY: Calder & Boyars. 8–60.

— (1972). *Three Screenplays: L'eternel retour, Orphée, La belle et la bête*. Transl. Carol Martin-Sperry. New York, NY: Grossman.

— (1992). "*Orphée*". *The Art of Cinema*. Eds. André Bernard, Claude Gauteur. Transl. Robin Buss. London/New York, NY: Marion Boyars. 155–160.

Coleridge, Samuel Taylor (1817/1965). *Biographia Literaria*. Ed. George Watson. London: Dent.

Curtis, Robin (2008). "Immersion und Einfühlung: Zwischen Repräsentation und Materialität bewegter Bilder". *montage AV* 17/2: 89–107.

—, Christiane Voss (2008). "Theorien ästhetischer Immersion". *montage AV* 17/2: 4–10.

Dyson, Frances (2009). *Sounding New Media: Immersion and Embodiment in the Arts and Culture*. Berkeley/Los Angeles, CA: University of California Press.

Falkenhausen, Susanne von (2008). *KugelbauVisionen: Kulturgeschichte einer Bauform von der Französischen Revolution bis zum Medienzeitalter*. Bielefeld: transcript.

Friedberg, Anne (2006). *The Virtual Window: From Alberti to Microsoft*. Cambridge, MA/London: MIT Press.

Gerrig, Richard J. (1993). *Experiencing Narrative Worlds: On the Psychological Activities of Reading*. New Haven, CT: Yale UP.

Gombrich, E. H. (1960/ 2000). *Art and Illusion: A Study in the Psychology of Pictorial Representation*. Princeton, NJ/Oxford: Princeton UP.

Grau, Oliver (2001). *Virtuelle Kunst in Geschichte und Gegenwart: Visuelle Strategien*. Berlin: Reimer.

— (2003). *Virtual Art: From Illusion to Immersion*. Transl. Gloria Custance. Cambridge, MA/London: MIT Press.

— (2005). "Immersion & Emotion: Zwei bildwissenschaftliche Schlüsselbegriffe". Oliver Grau, Andreas Keil, eds. *Mediale Emotionen: Zur Lenkung von Gefühlen durch Bild und Sound*. Frankfurt am Main: Fischer. 70–106.

Griffiths, Alison (2008). *Shivers Down Your Spine: Cinema, Museums, and the Immersive View*. New York, NY: Columbia UP.

Grizelj, Mario, Oliver Jahraus, Tanja Prokić (2014). *Vor der Theorie: Immersion – Materialität – Intensität*. Cologne: Königshausen & Neumann.

Huhtamo, Erkki (1995). "Encapsuled Bodies in Motion: Simulators and the Quest for Total Immersion". Simon Penny, ed. *Critical Issues in Electronic Media*. New York, NY: State University of New York Press. 159–186.

— (2011). "Media Archaeology as Topos Study". Erkki Huhtamo, Jussi Parikka, eds. *Media Archaeology: Approaches, Applications, and Implications*. Berkeley/Los Angeles, CA: University of California Press.

Koch, Gertrud, Christiane Voss, eds. (2006). *... kraft der Illusion*. Munich: Fink.

Manovich, Lev (2001). *The Language of New Media*. Cambridge, MA/London: MIT Press.

McMahan, Alison (2003). "Immersion, Engagement, and Presence: A Method for Analyzing 3-D Video Games". Mark J. P. Wolf, Bernard Perron, eds. *The Video Game Theory Reader*. Vol. 1. New York, NY/London: Routledge. 67–87.

Murray, Janet H. (1997). *Hamlet on the Holodeck: The Future of Narrative in Cyberspace*. New York, NY: The Free Press.

Novak, Marcos (1991). "Liquid Architectures in Cyberspace". Michael Benedikt, ed. *Cyberspace: First Steps*. Cambridge, MA/London: MIT Press. 225–254.

Papenburg, Bettina (2011). "Touching the Screen, Striding Through the Mirror: The Haptic in Film". Stefanie Kiwi Menrath, Alexander Schwinghammer, eds. *What Does a Chameleon Look Like? Topographies of Immersion*. Cologne: Halem. 113–136.

Recuber, Tim (2007). "Immersion Cinema: The Rationalization and Reenchantment of Cinematic Space". *Space and Culture* 10/3: 315–330.

Ryan, Marie-Laure (2001). *Narrative as Virtual Reality: Immersion and Interactivity in Literature and Electronic Media.* Baltimore, MD: Johns Hopkins UP.

Shaw, Jeffrey (2002). "Movies after Film: The Digitally Expanded Cinema". Martin Rieser, Andrea Zapp, eds. *New Screen Media: Cinema/Art/Narrative*. London: British Film Institute. 268–275.

Simmel, Georg (1902/1995). "Der Bildrahmen: Ein ästhetischer Versuch". *Aufsätze und Abhandlungen 1901–1908*. Vol. 1. Eds. Rüdiger Kramme, Angela Rammstedt, Otthein Rammstedt. Frankfurt am Main: Suhrkamp. 101–108.

— (1994). "The Picture Frame: An Aesthetic Study". *Theory, Culture & Society* 11/1: 11–17.

Sloterdijk, Peter (2006). "Architektur als Immersionskunst". *Arch+* 178: 58–61.

— (2007). *Der ästhetische Imperativ*. 2nd ed. Hamburg: Philo & Philo Fine Arts.

— (2011). "Architecture as an Art of Immersion". Transl. A.-Chr. Engels-Schwarzpaul. *Interstices* 12: 105–109.

Stoichita, Victor I. (1993). *L'instauration du tableau: Métapeinture à l'aube des temps modernes*. Paris: Méridiens Klincksieck.

— (1997). *The Self-Aware Image: An Insight into Early Modern Meta-Painting*. Transl. Anne-Marie Glasheen. Cambridge: CUP.

Thon, Jan-Noël (2008). "Immersion Revisited: On the Value of a Contested Concept". Olli Leino, Hanna Wirman, Amyris Fernandez, eds. *Extending Experiences: Structure, Analysis and Design of Computer Game Player Experiences*. Rovaniemi: Lapland UP. 29–43.

Walton, Kendall L. (1990). *Mimesis as Make-Believe: On the Foundations of the Representational Arts*. Cambridge, MA: Harvard UP.

Weibel, Peter (1997). "Neurocinema: Zum Wandel der Wahrnehmung im technischen Zeitalter". Brigitte Felderer, ed. *Wunschmaschine Welterfindung: Eine Geschichte der Technikvisionen seit dem 18. Jahrhundert*. Vienna/New York, NY: Springer. 167–184.

— (2003). "The Intelligent Image: Neurocinema or Quantum Cinema?" Jeffrey Shaw, Peter Weibel, eds. *Future Cinema: The Cinematic Imaginary After Film*. Exh. cat. Karlsruhe: ZKM, 16 November 2002 – 30 March 2003. Cambridge, MA/London: MIT Press. 594–601.

Wolf, Werner (1993). *Ästhetische Illusion und Illusionsdurchbrechung in der Erzählkunst: Theorie und Geschichte mit Schwerpunkt auf englischem illusionsstörenden Erzählen*. Tübingen: Niemeyer.

— (2006). "Introduction: Frames, Framings and Framing Borders in Literature and Other Media". Werner Wolf, Walter Bernhart, eds. *Framing Borders in Literature and Other Media*. Studies in Intermediality 1. Amsterdam/New York, NY: Rodopi. 1–40.

, ed. (2009). *Metareference across Media: Theory and Case Studies*. Studies in Intermediality 4. Amsterdam/New York, NY: Rodopi.

—, ed. (2011). *The Metareferential Turn in Contemporary Arts and Media: Forms, Functions, Attempts at Explanation*. Studies in Intermediality 5. Amsterdam/New York, NY: Rodopi.

— (2013). "Aesthetic Illusion". Werner Wolf, Walter Bernhart, Andreas Mahler, eds. *Immersion and Distance: Aesthetic Illusion in Literature and Other Media*. Studies in Intermediality 6. Amsterdam/New York, NY: Rodopi. 1–88.

Part 1:
Materials and Sensations of Immersion

Illustrations 1 and 2:
Film stills from Björk, "Wanderlust" *(2007).*
Music video by Encyclopedia Pictura.

Water, Steam, Light
Artistic Materials of Immersion

Burcu Dogramaci

In 1968, in the catalogue of the Philadelphia Arts Council's exhibition *Air Art*, Willoughby Sharp wrote: "[...] one of the primary accomplishments of the new art is that it has enabled the spectator to feel more a part of his physical environment. He actually can enter the work." To take this idea of the activation of the art viewer further, the term 'immersion' – the plunging into perceptual worlds – must be adapted for installation art. In this context, this essay examines the immersive qualities of various materials; the main focus will be placed on water, steam, and fog. Here, the examination of the viewer's relation to the work, material, and body is of particular importance. To what extent is a material responsible for the breaking down of barriers, the dissolution of transitions, and thereby for pulling the viewer into the work?

1. Water Images

Immersion is often related to the impression of being drawn into the world of the text (cf. Neitzel/Nohr 2006: 16) or to the metaphorical act of 'diving into' fictional or factual worlds (cf. Wolf 2013: 32f.). In this way, it is placed in the context of video games or 3-D animation (see Thon 2008). Perceptive, psychological, and spatial immersion have been intensely discussed by researchers[1]. In addition, there are models of narrative and social[2] immersion that may be important to the act of diving into fictional worlds. It is interesting that, while materials have attracted attention in the discourses surrounding immersion, the focus has almost exclusively been placed on the fluid medium of water in film with regard to aesthetic- and narrative-related questions (see Heller 2010). In material iconography – a field of research established by the art historian Monika Wagner from Hamburg (see 2001) – the immersive qualities of

1 Here, 'perceptive immersion' refers to a superimposition of the perception of reality. According to the current definition held by researchers, so-called psychological immersion describes the shift of the recipients' attention to media content, such as computer games, films, and the like (cf. McMahan 2003: 77f.; cf. also Thon 2008: 31f.).

2 This is in reference to the player's and his or her alter ego's communication skills.

materials are taken into account; however, they are not the focus. Rather, materials are analyzed within the context of the changing and expanding definition of art in the 20th century. In light of the fact that a survey of immersive materials has yet to be compiled, this essay will provide an initial perspective and address the immersive qualities of materials such as water, light, and mist (these materials were selected knowing full well that oil, quicksilver, and bodily fluids could have been discussed as well). Here, the illustrated or virtually generated material has been placed at the beginning of the examination so that the immersive effects of the materials mentioned in installations without a cinematic or electronic component can subsequently be discussed.

'Wanderlust' is defined as a "strong desire for travel" (*Oxford Dictionaries* 2013). As a German loanword, 'wanderlust' has been used in English since 1902 to describe what is considered a typically German characteristic – the desire for and enjoyment of hiking – and supposedly refers back to the Romantic era. 'Wandern' itself is the act of physically moving through a landscape, not strolling, but powerfully, rapidly walking in nature. "Wanderlust" is also the name of a single by the Icelandic singer Björk from her studio album *Volta*, released in 2007. Björk begins her song with the words, "I am leaving this harbor", thereby clarifying that, here, she is not referring to a means of traveling on foot. In another line, she sings, "Sailing into nature's laws and be held by ocean's paws". Björk already projects the metaphor of water onto the term 'wanderlust' in her lyrics. In the song's music video, Encyclopedia Pictura, an animation studio, transfers Björk's "Wanderlust" into a fantastical, primeval context. Björk appears in Mongolian attire as the shepherd of a herd of yaks (see *Illustration 1*), setting off on a journey down a raging river. In this music video, water serves as a means of transportation and a mystical place in which Björk encounters the 'pain-body' that grows out of her backpack – an attribute of the traveler/hiker. The video flows into an encounter with a water deity who creates a waterfall.

The pull that the animated water (see *Illustration 2*) in the "Wanderlust" music video seems to exert on the viewer is certainly also due to the perspective he or she is given. The viewer is positioned on the same side as the travelers and follows the raging river that is depicted in one-point perspective flowing into a fantasy landscape; the beats of the electronic music also course along. The journey down the river and the motif of travel are well established in the cinematic theory of immersion. In this context, Marie-Laure Ryan talks about a "space-travel-mode" (2001:

Illustration 3:
Animation still showing moving hair (2005).
3-D computer graphics by Softimage/XSI.

103), a manner of travel in which consciousness crosses over into the other world of the film.

For the video, Encyclopedia Pictura constructed a life-size yak out of modeling clay that was operated by two people. The yak was filmed from various perspectives and digitally multiplied to create the herd (see McGorry 2008). Björk's archaic outfit was, in fact, also handmade. The river itself, however, which she creates by digging a path through the earth, was created and animated by a computer program called Softimage/XSI-Hair (see Bayne et al. 2005) that was developed to generate human hair or animal fur (see *Illustration 3*). For this video, they worked with a total of 37 water shots. It is amazing that a program designed to depict hair was used to simulate water. An art-historical connection between water and hair can particularly be found in the art of the 19th century, such as in John Everett Millais's *Ophelia* (1851–1852) and John William Waterhouse's *Undine* (1872). It is presumably this very association of a powerful current with the flowing of long hair that contributes to viewers' intense involvement in Björk's 3-D music video and their ability to immerse themselves in this fantastic landscape with the strange eschatological cast of characters. Next to the main character, the singer, the water is a central protagonist in the video; it seems virile and develops its own dynamic. It is noteworthy that, although water is employed here as a predestined immersive material, it is not shown as being transparent and light but is given a physical appearance. This computer-generated water plays a decisive role in shaping the video's dramaturgy.

Whereas simulated water is seen in Björk's music video, in his piece *Bondi Beach* (see *Illustration 4*) Beat Streuli works with projected photographs of the beach and the ocean that are orchestrated in a darkened room using a cross-fade technique and accompanied by corresponding background noises. For this, Streuli uses photographs that he arranges into groups, whereby the cross-fade technique creates a state between static and moving image. The movement here does not appear smooth, but discontinuous. The arrangement of the projections on several walls in the room places viewers directly in the center of events. The water seems to be in motion; in addition, the pictures look

Illustration 4:
Beat Streuli, Bondi Beach *(1999).*
Five-screen slide installation.

as though they are emitting their own light (cf. Pfab 1999: 7), which strengthens the impression of movement. The surf and the people involved in actions within it surround the visitors; even the clearly audible switching of slides does not disrupt viewers from immersing themselves in *Bondi Beach.* On the contrary, viewers are clearly aware of their exclusion from what is being viewed. However, this very awareness of being outside allows for the relaxed, extensive viewing of the bodies in the water. In the context of cinematic immersion, this rational realization of the distance between the viewer and that which he or she is viewing is not considered by some authors to be an underlying reason for a successful immersion. In this regard, I would agree with Christiane Voss's thesis that, in an immersive experience, consciousness is not turned off or trapped (see 2009)[3].

3 An opposing standpoint that declares film and the video game as completely absorbing instruments of seduction is often found. See, for example, Boris Groys, who writes: 'At the movie theater, viewers are transported into a situation of absolute powerlessness, paralysis, physical immobility. In the case of a regular film screening, the cinematic image is the only thing moving, temporally developing, whereby the viewers remain passive. For the viewers, the movement of the cinematic image replaces the movement of thought and language. The viewers are not only physically but mentally immobilized – they are, as many say, internally "bound" by the film and, through this, transform themselves into mental robots in whose heads a program predetermined from the outside is played. […] During this time, the moviegoers are ripped out of the usual milieu in which they live, the course of their lives interrupted; they lose control of their attention and their freedom of movement.' Unless otherwise indicated, all translations are mine. ("Beim Kinobesuch wird der Betrachter nämlich in die Situation der absoluten Ohnmacht, der Paralyse, der körperlichen Immobilität versetzt. Bei der üblichen Filmvorführung ist es allein das Kinobild, das sich bewegt, sich zeitlich entfaltet, wobei der Betrachter passiv

Even if only an imagined immersion in water takes place, one associates the stored experience of body-water contact with the image of flowing water. Hellmut Stoffer examined these water feelings, in other words, the evocation of emotions through interactions with fluidity, in his study on the magic of water (cf. 1966: 126–130). With regard to the transfer of what has been seen to memories of what has been experienced and felt – as a continuation of the concepts of Gaston Bachelard (see 1983) and Hartmut Böhme (1988: 22) – one could speak of an 'imagology', the migration of experiences in the outside world into processes of the imagination via the element of water. Hereby, an original experience of contact with water also plays into the imagination: in the context of diving or scuba diving, immersion refers to a reflex that all mammals share. As soon as a mammal's cheeks come into contact with water, its body reacts by reorganizing its supply of oxygen and slowing down its heartbeat so the use of oxygen can be reduced (see Pelzer 1996). In his book *Schwimmen*, the novelist John von Düffel describes the fusion between the crawling swimmer and the water surrounding him:

> My horizon is water itself, its depth and the dreamscape of its floor. I no longer separate air and water; I have become part of the water world. And when I take a breath, I try to close the side that is open as much as possible; I only breathe through a thin, disappearing slit, through the crack in a door that I slammed behind me. I enjoy being surrounded by water, for that is the goal of my path: not to touch the pool's edge, to reach the shore or any other kind of land, but to become one with water and motion, to belong to this element. I strive to be the same as water.[4]

---

bleibt. Die Bewegung des Kinobildes ersetzt beim Betrachter die Bewegung des Denkens und der Sprache. Der Betrachter wird nicht nur physisch, sondern auch geistig immobilisiert – er wird, wie man so sagt, innerlich vom Film 'gefesselt' und verwandelt sich dadurch in einen geistigen Automaten, in dessen Kopf ein ihm von außen vorgegebenes Programm abläuft. […] Während dieser Zeit wird der Kinobesucher aus seinem üblichen Lebensmilieu herausgerissen, der Verlauf seines Lebens wird unterbrochen, er verliert die Kontrolle über seine Aufmerksamkeit und seine Bewegungsfreiheit"; 1999: 16).

4 "Mein Horizont ist das Wasser selbst, seine Tiefe und die Traumlandschaft des Grundes. Ich trenne Luft und Wasser nicht mehr, ich bin ein Teil der Wasserwelt geworden. Und ich versuche, die offene Seite beim Luftholen so weit wie möglich zu schließen, ich atme nur noch durch einen verschwindend dünnen Spalt, durch die Ritze einer Tür, die ich hinter mir zugeschlagen habe, und ich genieße das Umschlossensein vom Wasser, denn das ist das Ziel meiner Strecke: nicht der Anschlag am Beckenrand, das Erreichen des Ufers oder irgendein Ende an Land, sondern die Einheit von Wasser und Bewegung, die Zugehörigkeit zu diesem Element. Ich strebe Wassergleichheit an." (Düffel 2011: 54)

Illustration 5:
Vija Celmins, Sea #9 *(1975). Graphite on acrylic ground on paper, 30.5 x 38.5 cm. Private collection.*

This intense physical adjustment to fluid is stored in the memory and is recalled by images of water: Beat Streuli synthesizes the motif of water with the technique of cross-fading and, in doing so, evokes movement – an important tool in achieving an immersive effect. Inversely, 20th-century art history offers many depictions of surfaces of water that 'freeze' movement. In the early 20th century, Wenzel Hablik and Emil Nolde frequently painted detailed views of the ocean that exhibit a high level of abstraction and avoid central perspective. Water and waves take up almost the entire pictorial area; a position or a specific standpoint from which the scene is being viewed has become almost impossible to determine. The seascapes by Gerhard Richter, created beginning in the late 1960s, as well as the graphite and ink drawings, engravings, and etchings created by the American artist Vija Celmins since 1967, also translate water surfaces into images (see *Illustration 5*). Here, one can speak of a double translation process: water is first photographed and then transferred into a smeared or blurred painting (Richter) or, through a painstaking process, into detailed drawings or prints (Celmins).

Vija Celmins's own photographs of the Pacific taken at her place of work in Venice, California, were the starting point of her artistic transformation of pictures of the ocean. In these usually small-format works of Celmins's, there is no horizon, no shore, no people, no animals in or on the water that would make it possible for the viewer to determine his or her perspective[5]. Whereas the chosen technique of accurate drawing and its careful, microscopically precise execution formally freeze the water's restlessness, allowing it to become a deep and pure surface, movement, as a prolongation of time, is brought into the picture on another level. The water's boundless expansion clear to the edge of the

5 A similar, though photographic, approach to water – ocean or river – can be found in works by Roni Horn (see 2000) and Peter Schanz (see 2003), who both aim their cameras at a moving surface of water that takes up the entire image space.

picture and – imaginarily – beyond it, the negation of a compositional framing through a shore or a horizon, the drawing's 'all-overness', and the constant repetition and rhythmization of the movement of the waves imply an endless pictorial space of many shades of gray into which the viewer's gaze is drawn[6]. Thus, although no depth is created, Celmins clearly emphasizes the pictorial nature of the scenes. Her works convey an impression of distance that exerts a pull on the viewer – the totality of the 'ocean' experience leads to "a dissolving of [...] boundaries that undoes every certainty about spatial dimension, location and orientation" (Butin 2011: 37). In 1967, at a pivotal point in her creative work – shortly after earning her master's degree in painting from Yale – Vija Celmins rented a studio in Venice right on the Pacific. It was during this time that the artist met James Turrell and Doug Wheeler. Their discussions about space and light, their group outings, and their walks along the ocean linearly led to the series of ocean and star pictures that Celmins continues to create today. In 1967, the artist recorded the following in her diary-like chronicle:

> I meet James Turrell and Doug Wheeler, who do not make paintings but who also love the space and light of the desert. They both fly airplanes so we do some flying together. [...] I sit in my big, empty studio and do moon-shot and ocean-drawings. I spend every evening walking with my big Malamut dog by the ocean. Doug sometimes joins me with his German shepherd, Zero. I watch the light on the water and sky, and keep a diary of my observations. I look at the ocean through my camera. (2011: 147)

2. From Water to Light

According to Vija Celmins's notes, the physical and photographic experience of nature was fundamental for her drawings. It is interesting that James Turrell, who works with time and immateriality in a way probably unlike any other artist of his time, has a special place in Vija Celmins's reminiscences. Whereas Celmins's flat works on paper and Turrell's three-dimensional installations are different in

6 James Lingwood has expressed himself very descriptively on the dramaturgy of Celmins's seascapes: "The centre of attention is no longer the centre of the picture, it is anywhere and everywhere. Each part has equal weight, and no particular fragment outweighs another. There is no horizon, no perspective, no vanishing point. Looking at these detailed surfaces, we are absorbed into a compressed expanse of liquid space and drawn into an experience of time far removed from the quotidian" (1996: 27).

terms of spatiality, media, and how they address the viewer, both obviously share a common starting point for their work in their socialization on the California coast. Their works also show the diverse immersive qualities of water as a material. In its translation to paper, the immersive experience can be traced back, in particular, to sight. The haptic quality Celmins creates with her drawing skills remains visual. Turrell, on the other hand, works with a physically involved recipient in his installations – materials such as water and light are the ingredients of an immersive experience. In James Turrell's installation *Heavy Water* (see *Illustration 6*), which he showed in an alternative music center in Poitiers, France, in 1991, visitors were invited to swim through a pool of water (in a windowless room) to another room. They could only accomplish this by diving in. Upon surfacing, this unknown room revealed itself to be a construction that was open on the top and whose sides were illuminated by colored lights. Here, Turrell brings together "the plunging of the gaze into the lucid dimensions of the Skyspace with the plunging into another transparent medium: water" (Sinnreich 2009: 23). The visitor's actual experience of swimming through the water – the experience of immersion in the original sense – ended with a glimpse into the sky, into a framed patch of blue.

When speaking of 'immersion', water is a central material, in that the term originally comes from the sport of swimming and means 'to dive in', an action that is most successful in liquids such as water. In her early and fundamental definition, Janet Murray also calls upon the image of water to describe 'immersion':

> Immersion is a metaphorical term derived from the physical experience of being submerged in water. We seek the same feeling from a psychologically immersive experience that we do from a plunge in the ocean or swimming pool: the sensation of being surrounded by a completely other reality, as different as water is from air, that takes over all of our attention, our whole perceptual apparatus [...]. (1997: 98f.)

In *Heavy Water*, Turrell follows the first immersive experience – immersion in water – with a second: looking into the light when reemerging, which acts like a transcendental moment of awakening. In the experience of the weightlessness of space, the fluid element of water becomes a heavy material – a 'heavy water'. Although light shapes part of the immersive effect in this installation, in the artist's other projects, it becomes an encompassing, central element. Particularly in the case of installations

Illustration 6:
James Turrell, Heavy Water *(1991).*
Le Confort Moderne, Poitiers.

that use light to mold a room, such as James Turrell's 2009 *Wolfsburg Project*, immersive strategies can be found. Light is lexically defined as 'in general: the reason there is sight; in common speech: brightness, illumination. 2. Physics: a radiation that, in an empty room, spreads itself out linearly'[7]. From the dissolution of space and the absorption of the viewer's body to a dismantling of the threshold – all this can be observed in many light installations that work with irritating the viewer's vision. In James Turrell's installations, light is employed as an element that both creates and dissolves space. Turrell's installations lead the viewers to themselves and their physical experiences. Georges Didi-Huberman attempts to describe the immateriality of light in the artist's work that is intangible and yet spatial using terms of disembodiment and desolateness, such as 'absence', 'emptiness', and 'nothingness'. At the same time, he speaks of places that people walk through in which they experience light and enlightenment (see 2001).

In 1993, at the exhibition *Feuer, Erde, Wasser, Luft*, Turrell's works made a very early international appearance at the Deichtorhallen in Hamburg as part of the media-art festival Mediale, a large show dedicated to media and the elements curated by Wulf Herzogenrath and Zdenek Felix. There, along with water, light was given a very prominent position and, in the process, its mystical qualities were called upon: ether, as in the 'upper air' in Greek mythology in which the gods live, leads directly to luminiferous ether, a hypothetical, fine material that pervades the universe (cf. Herzogenrath 1993: 53). According to Aristotle, ether and light are closely connected with one another. In his text *De anima* (*On the Soul*), he synthesizes the heavenly element with that which shines through it (cf. 1907: 418b6f.; cf. also Böhme/Böhme 1996:

7 "[...] allgemein: die Ursache der Sehwahrnehmungen; im gewöhnlichen Sprachgebrauch: Helligkeit, Beleuchtung. 2. Physik: eine Strahlung, die sich im leeren Raum geradlinig ausbreitet" (Finckh 1993: 8).

145). According to Heinz Mack, this thought leads to light mysticism and spirituality. Mack was involved in several collective works done by the group ZERO, including the so-called *Light Room* at the documenta III in Kassel in 1964. While many of Turrell's installations involve spherical light spread throughout a room in which he works with the suppression of other visual impressions and shapes the room predominantly through light, in ZERO's *Light Room*, one finds an entirely different concept of viewer inclusion. The installation is composed of an arrangement of seven apparatuses by the artists Mack, Otto Piene, and Günther Uecker. The constructions, some of which were created individually, some as group projects, are either placed on pedestals, stands, scaffolding, or tables, or laid on the floor. All of the individual objects are equipped with lights on the inside and also externally illuminated by the kind of work lights used in railroad construction. Perforations in the works allow the light to be dispersed point-by-point and scattered. All of the objects are in motion and circulate or rotate at different speeds. Other objects, on the other hand, incorporate projection. For the visitor entering the installation, the composite creates a constantly moving total picture:

> All seven light machines are thus in a constant flow of circulating spheres of light and shadow that constantly alter the space. The images created by the light and shadows not only are visible on the walls, the floor, and the ceiling but seize the objects themselves – above all, the individual works by Mack and Uecker.[8]

To this observation of Stephan von Wiese, one must add that the viewers were also inscribed by light and shadow. The artistic technique described by Mack as 'emanation' or light painting, which affects objects and dematerializes them (cf. Honisch 1996: 10), can also be questioned with regard to its immersive qualities: the viewer looks at luminous and illuminated objects that are in motion, which, as a result, also project a changing pattern and grid onto the viewer, who is thus physically involved and whose vision is shaped by the constant alternation of light and shadow.

8 "Alle sieben Lichtmaschinen stehen also im ständigen Fluß eines kreisenden Licht- und Schattenfeldes, das den Raum ständig verändert. Die Licht- und Schattenzeichnung ereignet sich aber nicht nur auf den Wänden, dem Boden, der Decke, auch die Objekte selbst sind davon ergriffen – vor allem die Einzelarbeiten von Mack und Uecker." (Wiese 1992: 31)

3. In the Midst of Clouds and Mist

In the 1960s and 1970s, intensive material experiments were conducted in Minimal Art, Land Art, and Arte Povera that employed steam in the creation of ephemeral sculptures. In the process, the definition of 'art' was called into question and expanded[9]. As a result, over the past several years, many artists and artist collectives have begun to increasingly test the dimensions of perception of steam, mist, and smoke. These installations were clearly prefigured in the artistic-political actions by concept artists in the 1950s to 1970s: noteworthy (without going into further detail) are Hans Haacke's *Water in Wind* from 1968, which was first shown on the roof of the artist's studio in New York (cf. Höck 1972: ill. 56)[10], and Sadamasa Motonaga's action *Kumuri* (*Smoke*), part of the artist group Gutai's[11] first show on the stage of the Sankei Hall in Osaka in 1957, in which light and smoke were used together. On the stage, Motonaga created large, colorfully illuminated smoke rings that dissipated above the heads of the audience members. Later, at a second stage performance, he repeated the action using a rubber cannon out of which the smoke rings were shot (cf. Bertozzi et al., eds. 1991: 42f.). In contrast to these two perform-

9 In material iconography, steam, above all, is viewed as an immaterial material, thus as a material for sculptures, such as *Steam* by Robert Morris from 1957/1974 in Bellingham (Western Washington University): 'In art, steam is one of the youngest materials: its contourless, barely controllable shape that dissipates in space plays a role for those artists who, around the 1960s, abandoned the traditional pictorial genres in order to develop a processual form of art that is determined by material.' ("In der Kunst ist Dampf eines der jüngsten Materialien: Seine konturlosen, kaum kontrollierbaren, sich im Raum verflüchtigenden Gebilde spielen vor allem für jene Künstler eine Rolle, die um 1960 die traditionellen Bildgattungen verlassen, um eine prozessuale, vom Material bestimmte Kunst zu entwickeln"; Westheider 2002: 60).

10 Hans Haacke, *Water in Wind*, 1968; roof of the studio on 95 East Houston Street, New York; fog jet, nozzles, pump, water, wind.

11 Since the 1950s, the members of the Gutai group have continuously experimented with water, wind, and earth. In the large 1965 exhibition *Nul* in Amsterdam, Gutai was involved with artists working outside of a formal, object-oriented form of art. Also noteworthy in this context is the 1965 exhibition *ZERO on Sea*, an event/festival that was to take place on the pier and beach of Scheveningen, Holland, but was canceled due to weather conditions. Haacke suggested several projects, including a pump-run water geyser and the positioning of two colliding streams of water.

ance actions in which viewers took on a rather observational role, in the following installations, the relationship between viewers and what they were looking at was different. Important here, in my opinion, was the positioning of the visitor within the installation, in the material. The immersion set in with the viewer's shift into the center of the action, whereby the often processual alteration of the material's quality and quantity developed a gradual immersive effect.

In 1991, the artist Maria Eichhorn opened her exhibition *Meer. Salz. Wasser. Klima. Kammer. Nebel. Wolken. Luft. Staub. Atem. Küste. Brandung. Rauch* (see *Illustration 7*) in the Wewerka & Weiss Gallery in Berlin. A brochure from a company that produces ultrasonic atomizers inspired the form and content of the invitation. Ultrasonic atomizers are used in health and wellness clinics in therapy treatments for lung diseases; Eichhorn incorporated one of these machines in her installation. In the first room, there were five plastic chairs, reminiscent of the waiting room of a doctor's office. The aforementioned ultrasonic atomizer, which converted a mixture of distilled water and sodium chloride into a mist and sprayed it into the air, was situated in the second room. Via a pipe and an opening in the wall, the very fine dispersion made its way into the first room, making the air there increasingly cloudy. Over time, the dispersion became thicker and thicker. With the increasing cloudiness of the air, the visitors' self-perceptions and their perceptions of others changed. Surrounded by the mist, they could sense these changes very clearly. Not only were they no longer able to make out the outlines of their own bodies and those of the other visitors, but – quite unusually – another detail in the room simultaneously became more and more focused and was given a shape: Eichhorn had the title of the exhibition, all terms associated with the topic of the climatic chamber or inhalation therapy, stenciled onto the white walls of the exhibition space in white plaster. As the humidity increased, the letters became increasingly darker and were made visible by the addition of the aerosol. In my opinion, this component points to the fact that, on the one hand, it was about changes in perception for Eichhorn, about altering taste (the mist tasted salty) and vision (blurred due to the mist but sharpened with regard to the letters). On the other hand, however, she was interested in eliminating distance, placing the viewers, who could not escape with any of their senses and who found themselves in a state of immersive appropriation, directly in the midst of things. In emotional terms, one could even say that visitors breathed in the ingredients of the work as if they were assimilating the pigments of a painting. If we think about the image of the entrance into the immersive world, the threshold can barely be marked. The entrance into the gallery room is certainly a primary entrance, but the actual immersive act of diving in did not occur until the viewer was already in the room. The way the visitors were slowly enveloped also seems important in this context. Eichhorn's environmental chamber stands in a longer tradition, namely that which includes works such as the *Nebelräume* created by Gotthard Graubner in the late 1960s – for example, the one presented in an exhibition by the Modern Art Museum München in the Villa Stuck in 1968[12]. Graubner's *Nebelräume* aimed at unnerving viewers who, enveloped in wafts of mist, would lose their orientation and were thus cast back at themselves.

Illustration 7: Maria Eichhorn, Meer. Salz. Wasser. Klima. Kammer. Nebel. Wolken. Luft. Staub. Atem. Küste. Brandung. Rauch *(1991). Wewerka & Weiss Gallery, Berlin.*

In the early 2000s, artists and architects experimented with obfuscation in a far more spectacular way than even that which is seen in Eichhorn's installation. Like Eichhorn's work, *The Mediated Motion* by Olafur Eliasson and Günther Vogt at the Kunsthaus Bregenz in 2001 and *The Blur Building* by Diller and Scofidio at the 2002 Swiss National Exhibition in Yverdon-les-Bains, Switzerland, point to phenomena in nature. While Eliasson used nature as a space of imagination 'inside the white cube', at the Kunsthaus Bregenz, Diller and Scofidio placed their *Blur Building* on a lake and, in doing so, took a stronger approach to the outside world. In this respect, the spatial experience in *Cloudscapes* by Tetsuo Kondo and Transsolar at the Arsenale of the 12th Architecture Biennale in Venice in 2010 (see *Illustration 8*) is particularly impressive.

12 A recreation of the *Fog Space* in Munich was exhibited in the 2012 show *Die Sammlung Gunter Sachs: Von Max Ernst bis Andy Warhol* at the Villa Stuck in Munich. For Graubner's *Fog Space*, cf. Schmied, ed. 1969: 7 and 98f.

Illustration 8: Tetsuo Kondo and Transsolar, Cloudscapes *(2010). Architecture Biennale, Venice.*

The concept of a cloudscape contains references to cloud painters such as Carl Gustav Carus and William Turner, who were inspired not only by their interest in meteorology but also by their desire for the immaterial. In analyzing the microclimatic conditions in the Arsenale, the Transsolar engineers created an artificial cloud, a collection of very fine droplets of water that they held in place at a certain height in the room. A ramp designed by Kondo led visitors into the center of this cloud that they physically touched, inhaled, and felt, then to the space above the cloud, and back down again. Along this path, visitors could distinctly feel the three climate layers in the room: the dry air on the ground floor, the warm air in the midst of the cloud, and the hot air above the cloud (see Kim 2010). Although the installations mentioned here – Eichhorn's *Meer. Salz. Wasser. Klima. Kammer. Nebel. Wolken. Luft. Staub. Atem. Küste. Brandung. Rauch*, the *Blur Building*, and the installation *Cloudscapes* – have their own individual intentions and conceptual foundations with artistic, ecological, or site-specific focuses, similarities between them can be found. All of these installations create a spatial stage, a setting into which the visitor first must enter. The installations work together with the moving viewer.

The special immersive qualities of the water-based materials of steam and mist lie in the fact that the individual is gradually 'swallowed', absorbed by the material, so that parts of his or her body remain visible, while other parts have already been enveloped in the steam or mist, rendering them invisible. Here, immersion becomes something one actually physically experiences. While in theories of fictional immersion – in an extension of the classical notion of a 'willing suspension of disbelief' – film's fictional or aesthetic ability to absorb viewers is argued[13], in instal-

13 'One can speak of fictional immersion if a large part of the viewer's attention is taken away from the surroundings and directed entirely on the artifact.' ("Wird ein Großteil der Aufmerksamkeit des Rezipienten von der Umgebung abgezogen und ganz auf das Artefakt gelenkt, kann man von fiktionaler Immersion sprechen"; Voss 2009: 127).

lations that use steam or mist as a material, there is often no longer a barrier between here and there. This means that viewers or visitors are, in fact, captured by the work, absorbed, and physically become part of the installation by which they are consumed. Here, one should differentiate between the internal perspective of those affected and the external perspective of other visitors. While the self becomes part of the work, it also observes the other visitors who are visible or invisible. Only through the observation of others can one truly perceive one's own disappearance and synthesis with the material.

The physical and psychological experiences are to be viewed as being equal, which contradicts the definition of 'immersion' supported by the art historian Oliver Grau, for example, who speaks of a mental absorption and a reduction of critical distance. According to his understanding, immersion is a means of empowerment, of establishing "regimes of perception" (2004b: 13) ("Regime der Wahrnehmung"; 2004a: 14). The starting point for the installations I have mentioned here and for their creators is presumably a loss that is, however, less a loss of rationality or the ability to think or distance oneself but a temporary disappearance of one's own body in the material. Assumedly, this process of absorption is still a far more literal form of immersion than what one encounters with images. The destabilization of one's own self in favor of an encompassing new experience of the world is a facet of the immersive[14] that can be found in installations involving steam and mist.

In the cases of steam, mist, and installations that work with the material of light, one can use phenomenological theories that focus on the relationship between sight and physical existence in the world as an argument. These also apply in considering the constitution of spaces throughout the body (see Merleau-Ponty 1945 and 1962). With regard to the aforementioned steam installations, one could speak of a specific material space, the sides of which are flexible because no thresholds or transitional zones exist. Here, the dissolution of boundaries sets in that, according to many different definitions, should be assessed as an important paradigm of the immersive.

14 Susanne von Falkenhausen describes this destabilization and confusion of the viewer in relation to the immersive design of the Pepsi-Cola Pavilion at the 1970 Expo in Osaka (cf. 2008: 136f.).

References

Aristotle (1907). *De anima*. Transl. Robert Drew Hicks. Cambridge, MA: CUP.

Bachelard, Gaston (1942). *L'eau et les rèves: Essai sur l'imagination de la matière*. Paris: Corti.

— (1983). *Water and Dreams: An Essay on the Imagination of Matter*. Transl. Edith R. Farrell. Dallas, TX: Pegasus Foundation.

Bayne, Judy, et al. (2005: online). *Softimage/XSI Hair*. http://softimage.wiki.softimage.com/images/3/35/Hair.pdf. [25/12/2011].

Bertozzi, Barbara, et al., eds. (1991). *Gutai: Japanische Avantgarde / Japanese Avant-Garde 1954–1965*. Exh. cat. Darmstadt: Mathildenhöhe, 24 March – 5 May 1991. Darmstadt: Institut Mathildenhöhe.

Böhme, Gernot, Hartmut Böhme (1996). *Feuer, Wasser, Erde, Luft: Kulturgeschichte der Elemente*. Munich: Beck.

Böhme, Hartmut (1988). "Umriß einer Kulturgeschichte des Wassers: Eine Einleitung". Hartmut Böhme, ed. *Kulturgeschichte des Wassers*. Frankfurt am Main: Suhrkamp. 7–42.

Butin, Hubertus (2011). "Here, Look at This. And Look at It Again and Look at It Again: Vija Celmins' Desert, Sea and Star Pictures". Friedrich, ed. 34–39.

Celmins, Vija (2011). "Chronology". Friedrich, ed. 146–149.

Didi-Huberman, Georges (2001). *L'homme qui marchait dans la couleur*. Paris: Editions de Minuit.

Düffel, John von (2011). *Schwimmen*. Munich: dtv.

Falkenhausen, Susanne von (2008). *KugelbauVisionen: Kulturgeschichte einer Bauform von der Französischen Revolution bis zum Medienzeitalter*. Bielefeld: transcript.

Finckh, Gerhard (1993). "Licht-Räume". Gerhard Finckh, ed. *Licht-Räume*. Exh. cat. Essen: Museum Folkwang, 28 November 1993 – 16 January 1994. Essen: Museum Folkwang. 8–25.

Friedrich, Julia, ed. (2011). *Vija Celmins: Wüste, Meer & Sterne / Desert, Sea & Stars*. Exh. cat. Cologne: Museum Ludwig, 15 April – 17 July 2011. Cologne: Walther König.

Grau, Oliver (2004a: online). "Immersion und Interaktion: Vom Rundfresko zum interaktiven Bildraum". *Medien Kunst Netz*. http://

www.medienkunstnetz.de/themen/medienkunst_im_ueberblick/immersion/. [14/07/2013].
— (2004b: online). “Immersion and Interaction: From Circular Frescoes to Interactive Image Spaces”. Transl. Gloria Custance. *Media Art Net*. http://www.medienkunstnetz.de/themes/overview_of_media_art/immersion/. [14/07/2014].
Groys, Boris (1999). “Die Dauer der Bilder”. Pfab, ed. 13–19.
Heller, Franziska (2010). *Filmästhetik des Fluiden: Strömungen des Erzählens von Vigo bis Tarkowskij, von Huston bis Cameron*. Munich: Fink.
Herzogenrath, Wulf (1993). “Vier Elemente: Das Gleiche im Wandel – vom Materiellen zum Immateriellen”. Klaus Meyer, ed. *Mediale Hamburg*. Exh. cat. Hamburg: Deichtorhallen, 5 February – 28 March 1993. Hamburg: MACup. 52–57.
Höck, Wilhelm (1972). *Hans Haacke*. Cologne: DuMont.
Honisch, Dieter (1996). “Eine eingelöste Vision”. Dieter Honisch, ed. *Mack: Licht im Blick*. Exh. cat. Stuttgart: Galerie Landesgirokasse, 14 May – 5 July 1996. Ostfildern-Ruit: Hatje Cantz. 7–12.
Horn, Roni (2000). *Another Water: The River Thames, for Example*. Zurich: Scalo.
Kim, Erika (2010: online). “Transsolar + Tetsuo Kondo Architects: *Cloudscapes*, at Venice Biennale”. *Designboom*. http://www.designboom.com/weblog/cat/9/view/11396/transsolar-tetsuo-kondo-architects-cloudscapes-at-venice-biennale.html. [01/06/2011].
Lingwood, James (1996). “Pictures of Facts: Vija Celmins’ Work from the 60s”. James Lingwood, ed. *Vija Celmins*. Exh. cat. London: Institute of Contemporary Arts, 1 November – 22 December 1996. London: Institute of Contemporary Arts. 22–27.
McMahan, Alison (2003). “Immersion, Engagement, and Presence: A Method for Analyzing 3-D Video Games”. Mark J. P. Wolf, Bernard Perron, eds. *The Video Game Theory Reader*. Vol. 1. New York, NY/London: Routledge. 67–86.
McGorry, Ken (2008: online). “Making a Splash”. *Post Magazine*. http://www.bjork.fr/Wanderlust-Post-Magazine. [11/09/2012].
Merleau-Ponty, Maurice (1945). *Phénoménologie de la perception*. Paris: Edition Gallimard.
— (1962). *Phenomenology of Perception*. Transl. C. Smith. London: Routledge & Kegan Paul.
Murray, Janet H. (1997). *Hamlet on the Holodeck: The Future of Narrative in Cyberspace*. Cambridge, MA/London: MIT Press.

Neitzel, Britta, Rolf F. Nohr (2006). "Das Spiel mit dem Medium: Partizipation, Immersion, Interaktion". Britta Neitzel, Rolf F. Nohr, eds. *Das Spiel mit dem Medium: Partizipation – Immersion – Interaktion*. Marburg: Schüren. 9–19.

Oxford Dictionaries (2013: online). "wanderlust". http://oxforddictionaries.com/definition/english/wanderlust?q=wanderlust. [13/12/2013].

Pelzer, Michael (1996). *Einfluß von Immersion, Submersion und Tauchen auf Herzfrequenz und Herzfrequenzvaribilität*. MD thesis, University of Düsseldorf.

Pfab, Rupert (1999). "Photographien des modernen Lebens". Pfab, ed. 4–11.

—, ed. (1999) *Beat Streuli: City*. Exh. cat. Düsseldorf: Kunsthalle Düsseldorf, 24 April – 27 June 1999. Ostfildern-Ruit: Hatje Cantz.

Ryan, Marie-Laure (2001). *Narrative as Virtual Reality: Immersion and Interactivity in Literature and Electronic Media*. Baltimore, MD: Johns Hopkins UP.

Schanz, Peter (2003). *87 Tage Blau: Logbuch einer Erdumrundung in Text und Fotografie*. Munich/Vienna: Sanssouci.

Schmied, Wieland, ed. (1969). *Gotthard Graubner*. Exh. cat. Hannover: Kestner Gesellschaft, 9 October 1969 – 11 February 1970. Hannover: Vandrey.

Sinnreich, Ursula (2009). "Between Heaven and Earth". Ursula Sinnreich, ed. *James Turrell: Geometrie des Lichts / Geometry of Light*. Exh. cat. Unna: Zentrum für internationale Lichtkunst, 31 January – 31 May 2009. Ostfildern-Ruit: Hatje Cantz. 21–23.

Stoffer, Hellmut (1966). *Die Magie des Wassers*. Meisenheim am Glan: Hain.

Thon, Jan-Noël (2008). "Immersion Revisited: On the Value of a Contested Concept". Olli Leino, Hanna Wirman, Amyris Fernandez, eds. *Extending Experiences: Structure, Analysis and Design of Computer Game Player Experiences*. Rovaniemi: Lapland UP. 29–43.

Voss, Christiane (2009). "Fiktionale Immersion". Gertrud Koch, Christiane Voss, eds. *"Es ist, als ob": Fiktionalität in Philosophie, Film- und Medienwissenschaft*. Munich: Fink. 127–138.

Wagner, Monika (2001). *Das Material der Kunst: Eine andere Geschichte der Moderne*. Munich: Beck.

Westheider, Ortrud (2002). "Dampf". Monika Wagner et al., eds. *Lexikon des künstlerischen Materials: Werkstoffe der modernen Kunst von Abfall bis Zinn*. Munich: Beck. 60–64.

Wiese, Stephan von (1992). "Lichtraum: Hommage à Fontana; der ZERO-Raum für die documenta III". Hans Albert Peters, Stephan von Wiese, eds. *Heinz Mack, Otto Piene, Günther Uecker: Lichtraum (Hommage à Fontana) 1964*. Exh. cat. Düsseldorf: Kunstmuseum Düsseldorf. Berlin: Kulturstiftung der Länder. 20–40.

Wolf, Werner (2013). "Aesthetic Illusion". Werner Wolf, Walter Bernhart, Andreas Mahler, eds. *Immersion and Distance: Aesthetic Illusion in Literature and Other Media*. Amsterdam/New York, NY: Rodopi. 1–63.

Picture Credits

Ills. 1, 2: http://vimeo.com/9021557. [30/07/2013]; Ill. 3: http://softimage.wiki.softimage.com/images/3/35/Hair.pdf. [30/07/2013]; Ill. 4: *Beat Streuli: Bondi Beach/Parramatta Road.* (1999). Exh. cat. Hannover: Sprengel Museum Hannover, 27 January – 7 March 1999. Hannover: Sprengel-Museum. [n. p.]; Ill. 5: Julia Friedrich, ed. (2011). *Vija Celmins: Wüste, Meer & Sterne / Desert, Sea & Stars*. Exh. cat. Cologne: Museum Ludwig, 15 April – 17 July 2011. Cologne: Walther König. 57; Ill. 6: Peter Noever, ed. (1998). *James Turrell: The Other Horizon*. Exh. cat. Vienna: MAK – Österreichisches Museum für angewandte Kunst, 2 December 1998 – 21 March 1999. Ostfildern-Ruit: Hatje Cantz. 141; Ill. 7: Maria Eichhorn (1996). *Abbildungen, Interviews, Texte*. Munich: Silke Schreiber. 35; Ill. 8: http://www.designboom.com. [30/07/2013].

Illustration 1:
Publicity drawing by Karl Leydenfrost
for the film This Is Cinerama
(dir. Merian C. Cooper, USA 1952).

Immersion and Abstraction as Measures of Materiality

Robin Curtis

Is immersion to be understood merely as a result of, and thus little more than a synonym for, realism? If so, what kind of simulation would this imply? This essay posits that two distinctly different modes, namely external and internal realism, could be responsible for the emergence of immersive experience, and, in particular, examines the effect of the latter. In this context, the specific characteristics of the potential for abstraction inherent in the moving image will be emphasized in order to analyze a wide and perhaps surprising variety of characteristics that point to its immersive potential.

1. The Terms of Engagement

Over the last decade, the term 'immersion' has increasingly been called upon to provide a label for the particularly visceral, 'here and now', contemporary quality of various sorts of present-day aesthetic experience. Despite this prevalence, 'immersion' nevertheless remains a relatively unspecific placeholder in present-day discourse. One rather one-sided account of what is at the root of immersive experience that is in general circulation highlights the effects of the representational features of a variety of media and the texts made available via these media; in this account, immersion and realism are virtually synonymous with an ever more detailed realist representation of the world (whether this realism be an effect of the parameters of a medium or a given text), allowing for ever greater immersion. In contrast, I would like to turn attention away from the goal of representational realism as the basis for the immersive characteristics of a text or a medium and instead focus attention on various forms of abstraction that can also invite immersive engagement, and thereby highlight other processes at work that may be at the root of immersive experience but were heretofore neglected.

A brief but lively debate about the nature of immersion took place in 2009 on the collaborative academic website *In Media Res*. One particular question posed there will help to elucidate the range of issues at stake in a discussion of that term. The wide range of topics that were raised in the discussion on *In Media Res* points to a fundamental indeterminacy that would seem to dwell within the notion of immersion. One participant in that discussion first stated that "immersion is mediational and multiperspectival" and then wondered,

> how can we explain it in a way that accounts for these *multiple perspectives and intentionalities?* is it enough to explain it as a characteristic of certain types of media? or should our discussions of immersion account for players' intentions? technological affordances and constraints? the consumerist orientation of most computer games and other immersive media? given these questions, what might meaningful studies of immersion look like? (Moeller 2009 [my emphasis])

The response that followed encouraged an approach that would look beyond the characteristics and structures of the media or even individual aesthetic 'texts' that are the objects of an immersion scholar's attention at any given moment; this second participant in the debate replied:

> No, it is not enough to explain immersion as a characteristic of certain media types because immersion is not a component of any medium. Rather, I'm thinking that immersion is purely an invention of the mind of the one immersed. And for this reason there is no negotiation because immersion is a figment of the imagination. The game is not negotiating; the game is simply stating the terms for engagement. (McAllister 2009)

But how may such "terms for engagement" with the moving image be conceptualized? These two contributions point to an aspect of immersive experience – whether inspired by engaging with a game, reading a text, looking at or watching a still or moving image, or entering into a space mediated by any other aesthetic device, or any combination thereof – that is too often neglected. The source of immersive experience is oftentimes sought exclusively within the medial or textual characteristics (i. e., within the 'dispositif') of what has been determined to be an 'immersive' aesthetic object. Conversely, if we do take up the challenge to view immersion as an 'invention of the mind', this should not be taken to imply the participation of a veritable black box in which immersive processes are generated; this would only replace one placeholder, immersion itself, with another, the operations of the imagination, which are deemed inscrutable (cf. Scarry 2001: 1–22). Instead, a consideration of the role of imagination in immersion points to an interaction between subject and aesthetic object that has the potential to create something unexpected. I would like to outline several imaginative and associative processes that may be responsible for one particular type of immersion based in our varied experiences of materiality, abstraction, and scale and that can have a profoundly thrilling as well as disconcerting effect.

Consider the visceral power that our experience of space in an aesthetic context can have and our complex reaction to it, particularly when, as is the case with moving images, one cannot enter the space of the image visible on the screen: the moving image nonetheless remains the source of a host of somatic effects that may even threaten to take on existential qualities. And yet I would argue against a perspective that sees the illusory quality of the moving image as the sole source of such effects, since it does not seem to be the case that the viewer or user of such images is truly confounded, confused, or deceived by their status but rather that the viewer engages in a particular way with that representation. I would suggest that, in order for immersion to take place, a kind of visceral, attentional investment must take place that allows the specific terms for engagement defined by a given work to be brought to bear upon the reception situation. In cases such as these, it is imagination rather than simply illusion that is called upon.

I have previously taken up two analogies for immersive media, the roller coaster and the fun house, which each define specific qualities responsible for the affective power of moving images and have specific implications for the immersive experience (see Curtis 2010). I would like to raise these two models again here, in order to better elucidate their implications, not only for forms of representation within specific texts but also for forms of imaginative engagement, which may be employed either distinctly or in combination.

2. The Roller Coaster

It is perhaps due to the long association between train travel and the experience of the cinema in general that it has become something of a cliché to associate immersion with the experience of a roller coaster[1]. The jarring new experience of train travel is described by Wolfgang Schivelbusch as one of the most fundamental perceptual shifts of modernity, akin to the effect of montage in the cinema in its ability to

1 For an overview of the relationship between the cinema and the train, see Kirby 1997.

shrink space and compress time. This analogy is mentioned but left underdeveloped in Schivelbusch's seminal study of the train's place in modernity (see 1979/1986). He labels the form of vision that originates in this mode of travel "panoramic vision" (ibid.: 64), a perspective on the world that separates the viewer from that which is seen as vision is filtered through the apparatus, which is the train itself. Ironically, following the advent of the cinema, the two 'media' of vision, trains and films, are brought together to create a sensation of intense involvement, of presence. It is, of course, the train pulling into the station at La Ciotât that has left one of the most indelible impressions of early cinema, particularly with regard to our notion of the impact of that new medium in retrospect[2]. However, in contrast to the perspective of the Lumière brothers' film – which was shot with a static camera as the train approached, moving from the upper right to the lower left edge of the screen as it entered the station – film's immersive power has long been linked to the perspective from the moving vehicle itself. This latter, more kinetic view of the world was soon taken up by early cinema makers and has proved to be an enduring visual motif. And yet, unlike Schivelbusch's panorama perspective, this model for cinematic perspective inspired by the train does not record movement lateral to the viewer, as if he or she were gazing out the window of a train, but rather from the front of a moving vehicle, directed toward the vanishing point. The popularity of this perspective throughout the early years of the cinema can be seen in both the phantom-ride genre, which replicated such a perspective, shot from a train, subway car, or streetcar, and the complex apparatus assembled for the Hale's Tours attractions, which seated the audience in a prop designed to look like a railway car and projected phantom-ride films for their viewing pleasure[3].

2 The account of the first public screening of films offered by the Lumière brothers at the Grand Café in Paris in December 1895 that envisions the crowds running from the screening room in fear remains a persistent myth of the cinema that is often reproduced without question, particularly in the context of histories of immersion. Both Tom Gunning (see 1989) and Martin Loiperdinger (see 2004) have provided detailed accounts of that historic screening that discount such naïveté on the part of the first audiences while considering the function of that myth for the history of the filmic medium.

3 Kirby (see 1997) offers a detailed account of the Hale's Tours attractions in the early years of the 20th century. For a detailed examination of the role of the phantom ride and the travelogue in general in the early years of the cinema, see Peterson 2013.

These films function on the basis of the information they provide about the wider world, but more importantly, for the purposes of a discussion of immersion, they simulate the experience of kineticism and particularly kinetosis, or motion sickness, which, in the case of simulated motion, notably is termed 'virtual reality sickness'. The source of kinetosis in the case of simulated motion is the misalignment between the visual system in the human body and the other systems of information input, in particular the vestibular system. The criteria that have until now traditionally been understood to be necessary for the production of an immersive experience (i. e., those that are based in an ever greater degree of realism) are also responsible for inducing such effects in that they attempt to occupy the viewer's entire field of vision and thus exclude real-world points of reference. Corporeally immersive effects such as motion sickness can be induced by large-scale screens, such as those generally installed in IMAX film theaters, or the 360-degree image environments provided by a head-mounted display or suggested by media formats that utilize rounded projection surfaces, such as the wide-screen formats of the mid-20th century or the contemporary OMNIMAX IMAX format.

It is the objective of *This Is Cinerama* (dir. Merian C. Cooper, USA 1952), the film with which the wide-screen format Cinerama was advertised at its introduction in the 1950s, to give the viewer the impression of having been placed, theater seat and all, in the midst of a variety of situations outside of the cinema and thus transported by the experience into a fictional space. Most famously, this particular film used the roller coaster as its central metaphor for engaged and spatially involved viewing (see *Illustration 1*)[4]. Although it functions to induce a corporeal response most reliably if the screen extends to the limits of the viewer's vision, the movement of the image itself can be sufficient to cause motion sickness. This particular perspective, already familiar from the phantom rides of early cinema, has reappeared periodically throughout the 20th century.

Claude Lelouch's short film *C'était un rendez-vous* (France 1976) consists of a single take (see *Illustration 2*), which was ostensibly shot in the early morning hours on the empty streets of Paris, thus allowing the car on which the camera was perched at a very low

4 For a contemporary account of the virtues of the wide-screen format, see MacGowan 1957. For a very detailed account of the variety of wide-screen formats available in the mid-20th century, see Belton 1992.

angle close to the ground to travel at a high speed through the streets of the city, ignore red traffic lights, and avoid the few pedestrians who appear. During this apparently real-time trip through the city, a number of other vehicles cross the path of the car and, several times, a collision seems to be just barely avoided. The sound effects provided in the film support the sense of velocity. The visceral effects produced in the viewer in a case such as this have less to do with imagination and more to do with physiology.

The IMAX film entitled *North of Superior* (dir. Graeme Ferguson, Canada 1971), which was commissioned in 1971 for the world's first IMAX cinema, the Cinesphere, located at Ontario Place in Toronto, utilized a similar aesthetic strategy to produce a sense of real motion (and real nausea in the viewer) and combined that content-based strategy with a screening venue that allowed the screened image to occupy the majority of a viewer's field of vision. The opening images of the film, shot from the front of a light aircraft flying at a low altitude over the landscape of the geological formation known as the Canadian Shield above Lake Superior, move rapidly and inevitably produce a feeling of vertigo in the viewer[5].

This particular non-volitional, corporeally based form of viewer involvement has become standard practice in the blockbuster action film of the turn of the 21st century. Constance Balides has termed this feature of film aesthetics the "movie ride" and draws a direct link between the phantom rides of early cinema and the inclination of more recent cinema to provide the viewer with a break from the narrative and focus instead on the pure kineticism provided by the image. She dates this aesthetic development within narrative film to George Lucas's *Star Wars* (USA 1977) in that it was the first major film in which the pure kinetic thrill of the flight of a spaceship occupies the attention of the viewer beyond the parameters of the narrative. Luke Skywalker's at-

5 For an overview of the IMAX format, see Whitney 2005.

Illustration 2:
Film stills from C'était un rendez-vous
(dir. Claude Lelouch, France 1976).

tack on the Death Star, which is depicted from the same frontal perspective as the phantom rides were, inaugurates the "movie ride". Balides describes it as follows:

> The "sense of immersion" resulting from the "tight linkage between visual, kinesthetic and auditory modalities" [Brenda Laurel, qtd. Lunenfeld 1993: 6] [...] extends beyond virtual reality as well as computer graphic images to include a wide range of cultural technologies such as computer games, motion simulator theme park rides, and "movie ride" films, which are films containing scenes approximating the experience of theme park rides. (2003: 316f.)

According to Balides, the "movie ride" films of the present restage the experience of theme-park rides through "imperatives of pure sensation" that "leave audiences staggering back into daylight like passengers unsteadily exiting" (Bruce Handy, qtd. ibid.: 318). Thus, she understands contemporary entertainment to be based on a form of corporal involvement that depends on the "blurring of boundaries". In an analogy to Siegfried Kracauer's analysis of the Tiller Girls' dance routines of the 1920s (cf. 1995: 75–86) as spectacles that offered the workers of the day a display appropriate and analogous to their labor, Balides sees the present-day immersive strategy of the "movie ride" as an "aesthetic reflex of the rationality to which the prevailing economic system aspires" (2003: 325). According to Balides, the neo-Fordism of the present period shifts its emphasis from the fragmentation of bodies found in Kracauer's day (shaped by Taylorism) to an emphasis on the "blurring of boundaries of various kinds, for example between spaces of production and reproduction, between work and leisure, and between person and machine" (ibid.: 327). I will soon return to the implications of the blur that is highlighted by Balides in the contemporary aesthetic inclination toward "the blurring of spatial and temporal boundaries expressed in terms of speed [...] and in the movement towards indeterminate space" (ibid.). However, the crucial element of this aesthetic strategy, whether in *Star Wars* or in more contemporary blockbusters, such as any one of those made by the director Michael Bay (from the *Bad Boys* to the *Transformers* franchise), is the experiential similarity between the effects of real, kinetic experience and those instilled by the movement of the filmic image.

In her book *Shivers Down Your Spine: Cinema, Museums, and the Immersive View*, Alison Griffiths similarly emphasizes the corporeality of immersive reception. She defines immersion as

> the sensation of entering the space that immediately identifies itself as somehow separate from the world and that eschews conventional modes of spectatorship in favour of a more bodily participation in the experience, including allowing the spectator to move freely around the viewing space (although this is not a requirement). (2008: 2)

Although Griffiths considers realism to be a key component of immersive experience, she distinguishes between what she terms "*representational* realism" and "*experiential* realism" (ibid.: 285) and considers immersion to ideally come about through a blending of these two properties. If we are to avoid a definition of immersion that is dependent on the given apparatus-based parameters of a particular medium, the notion of experiential realism and the part it plays in the creation of an immersive experience should be accorded more attention than Griffiths ultimately accords it here.

But how may one better approach experiential realism? In his book *The Language of New Media*, Lev Manovich points out that the triggers that bring about immersion are neither transhistorical nor transhistorically available to experience but instead operate in conjunction with what are familiar aesthetic forms at a given moment. This means, for instance, that new media ape the effective characteristics of older, already familiar media in order to produce effects that signify experiential realism. Manovich writes:

> The paradox of digital visual culture is that although all imaging is becoming computer-based, the dominance of photographic and cinematic imagery is becoming even stronger. But rather than being a direct, "natural" result of photo and film technology, these images are constructed on computers. 3-D virtual worlds are subjected to depth of field and motion blur algorithms; digital video is run through special filters that simulate film grain; and so on. (2001: 180)

However, while these characteristics may signify experiential realism at a particular moment in time, how may we better understand the full range of possibilities encapsulated by such a notion? Must experiential realism align itself with the characteristics of representational realism or can it diverge widely from it? To assume that it may would be a departure from the mainstream of immersion theory, which tends to agree that whether film, video game, or virtual-reality environment, as far as the creation of immersion is concerned, the more detailed the audio-visual representation of a space is, the more immersive the experience of it will be[6].

3. The Fun House

To counter these assumptions, I would like to consider some ways in which abstract images can also bring about immersive experiences and thus suggest that our perspective on immersion has been too narrowly conceived to date. The roller coaster as an analogy for immersive experience functions on the basis of a dynamic kineticism and aims to engage the nervous system of the viewer directly, often by means of a disjunction between visual and vestibular cues. As an alternative, and indeed corrective, to this strategy, the fun-house model suggests an even deeper sense of dislocation, since it not only challenges the viewer's sense of balance and gravity but also, and more fundamentally, examines the state of the viewer's subjectivity itself and the parameters on which it is based.

In *Hamlet on the Holodeck*, published in 1997, Janet Murray already proposed the fun house as a model for immersive experience, emphasizing its implications for narrative structure. She focuses attention within her model on the temporality of the fun house, making reference to the "visit metaphor", which provides very clear limits on a viewer's experience of time and space. Murray writes:

> The fun house has an entrance and an exit that mark the beginning and the end of the story. As the visitor progresses on a moving platform, the dramatic tension builds from small surprises and hints of danger; then there are thrills and a mounting sense of threat or terror, which culminates in a big finish such as a free fall or an attacking beast. […] A fun house is a movie made into a machine that you travel through. (1997: 106f.)

6 Indeed, the accessibility of the space to the viewer is precisely what, according to Manovich, distinguishes interactivity from illusion, since the navigation of a 3-D space is "something one cannot do with an illusionistic painting" (2001: 184). I would suggest, however, that the distinction between illusion and non-illusion is something of a red herring in the discussion of immersion, since it clearly is not, and has never been, the case that viewers are deluded about the status of what they see.

To my mind, this account of the fun-house attraction is inadequate in that it does not examine the attractions housed by a fun house and the more fundamental encounters with embodied existence that they offer; the specific qualities of a fun house have less to do with the temporally defined experience of navigating a narrative with a clear trajectory than with a series of individually orchestrated corporeal challenges and thrills.

In his analysis of the Pleasure Beach in Blackpool, England, Tony Bennett highlighted some of these pleasures (and, one should note, in 1983, the fun house was a far more prevalent attraction than it is today). For instance, in the hall of mirrors, a common component of the fun house, it is not only the body, according to Bennett, "it is the psyche that is (flirtatiously) exposed to assault" (1983: 150). He continues:

> The Fun House is especially worthy of mention as it inverts the usual relations between the body and machinery at the Pleasure Beach. On most thrill-rides, the body is surrendered to the machinery which liberates it from normal limitations. In the Fun House, the body competes with the machinery, tries to conquer it and is forcibly reminded of its limitations. Most of its activities involve trying to get the better of various mechanical devices – walking through a revolving drum, attempting to stay at the centre of a spinning wheel, crawling to the centre of a centrifugal bowl or climbing impossibly slippery slopes. The sense of crossing a threshold in the Fun House is quite strong. Before getting into the main entertainment area, the body is subjected to a number of ritual assaults – you are buffeted by skittles, the floor shifts beneath your feet and you have to cross a series of revolving discs. These obstacles also mark a boundary between the Fun House and the rest of the Pleasure Beach – a sign of a reversal of the relations between the body and machinery, a warning that in the Fun House the body will be opposed by machinery rather than assisted or transported by it, and that the body must resist machinery and struggle against it rather than surrender itself to it. (Ibid.: 150f.)

Bennett thus establishes an opposition between the roller coaster and the fun house as attractions that I would relativize to some extent: the relationship between the visitor and the environment that is provoked by the fun house does not always, or only, result in a recognition of the strict division between the human and the apparatus, which Bennett sees at the heart of the many tests to which the visitor is subjected at the Pleasure Beach. Instead, I would emphasize that these attractions, in general, and the fun house, in particular, seek to enable a temporary rearrangement of the senses. When one enters a fun house, one enters an environment in which the standard rules regulating the configuration of space and the self's relationship to that space are overturned; thus one encounters not only an opportunity to transcend these rules of spatial negotiation but also an opportunity to enter into a slightly different world (and one may remain there as long as one likes, since the time spent in the fun house is self-determined).

In the same fashion as the fun-house attraction, immersive experiences can also offer the viewer or user the opportunity not only to transport the intact self to another pre-constituted place but also to challenge and transform the parameters of that self. These transformational aspects of immersion may oftentimes thus have less to do with the richness or fullness of the simulated space into which a viewer or user projects himself or herself than with a situation of empathetic alignment. While such an alignment with an avatar in a gaming situation or with a fictional or nonfictional character in a narrative or documentary film may seem to be a self-evident part of immersion, I have argued elsewhere in greater detail for the opportunities presented by a reexamination of traditional empathy aesthetics (or, 'Einfühlungsästhetik') in the context of immersion theory (see Curtis 2008; 2011; 2012). Suffice it to say here that the debates considering 'Einfühlung' as a basis for aesthetic involvement, which were particularly lively around the beginning of the 20th century, offer a new perspective on the ways in which one may engage with aesthetic objects as arrangements of form rather than as realist representations. As such, they are not taken merely as copies of objects in the everyday world, but facilitate a heightened corporeal engagement with the world, its objects, and its forms by reminding one of the various ways in which one experiences one's own vitality in embodied experience[7]. This form of reminiscence of the specific parameters dictated by embodiment links us to the world around us through analogy and has great consequences for an account of the reception of moving images, regardless of the media format in which one encounters them. An immersive engagement should thus not be conceived of as the insertion of the subject onto a three-dimensional realistic stage, just like a doll is positioned within a dollhouse. Instead, we need to consider a broader range of experiences that describe our multifaceted engagement with the world around us in both aesthetic and everyday settings.

If immersive experience is indeed historically specific, an examination of filmic immersion should begin at the advent of the cinema and may well uncover forms of immersion that are no longer readily available

7 This account is most closely in line with that proposed by Theodor Lipps, who views aesthetic experience in general, and Einfühlung in particular, as a result of what he calls objectified self-enjoyment, an enjoyment of the formal characteristics of the world in analogy to oneself (see, for instance, Lipps 1905/1985).

Illustration 3:
Film stills from Rough Sea at Dover
(dir. Birt Acres, UK 1896).

to present-day viewers. The first audiences of the public film screenings beginning in 1895 were quick to note and appreciate the completely new type of spatial experience that the cinema facilitated. In his influential account of the form of spectatorship common to early cinema, which he named the "cinema of attractions" (1990), Tom Gunning emphasizes that it was not the realism of the representation that so fascinated and thrilled early audiences. Instead, the astonishment to which they often attested was, according to Gunning, due far more to the more abstract qualities of the image and the experience of 'movere', or an affective exhilaration, brought about by the movement of the image itself (see ibid)[8]. Film records a kind of flow that fundamentally defines the spatial experience of the viewer; filmic space should not be understood to merely reproduce architectural space, as a container of objects in which activities take place, but rather as a kind of kaleidoscopic space in which the things of the world sway, lose their original form, and take on new forms.

Keeping Gunning's perspective on early cinema in mind one may better understand the published accounts of the experience of seeing a film in these first years of the cinema offered by those turn-of-the-20th-century viewers who were so fascinated by steam or smoke, by the quivering leaves of a tree or the waves of the ocean (see *Illustration 3*). In this way, images of these objects could themselves be the source of this kind of exhilaration or astonishment, despite their ostensibly unspectacular subject matter, because of the pure kinetic enjoyment they provided. The everyday items visible in the images dissolve into objects of pure rhythmic intensity. Siegfried Kracauer's account of his own first encounter with a film offers support for this perspective. At the end of his preface to his *Theory of Film: The Redemption of Physical Reality*, he writes:

8 For a detailed examination of this question, see Gunning 2006 and Sobchack 2006.

> I was still a young boy when I saw my first film. The impression it made upon me must have been intoxicating, for I there and then determined to commit my experience to writing. To the best of my recollection, this was my earliest literary project. Whether it ever materialized, I have forgotten. But I have not forgotten its long-winded title, which back home from the moviehouse, I immediately put on a shred of paper. *Film as the Discoverer of the Marvels of Everyday Life*, the title read. And I remember, as if it were today, the marvels themselves. What thrilled me so deeply was an ordinary suburban street, filled with lights and shadows which transfigured it. Several trees stood about, and there was in the foreground a puddle reflecting invisible house facades and a piece of the sky. Then a breeze moved the shadows, and the facades with the sky below began to waver. The trembling upper world in a dirty puddle – this image has never left me. (1960: xi)

This description of Kracauer's early encounter with the cinema (he was born in 1889) has often been taken for a sign of filmic realism, in other words, that film offers an encounter with the world in a naturalistic sense; it should, however, equally be understood as a description of the kind of encounter with the world that film makes accessible. In short: rather than as an example of representational realism, it should be viewed as one of experiential realism. "The trembling upper world in a dirty puddle" is indeed a form of representation but an obscure, blurred, kinetically transformed one. In a word, it is a distracted perspective on the world.

The form of abstraction that is at play in films such as this is, however, quite different from that which is generally meant when one speaks of abstract film. In a recent book that investigates Wassily Kandinsky's development of his notion of abstraction, the art historian Matthias Haldemann offers a reevaluation of the term, which somewhat softens the divide between the representational and the abstract. In it, Haldemann wonders, crucially: When one speaks of abstraction, what is it exactly that has become abstracted? To answer this question, he returns to Kandinsky's original ruminations on the issue and finds therein a significant contribution to a theory of the nature of the image or what the image does (to a 'Bildwissenschaft' avant la lettre, that is): for Kandinsky, abstraction takes place on the level of the effects caused by the image in its observer. The experience of abstraction makes reference to the 'sensually accessible world and not only to its negation'[9]. As such, viewers may also find abstraction within representational images (as the early film viewers seem to have been able to do, those film viewers who were in fact Kandinsky's contemporaries). According to Haldemann,

> Kandinsky first spoke in 1909 of the 'abstract' effect of a work that is generally accepted to be representational. In 1912 he recognized that the 'abstract reverberations' of a physical form do not necessarily result in a 'destruction of the object'. Even an image that is quite *representational* could nonetheless be viewed as *abstract*! It is possible to see both the "object and the painting" at the same time. The abstract is synonymous here with the effect on the observer. [...] As such a significant content-based displacement took place: if the abstract had heretofore only been used in reference to nonrepresentational elements, after 1909 it also began to be used in reference to the perceptual effects brought about by an image and the faculty of imagination in both the artist and the viewer.[10]

Haldemann's reinterpretation of the notion of abstraction within Kandinsky's writings points to the necessity of an analogous shift of our attention regarding the manner in which one sees a moving image: we should be less attentive to the processes that seek to semantically identify objects present in images and more attentive to the ever-changing effects of the image itself. Thus, the image would oftentimes be more properly identified as being in a state of constant flux or oscillation between the representational and the abstract. Such a shift in our assumptions about whether an image is either abstract or representational is particularly significant in the case of the moving image, since the relationship between what constitutes a line and a surface and what constitutes a representational object is far more complex there than in a still image.

9 "[...] sinnlich erfahrbare Wirklichkeit, nicht allein [auf] deren Negation [...]" (Haldemann 2001: 13). Unless otherwise indicated, all translations are mine.

10 "Zum ersten Mal sprach Kandinsky 1909 von der 'abstrakten Wirkung' eines weitgehend noch als gegenständlich begriffenen Werks. 1912 stellte er fest, dass das 'abstrakte Klingen' einer körperlichen Form keine 'Zerstörung des Gegenstands' brauchte. Selbst ein an sich *gegenständliches* Bild könne demzufolge *abstrakt* gesehen werden! Es sei möglich, 'Objekt und Malerei' gleichzeitig zu erkennen. Abstrakt ist hier mit Wirkung gleichgesetzt. [...] Folglich fand eine bedeutsame inhaltliche Verlagerung statt: Hatte abstrakt zunächst allein gegenstandslose Elemente bezeichnet, bezog sich der Begriff ab 1909 ebenso auf die Wirkungseigenschaften eines Bildes und auf das Vorstellungsvermögen von Künstler und Betrachter." (Ibid.: 21 [emphases in the original])

But how does a contemporary viewer enter into a similar state of potentially immersive exchange with the moving image? Is it simply no longer available to us, because we have grown accustomed to film's marvels? This kind of visual complexity is neatly demonstrated by Larry Gottheim's eleven-minute silent film *Fog Line* (Canada 1970), shot with an entirely static camera, which begins with a frame filled by a fog nearly completely obscuring the contours of a landscape (see *Illustration 4*). Two cables are visible throughout the film, which seem to be part of an unseen system of electrical masts in this landscape, neatly trisecting the image more or less horizontally. Thus the image recalls image structures familiar from constructivist paintings and photomontages from the early part of the 20th century, although one could hardly refer to this film as dynamic. Nevertheless, although the camera is static, the image is not: one views this image as it changes throughout the eleven minutes from a single plane, trisected by the cables into a three-dimensional space, into a three-dimensional landscape. Gottheim documents the discovery of a landscape hovering between abstraction and representation, highlighting the interstitial spaces between these categories of perception made available by the moving image, allowing objects to dissolve and take shape once more, moving between representation and rhythm, formal rigor, and pure intensity.

Illustration 4: Film still from Fog Line *(dir. Larry Gottheim, Canada 1970).*

In Scott MacDonald's account of the film, he highlights the viewer's intense engagement with the movement of the image itself rather than with the realist representation of space that slowly becomes available there. He writes:

> For a few moments at the beginning of this film, viewers cannot be sure that the image they're looking at is a motion picture. Indeed, it is only once the fog has thinned enough for an identification of the image to be possible that we can recognize that something other than the movie projector – the fog itself – is moving. (2001: 9)

Viewed in the light of more traditional accounts of immersion, the experience of watching *Fog Line* would be seen as either not at all immersive or, at most, slowly immersive in that one would slowly be able to insert oneself into the three-dimensional space that slowly becomes manifest within the image. An alternative reading of the kind of investment that is made by a viewer of *Fog Line* has recently been offered by Justin Remes, who takes up what he calls a "cinema of stasis" and the opportunity for contemplation offered by a great many films that highlight the temporality of the viewer's experience rather than the motion that is visible within the film's image. Remes suggests that it might be true that "static films are even more insistent on spectatorial contemplation than traditional visual art" (2012: 267), adding that "the majority of works within the cinema of stasis aim to create a space for meditation, for immersion in an image, for sober reflections on the nature of movement and stasis, time and space, cinema and art" (ibid.: 268). I would like to consider the immersive qualities of this form of contemplation more closely than Remes does and suggest a different kind of investment available in this image, one that is conceptual rather than based on the realistic representation of space but is, nonetheless, concerned not only with the temporality of the filmic image but also with its capacity to suggest movement.

In order to better elucidate the manner in which such a sense of immersive investment may come about, I would like to finally take a closer look at how the consideration of relationships of scale may be highlighted by the moving image and may thus provide a more abstract experience of immersion. An ideal venue for considerations of scale is the planetarium. Due both to the large-scale projections onto its domed ceiling and to the more intense darkness (compared with that commonly experienced in a cinema) of the room in which the presentation takes place, the planetarium format is often included among media with immersive qualities. Alison Griffiths compares the experience to that available in a panorama, writing:

> Like the panorama, the planetarium experience takes place inside a dome […] where a "virtual" reality is illusionistically constructed; spectators are to imagine that once they take their seat, they are magically transported to outer space and possibly another time, depending on the subject of the planetarium performance or panoramic painting. (2008: 116)

However, it would be incorrect to assume that the planetarium as an institution continues to present the same perspective on our surroundings that was facilitated by the 19th-century panorama. The goals of the contemporary planetarium are both more ambitious and more complex than they are given credit for in Griffiths's account. Planetariums do not merely offer a grand overview of the world, or indeed the universe, but also challenge the perspective of each viewer by attempting to offer more than an immersive experience in absolute time and space in a Newtonian sense.

But what could such an immersive experience look like? A contemporary presentation at the Zeiss Planetarium in Bochum, Germany, entitled *Chaos & Order*, for instance, takes up the notion of fractals and their place within our experience of the world[11]. The roughly sixty-minute large-scale round image projection onto the domed ceiling of the planetarium investigates the various types of depth experience suggested by abstract and representational images ranging from human figures moving through recognizable public spaces in Germany to abstract forms and patterns, such as cubes and spheres, in various arrays to a variety of fractal figures, providing visualizations of mathematical concepts. However, all of these images are prefaced by a quotation at the start of the presentation: the first thing made visible on the dome's surface is a sentence attributed to the MIT physicist (and cosmologist) Max Tegmark: "The universe is made of math." This famous claim made by Tegmark attempts to account for what he assumes should be the fundamental simplicity of any notion that one may propose as a hypothesis to account for the structure of the universe. Most famously, Einstein's theory of relativity challenged a perspective on space and time that allowed for human perception and its intervention in the universe through observation and measurement to be equal to the task of representing space and time adequately. As Tegmark puts it, "If a reality exists independently of us, it must be free from the language that we use to describe it. There should be no human baggage" (qtd. Frank 2008). Hence Tegmark argues that mathematics not only describes reality but rather is reality: "Mathematical things actually exist, and they are actually physical reality" (qtd. ibid.). In order to explain this notion, in the face of embodied experience as the basis for our access to the world, Tegmark suggests imagining two perspectives on reality: one that is exterior to that reality, an overview that he likens to a physicist studying reality's mathematical structure, which he terms a "bird's eye

11 A short clip from *Chaos & Order* has been uploaded by Rocco Helmchen on vimeo: http://vimeo.com/44867264. [06/02/2014].

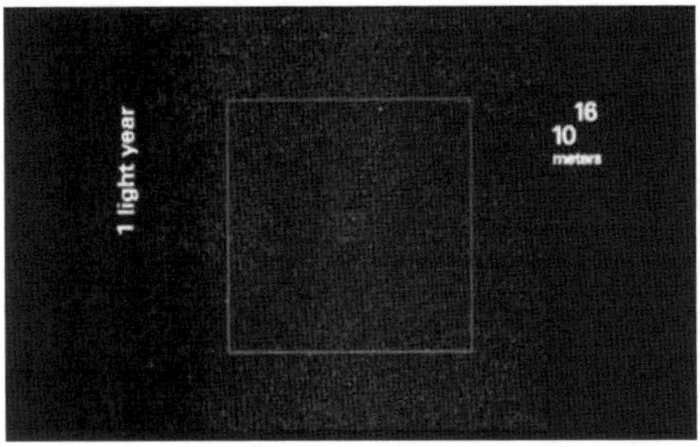

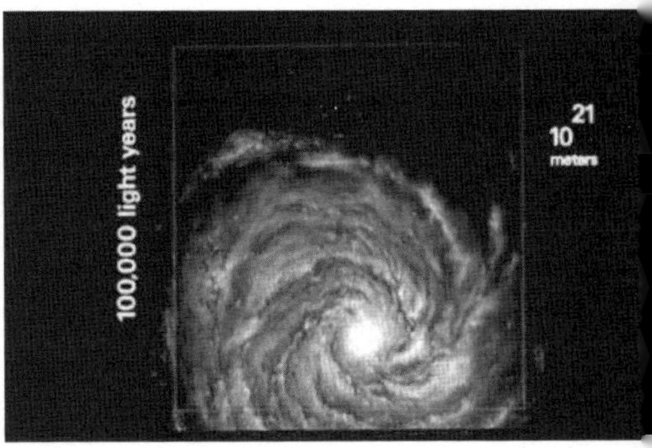

view"; the other, aligned with our own embodied experience within our own frame of reference and thus within the structure of reality itself, he terms a "frog's eye view". The two perspectives, one from within reality and one from a position external to it, are connected to one another through time. He continues:

> Einstein's theory taken as a whole represents the bird's perspective. In relativity all of time already exists. All events, including your entire life, already exist as the mathematical structure called space-time. In space-time, nothing happens or changes because it contains all time at once. From the frog's perspective it appears that time is flowing, but that is just an illusion. The frog looks out and sees the moon in space, orbiting around Earth. But from the bird's perspective, the moon's orbit is a static spiral in space-time. (Qtd. ibid.)

To this the interviewer responds, "the frog feels time pass, but from the bird's perspective it's all just one eternal, unalterable mathematical structure" (qtd. ibid.).

And it is this contrast between the relative perspectives of the frog and the bird that Rocco Helmchen attempts to visualize in *Chaos & Order*: he contrasts shadowy human figures in everyday situations (moving, for instance, in slow motion through the space of the 'Hauptbahnhof' in Berlin) with a vast array of interstitial spaces, including the stars visible from Earth, which are more typically the subject of planetarium shows, culminating finally with the representation of fractals. Fractals are generally defined as self-identical structures that repeat their form infinitely. By means of the various contrasts visible in this presentation of types of movement, both through realistic representations of space on the surface of the Earth and through digital special-effect animations of geometrical shapes including fractals, *Chaos & Order* suggests an alternative kind of abstract immersion to its viewer from that which was described as present in *Fog Line* in

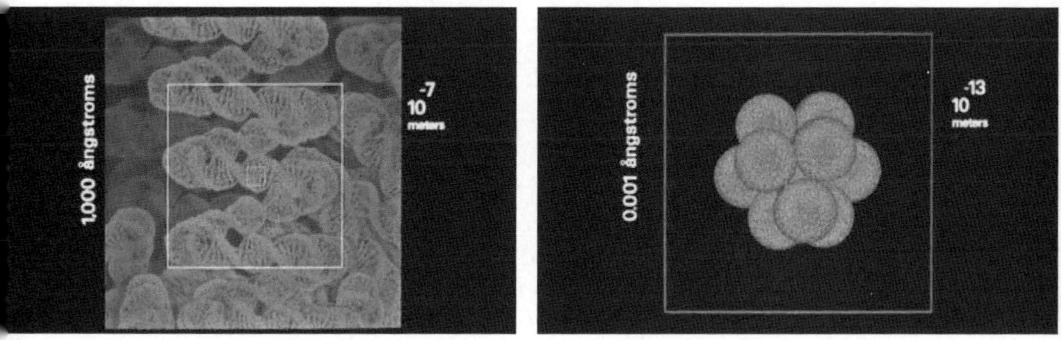

Illustration 5: Film stills from Powers of Ten *(dir. Charles and Ray Eames, USA 1977).*

that it is primarily conceptual in nature. In essence, it takes up the relationship between the perspectives of the frog and the bird that were described by Tegmark above in that it contrasts movement within space and time with fractal figures. Thus *Chaos & Order* seeks to offer what in German is termed a 'Denkfigur', or a tangible model for complex thought, regarding space, time, and the shape of the universe.

In order to clarify what *Chaos & Order* is attempting to represent, let me contrast it with a much older film that explicitly takes up the notion of scale: *Powers of Ten* (USA 1977) by Charles and Ray Eames[12]. The film begins with a nearly static image of a woman and a man sitting on a blanket having a picnic in a park in Chicago and begins to zoom out slowly from a view of the man resting on the blanket that measures ten meters across, to one that is expanded by the power of ten every ten seconds (see *Illustration 5*). This continuous zoom is narrated by a voice-over, which identifies both the present location of the camera relative to the original couple in its journey through space and the specific calculations, each to the power of ten, that represent the change in perspective that is marked every ten seconds. The journey outwards takes the viewer finally out to a view at the edge of our known universe. The voice-over guiding us on this journey states the following: "As we approach the limit of our vision, we pause to start back home. This lonely scene, the galaxies like dust, is what most of space looks

12 The film was made in two iterations, in 1968 and 1977. The later, final, version, which lasts nine minutes, is the best-known version, and I make reference to that version here.

like. This emptiness is normal. The richness of our own neighborhood is the exception."

At this point, the camera begins to rapidly zoom in again until it closes in once more on the couple on the blanket and, finally, on a close-up of the hand of the man resting there. A second voyage is initiated at this point, marked every ten seconds by a movement by the power of ten inwards (thus reducing the perspective offered by 90 percent every ten seconds), into the interior of the man's hand through a similarly extensive zoom inwards until a single proton is the focus of the image. Finally, the similarity of this inner space to the outer reaches of what was known to us of outer space in the 1960s is highlighted by the voice-over, which states: "As we draw toward the atom's attracting center, we enter upon a vast inner space – at last the carbon nucleus! [...] We are in a domain of universal modules. There are protons and neutrons in every nucleus, electrons in every atom, atoms bonded into every module out to the farthest galaxy."

The film highlights the visual similarity of the inner- and outermost realms visited on this phantom ride through space (both inner and outer), where the emptiness of the smallest and the most distant realms, those least known or understood, is similarly black and void. But the calculations represented by the film, the temporal constant of the power of ten by which the movement inwards and outwards is gauged, represent a reassuring anthropomorphic presence within the film: that of scale. The movement is smooth and the space traversed is increasingly empty but, nonetheless, wholly available to the gaze of the camera, which is able to provide us with a complete overview.

In recent years, Mary Ann Doane (see 2003) has been investigating the significance of scale for the cinema particularly as represented within the various meanings ascribed to the close-up. She distinguishes between two opposing tendencies within discussions of the close-up in film theory and practice. One tendency, associated with the American cinema, views the close-up in terms of perspective or point of view, implying an identification between the camera and the viewer. This take on the close-up suggests a relationship to that which is pictured akin to taking possession of that person or thing. The other tendency, associated with the Soviet and French cinemas, views the close-up as a quality inherent to the image, representing the notion of scale, highlighting either the gigantic or the miniature. This latter model assumes a relationship to what is represented in terms of what Doane labels "transcendence (the image is truly 'larger than life'), a scale that guarantees unattainability" (ibid: 93). It is not Doane's goal to endorse one or the other of these tendencies but rather to suggest that the power of the cinema, particularly as a modernist palliative, lies in its dual allegiance to these notions. She writes: "The close-up, with its contradictory status (as both detail of a larger scene and totality in its own right – a spectacle of scale with its own integrity) responds to this need [for a simulacrum of wholeness]" (ibid.). The component parts of this simulacrum are in permanent oscillation with one another: "detail and enormity, miniature and gigantic", Doane concludes, "are inextricable in the cinema" (ibid.: 110). Doane's account of the close-up sees it as the hinge in cinema's flirtation with issues of scale, which both appeal to and hinder the viewer's desire for an immersive experience in the cinema, or what Doane herself terms "the lure of absorption into the image, of losing oneself" (ibid.). This is both the pleasure and the threat raised by the historical discourse on the close-up:

> Its unspeakability is no doubt linked to the desire to make it a corporeal experience, a matter of touching, feeling, tasting as well as seeing. Yet the historical trajectory of classical cinema was to defeat that body by annihilating its space, its ability to act as a measure of scale. (Ibid.)

Indeed, scale, as a concept, is inconceivable if separated from its reference to and implicit inscription of the human body as the measure of all things.

Both of these films appeal to us to imagine the relationship between the micro and the macro; however, they approach this challenge differently. *Powers of Ten* employs scale as a kind of rail upon which the viewer travels to partake of a phantom ride from a perspective familiar from everyday life, outwards and then inwards, highlighting the visual parallels between the macro and micro perspectives while emphasizing the distance that lies between them. In contrast, *Chaos & Order* highlights the incommensurability of the frog's and the bird's perspectives on space and thus does not provide a reassuring overview of these points of view. Furthermore, fractals themselves challenge the very notion of scale in that they are identical at every level of measure: parts are indistinguishable from the whole.

Thus films such as these final cosmic examples do not invite viewers to immerse themselves in them in the traditional sense, by being transported into the spaces represented within the films. Instead, viewers are more likely to be confounded by the vastness (and minuteness) of the objects on display and by the two films' approaches to the contrast between the large and the small, the near and the far. The reflection on the relationship between the edges of the universe and the proton offered in both of these films can provoke a variety of forms of spatial experience and offer a template for an engagement with space that is not based in illusion but rather in conceptual immersion and contemplation. Such films as these should raise doubt regarding any simple description of the way in which immersive spatial experience is brought about by way of the moving image. They should encourage us to investigate more than only the most obvious explanations for our engagement with the moving image and consider the complex manner in which representation and abstraction interact to suggest a third, perhaps more conceptual, form of fascination. We must consider alternatives to the evidence offered by the contemporary blockbuster, for the spatial experience offered by the moving image goes beyond that which may be explained through the analogy of the roller coaster; by way of our engagement with the moving image, we enter the fun house of aesthetic experience.

References

Balides, Constance (2003). "Immersion in the Virtual Ornament". David Thorburn, Henry Jenkins, eds. *Rethinking Media Change: The Aesthetics of Transition.* Cambridge, MA/London: MIT Press. 315–336. (Previous version available online: "Virtual Spaces and Incorporative Logics: Contemporary Films as 'Mass Ornaments'". *Media in Transition.* http://web.mit.edu/m-i-t/articles/index_balides.html. [10/01/2013]).

Belton, John (1992). *Widescreen Cinema.* Cambridge, MA: Harvard UP.

Bennett, Tony (1983). "A Thousand and One Troubles: Blackpool Pleasure Beach". Tony Benett et al., eds. *Formations of Pleasure.* London: Routledge & Kegan Paul. 138–155.

Curtis, Robin (2008). "Immersion und Einfühlung: Zwischen Repräsentationalität und Materialität bewegter Bilder". *montage AV* 17/2: 89–107.

— (2010). "Bewegung, Rhythmus, Immersion: Räumliche Wirkung der Abstraktion". Robin Curtis, Marc Glöde, Gertrud Koch, eds.

Synästhesie-Effekte: Zur Intermodalität der ästhetischen Wahrnehmung. Munich: Fink. 131–150.
— (2011). "Learning to Live with Abstraction: Filmic Abstraction and Sensory Intermodality". Joerg Fingerhut, Sabine Flach, Jan Söffner, eds. *Habitus in Habitat III: Synaesthesia and Kinaesthetics.* Bern: Peter Lang. 155–170.
— (2012). "'Einfühlung' and Abstraction in the Moving Image". *Science in Context* 25/3: 425–446.
Doane, Mary Ann (2003). "The Close-Up: Scale and Detail in the Cinema". *differences* 14/3: 89–111.
Frank, Adam (2008: online). "Is the Universe Actually Made of Math? Cosmologist Max Tegmark Says Mathematical Formulas Create Reality". *Discover Magazine.* http://discovermagazine.com/2008/jul/16-is-the-universe-actually-made-of-math#.UPKYfaW0eCh. [10/01/2013].
Griffiths, Alison (2008). *Shivers Down Your Spine: Cinema, Museums, and the Immersive View.* New York, NY: Columbia UP.
Gunning, Tom (1989). "An Aesthetic of Astonishment: Early Film and the (In)Credulous Spectator". *Art and Text* 34: 31–45.
— (1990). "The Cinema of Attractions: Early Film, Its Spectator and the Avant-Garde". Thomas Elsaesser, ed. *Early Cinema: Space Frame Narrative.* London: British Film Institute. 56–62.
— (2006). "Attractions: How They Came into the World". Strauven, ed. 31–41.
Haldemann, Matthias (2001). *Kandinskys Abstraktion: Die Entstehung und Transformation seines Bildkonzepts.* Munich: Fink.
Kirby, Lynne (1997). *Parallel Tracks: The Railroad and Silent Cinema.* Durham, NC: Duke UP.
Kracauer, Siegfried (1960). *Theory of Film: The Redemption of Physical Reality.* Princeton, NJ: Princeton UP.
— (1963). *Das Ornament der Masse: Essays.* Frankfurt am Main: Suhrkamp.
— (1995). *The Mass Ornament: Weimar Essays.* Ed. and transl. Thomas Y. Levin. Cambridge, MA: Harvard UP.
Lipps, Theodor (1905/1985). "Empathy and Aesthetic Pleasure". Karl Aschenbrenner, Arnold Isenberg, eds. *Aesthetic Theories: Studies in the Philosophy of Art.* New Jersey, NJ: Prentice-Hall. 403–412.
Loiperdinger, Martin (2004). "Lumière's Arrival of the Train: Cinema's Founding Myth". *The Moving Image* 4/1: 89–118.

Lunenfeld, Peter (1993). "Digital Dialectics: A Hybrid Theory of Computer Media". *Afterimage* 21/4: 5–7.
MacDonald, Scott (2001). *The Garden in the Machine: A Field Guide to Independent Films about Place.* Berkeley, CA: University of California Press.
MacGowan, Kenneth (1957). "The Wide Screen of Yesterday and Tomorrow". *The Quarterly of Film Radio and Television* 11/3: 217–241.
Manovich, Lev (2001). *The Language of New Media.* Cambridge, MA/London: MIT Press.
McAllister, Ken (2009: online). "Comments: Media Immersion: Ignis Fatuus?" *In Media Res: A Media Commons Project.* http://mediacommons.futureofthebook.org/imr/2009/04/14/multiple-perspectives-player-immersion. [23/12/2012].
Moeller, Ryan (2009: online). "Multiple Perspectives on Player Immersion". *In Media Res: A Media Commons Project.* http://mediacommons.futureofthebook.org/imr/2009/04/14/multiple-perspectives-player-immersion. [23/12/2012].
Murray, Janet (1997). *Hamlet on the Holodeck: The Future of Narrative in Cyberspace.* New York, NY: The Free Press.
Peterson, Jennifer Lynn (2013). *Education in the School of Dreams: Travelogues and Early Nonfiction Film.* Durham, NC: Duke UP.
Remes, Justin (2012). "Motion(less) Pictures: The Cinema of Stasis". *British Journal of Aesthetics* 52/3: 257–270.
Scarry, Elaine (2001). *Dreaming by the Book.* Princeton, NJ: Princeton UP.
Schivelbusch, Wolfgang (1979). *Geschichte der Eisenbahnreise: Zur Industrialisierung von Raum und Zeit im 19. Jahrhundert.* Frankfurt am Main: Ullstein.
— (1979/1986). *The Railway Journey: The Industrialization of Time and Space in the 19th Century.* 2nd ed. Berkeley, CA: University of California Press.
Sobchack, Vivian (2006). "'Cutting to the Quick': Techne, Physis, and Poiesis and the Attractions of Slow Motion". Strauven, ed. 337–355.
Strauven, Wanda, ed. (2006). *The Cinema of Attractions Reloaded.* Amsterdam: Amsterdam UP.
Whitney, Allison (2005). *The Eye of Daedelus: A History and Theory of IMAX Cinema.* PhD thesis, University of Chicago.

Illustration 1:
Jeffrey Shaw, The Legible City *(1988–1991).*
Interactive installation, Collection of ZKM.

Immersed in Reflection?
The Aesthetic Experience of Interactive Media Art

Katja Kwastek

In (media) art, immersion is not only effective as a visual-spatial illusion, but also in the sense of cognitive immersion in illusory worlds or artistically staged processes. This is particularly true in the case of interactive art, which requires an active awareness of offers of interaction and places the focus on the participant's actions. In this way, it enables effects that the psychologist Mihály Csíkszentmihályi refers to as 'flow' – the sense of becoming absorbed in one's own actions caused by intrinsic motivation. Here, the focus is not on a withdrawal from everyday life, but rather on the emotional and cognitive intensity of the experience. However, connecting the psychological concept of flow with theories of reception in art seems difficult, because the potential for aesthetic experience is usually attached to a fundamental requirement: aesthetic distance. According to this theory, the aesthetic object is only constituted through the viewer's contemplation. In interactive art, however, how the living, breathing participant actually acts is crucial to the realization of the artistic concept, which, in its realization, asks to be both experienced and contemplated. This essay poses the question of which strategies interactive art develops to bring together the supposed opposites of immersion and reflection, aesthetic experience and flow.

1. Immersion and Virtual Reality

Interactive art calls for the viewer to actively engage with an interactive system designed by an artist or artist group. This dependence on the physical participation of the audience distinguishes interactive art from most other forms of artistic expression, which invite the audience to become cognitively active but do not engage them in the physical realization of the work. As a consequence, interactive art's quest for the viewer's physical participation necessitates a reconsideration of the possible modes of aesthetic experience in the reception of art. This essay will discuss the relevance of the concept of immersion for the participatory reception of interactive media art.

As several other essays in this volume show, the reception of art (including music, theater, film, and architecture) may be informed by different kinds of immersive experiences. In the context of new media and new media art, the concept of immersion has traditionally

Illustration 2:
Char Davies, Tree Pond, Osmose *(1995). Digital still captured in real time through HMD (head-mounted display) during live performance of the immersive virtual environment.*

(especially in the 1990s) been closely associated with virtual reality. Virtual reality denotes a computer-generated environment that the participant feels part of or surrounded by and that opens up possibilities of interaction[1]. This is true for some of the 'classics' of interactive media art, such as Jeffrey Shaw's *The Legible City* (1988–1991; see *Illustration 1*), or Char Davies's *Osmose* (1995; see *Illustration 2*). *The Legible City* is based on the presentation of an artificial urban landscape that – instead of buildings – consists of three-dimensional letters. While navigating this artificial city by means of an interface resembling a stationary bicycle, the visitor can 'read' sentences lined up along the city streets. *Osmose*, on the contrary, invites the visitor to 'fly' through different formations reminiscent of natural forms like clouds and leaves. It thus stages immersion literally as the diving into substances or instances of matter.

Both examples show that, in the context of mediated environments, immersion does not necessarily require a mimetic representation of the physical world and a remodeling of its principles but may instead be staged as a journey through alternative worlds that offers experiences different from those present in our everyday lives. The 'reality' referenced by the paradoxical notion of 'virtual reality' thus does not denote that which is physically possible but the phenomenon of 'taking something for real', namely, the illusionary.

But immersion may even do without visual illusion altogether. Concerning video games, game theorists Katie Salen and Eric Zimmerman

1 According to Christiane Paul, the original meaning of virtual reality was "a reality that fully immersed its users in a three-dimensional world generated by a computer and allowed them an interaction with the virtual objects that comprise that world" (2003: 125).

expose the primacy of realistic illusion as an "immersive fallacy". They hold that an intensive experience of play does not necessarily require the illusion of acting within an artificial world (cf. 2004: 450). This is why Staffan Björk and Jussi Holopainen, again in the context of game studies, suggest a distinction between spatial, sensorimotor, cognitive, and emotional immersion (cf. 2005: 206). Visual illusion based on the three-dimensional presentation of navigable environments is thus only one possible facilitator of immersion within digital systems. 'Immersion', in this reading, serves as a kind of generic term for various phenomena of absorption into processual experiences. In the following, I will discuss one aspect of such immersive experiences described by the concept of 'flow'.

2. Flow

'Flow' describes the cognitive and emotional aspects of being immersed in or carried away with an action. Like immersion, it draws on the metaphor of liquidity to denote its absorbing potential, but its emphasis is on the processuality and intensity of an experience. The term was coined by the American psychologist Mihály Csíkszentmihályi, who defines "flow" as a state in which

> action follows upon action according to an internal logic which seems to need no conscious intervention on our part. We experience it as a unified flowing from one moment to the next, in which we feel in control of our actions, and in which there is little distinction between self and environment; between stimulus and response; or between past, present, and future. (1975: 58)

Thus, the issue here is not mental or sensual illusion but the emotional and cognitive intensity of an experience. The concept of flow focuses on processes of individual perception. It describes a subjective experience, not a staged situation or the aesthetic potential of a specific medium. Csíkszentmihályi identifies several factors as constitutive for the experience of flow: focused concentration on the action, loss of self-consciousness, merging of action and awareness, intrinsic motivation, clearness and achievability of goals, and control over the situation (cf. ibid.: 40–47).

I consider the concept of flow as key to an analysis of the aesthetic experience of interactive art, as it relates experiences based on intrinsic motivation – a central characteristic of any kind of reception of art in general – to action-based experiences, which have been identified as distinctive of the reception of interactive art.

3. Aesthetic Distance

The suggested framing of action-based experiences as aesthetic experiences touches upon a central issue of aesthetic theory. The reason is that the association of aesthetic experience with physical activity challenges a fundamental condition to which the possibility of aesthetic experience of any art form is usually linked – that of aesthetic distance (cf. Wolf 2013: 14f.). The aesthetic object – according to the prevailing theory – is constituted only in the contemplative act of the viewer. For the literary scholar and founder of reception aesthetics Hans Robert Jauß, for example, the detachment of the reception situation from normal, everyday behavior is a fundamental condition of the aesthetic experience (cf. 1982: 31).

In contrast, Hans-Georg Gadamer describes the aesthetic experience of art as a transformation. Gadamer describes the artwork as "a true being in the fact that it becomes an experience that changes the person who experiences it" (2004: 103)[2]. He distinguishes the knowledge attained through aesthetic experience from logical judgment as a transformation that can be controlled only partially. The spectator's experience, according to Gadamer, must not be equated with a distanced judgment. On the contrary, the experience is interrupted if the spectator "reflects about the conception behind a performance or about the proficiency of the actors" (ibid.: 116)[3]. While he goes on to say that aesthetic reflection has its own value, he does not consider it essential to aesthetic knowledge. For Gadamer, aesthetic knowledge is primarily based not on reflective judgment but on the process of transformation described above.

This admittedly brief citation of two key theoretical positions must suffice as evidence of the ambivalent assessment of aesthetic distance (cf. Wolf 2013: 14f.) within theories of aesthetic experience. It is here that the possibility of becoming directly absorbed in an aes-

2 "[...] eine echte Erfahrung am Werke, die den, der sie macht, nicht unverändert lässt" (Gadamer 1960: 95).

3 "[...] über die Auffassung, die einer Aufführung zugrunde liegt, oder über die Leistung der Darsteller als solche reflektiert" (ibid.: 112).

thetic experience comes into conflict with the possibility of acquiring knowledge, which is commonly thought to be dependent upon a distancing of the self from the object of understanding. This tension is not restricted to the realm of interactive art but is accentuated here by the merging of action and experience. In this category of art, not only the relationship between aesthetic experience and knowledge but also that between aesthetic experience and action must be reconceived. The embodied action of the participant is indispensable for the fulfillment of the artistic concept, which is intended to be experienced and reflected upon while being unfolded.

In the following, I will explore the complex interrelations of immersion and reflection at stake in the experience of interactive media art by drawing upon three close readings of exemplary works.

4. Frame Collisions: Stefan Schemat's *Wasser*

Visitors to Stefan Schemat's work *Wasser* (2004; see *Illustration 3*) are given a small backpack containing a laptop equipped with a GPS device and headphones. They are invited to explore a section of coastline near Cuxhaven, Germany, where the Elbe River enters the North Sea. Based on the visitor's exact location, as established by the GPS device, the computer plays back different audio-recorded text fragments. Together, these make up a story, though not a linear one. Rather, it takes the form of a mesh of situations, actions, memories, and observations. The participant's movement shapes its course, by the direction in which he or she walks, and by his or her endurance in exploring the area. The story's basic framework is a criminal investigation: a woman has disappeared and the participant is asked to find her. The participant is invited to close his or her eyes and to assume the role of a blind detective.

The different audio texts range from concrete instructions ('Come on, get going!'), through personal reminiscences ('But why did you run away?'), to scientific and philosophical observations on natural phenomena, which often lead to musings about transformation and metamorphosis ('As a shell, I am deaf and blind.')[4]. The narrators sometimes appear to be detached observers, at other times

4 ("Los, geh' schon los!"), ("Aber warum bist du bloß weggelaufen?"), ("Als Muschel bin ich blind und taub."). Unless otherwise indicated, all translations are mine.

Illustration 3:
Stefan Schemat, Wasser *(2004).*
Augmented reality fiction,
site of work, Cuxhaven, Germany.

characters in the story. At the same time, the story is closely tied to the landscape in which it is being presented. Aspects of the scenery are mentioned and observations are made about the weather. Events are described that took place or could have taken place at locations the visitor is passing at that very moment. The landscape thus becomes the setting for the plot; it provides the imagery to accompany the text, and the participant has the sensation of being in a film – except that he or she is actor and audience at the same time. Although the work might at first sight be considered as belonging to the genre of digital literature or radio play, visuality plays a central role. Landscape and texts become a fabric woven from reality and fiction, within which the participant has to actively position him- or herself, even beyond deciding whether or not to assume the role of blind detective.

In the reception of *Wasser*, experiences of flow may be caused by the multi-sensorial stimulation of the participant, his or her assignment of an active role, and the close interweaving of different semantic situations. The visitor is invited to actively explore and individually construct a spatially structured web of thoughts, of real and narrated events, within which he or she might, at least momentarily, feel fully engaged. In the long run, however, it is nearly impossible to experience the interaction as a seamless process, since total immersion in the fictional plot is constantly impeded. First of all, this is due to the multi-perspective faceting of the story, within which assuming a stable role is nearly impossible. The visitor may also defy diegetic rules of the work, such as closing his or her eyes, because he or she does not find them to be binding. In fact, the work itself encourages participants to violate this rule, because despite the clear order at the beginning to keep their eyes closed, they are later explicitly encouraged to open them.

At the same time, the work constantly prompts the participant to traverse the boundary from art to everyday life and vice versa. To an external observer, the participant is no different from any normal person walking on the beach, whereas the participant quickly becomes aware of his or her double role as a walker (a participant in the everyday life of the seaside area), on the one hand, and as a recipient of art (an aesthetic observer of the activities he or she is carrying out), on the other. The ambivalence between the activities of contemplating art and strolling along the beach guides the participant's reception of the work. Furthermore, concerning the media-based presentation of the story, it is extremely unlikely that the participant really believes he or she is participating in an actual dialogue, as he or she is merely playing back prerecorded audio files.

The oscillation between executing and abstaining from an action, between observing rules and freely exploring the proposed interaction, and between identifying with the narrative and reflecting on it from a distance all contribute to the participant's becoming aware of his or her own ambivalent point of view within the complex fabric of fictional elements, associations, and materialities the work presents. This multi-sensorial and semantically complex work pulls the participant, again and again, from experiences of flow into distanced positions of self-observation, reflection, or distraction. Such disruptions, which have been described by Erika Fischer-Lichte as "frame collisions" (2008: 48) ("Kollision von Rahmen"; 2004: 341, referring to Erving Goffman's theory of frame analysis; see 1974), are a key aspect of the aesthetic experience of this work.

Although *Wasser* by Stefan Schemat fulfills many of the constitutive factors of flow identified by Csíkszentmihályi, it defies others, especially the clearness and achievability of goals and the possibility of exercising control over the situation. In Schemat's work, the ambivalence between flow and reflection is based on disruptions resulting from the challenges of the presented narrative, the role assigned to the visitor, and the merging of the artificial and everyday environments. In the following, I will discuss two further interactive artworks that differ from the first insofar as they forgo any form of narrative or assignment of roles. Furthermore, they are interactive installations/environments intended for exhibition in enclosed spaces.

5. Remarks on Methodology

With regard to methodology, however, the analysis of the following examples will be based on a different premise. As the reader may have noticed, I have, so far, outlined my argument by means of a close reading based on personal experience and visitor observation, but devoid of any empirical data that would support my analysis. This approach will probably not have irritated the reader, as this form of analysis based on personal observation is common in art history. Nevertheless, especially concerning analyses focusing on the aesthetics of reception, we might ask to what extent we can do justice to the variety of possible audience experiences. Therefore, the following descriptions pursue a different method of data collection. They rely on empirical data collected during a research project I had the opportunity to conduct at the Ludwig Boltzmann Institute Media.Art.Research in 2009.

Illustration 4: Setup for the video-cued recall interviews, Lentos Kunstmuseum Linz, 2009.

Within this project, we applied the video-cued recall (VCR) method. Lizzie Muller and Caitlin Jones, with whom I collaboratively conducted this research, had already applied this method in the past. In VCR, the participant is filmed during the interaction and is subsequently asked to comment on his or her actions and perceptions while watching this video recording of him- or herself (see *Illustration 4*) (cf. Muller 2008: 4). An in-depth interview with the participant is carried out only after this procedure, and is paralleled with an extensive artist interview. The self-commentary encouraged in the VCR method proved to be very informative, in part because the video-supported self-observation allowed pauses in the conversation, which gave the participants the opportunity to recall details and enough time to verbalize their experiences.

It goes without saying that this method of research is also based on a kind of laboratory setting. The awareness of being filmed, the retroactive description of experiences, and – above all – their verbalization all account for a biased outcome. Nevertheless, I hold that if we want to scientifically research individual aesthetic experience, this method is a promising option.

6. Creative Flow: Tmema's *Manual Input Workstation*

My second example is a 'classical' interactive installation intended for exhibition indoors. It combines a gestural input interface with audiovisual output. This output is neither narrative nor representational, but abstract – even its abstract forms and sounds can be considered extremely minimalistic. I consciously selected this work to corroborate my argument, as it helps to illustrate that within interactive media art, immersive situations can be created without any reference to narrative, spatial, or representational systems.

The *Manual Input Workstation* was constructed by the artist duo Tmema (Golan Levin and Zachary Lieberman) in 2004 (see *Illustration 5*). It can be described as an interactive installation that allows users to create and manipulate abstract images and sounds. At first glance, it resembles an ordinary overhead projector with some cut-out cardboard shapes lying next to it. Visitors can place the shapes on the glass surface, thereby projecting the shadows of the shapes onto the facing wall. But the work does more than simply project the shadows – it also records them with a video camera attached to a computer. The software analyzes the video data and generates both sounds and animated objects that correspond to the shapes, which are then superimposed via a data projector onto the overhead projection. Thus, visitors see the silhouettes of the shapes overlaid by computer animations and accompanied by sounds. Most visitors quickly realize that they can create images using not only the shapes that have been provided, but also other objects, such as – and especially – their own

Illustration 5:
Tmema (Golan Levin and Zachary Lieberman), Manual Input Workstation *(2004–2006). Interactive installation, exhibition view at Ars Electronica Center, Linz.*

hands. In fact, visitors can use hand movements and gestures to discover not only different but also more sophisticated ways of creating dynamic shapes.

The installation has different program modes: the Rotuni mode generates sound-image formations directly based on the shadows created by the participant. Starting from the center of the shape and extending only as far as its contours, a green radar arm rotates clockwise in a steady rhythm. Each advance of the arm generates a tone, the pitch of which is determined by the length of the arm (which depends, in turn, on the extension of the contours of the underlying shape). In addition, when a very high note sounds, the entire shape briefly lights up. Another mode, NegDrop, invites the participant to create closed contours that the system then fills with colored shapes. If the contour is opened, the shape inside drops to the bottom of the screen and bounces repeatedly, each time triggering a sound, which varies depending on the size, form, and rate of fall of the shape.

As part of the aforementioned research project, we empirically documented audience interactions with the work using the VCR method.

One visitor, who described himself as musical, was initially mainly attracted to the acoustic phenomena (see Kwastek/Muller/Spörl 2009a). When he arrived, the work was in the Rotuni mode, and he immediately began to move his fingers in time to the sounds as though plucking the strings of a guitar. While observing himself on video afterward, he said he had found the overhead projector to be a physical hindrance and was surprised at how little he had moved. He also explained that he had found it difficult to coordinate his hands with the mirror-inverted projection, a problem he had often noticed in his job as a teacher as well. While formulating his reflections retroactively during the video-supported self-observation, this teacher said that, while interacting, he had, for the most part, felt immersed in the work. His evident enthusiasm for the process of interaction is also suggested by the fact that even while watching the recording of his interaction, he spontaneously commented on the shapes he was creating, saying, "doesn't this look cool?" (qtd. ibid.). Another participant also reported her enchantment with the constellations that emerged:

> That was fascinating when all these little things fell down, and I knew they were coming from my hands; I liked that very much. I just liked the colors, and I saw them falling. I didn't think so much about the music then, it was more the colors, the shapes that were fascinating me, so I tried them very often, because [laughs] I thought it was really nice. (Qtd. Kwastek/Muller/Spörl 2009b)

A third participant, who described himself as a media theorist, explored the workings of the different modes in great detail. For example, he characterized the Rotuni mode as the least interactive of the three, because all it did was set off an automatic process (see Kwastek/Muller/Spörl 2009c). It quickly became clear through his self-observations and self-description that he was used to dealing with interactive art and was able to apply appropriate strategies, for instance, when he explained how he had approached the work: "I think my first approach was to try and figure out how it worked more or less and then to use it as an expressive device. That's what I was hoping to do" (qtd. ibid.). This is also evident when he describes the situation after about three minutes of interaction as follows: "Up until now, I was really laboring a lot to try and figure out, ok, what are the rules of interaction and hopefully they will be more interesting than something you just do once and then it's over" (qtd. ibid.). At another point in the recording, he recalls that his main aim had been to find out the most efficient way of generating something new "as opposed to sort of repeating the same thing over and over again" (qtd. ibid.). Thus, his self-description focused on the exploration of the system's functionality, while he was also interested in discovering the limits of the work. For example, he spent a lot of time trying to find out whether there were interim steps between two modes or whether these could be created, with the intention of making the Rotuni mode more interesting: "Here, again, I am perhaps too stubbornly insisting on trying to do something different with mode number two [laughs]" (qtd. ibid.). He also verbalized the difference between immersing himself in the activity and reflecting on it:

> This is like an interesting tension between, on the one hand, trying to deal with it in a sort of right-brain kind of way, as here for example, just sort of playing with it, and then, on the other hand, sort of a left-brain kind of way, to try to figure out what some of the algorithmic logic and intuition there is. (Qtd. ibid.)

Whereas this visitor explicitly verbalized the oscillation in the aesthetic experience between exploration, creativity, and immersion, the other two visitors tended to reflect on single aspects of their experience, such as their gestures or their focus on either acoustic or visual feedback.

Such individual self-observations not only reveal how greatly aesthetic experiences can vary from one visitor to another, but also how much they depend on formative influences and previous experiences on the part of the participants. As the reactions of these three visitors show, each developed their own strategies of interaction. As diverse as these interactions are, they are all based on an alternation between flow and reflection.

Nevertheless, flow, in this context, is not based on the identification with a role or the absorption in a fictional world or multi-sensorial stimuli but on a kind of creative play, on the expressive manipulation of forms and sounds, which results in observable formations. Golan Levin actually describes the ideal reception of the work as a state of creative flow – a kind of rapture. He believes that participants may become engrossed by the feedback loop in progress and enchanted by the emerging possibilities and relationships that become apparent between the self and the system (cf. Kwastek/Muller 2009: question 6). But as the VCR interviews show, flow is, again, paralleled or followed by moments of reflection.

As has been shown by these interactions with the *Manual Input Workstation*, flow is not aroused by the identification with a narrative but by processes of explorative creation. Furthermore, the characteristics provoking reflection here differ from those found in Schemat's work, which have been identified as semantic or contextual frame collisions. In the *Manual Input Workstation*, reflection is encouraged as part of explorative creation itself. While exploring the workings of the system, visitors start to reflect on the characteristics of different media and the interrelations of the visual and the auditory.

7. Resonance: David Rokeby's *Very Nervous System*

My third example is better described as an interactive environment than as an installation, since the first thing visitors encounter is an empty, silent space. In David Rokeby's *Very Nervous System* (1983 to present; see *Illustration 6*), there is no visual feedback, only auditory. When visitors inside the room move, they hear sounds – either the timbres of different musical instruments or everyday noises such as human breathing or gurgling water. The system records the visitors' movements and gestures via video camera, analyzes them digitally, and responds to them by emitting sequences of sound.

Rokeby emphasizes that his interest in interactivity is not focused on the straightforward and intellectually comprehensible control of processes. He objects to interpretations of interaction as control. His aim is to create a system based on intuitive body movements in order to challenge the perception of the computer as a logical machine with no connection to the human body. Rokeby is interested not in control, but in resonance; not in power, but in the adjustment of the participant and the system to one another (see 1990). He describes an imaginary ideal participant as someone who "tries to control it [...] hard to tell [...] then lets go of that and starts to relax into the piece [...] sound moves against her body" (qtd. Muller/Jones 2009: question 1). Ideally, Rokeby explains, the feedback loop functions faster than it can be consciously perceived: "The body starts to lead in a way that does not seem to be guided by consciousness. So the body is responding to sounds that are produced by movements you still haven't taken possession of consciously" (qtd. ibid.: question 3). Rokeby uses the term 'resonance' to emphasize the way that recipients' actions can actually take place subconsciously. As soon as visitors allow themselves to spontaneously react to the sounds emitted by the system, they are "played by the installation [...] allowing the music of the system to speak back through [their bodies] directly, involving a minimum of mental reflection" (Rokeby 1990).

Thus, according to the artist's intention, the aesthetic potential of the *Very Nervous System* is primarily based on the possibilities for transformation as described by Gadamer, in the sense of a self-knowledge achieved through new forms of experience. These experiences are found on the boundary between physical and cognitive awareness and between conscious control and unconscious reaction. As a result, the work has practically no consciously implemented disruptions that explicitly seek to provoke an oscillation between reflection and absorption.

In fact, two of the participants who were filmed and interviewed as part of the aforementioned research project pointed out that it was not really possible to control the work. Nonetheless, neither of them, contrary to the artist's intention, seems to have entirely abandoned her- or himself to the interaction. They simply limited themselves to the further exploration of the system's workings. One of them described her attitude toward the installation as intellectual as opposed to emotional (see Muller 2009a; 2009e).

Another visitor experienced the difference between Rokeby's installation and traditional artworks as a feeling of closer proximity to the work. He believed that this depended not only on the invitation to actively participate, but also on the fact that the work did not require interpretation in the usual sense. He further explained that, whereas with traditional art, it is difficult to liberate oneself from existing discourses and that one always seeks to understand artworks, this work was very accessible and simply fun to interact with (see Muller 2009b). At the same time, he pointed out several times that he had tried to find out how the system worked and where its spatial boundaries lay. Nonetheless, he found the experience of exploration playful and enjoyable. Another visitor also tried to investigate how the installation responded to her, but entirely ignored its technical workings (she reported that, throughout the entire interaction, she had never figured out how it worked). However, it was also clear from her interview that understanding the workings of the piece was not important to her. She actually experienced the interaction as a, at least potential, form of resonance with the system: "I didn't quite find out whether the sounds wanted to make me move or not, but it was more enjoyable all the time" (qtd. Kwastek 2009). At another point, she described how her own movements merged with the sounds produced by the system and spoke of a sense of abandoning herself to the sounds. Other participants compared their enjoy-

Illustration 6:
David Rokeby, Very Nervous System *(1983 to present). Interactive installation, exhibition view at Lentos Kunstmuseum Linz, 2009.*

ment of the interaction with that of a child trying out a new toy (see Muller 2009c) and described the meditative effect of the installation, which they said had made them slow down (see Muller 2009d).

Again, the reported artistic intentions and visitor experiences share many characteristics with the experience of flow as described by Csíkszentmihályi: focused concentration, a loss of self-consciousness, and a merging of action and awareness. However, they also differ insofar as the artist explicitly attempts to preclude the possibility of the participants' taking control of the situation. The participants, on the other hand, report that the interest in understanding the workings of the system repeatedly led to attitudes of distanced reflection. Again, it turns out that characteristics of flow significantly inform the aesthetic experience of the work, but are complemented by intentional or unintentional disruptions, and thus by moments of distancing and reflection.

8. Conclusion

As I hope to have proven by means of the three examples discussed above, the aesthetic experience of interactive (media) art is often based on an oscillating process between flow and reflection; between absorption in the activity and distanced (self-)perception. All three works described require action-based reception in the form of explorative walking, gestural creation, or full-body movement. They do, however, differ substantially concerning their semiotic contexts: one offering a narrative setting, the second based on abstract formations, the third creating an atmospheric aural environment for interaction. Accordingly, the quality of the participants' activity and its contextualization differ substantially. Nevertheless, in all three examples, aesthetic experience is informed by an interplay of flow and reflection.

Not all theorists agree, however, that reflection is possible during absorption in an activity. Marvin Carlson claims that states of flow impede reflexivity through the merging of action and awareness, the total concentration on the pleasure of the moment, and the loss of a sense of self and any type of goal pursuit (cf. 1996/2004: 22). Csíkszentmihályi, on the contrary, sees moments of reflection as a necessary counterpart to flow. He believes that specifically because flow prevents reflections on one's consciousness, interruptions to this state, however minimal, are essential: "Typically, a person can maintain merged awareness with his or her actions for only short periods, which are broken by interludes when he adopts an outside perspective" (1975: 38). In the same vein, John Dewey describes a rhythm of surrender and reflection. He believes that the moment of surrender is interrupted in order to ask where the object of the surrender is leading and how it is leading there. Because surrendering to the object consumes the viewer by way of "cumulation, tension, conservation, anticipation, and fulfillment", one must distance oneself enough to be able to "escape the hypnotic effect of its total qualitative impression" (Dewey 1934: 150).

Both Csíkszentmihályi and Dewey thus posit an alternation between states of flow and reflection. Goffman, by contrast, believes the two can actually occur in parallel. He argues that a person can be simultaneously active in different channels of activity – observing and reacting to other occurrences while engaged in a concentrated action, and even communicating in a "concealment channel" (1974: 219)[5].

Whether the dominant mode in the active realization of interactive art is an alternating or a parallel manifestation of reflective and immersive moments is ultimately difficult to determine. What matters in this context, and what I have tried to explain through these examples and their analysis via my own observations and visitor interviews, is that aesthetic distance or reflection and immersive experiences of flow are not mutually exclusive in the experience of interactive art, but essential counterparts[6].

References

Björk, Staffan, Jussi Holopainen (2005). *Patterns in Game Design.* Boston, MA: Charles River Media.

Carlson, Marvin A. (1996/2004). *Performance: A Critical Introduction.* 2nd ed. New York, NY/London: Routledge.

Csíkszentmihályi, Mihály (1975). *Beyond Boredom and Anxiety:*

5 Mark B. N. Hansen reminds us that simultaneity of object awareness and consciousness of one's own perception is already described in Husserl's theory of double intentionality (cf. 2004: 252).

6 This paper is part of a larger research project conducted by the author (see Kwastek 2013).

The Experience of Play in Work and Games. San Francisco, CA: Jossey-Bass.
Dewey, John (1934). *Art as Experience*. New York, NY: Minton, Balch & Company.
Fischer-Lichte, Erika (2004). *Ästhetik des Performativen*. Frankfurt am Main: Suhrkamp.
— (2008). *The Transformative Power of Performance: A New Aesthetics*. Transl. Saskya Jain. New York, NY/London: Routledge.
Gadamer, Hans-Georg (1960). *Wahrheit und Methode: Grundzüge einer philosophischen Hermeneutik*. Tübingen: Mohr.
— (2004). *Truth and Method*. 2nd rev. ed. Transl. Joel Weinsheimer, Donald G. Marshall. New York, NY/London: Continuum.
Goffman, Erving (1974). *Frame Analysis: An Essay on the Organization of Experience*. London: Harper & Row.
Hansen, Mark B. N. (2004). *New Philosophy for New Media*. Cambridge, MA/London: MIT Press.
Jauß, Hans Robert (1977/1982). *Ästhetische Erfahrung und literarische Hermeneutik*. Frankfurt am Main: Suhrkamp.
— (1982). *Aesthetic Experience and Literary Hermeneutics*. Transl. Michael Shaw. Minneapolis, MN: University of Minnesota Press.
Kwastek, Katja (2009: online). "*Very Nervous System*: Documentary Collection: Video-Cued Recall with Birgitt, Linz 2009". *La Fondation Daniel Langlois*. http://www.fondation-langlois.org/html/e/page.php?NumPage=2193. [15/08/2014].
— (2013). *Aesthetics of Interaction in Digital Art*. Cambridge MA/London: MIT Press.
—, Lizzie Muller (2009: online). "*The Manual Input Workstation*: Documentary Collection: Interview with Golan Levin, Linz 2009". *La Fondation Daniel Langlois*. http://www.fondation-langlois.org/html/e/page.php?NumPage=2221. [15/08/2014].
—, Lizzie Muller, Ingrid Spörl (2009a: online). "*The Manual Input Workstation*: Documentary Collection: Video-Cued Recall with Helmut, Linz 2009". *La Fondation Daniel Langlois*. http://www.fondation-langlois.org/html/e/page.php?NumPage=2225. [15/08/2014].
—, Lizzie Muller, Ingrid Spörl (2009b: online). "*The Manual Input Workstation*: Documentary Collection: Video-Cued Recall with Heidi, Linz 2009". *La Fondation Daniel Langlois*. http://www.fondation-langlois.org/html/e/page.php?NumPage=2225. [15/08/2014].

—, Lizzie Muller, Ingrid Spörl (2009c: online). "*The Manual Input Workstation*: Documentary Collection: Video-Cued Recall with Franzisko, Linz 2009". *La Fondation Daniel Langlois.* http://www.fondation-langlois.org/html/e/page.php?NumPage=2225. [15/08/2014].

Muller, Lizzie (2008: online). "Towards an Oral History of New Media Art". *La Fondation Daniel Langlois.* http://www.fondation-langlois.org/html/e/page.php?NumPage=2096. [15/08/2014].

— (2009a: online). "*Very Nervous System*: Documentary Collection: Video-Cued Recall with Susanna, Linz 2009". *La Fondation Daniel Langlois.* http://www.fondation-langlois.org/html/e/page.php?Num Page=2193. [15/08/2014].

— (2009b: online). "*Very Nervous System*: Documentary Collection: Video-Cued Recall with Markus, Linz 2009". *La Fondation Daniel Langlois.* http://www.fondation-langlois.org/html/e/page.php?Num Page=2193. [15/08/2014].

— (2009c). "Interview with Alexander, Linz 2009". Private Archive.

— (2009d). "Interview with Claudia, Linz 2009". Private Archive.

— (2009e: online). "Very Nervous System: Documentary Collection: Video-Cued Recall with Elfi, Linz 2009". *La Fondation Daniel Langlois.* http://www.fondation-langlois.org/html/e/page.php?Num Page=2193. [15/08/2014].

—, Caitlin Jones (2009: online). "*Very Nervous System*: Documentary Collection: Interview with David Rokeby, Linz 2009". *La Fondation Daniel Langlois.* http://www.fondation-langlois.org/html/e/page.php?NumPage=2187. [15/08/2014].

Paul, Christiane (2003). *Digital Art.* London: Thames & Hudson.

Rokeby, David (1990). "The Harmonics of Interaction". *MusicWorks* 46: 24–26. (Online: Website of the Artist. http://www.davidrokeby.com/harm.html. [15/08/2014]).

Salen, Katie, Eric Zimmerman (2004). *Rules of Play: Game Design Fundamentals*. Cambridge, MA/London: MIT Press.

Wolf, Werner (2013). "Aesthetic Illusion". Werner Wolf, Walter Bernhart, Andreas Mahler, eds. *Immersion and Distance: Aesthetic Illusion in Literature and Other Media.* Amsterdam/New York, NY: Rodopi. 1–63.

Illustration 1:
Pieter Bruegel the Elder, Landscape with the Fall of Icarus *(ca. 1558), detail. Oil on canvas, 73.5 x 112 cm, Royal Museums of Fine Arts of Belgium.*

Neither Here nor There
The Paradoxes of Immersion

Fabienne Liptay

In "Leaving the Movie Theater" Roland Barthes speaks of the twofold fascination of the cinema, which affects viewers both as an image and as a surrounding. For him, watching a film means experiencing the illusion of having "two bodies at the same time", of being inside the film's space and at the same time outside in the theater. The resulting concurrence of conflicting sensory perceptions is constitutive for situations in which viewers immerse into an artificial image space without ever completely blocking the coordinates of the real environment from their consciousness. The correlation of these conflicting perceptions occasionally causes more sensitive viewers to experience dizziness and nausea, an unsettling yet – to a certain degree – pleasurable feeling, which is significantly intensified in media environments such as 3-D films and virtual reality. Based on these observations, dizziness will be illuminated as a visual formula of immersion as it is captured by Alfred Hitchcock's *Vertigo* effect: an antidromic motion by which the camera zooms forward while tracking backward. The article discusses examples from the fields of mainstream cinema, experimental cinema, and video art that self-consciously deploy dizzying effects in order to reflect upon their medial conditions and potentials. Considering the viewer's experience of these works, this article suggests understanding immersion as a paradoxical experience: an experience of being neither here nor there, but in an unstable, perceptual 'in-between' zone.

1. The Viewer's Two Bodies

In his short essay "Leaving the Movie Theater", written in 1975, Roland Barthes draws attention to cinema's power of fascinating the viewer twice over:

> [...] by the image and by its surroundings – as if I had two bodies at the same time: a narcissistic body which gazes, lost, into the engulfing mirror, and a perverse body, ready to fetishize not the image but precisely what exceeds it: the texture of the sound, the hall, the darkness, the obscure mass of the other bodies, the rays of light, entering the theater, leaving the hall; in short, in order to distance, in order to "take off," I complicate a "relation" by a "situation." What I use to distance myself from the image – that, ultimately, is what fascinates me:

> I am hypnotized by a distance; and this distance is not critical (intellectual), it is, one might say, an amorous distance [...]. (1995: 421)[1]

Here, cinema is described as a realm of experience in which the viewer's senses simultaneously extend between the screen and the movie theater. When Barthes speaks of a narcissistic interest in the screen and a fetishistic interest in the movie theater, he draws upon the vocabulary of psychoanalysis in order to describe a paradox that is constitutive for the cinematic experience in general. Theories of immersion commonly focus on strategies and techniques of resolving this paradox, but, as I will argue, it is precisely in viewers' experiences of immersive media that this paradox resurfaces as a challenge to the theories themselves. Provided that we understand immersion as an act of relocation in an artificially created space while awareness of the real environment is almost completely blocked out, we may, of course, question whether the assumption of conflicting interests in the image and its surroundings can logically be maintained here. Through digital image and sound technologies, the cinematic experience has become more and more spatial. In the case of 3-D cinema, the image is even no longer identical to the screen, but seems to extend to both sides of the projection surface into space. However, even though the image increasingly inhabits its surroundings, screen space and viewing space are far from being experienced as one and the same. Their relationship can be described as that of an unstable correlation, without its resulting contradictions resolving in favor of one space or the other (see Bieger 2007)[2]. Consequently, the impression of having two bod-

1 "[...] par l'image et par ses entours, comme si j'avais deux corps en même temps: un corps narcissique qui regarde, perdu dans le miroir proche, et un corps pervers, prêt à fétichiser, non l'image, mais précisément ce qui l'excède: le grain du son, la salle, le noir, la masse obscure des autres corps, les rais de la lumière, l'entrée, la sortie: bref, pour distancer, 'décoller', je complique une 'relation' par une 'situation'. Ce dont je me sers pour prendre mes distances à l'égard de l'image, voilà, en fin de compte, ce qui me fascine: je suis hypnotisé par une distance; et cette distance n'est pas critique (intellectuelle); c'est, si l'on peut dire, une distance amoureuse [...]." (Barthes 1975: 106f.)

2 In this sense, Laura Bieger speaks of a choreography of immersing and emerging that evokes a feeling of being 'in-between': 'In this way, the impression of a heightened reality through being simultaneously present in two different locations is temporally extended. This is because, as long as you submit yourself to a game of oscillating between fiction and reality, immersing and emerging, the space around you lingers in a receptive limbo.' ("Der Eindruck einer gesteigerten Wirklichkeit durch gleichzeitige Anwesenheit an zwei unterschiedlichen Orten wird auf diese Weise zeitlich ausgedehnt,

ies at the same time is not lifted in immersive environments, but even more amplified. Similar to the trompe l'oeil, the appeal of these environments lies precisely in conveying the illusion of spatial depth and physical volume while simultaneously allowing the viewer to see through it (cf. Wolf 2013: 16f.). Therefore, the cinematic experience almost inevitably relies on the precondition that the sensation of immersion and the thwarting of this sensation always coexist (see Schweinitz 2006)[3].

Even in situations in which the image and its surroundings share a common space, film viewers experience having two bodies when they find themselves in the midst of the film and, at the same time, outside in the viewing space. In sensitive viewers these competing sensations occasionally arouse feelings of dizziness and nausea. When the stimulus discrepancy is felt particularly severely, because the body is receiving contradictory information about its position and movement in space, one speaks of visually induced motion sickness (VIMS) (see Bos/Bles/Groen 2008; Kennedy/Drexler/Kennedy 2010; Solimini 2013)[4]. While the eye is taken along with the camera and darts around the film's space, the vestibular system in the inner ear remains in a steady seated position, which causes the so-called visual-vestibular conflict. It is significant that the vestibular system was not discovered as an independent organ until the late 19th century, when, in the course of industrialization and urbanization, the body's reaction to acceleration, in particular, became a focus of attention (cf. Simmen 1990: 18f.). The symptoms viewers can experience in media-based environ-

denn solange man sich dem Spiel eines Oszillierens zwischen Fiktion und Wirklichkeit, Ein- und Auftauchen hingibt, verweilt der Raum um einen herum in einem rezeptiven Schwebezustand"; 2007: 224). Unless otherwise indicated, all translations are mine.

3 Jörg Schweinitz describes this effect as the 'oscillating simultaneity of intense immersion and the not-disabled awareness that one is dealing with a product of art' ("oszillierende Gleichzeitigkeit von hochgradiger Immersion und dem nicht ausgeschalteten Bewusstsein, es mit einem Kunstprodukt zu tun zu haben"; 2006: 147).

4 "Those symptoms [nausea (nausea, increased salivation, sweating) and disorientation (dizziness, vertigo, fullness of the head)] are indicative of VIMS, a condition that may onset during or after viewing dynamic images while being physically still, when images induce in the stationary spectator a sense of vection (i. e. illusion of self movement). The most accepted explanation for VIMS is the classical conflict theory based on the mismatch between the visual, the proprioceptive and the vestibular stimuli. In this case, the visual system feels vections while the vestibular and proprioceptive systems do not transmit signals consistent with motion" (Solimini 2013: 2).

ments, including dizziness and nausea, are related to those caused by motion sickness (kinetosis), which is also brought on by a contradiction of sensations (cf. Rabinovitz 2006: 45). They occur more prominently in cases in which the image space occupies the viewer's entire field of vision or even surrounds his or her body. This is why these symptoms have been observed in the past in visitors to the panoramas of the 19th century (see Buddemeier 1970; Huhtamo 2013)[5] as well as in more recent times in viewers of 3-D movies (see Solimini et al. 2012; Solimini 2013; Bos et al. 2013)[6]. If one understands 'immersion' as the impression of being relocated to or surrounded by another world caused by perceptual and psychological effects (cf. Murray 1997: 98; Ryan 2001: 103), this impression does not, however, inevitably have to amplify the sense of being there. On the contrary, it is perceived as impairing the experience of presence especially in those instances in which dizziness and nausea mix in with the viewer's perception (see Ijsselsteijn/Riva 2003; McMahan 2003).

However, we do not need to go to a 3-D movie, climb into a flight simulator, or navigate through cyberspace to get dizzy. Similar side

5 In 1807, in *Handbuch der Ästhetik*, Johann August Eberhard noted: 'The preciseness of the perspective, the accuracy of the drawing, the verity of the contrast and expression set me, through their collective enchantment, in the true natural world, but the bleak, deathlike silence and lifeless motionlessness cast me back out. I oscillate between reality and non-reality, between nature and non-nature, between truth and illusion. My thoughts, my spirits take on a swinging, wavering, swaying movement, which has the same effect as going around in circles or the rocking of a ship. It is in this way that I explain the dizziness and nausea that overcome the steadfast viewer of the panorama.' ("Die Genauigkeit der Perspective, die Richtigkeit der Zeichnung, die Wahrheit des Helldunkels und der Haltung versetzen mich durch ihre vereinten Zauber in die wirkliche Natur, aber die öde Todesstille und die erstorbene Bewegungslosigkeit stoßen mich daraus zurück. Ich schwanke zwischen Wirklichkeit und Nichtwirklichkeit, zwischen Natur und Unnatur, zwischen Wahrheit und Schein. Meine Gedanken, meine Lebensgeister erhalten eine schwingende hin und her gestoßene, schaukelnde Bewegung, die eben so wirkt, wie das Herumdrehen im Kreise und das Schwanken des Schiffs. Und so erkläre ich mir den Schwindel und die Uebelkeit, die den unverwandten Anschauer des Panorama überfällt"; qtd. Buddemeier 1970: 175).

6 In a comparable study of 497 subjects who watched the film of their choice in 2-D or 3-D in the movie theater, Angelo G. Solimini came to the following conclusion: "Viewing 3D movies can increase rating of nausea, oculomotor and disorientation. Analogous to riding a roller coaster, for most individuals the increase in symptoms is part of the 3D experience and enjoyment and this experience is not necessarily an adverse health consequence. However, some viewers will have responses that in other contexts might be unpleasant" (Solimini et al. 2012: 8).

effects can already be experienced by looking at works of art in high concentration, particularly in Florence, where Stendhal suffered from an illness that was later named after him. In his travel journal from 1817, he notes its symptoms, which troubled him after a visit to the Franciscan church Santa Croce: "I had reached that stage of emotion where *celestial sensations* given by art and passionate feeling meet each other. Upon leaving *Santa Croce* I had heart palpitations, which in Berlin are called nerves; I was totally exhausted, I was afraid of falling as I walked" (qtd. Ross 2010: 93)[7]. The psychiatrist Graziella Magherini, who treated many such cases on an ambulatory basis in the Hospital of Santa Maria Nuova in Florence, gave Stendhal syndrome its name and described its causes in her clinical study published in 1989[8]. Inspired by her medical treatise, Dario Argento's film *La sindrome di Stendhal* (*The Stendhal Syndrome*, Italy 1996) features a protagonist who is afflicted with this Florentine art sickness. When detective Anna Manni (Asia Argento), trying to track down a murderer preying on women, goes to the Uffizi, the paintings suddenly come to life. At first, the young woman hears the sounds of what is depicted in the paintings and frescos: the clamor in Paolo Uccello's *The Battle of San Romano* (ca. 1440) and the divine wind in Sandro Botticelli's *The Birth of Venus* (ca. 1486). Gripped by dizziness, she then plunges into the floodwaters in Pieter Bruegel the Elder's *Landscape with the Fall of Icarus* (ca. 1558) – which, incidentally, is not located in the Uffizi in Florence but in the Royal Museums of Fine Arts of Belgium

7 "J'étais arrivé à ce point d'emotion où se recontrent les *sensations célestes* données par les beaux-arts et les sentiments passionnés. En sortant de *Santa Croce*, j'avais un battement de cœur, ce qu'on appelle des nerfs à Berlin; la vie était épuisée chez moi, je marchais avec la crainte de tomber" (Stendhal 1826/1987: 272 [emphasis in the original]).

8 In an interview, Graziella Magherini spoke about the potential causes: "The Stendhal Syndrome is a normal aspect of artistic-aesthetic awareness. I have treated 106 cases in the last 10 years. They are very important, because they represent the tip of the iceberg in a process that is in fact very common, striking anyone who goes to see a work of art with an open mind and a desire to feel emotions. [...] An important aspect of the degree to which people can become confused by looking at art is a feeling of being completely overwhelmed. The Stendhal Syndrome occurs most frequently in Florence, because we have the greatest concentration of Renaissance art in the world. People seldom see just a single work, but overload themselves with hundreds of masterpieces in a short period" (qtd. Barnas 2008).

(see *Illustration 1*)[9]. Her gaze, as if caught in an undertow, is pulled into the painting as the camera flies through cloud vapor over the water's surface and into the bay. Barthes' metaphor of the viewer's two bodies is made explicit in a shot sequence that alternates between views of Anna in the actual space of the museum and in the imaginary space of the painting, showing how she synchronously falls unconscious here and sinks to the sea floor there. Argento, however, does not leave it at exhibiting Stendhal syndrome as an achievement of the painting's illusionism that allows us to perceive and experience the depicted world from within (cf. Wolf 2013: 11f.). The film's shocking effects derive from the visual evidence that whenever the detective enters pictorial spaces it appears as though she were truly, and not merely imaginarily, crossing over the threshold of the frame (cf. Barck 2009: 220f.). It remains a privilege of fiction to invent such scenarios of total immersion, in which the image ceases to be an image and crosses the boundaries of aesthetic illusion toward a real experience.

2. The Double Meaning of Vertigo

Here, however, I am interested neither in the potential side effects of looking at images under certain circumstances, nor in the curious series of motifs that led from Stendhal's trip to Florence to Argento's psychological thriller. Instead, I am interested in dizziness and nausea as recurring symptoms of change within the history of media. Wherever they are explicitly addressed or depicted in the arts and media, they always relate to the specific cultural and historical context that 'caused' them. In this sense, dizziness and nausea are not merely psycho-physical constants in the history of image perception, whose periodic amplified occurrence can be explained by the overstimulation of the senses in the face of new and unfamiliar media. Rather, they may be considered as indicators of cultural-historical shifts, as markers of those 'secret transfer points at which modulations are no longer based on the old but a new quality is set' ("geheimen Umschlagplätze, wo Modulationen nicht mehr aufs Alte bezogen [sind], sondern eine neue Qualität sich setzt"; Simmen 1990: 23; see also Edwards/Bailey 2012).

9 For a reading of Bruegel's landscape paintings as immersive images, cf. Schulz 2011: 77f.

It is no coincidence that, in cinema, these symptoms appear particularly in self-reflexive instances in which the relationship between image and viewer is renegotiated under socially and technologically altered conditions of perception. Considering the fact that Argento's film was the first to make use of computer-generated imagery (CGI) in the history of Italian cinema, we perceive its digital effects not only as a means of displaying a new visualization technology but also as a means of addressing a shift within the image-viewer relationship itself: the viewer no longer stands across from an imaginary window, but plunges into a digitally liquefied image that dissolves into its surroundings (cf. Balides 2003: 317)[10]. In the process, screen and canvas converge into an interface between the image and the viewer, transforming into a site on which the metamorphosis of their relationship is carried out.

The symptoms of dizziness and nausea experienced by the protagonist of Argento's film are closely linked to the motif of water. Water's motion characteristics also connote the medical term 'vertigo', which *Webster's Revised Unabridged Dictionary* from 1913 defines as a "swimming of the head", a sensation according to which "objects, though stationary, appear to move in various directions, and the person affected finds it difficult to maintain an erect posture" (Porter, ed. 1913: 1605)[11]. The equivalent German term 'Schwindel' dispenses with this connotative proximity to water, but it opens up other semantic dimensions, for it can equally mean 'dizziness' or 'vertigo' as well as 'deceit' or 'swindle'. Etymologically speaking, the definition of physical discomfort is older than that of deceitful appearance, which

10 With regard to the film, Constance Balides speaks of an 'imaginary' immersion, which she differentiates from a 'virtual' immersion of computer-simulated surroundings – namely, that the former requires an image space that is not strictly three-dimensional or interactive. Viewers neither dive into the world of the film with their entire bodies nor can they independently navigate within it or change it.

11 The original trailer for Alfred Hitchcock's 1958 film *Vertigo*, which begins with the opening of a dictionary to explain the film's title, is based on this definition. On the pages of the book it reads: "ver'-ti-go – a feeling of dizziness … a swimming in the head … figuratively a state in which all things seem to be engulfed in a whirlpool of terror". The motion of a whirlpool is referred to here with the image of a spiral, which graphically depicts dizziness. This linking of motifs is used once again in Hitchcock's *Psycho* (USA 1960). In the shower scene, a shot of bloodstained water spiraling into the drain dissolves into a shot of the wide-open eye of the murdered protagonist from which the camera, also moving in a spiral, rotates as it zooms out.

has only gradually begun to develop since the 16th century (cf. Braun 2001: 14f.)[12]. However, between the term's seemingly competing notions there is an inner connection in that both imply a moment of illusiveness or pretense (see Janz/Stoermer/Hiepko, eds. 2003)[13]. In any of its uses, 'Schwindel' relates to an irritation of sensory perception and a destabilization of the order of reality, in which the viewer's vertigo and the picture's deceptive effects are closely related. Indicative of this is the fact that the viewer's psycho-physical experience corresponds with the picture's genuine accomplishment of presenting something so vividly that it seems real. No other film presented this correspondence in a more eye-catching manner than Alfred Hitchock's *Vertigo* (USA 1958), in which the protagonist's fear of heights is intrinsically linked to the deception to which he falls victim (cf. Braun 2001: 13; Teja Bach 2006: 380)[14]. Tellingly, the moment in which he

12 According to Christina von Braun, the different meanings of 'Schwindel' – as a syndrome and as a deception – both relate to the question of sensory perception: 'On the one hand, the symptom of vertigo is often traced back to an irritation of one's vision; on the other hand, seeing and vision are at the center of the great Western debate about the question of the collective perception of *reality*.' ("Einerseits wurde das Symptom des Schwindels sehr oft auf eine Irritation des Sehvermögens zurückgeführt; andererseits standen Sehen und Blick auch im Zentrum der großen abendländischen Debatten über die Fragen der kollektiven Wahrnehmung von *Wirklichkeit*"; 2001: 16f. [emphasis in the original]).

13 For Rolf-Peter Janz, Fabian Stoermer, and Andreas Hiepko, the meanings of 'Schwindel', in its literal and figurative senses, converge in this chatoyant character: 'It is clearly in the relativizing of the opposites of truth and lie, reality and illusion, characteristic of the figurative sense of the word "Schwindel", that the liberating moment in which constraints are discarded and the playing field of the possible expands – but also the uneasiness of a virtualization of the world lies. The experience of "Schwindel" in its literal sense seems to be characterized by the same ambivalence. The difference here, however, is that it does not apply to the coordinates of social reality but to the elementary order of the perceptual world.' ("In der für den Schwindel im übertragenen Sinne kennzeichnenden Relativierung der Gegensätze von Wahrheit und Lüge, Wirklichkeit und Schein offenbar das befreiende Moment der Dispension von Zwängen und der Erweiterung des Spielraums des Möglichen, aber auch das Beunruhigende einer Virtualisierung der Welt. Das Erleben des Schwindels im wörtlichen Sinn scheint von derselben Ambivalenz geprägt zu sein; nur bezieht sie sich hier nicht auf die Koordinaten der sozialen Wirklichkeit, sondern auf die elementaren Ordnungen der Wahrnehmungswelt"; 2003: 11f.).

14 'The overlapping of the two meanings also becomes clear in Alfred Hitchcock's film *Vertigo*, in which the male protagonist's dizzying fear of heights is put in relation to a complex web of deceit, pretense and simulation in which the hero is entangled.' ("Deutlich wird die Überlagerung der beiden Bedeutungen auch in Alfred Hitchcocks

discovers the deceit is also the moment he is cured of his vertigo; his fear of heights is thus by no means just an arbitrary, easily replaceable MacGuffin that sets the drama in motion. Precisely at the point at which media-generated illusions and simulations trigger cultural fantasies that mix in with the psycho-physical experiences of vertigo, it becomes apparent that what is being referred to is not merely an undesirable reaction to a technical stimulus. In this sense, the viewer's dizzying engagement is more than just a result of cinema's neat tricks and effects that are enhanced to the utmost degree with the newest media technology. Experiences of uncertainty and instability, of complexity and change provide the material out of which vertigo as an existential formula is composed (cf. Koebner 2003: 139f.)[15].

3. The Twofold Fascination of Film

Vertigo is the name for a deeply ambivalent experience that results from a destabilization of order, which itself traces back to the simultaneity of opposing perceptions. It is, once again, as if one would need two bodies at the same time to be able to confront these contradictions. In the case of cinema, however, this self-duplication not only entails correlating the experience of the image with that of its surroundings: the image alone exerts a twofold fascination in that it relocates the viewer in another world that is created by both audio-visual and narrative means. That these two facets of film are to be differentiated even in their interaction with one another is expressed by Béla Balázs, who advises the director to intensify the dramatic impact of his story through the evocation of pure physical sensations. Significantly, he refers to the "feeling of *vertigo*" (2010: 66) ("Schwindelgefühl"; 1924/2001: 83) as a prime example of such sensations that may

Film *Vertigo*, wo der Höhenschwindel des männlichen Protagonisten mit einem dichten Netz von Betrug, Verstellung und Simulation in Beziehung gesetzt wird, in das der Held verwickelt wird"; Braun 2001: 13).

15 It is in this sense that Michael Hagner also understands psycho-physiology's heightened interest in the 19th century in the experimental examination of dizziness in the context of 'cultural and aesthetic reactions to the drastic social and technological changes' ("kulturellen und ästhetischen Reaktionen auf die einschneidenden sozialen und technologischen Veränderungen"; 2001: 262) that characterize the experience of the modern era.

be induced by certain camera perspectives: "The greatest catastrophe depicted in a pictorial space that is separated from our own space will never have an impact comparable to the image that places us on the very edge of an abyss that opens up *before our very eyes*" (2010: 66 [emphases in the original])[16].

Considering Barthes' idea of the screen's "glue" (1995: 420) ("colle"; 1975: 105), we will have to distinguish between at least two different forms of viewers' fixation on film: in one case, it is an effect of audio-visual techniques; in the other, an effect of the story being told. In the case of cinema, viewers' immersive experience divides – put somewhat schematically – into their identification with the camera and their identification with the characters. If one wants to take this characteristic into account, film's immersive effects could basically be traced on the two different levels that Noël Burch has identified as "diegesis" and "narration" (see 1982). Calling into question the central importance of narrative for the viewer's engagement in a film, Burch assumes that the diegetic effect – which he also describes as the "cine-spectator's sense of *being-there*" (ibid.: 22 [emphasis in the original]) – can be achieved independently from the telling of a fictional or documentary story. The construction of an imaginary inhabitable world, as Étienne Souriau emphasizes (cf. 1953: 7; see also 1951), may be different from the media-related means of this construction; it is, however, inconceivable without them. Thus, for Burch, the viewer's engagement is achieved, first and foremost, through audio-

16 "Die größte Katastrophe, die in dem von unserem Raume geschiedenen Raume des Bildes sich abzuspielen scheint, wird nie so wirken, wie das Bild eines Abgrundes, der sich *vor unseren Augen öffnet*, als wenn wir selber über ihm stehen würden" (Balázs 1924/2001: 83). In this further context, Balázs mentions a scene from Friedrich Wilhelm Murnau's *Phantom* (Germany 1922) entitled "The Reeling Day". For this scene, Hermann Warm created a moving set, which sinks under the protagonist's dizzied senses as if pulled by an undertow: 'He [Alfred Abel] is in a state of tumbling; he is filled with and surrounded by a chase, a whirling. The psychological shock sent him into a chaotic state. This was nothing the actor himself could physically express; in order to show this state to the viewer, I came up with decorative, technical tricks.' ("Er [Alfred Abel] ist in einem Zustand des Taumelns, um ihn und in ihm ist ein Jagen und Wirbeln. Die seelische Erschütterung hat ihn in einen chaotischen Zustand versetzt. Vom Darsteller selbst war das mimisch nicht auszudrücken; um diesen Zustand dem Betrachter vor Augen zu führen, sind mir dekorative, technische Tricks eingefallen"; Warm 1979: 147f.). In his history of the film still, Barry Salt describes this scene as "the first attempt at what later became the standard method of suggesting a subjective feeling of dizziness, or vertigo, or loss of consciousness of a character in a film" (1983: 217).

visual techniques that relocate him or her in the space-time coordinates of the film:

> [...] gradations [between the fully diegetic film and the imperfectly or weakly diegetic film] depend not upon the absence or presence – or the relative degree of development – of narrative structures, but hinge, more fundamentally, on such factors as movement (both pro-filmic and camera), live sound, the readability of the picture track and even, to an extent, upon the use of shot-counter-shot and the other strategies of camera-ubiquity. (1982: 17)

The usually corresponding narrative and diegetic effects can sometimes diverge sharply – like in the case of Chris Marker's *La jetée* (France 1962), which Burch cites as an eccentric example of a weakening of the diegesis, thus as an experimental test of its limits (cf. ibid.: 27). It is primarily interesting because, on the diegetic level, the film withholds that which it promises on the narrative level: the complete immersion of the viewer in the image. *La jetée* is a 'roman-photo', a film that is composed exclusively of static black-and-white photographs, which are woven together into a science-fiction story by a voice-over narrator. The photographs seem to seal time and space in that they anticipate a dystopian future as having happened in the past (cf. Wollen 1984/2003: 79)[17]. Unlike the moving image, which is commonly said to show actions taking place in the present (cf., e. g., Gaudreault/Jost 1990: 101; for a critique of this position, cf. Bordwell 2004: 212f.), the photographs are assigned to the remembrance of the past; and it is only with the beginning of the time-travel experiments that the voice-over narrator switches from past to present tense. Whispers and noises are all that temporarily open this world to the viewer's present moment.

The Third World War has devastated the world and forced the survivors into subterranean catacombs. Prisoners of war are abused for scientific experiments, which send them via time travel into the past to bring back food, medicine, and energy. The time machine with which they are to travel is actually the memory film that plays under the subjects' wired eye masks as part of a fictional setting based on

17 Peter Wollen described the fictional diegetic time in *La jetée* as "past-of-the-future", which mixes itself with an "inbetween near-future", from the point of view of which the story is told (1984/2003: 79). From this, Wollen deduces that neither photography nor film exhibit a media-specific time form; consequently, one can speak neither of the fundamental past of photography nor of the present of film. Rather, both media have the ability to demark various times.

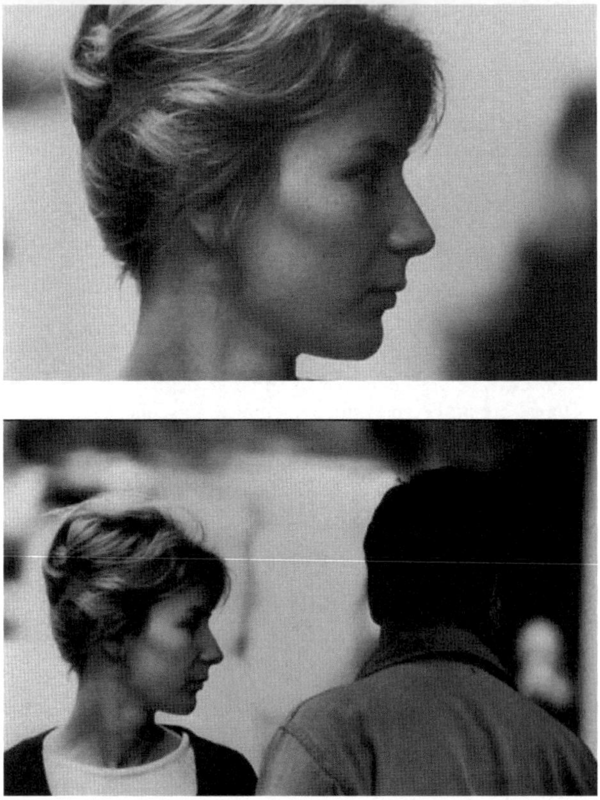

Illustration 2:
Film stills from La jetée
(dir. Chris Marker, France 1962).

the hypothesis that they may be able to actually inhabit the time they dream of. Thus, *La jetée*, like the film's first intertitle states, tells 'the story of a man marked by an image of his childhood' ("l'histoire d'un homme marqué par une image d'enfance") to such an extent that he is able to enter this image from his memory and permanently live in it. The point of entry into the memory film is a picture that first appears before the protagonist's (Jean Négroni's) inner eye before he himself can be seen in it (see *Illustration 2*).

In an intriguing film essay, Luc Lagier suggests that *La jetée* is about a cinephile's dream and lists several pieces of evidence in support of his reading: the fact that the film was shot in the catacombs below the Palais de Chaillot, where, just a year later, in 1963, the film archives of the Cinémathèque Française were to be housed; that the medical supervisor of the experiment was played by Jacques Ledoux, the then director of the Cinémathèque Royale in Brussels; that the protagonist is an immobile traveler and, as such, could also be an alter ego of the film viewer[18]. For Lagier, the film tells not only of a journey into the imaginary museum of memory but also of a journey into the imaginary museum of the cinema. Accordingly, the defining image from the protagonist's childhood that serves as this door to the past is simultaneously an echo of Hitchcock's *Vertigo*: like Madeleine (Kim Novak) – the Proustian name alone reveals her as a trigger of memories – the young woman por-

18 See the short film by Luc Lagier included in the bonus material on the *La jetée/Sans soleil* DVD, which was originally produced for the television program *Court-circuit* for the ARTE network, Criterion Collection 2007.

trayed in the picture (Hélène Chatelain) is shown in profile with her hair in an updo. And, like Scottie (James Stewart) and Madeleine, the man and woman in Marker's film look at the trunk cross-section of a sequoia tree to affirm their own position within and outside of time (only this time not in the Big Basin Redwoods State Park in California but in the Jardin des Plantes in Paris). In Marker's later film *Sans soleil* (France 1983), which embarks on a pilgrimage to the shooting locations used in the making of *Vertigo*, one can recognize this scene shot in the Jardin des Plantes in Paris: a reminder of the reminder of Hitchcock's film.

La jetée is a film about impossible memory, inspired by Hitchcock's motif of the spiral, which, for Chris Marker, actually represents a visual metaphor for the "vertigo of time" (1995: 123). In this spiral, the end coincides with the beginning of the film: in order to trace the woman whose image haunts his childhood memory, the man returns to the airport in Orly. It was there that, as a child, he had looked her in the eyes at a critical moment when both became witnesses to a man's murder. At the end, he finds out that he himself is, in fact, this man, who had traveled back into his past in order to watch his own death. Birgit Kämper writes: 'And now, we almost become dizzy ourselves, because if the child is actually on the jetty watching the scene as well, the film can start all over again.'[19] Here, the protagonist accomplishes that which is only possible in fiction: at the cost of his life, he enters the image completely. The viewer, on the contrary, is directed to his or her place outside of the image, wherefrom he or she can only ever desire that which remains unattainable. This rift between narration and diegesis establishes a deeply ambivalent image-viewer relationship in which immersion is *simultaneously* achieved and thwarted.

4. Neither Here nor There

Marker's *La jetée* is, without a doubt, a special case in the history of film. And yet, the simultaneous failure and success of total immersion in the image reveals a fundamental paradox of the film experi-

19 "Und jetzt wird uns selbst fast schwindelig, denn wenn das Kind vielleicht doch auf der Mole ist und die Szene mitansieht, dann kann der Film gleich wieder von vorn beginnen" (Kämper 1997: 238).

Illustration 3:
Film still from Vertigo *(dir. Alfred Hitchcock, USA 1958). Film Stills Archive, Museum of Modern Art, New York.*

ence in general. According to this paradox, we must doubt the possibility of immersion in the sense of a complete absorption. Or, as I would like to suggest, we must redraft the term: as the experience of the threshold of an instable in-between zone, wherein the viewer balances between different perceptual offerings (cf. Neitzel 2008: 147; Griffiths 2008: 3)[20]. On these grounds, it is exactly the viewer's experience of vertigo that rejects the claim that immersive media have a limitless "suggestive power" (Grau 2003: 65) and assigns it to the realms of myth and fiction. Bazon Brock calls attention to this when he reads Jeannot Simmen's reflections on the vertigo of modern art (see 1990) as an implicit contradiction to the positions of Paul Virilio, Jean Baudrillard, and Peter Sloterdijk. Under the condition, namely, that the viewer's body remains subject to the law of gravity, 'even the most refined space and time simulations with electronic media by no means lead to the random simulation of coordinateless states-of-being in the world'[21].

For viewers, the challenge in immersive surroundings lies in exposing themselves to a vertigo for which Hitchcock has found a distinctive formula: an opposing movement whereby the camera zooms forward while tracking in the reverse direction. The tunnel view that leads into the model of the bell tower based on designs by Henry Bumstead seems to stretch vertically, thereby creating the vertigo-like impression that one is being sucked into the chasm while simultaneously backing away from it (see *Illustration 3*).

In their book *Remediation*, Jay David Bolter and Richard Grusin referred to the *Vertigo* effect as a historically particularly virulent example of the interplay of involving and distancing forces in film viewing: "Because this effect is dislocating and 'unnatural,' *we may be drawn in, but we are distanced at the same time* – which is the

20 In his *Arcades Project*, Walter Benjamin calls to mind the fact that the threshold is to be strictly differentiated from the boundary: "A *Schwelle* 'threshold' is a zone. Transformation, passage, wave action are in the word *schwellen*, swell, and etymology ought not to overlook these senses" (1999: 494). ("Schwelle ist eine Zone. Wandel, Übergang, Fluten liegen im Worte 'schwellen' und diese Bedeutung hat die Etymologie nicht zu übersehen"; 1983: 618). In this sense, Thomas Koebner also describes vertigo as a 'step over the threshold' ("Gang über die Grenze"; 2003: 154) that 'requires a specific periodicity in order to be depicted' ("eine spezifische Periodik für die Darstellung"; ibid.).

21 "Simmen zeigt, daß selbst die raffiniertesten Raum- und Zeitsimulationen mit elektronischen Medien keineswegs zur beliebigen Simulation koordinatenloser Befindlichkeiten in der Welt führen" (Brock 1990: 8).

significance of this ambivalent track-out/zoom-in" (1999: 150 [my emphasis]). The *Vertigo* effect works as much as a reference to the psycho-physical instability of the protagonist, who is afflicted with a fear of heights, as it does to the medium of film itself. In this way, the viewer is both kept under the spell of the story being told and catapulted out of it: "We suddenly become aware of the film as medium in precisely the way that the Hollywood style tries to prevent. These are moments in which hypermediacy interrupts the aesthetic of transparency" (ibid.: 150f.)[22].

Johann Lurf, who studied under Harun Farocki at the Academy of Fine Arts of Vienna, made this opposing movement the structural principle of his video installation *Vertigo Rush* (Germany 2007). Here, a digitally controlled camera rides along tracks into and back out of a section of forest while zooming in the respective opposite direction. This occurs slowly at first but gradually accelerates until ultimately only vanishing-line-like, converging bundles of light can be seen, which form a perspectively distorted tunnel view in which the images are no longer seen but physically experienced (see *Illustration 4*). Because the movements of the dolly and the zoom are not synchronized but diverge arrhythmically, the viewer's experience of their interaction is particularly destabilizing. Hereby, the optical illusion that the section of forest is alternately contracting and expanding in the back-and-forth movement of the camera escalates to the visually induced impression of being subject to the push and pull of the film. The film

22 Bolter and Grusin differentiate between "immediacy" and "hypermediacy" (1999: chapter 1), by which they understand the respective transparency or opacity of media. As alternative strategies, "immediacy" and "hypermediacy" may occasionally converge when depictions of dreams, hallucinations, or intoxicated states serve as a display for the medium's self-awareness.

Illustration 4:
Film stills from Vertigo Rush *(dir. Johann Lurf, Germany 2007). Video installation, 35 mm, 19 min., Mono Color 24 f/s, 1:1.78.*

was shot over the span of one day and one night in one continuous take and compressed to a runtime of 19 minutes, whereby the impression of acceleration varies considerably due to a gradual increase of the exposure times of the individual frames to a maximum length of 30 seconds (see Payne 2010; qtd. Lurf 2014: 27). The video track is underscored by a synthetic signal, a test tone, which, at the beginning, is only barely audible in the bass region and then steadily raised in frequency and volume. As far as this tone illustrates anything at all, it is certainly not the nature scene but the abstract principle of this experimental setup, in which the film space seems proverbially to implode. One visitor to the Viennale described his experience with the film as follows:

> The film opens with a scene in the forest that reminds me of a painting I have seen the day before. *Forest at Dusk* by Albin Egger-Lienz, a beautiful, dark green leafiness with a sinister depth – a place you wouldn't want to get lost in when night falls. The thought made me shiver as my eyes wandered endlessly over the painting yesterday. On the screen, the scene in the wood is filmed in the bright daylight, the sun flashing through the branches. It is quiet and spacious enough to feel at peace. However, this calm is momentary as I notice that the camera's lens keeps zooming back and forth, ever so slowly at first, then increasingly faster. It feels a bit like being hypnotised. Through a series of dolly zooms, a technique using a succession of camera movements of forward and backward motion, caught in individual images while simultaneously zooming in the opposite direction, Johann Lurf's *Vertigo Rush* destabilises the normal human visual perception and provokes a kind of dizziness in the viewer. While the leafy background is forever shrinking and swelling, the front trees remain the same and my brain is getting confused, losing its sense of perspectives, while being compulsively attracted and repelled by the pendulum movement of the image. […] In-

> stead of the usual symptoms of increased heartbeats and moist hands and feet, however, I get a headache and a churning stomach. In any case, it does convince of the spectacular potential of this simple cinematographic 'craft'. (Qtd. Lurf 2014: 27)

Just how committed this video installation is to the experimental analysis of film space becomes clear, not least of all, in the comments of critics who felt reminded of Michael Snow's *Wavelength* (Canada/USA 1967) or Ernie Gehr's *Serene Velocity* (USA 1970) and saw *Vertigo Rush* as standing in the tradition of the structural films of the 1960s (see Payne 2010; qtd. Lurf 2014: 27). Lurf's installation is a continuation of these experimental investigations into film, into the threshold between screen space and viewer space. In the works discussed here, cinema's interface is spatially and temporally stretched, transformed into choreographies of back-and-forth movement that measure a zone neither here nor there. In this manner, the image becomes tangible as a pulsating field that challenges the viewer to explore it on the grounds of conflicting sensory perceptions. The vertigo that comes with subjecting oneself to this experience is more than just a merely discomforting or delightful side effect of immersive media: it lies at the very center of the investigation into the historically dynamic relation between the viewer and the image.

References

Balázs, Béla (1924/2001). *Der sichtbare Mensch oder die Kultur des Films*. Frankfurt am Main: Suhrkamp.

— (2010). *Béla Bálazs: Early Film Theory*: Visible Man *and* The Spirit of Film. Ed. Erica Carter. Transl. Rodney Livingstone. New York, NY: Berghahn Books.

Balides, Constance (2003). "Immersion in the Virtual Ornament: Contemporary 'Movie-Ride' Films". David Thorburn, Henry Jenkins, eds. *Rethinking Media Change: The Aesthetics of Transition*. Cambridge, MA/London: MIT Press. 315–336.

Barck, Joanna (2009). "Der Riss im Opaken des Bildes: Raumbilder in Spielfilmen". Gundolf Winter, Jens Schröter, Joanna Barck, eds. *Das Raumbild: Bilder jenseits ihrer Flächen*. Munich: Fink. 213–238.

Barnas, Maria (2008: online). "Confrontations: An Interview with Florentine Psychiatrist Graziella Magherini". *Metropolis M* 4. http://www.metropolism.com/magazine/2008-no4/confrontaties/english. [06/10/2014].

Barthes, Roland (1975). "En sortant du cinéma". *Communications* 23: 104–107.

— (1995). "Leaving the Movie Theater". Phillip Lopate, ed. *The Art of the Personal Essay: An Anthology from the Classical Era to the Present*. Transl. Richard Howard. New York, NY: Anchor Books. 418–421.

Benjamin, Walter (1983). *Das Passagen-Werk*. Vol. 1. Ed. Rolf Tiedemann. Frankfurt am Main: Suhrkamp.

— (1999). *The Arcades Project*. Transl. Howard Eiland, Kevin McLaughlin. Cambridge, MA/London: Belknap Press of Harvard UP.

Bieger, Laura (2007). *Ästhetik der Immersion: Raum-Erleben zwischen Welt und Bild. Las Vegas, Washington und die White City*. Bielefeld: transcript.

Bolter, Jay David, Richard Grusin (1999). *Remediation: Understanding New Media*. Cambridge, MA/London: MIT Press.

Bordwell, David (2004). "Neo-Structuralist Narratology and the Functions of Filmic Storytelling". Marie-Laure Ryan, ed. *Narrative Across Media: The Languages of Storytelling*. Lincoln, NE/ London: University of Nebraska Press. 203–219.

Bos, Jelte E., et al. (2013). "Cinerama Sickness and Postural Instability". *Ergonomics* 56/9: 1430–1436.

—, Willem Bles, Eric L. Groen (2008). "A Theory on Visually Induced Motion Sickness". *Displays* 29/2: 47–57.

Braun, Christina von (2001). *Versuch über den Schwindel: Religion, Schrift, Bild, Geschlecht*. Zurich/Munich: Pendo.

Brock, Bazon (1990). "Vorwort". Jeannot Simmen. *Vertigo: Schwindel der modernen Kunst*. Munich: Klinkhardt & Biermann. 7–8.

Buddemeier, Heinz (1970). *Panorama, Diorama, Photographie: Entstehung und Wirkung neuer Medien im 19. Jahrhundert*. Munich: Fink.

Burch, Noël (1982). "Narrative/Diegesis – Thresholds, Limits". *Screen* 23/2: 16–33.

Edwards, Mary D., Elizabeth Bailey, eds. (2012). *Gravity in Art: Essays on Weight and Weightlessness in Painting, Sculpture and Photography*. Jefferson, NC: McFarland.

Gaudreault, André, François Jost (1990). *Le récit cinématographique*. Paris: Nathan.

Grau, Oliver (2003). *Virtual Art: From Illusion to Immersion*. Cambridge, MA/London: MIT Press.

Griffiths, Alison (2008). *Shivers Down Your Spine: Cinema, Museums and the Immersive View*. New York, NY: Columbia UP.

Hagner, Michael (2001). "Psychophysiologie und Selbsterfahrung: Metamorphosen des Schwindels und der Aufmerksamkeit im 19. Jahrhundert". Aleida Assmann, Jan Assmann, eds. *Aufmerksamkeiten*. Munich: Fink. 241–263.

Huhtamo, Erkki (2013). *Illusions in Motion: Media Archaeology of the Moving Panorama and Related Spectacles*. Cambridge, MA: MIT Press.

Ijsselsteijn, Wijnand, Giuseppe Riva (2003). "Being There: The Experience of Presence in Mediated Environments". Giuseppe Riva, Fabrizio Davide, Wijnand Ijsselsteijn, eds. *Being There: Concepts, Effects and Measurement of User Presence in Synthetic Environments*. Amsterdam: IOS Press. 3–16.

Janz, Rolf-Peter, Fabian Stoermer, Andreas Hiepko (2003). "Einleitung: Schwindel zwischen Taumel und Täuschung". Janz/Stoermer/Hiepko, eds. 7–45.

—, Fabian Stoermer, Andreas Hiepko, eds. (2003). *Schwindelerfahrungen: Zur kulturhistorischen Diagnose eines vieldeutigen Symptoms*. Amsterdam/New York, NY: Rodopi.

Kämper, Birgit (1997). "*La jetée*". Birgit Kämper, Thomas Tode, eds. *Chris Marker: Filmessayist*. Munich: CICIM. 236–241.

Kennedy, Robert S., Julie Drexler, Robert C. Kennedy (2010). "Research in Visually Induced Motion Sickness". *Applied Ergonomics* 41/1: 494–503.

Koebner, Thomas (2003). "Schwindel, Sturz, Ekstase: Anmerkungen zum Vertigo-Motiv in der Filmgeschichte". Janz/Stoermer/Hiepko, eds. 139–155.

Lurf, Johann (2014: online). "Portfolio". *Website of the Artist*. http://www.johannlurf.net/portfolio_johann_lurf_2014-01.pdf. [06/10/2014].

Magherini, Graziella (1989). *La sindrome di Stendhal*. Florence: Ponte Alle Grazie.

Marker, Chris (1994). "A Free Replay (notes sur *Vertigo*)". *Positif* 400: 79–84.

— (1995). "A Free Replay (Notes on *Vertigo*)". John Boorman, Walter Donohue, eds. *Projections 4 ½*. London: Faber and Faber. 123–130.

McMahan, Alison (2003). "Immersion, Engagement, and Presence: A Method for Analyzing 3-D Video Games". Mark J. P. Wolf, Bernard Perron, eds. *The Video Game Theory Reader*. Vol. 1. New York,

NY/London: Routledge. 67–87.
Murray, Janet (1997). *Hamlet on the Holodeck: The Future of Narrative in Cyberspace*. New York, NY: Free Press.
Neitzel, Britta (2008). "Facetten räumlicher Immersion in technischen Medien". *montage AV* 17/2: 145–158.
Payne, Simon (2010). "Vienna Report". *Sequence* 1: 8–13.
Porter, Noah, ed. (1913: online). "Vertigo". *Webster's Revised Unabridged Dictionary*. Springfield, MA: C. & G. Merriam Co. http://machaut.uchicago.edu/classic/webster.form.html. [06/10/2014].
Rabinovitz, Lauren (2006). "From *Hale's Tours* to *Star Tours*: Virtual Voyages, Travel Ride Films, and the Delirium of the Hyper-real". Jeffrey Ruoff, ed. *Virtual Voyages: Cinema and Travel*. Durham, NC/London: Duke UP. 42–60.
Ross, Silvia M. (2010). "The Stendhal Syndrome, or The Horror of Being Foreign in Florence". *Tuscan Spaces: Literary Constructions of Space*. Toronto, ON: University of Toronto Press. 90–119.
Ryan, Marie-Laure (2001). *Narrative as Virtual Reality: Immersion and Interactivity in Literature and Electronic Media*. Baltimore, MD: Johns Hopkins UP.
Salt, Barry (1983). *Film Style and Technology: History and Analysis*. London: Starwood.
Schulz, Martin (2011). "The Immersive Image of Landscape: Space Voyages and Time Travel". Stefanie Kiwi Menrath, Alexander Schwinghammer, eds. *What Does a Chameleon Look Like? Topographies of Immersion*. Cologne: Halem. 77–93.
Schweinitz, Jörg (2006). "Totale Immersion und die Utopien von der virtuellen Realität: Ein Mediengründungsmythos zwischen Kino und Computerspiel". Britta Neitzel, Rolf F. Nohr, eds. *Das Spiel mit dem Medium: Partizipation – Immersion – Interaktion*. Marburg: Schüren. 136–153.
Simmen, Jeannot (1990). *Vertigo: Schwindel der modernen Kunst*. Munich: Klinkhardt & Biermann.
Solimini, Angelo G. (2013: online). "Are There Side Effects to Watching 3D Movies? A Prospective Crossover Observational Study on Visually Induced Motion Sickness". *PLoS ONE* 8/2: e56160. http://www.plosone.org/article/fetchObject.action?uri=info%3Adoi%2F10.1371%2Fjournal.pone.0056160&representation=PDF. [06/10/2014].
—, et al. (2012: online). "A Survey of Visually Induced Symptoms and Associated Factors in Spectators of Three Dimensional Stereo-

scopic Movies". *BMC Public Health* 12: 779. http://www.biomedcentral.com/1471-2458/12/779. [06/10/2014].

Souriau, Étienne (1951). "La structure de l'univers filmique et le vocabulaire de la filmologie". *Revue de filmologie* 7/8: 231–240.

— (1953). "Préface". Étienne Souriau, ed. *L'univers filmique*. Paris: Flammarion. 5–10.

Stendhal (1826/1987). *Rome, Naples et Florence*. Ed. Pierre Brunel. Paris: Gallimard.

Teja Bach, Friedrich (2006). "Der Schwindel des Sehens". Thomas Hensel, Klaus Krüger, Tanja Michalsky, eds. *Das bewegte Bild: Film und Kunst*. Munich: Fink. 373–396.

Warm, Hermann (1979). "Technische Trickeffekte für *Phantom*". Lotte H. Eisner. *Murnau*. Rev., enl., and authorized ed. Frankfurt am Main: Kommunales Kino. 147–149.

Wolf, Werner (2013). "Aesthetic Illusion". Werner Wolf, Walter Bernhart, Andreas Mahler, eds. *Immersion and Distance: Aesthetic Illusion in Literature and Other Media*. Amsterdam/New York, NY: Rodopi. 1–63.

Wollen, Peter (1984/2003). "Fire and Ice". Liz Wells, ed. *The Photography Reader*. London/New York, NY: Routledge. 76–80.

Illustration 1:
Film still from Enter the Void
(dir. Gaspar Noé, France/Germany/
Italy 2009).

Phantom-Drug-Death Ride
The Psycho-sensory Dynamic of Immersion in Gaspar Noé's *Enter the Void*

Jörg von Brincken

Gaspar Noé's cinematic oeuvre shows a desire to speak to the viewer primarily on an emotional and physical level. To do this, Noé, unlike any other director, blatantly employs immersive strategies of direct involvement but also mechanisms of aggressive image confrontation. Their combination results in a sort of manipulative and incredibly hard-hitting oscillating dramaturgy, which accounts for the actual manipulative potential of his films. This essay analyzes these strategies using the example of Noé's hallucinatory, psychedelic film *Enter the Void.*

1. Immersion as a Cultural Desire

Before *Enter the Void* (France/Germany/Italy 2009), Gaspar Noé had already worked with immersive effects evoked by the camera, sound, and special effects in two other projects – *Irreversible* (*Irréversible*, France 2002) and *We Fuck Alone* (USA/UK 2006) – that tear the viewer out of the sphere of familiar perception into an audio-visual danger zone. Noé's cinematic language affirms, in every respect, the right to destroy the comfortableness of cinematic reception and to turn watching and listening into precarious physical acts on the dangerous edge of total vertigo. It is, therefore, no surprise that the cinematic adventurer Noé loves to swim (see ZAK/Kaghado 2011). His incredibly somatically effective films, mostly underscored by droning and industrial sounds, might initially remind one of the movements of waves on a stormy sea or of the chaotic spinning of a violent whirlwind that tosses viewers' minds around, almost as violently as Poe's maelstrom.

With regard to the paradigm of immersion, the metaphor of moving bodies of water is very appropriate. The basic definition of the term 'immersion' refers only to the submersion of an object in a liquid (cf. Curtis 2008: 89; cf. Murray 1997/1999: 89f.). The definition that established itself in the context of media studies from the very beginning, however, involves the experience of being transported and, with this, the transformation of the immersed object. In this context, immersion is associated with a heightened physical and affective involvement of the viewer at the cost of his capacity for intellectual reflection (cf. Curtis 2008: 93). Oliver Grau writes: "[...] in most cases immersion is mentally absorbing and a process, a change, a passage from one mental state to another. It is characterized by diminishing critical distance to what is shown and increasing emotional involvement in what is happening" (2003: 13). Janet Murray also refers primarily to emotional moments and physical aspects when she writes:

> We seek the same feeling from a psychologically immersive experience that we do from a plunge in the ocean or swimming pool: the sensation of being surrounded by a completely other reality, as different as water is from air, that takes over all of our attention, our whole perceptual apparatus. We enjoy the movement out of our familiar world, the feeling of alertness that comes from being in this new place, and the delight that comes from learning to move within it. (1997/1999: 89f.)

Along with the aspects of separation and transportation, Alison Griffiths, by contrast, emphasizes the physical-affective aspect of a

> sensation of entering a space that immediately identifies itself as somehow separate from the world and that eschews conventional modes of spectatorship in favor of a more bodily participation in the experience. [...] One feels enveloped in immersive spaces and strangely affected by a strong sense of the otherness of the virtual world one has entered, neither fully lost in the experience nor completely in the here and now. (2008: 3)

Experiences of immersion are obviously not easy to come by. When they are successful, however, they can offer a profound psycho-sensory experience, an – irritating – expansion of daily perception, which touches upon the somatic detour around the conditions of aesthetic distance.

Even Noé himself has always emphasized that, for him, in spite of their copious amount of cinematic "magic tricks", his films are about placing instinct and emotion above the assumption of any kind of critical distance. They are also about the evocation of a "real" and "authentic" experience in the audience that this facilitates (qtd. ZAK/Kaghado 2011). In other words, his films intentionally disregard the two-dimensionality of the screen, thereby confounding the physical economy of traditional film reception. In an interview, Noé emphasized that his first cinematic experience of this kind was with Stanley Kubrick's *2001: A Space Odyssey* (USA/UK 1968):

> Because you can invent a world that almost looks real at the end and you would experience things that you wouldn't want or couldn't in real life but you still recreate them in a specific way which looks real at the end. So you are a kind of a magician or the Wizard of OZ who is showing the world haaaaaa! But I guess it all came from my first vision of the "2001 Space Odyssey". I was sharing the experience of the astronauts, planets and outer space, and at the end of the movie I was told it was all just a movie and it was all fake done from special effects but still the emotional experience of being there and going thru tunnels of light and going to other dimensions was real… and it was like having my first drug ever, and it was that movie. (Qtd. ZAK/Kaghado 2011)

Noé's main argument, with regard to the supposed clash between highly rationalized and instrumental film technology and authentic experience, is based on the idea of the inescapable reality of emotions, even when these obviously arise as a result of the viewer's confrontation with special-effect techniques. With this, along with his reference to the film's drug-like effect, he demonstratively places himself, as an artist and a filmmaker, in the center of a techno-cultural and bio-political 'dispositif'. In this 'dispositif', technology strives to become part of affect. In doing so, as Erkki Huhtamo asserts, 'technology gradually becomes second nature, an area that is both external and internalized and, at the same time, becomes an object of desire'[1]. At the same time, for Huhtamo this 'need for immersive experience', specifically, is 'a topos that is constantly reactivated – or even fabricated – in certain cultural and ideological instances'[2]. This naturally refers not only to the visual culture that has surrounded us for years, but also to the development of audio-visual technologies into environmental 'dispositifs' that surround peoples' entire bodies (cf. Huhtamo 2008: 45f.).

In our postmodern world, thickly interlaced with mobile data and material networks, authentic experience is more and more associated with a feeling of total embedding, in other words, physical embedding in a highly complex, media-technological context. According to Dieter Mersch, this context is composed of network spaces and 'fractal atopias': 'the spatial arrangement of which remains undefined and unidentifiable. […] Fractality thus functions as a meta-

---

1 "Technologie wird allmählich zur zweiten Natur, zu einem Bereich, der sowohl extern ist als auch internalisiert, und zugleich zu einem Objekt der Begierde" (Huhtamo 2008: 56). Unless otherwise indicated, all translations are mine.

2 "[…] das Bedürfnis nach immersiver Erfahrung [ist] ein Topos, der immer wieder in bestimmten kulturellen und ideologischen Momenten aktiviert – oder sogar fabriziert – wurde" (ibid.: 43).

phor for an equally branched in-betweenness and spatial dynamic without a center.'[3] Without question, this off-centeredness and undefinability push the 'irrational' moment into the foreground: the desire for immersion, psycho-sensory experience, and somatic tactility increasingly replaces the pursuit of an intellectual overview and discursive classification. Overall, however, the scenario of belonging in the realm of the somatic and affect – if we follow Huhtamo's thoughts on the ideological activation and fabrication of need – is encouraged to a large extent by the culture industry. In particular, one must not forget that today's economy is simply no longer based on the production of goods but on the production of worlds in which people and goods coexist both physically and affectively (see Lazzarato 2004). Here immersion becomes the preeminent thought-image for the special biopolitical constitution of our post-capitalist reality.

As far as the culture and film industries are concerned, audio-visual dynamics and intensity levels are churned out through technical means that provide for immersive and emergent effects that have a profound physical effect on the viewer. This is especially the case with mainstream blockbusters and action films. Among these techniques are the fast cut and the nervous camera, rapid changes in perspective, threatening or hammering attacks of sound, and, last but not least, 3-D technology, which not only creates spatial depth, but also makes objects and characters in the picture magically appear in the theater (cf. Blanchet 2003: 204f.). At times, this tactile roller-coaster aesthetic almost seems experimental; however, it has considerable retrospective, or more specifically, reassurance mechanisms that reterritorialize the floating movements of the images. Along with the main claim, namely that it is fictional, these include, above all, content-related aspects, such as the still significant schema of good versus evil, the rigid symbolism of the lone (usually male) hero, and a narrative – though mostly one-dimensional and woodcut-like – with macro-suspense. With all the turbulence in today's audio-visual aesthetics, there is one last stronghold from which, in the end, the viewer can regain comfortable sovereignty: even the most transgressive immersive experiences end with the viewer's awareness of a sense of security: "a chance to try on death without cost" (Griffiths 2008: 286). This kind of ultimately fic-

3 "[…] deren Raumanordnung unbestimmt bleibt und von denen man nicht sagen kann, was sie sind. […] Fraktalität fungiert mithin als Metapher für eine ebenso verzweigte Zwischenräumlichkeit wie Raumdynamik ohne Zentrum" (Mersch 2011: 58).

tional and representational realism of immersion is already deeply ingrained in the experimental moment. However, it is restrained, in a way, by the symbolic order of cinematic narrative style.

The question arises, however, of whether the affect strategies of the culture industry not only delimit the secure terrain within a more comprehensive 'dispositif' of cultural intensity, but if their internal tendency to overstep boundaries attacks the lines of demarcation between fiction and reality on a more fundamental level. Huhtamo, for example, points out that, in analogy to the entertainment industry's fictional strategies in film, television, and computer-game culture, more radical – and non-fiction-based – cultural forms of expression have enacted a search for psycho-sensory experiences. These forms of expression manifest themselves, for example, 'in neo-psychedelic or "cyberdelic" techno-house parties or in drug consumption, and in a new-age interest in "mental machines" and "psycho-technologies", including Eastern philosophy and shamanism'[4]. With regard to the disappearance of collective forms of expression after the collapse of the great political systems, Gilles Deleuze already named drug consumption a new possible form of collective expression. He closely relates drug experience to a postmodern culture of pictoriality, which erodes the stabile image in favor of pure audio-visual sensory sensations (cf. 1986/1997: 85).

In the context of my reflections on Noé's *Enter the Void*, the thought of influencing our pictorial culture through drug culture is essential. It is important in the sense that *Enter the Void* not only addresses drug consumption and its effect on perception, but also was filmed by Noé with the explicit intention of reproducing the effects of hallucinogenic substances, above all DMT, through cinematic means (see Peters 2010). At the same time, the film is loosely based on the path of the soul after death described in *The Tibetan Book of the Dead*. In this way, it shows the possible liaison between a highly technologized, post-capitalist culture, represented by the metropolis of Tokyo, and a metaphysical or mythological, maybe even – in Noé's own words – "shamanic", perspective (qtd. ZAK/Kaghado 2011).

4 "[…] bei […] neopsychedelischen oder 'kyberdelischen' Technohaus-Partys oder beim Drogenkonsum und beim New-Age-Interesse an 'mentalen Maschinen' und 'Psychotechnologien', inklusive östlicher Philosophie und Schamanismus" (Huhtamo 2008: 42).

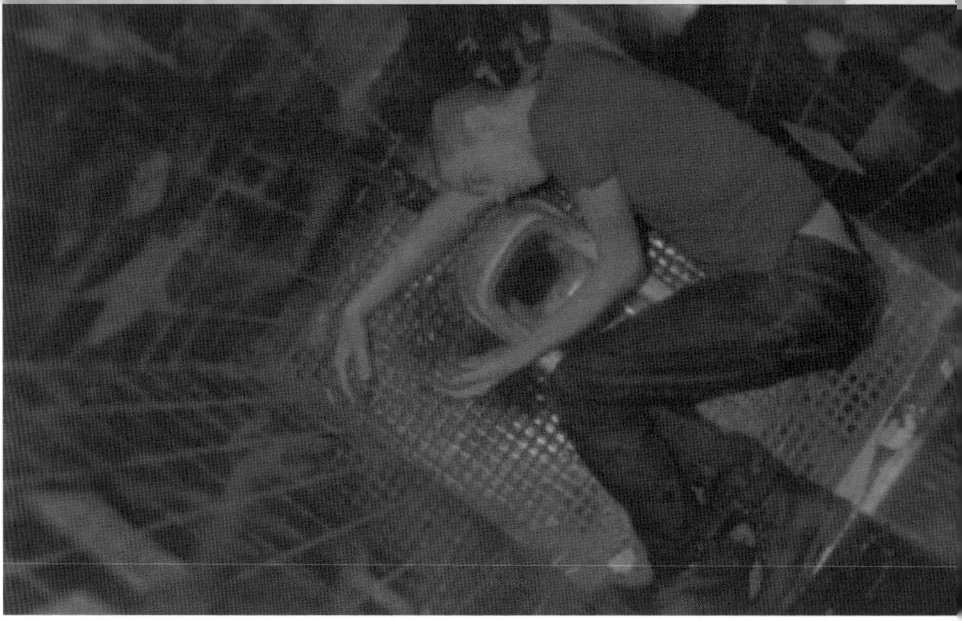

2. Drug Roller Coaster

Enter the Void is a great experimental film that breaks the boundaries of representation. Its essence lies in the identities of the cinematic experience and the drug experience. As the quotation above shows, Noé himself explains the basis of these identities through the shared 'magical' power of both cultures to evoke real emotion through purely fictional, or more specifically, purely hallucinatory perceptions.

At another point, Noé emphasized that *Enter the Void* was about the exact reproduction of the effect of psychedelic drugs (see Peters 2010). It thus becomes an experimental film, shot by a filmmaker who himself consumes drugs, who saw a point of entry to authentic transgressive experiences in the dimension of experience opened up by drug consumption and attempted to connect the two directly through his film aesthetic.

The fact that Noé refers to 'magic tricks' – that is, special effects and CGI technology, which are both used abundantly in *Enter the Void* – is in itself already quite revealing. For one, it shows the great extent to which he, as an advocate of an advanced film language, supports the principle of an already described culture of authenticity, for which the meeting of technology and the human body/affect no longer represents a clash of cultures, but, in fact, the opposite. His references to magic and shamanism underscore the manipulative power special effects have and the fact that they are capable of creating a *truly* boundary-breaking experience for the viewer.

What is crucial is that, with this, immersion leaves the sphere of representational realism – especially that which is represented by ac-

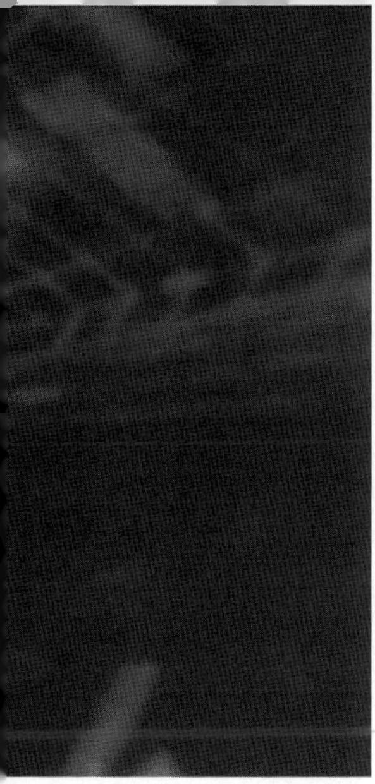

Illustration 2:
Film still from Enter the Void *(dir. Gaspar Noé, France/Germany/Italy 2009).*

tion movies and blockbusters – and enters the sphere of experimental realism (cf. Curtis 2008: 94). This occurs even though Noé, to a great extent, uses precisely those 'magic tricks' that are characteristic of the commercial action genre: rapid tracking shots; nervous, handheld camerawork; dynamic sound; digital special effects; et cetera. He emphasizes that, for him, it was about making a film that creates the same physical and psychological effect as a roller coaster (see Smith 2010). His hard-earned reputation as 'one of today's most dangerous directors' ("einer der gefährlichsten Regisseure der Gegenwart"; Peters 2010), however, is not only the product of the speed and dynamism of his films. It is also the result of the sensational themes and motifs that he so explicitly and drastically presents in both his narratives and his visuals: whether it be murder, violence, incest, rape, revenge, pornographic sex, or drug consumption, as is seen here. Without question, some of these motifs, as well as their drastic depiction, can also be found in corresponding film genres and are thus nothing new. However, Noé's choice of themes and motifs does not limit their respective depiction to a mere restaging of facts. Rather, it is about making the most extreme aspect of the motif the starting point of a psycho-sensory and thus existential experience that is shocking and physically involving. The movie theater is no longer a safe place in which viewers can have extreme experiences that, in the end, however, leave them existentially untouched. His dramaturgy is one of somatic involvement and psycho-sensory transgression; in other words, psyche and body are affected equally.

3. Through Oscar's Eyes

Oscar (Nathaniel Brown) ekes out a living in Tokyo as a small-time dealer and uses drugs himself. He is connected to his sister, Linda (Paz de la Huerta), who works as a stripper in a nightclub, by a close and fateful relationship: after their parents died in a car crash, they swore to each other that they would always stay together. The reason Oscar got involved in dealing drugs in the first place was so he could bring his sister to Tokyo. Then, however, betrayed by a friend with whose mother he was once involved, Oscar walks right into a trap set up by the police in a club called The Void. He flees to the bathroom and is shot while trying to flush the drugs he had on him down the toilet (see *Illustration 2*). His body is dead, but his spirit lives on and keeps the promise he once made to his sister: never to leave her. Thus, his ghost continues to float restlessly through the city.

The film consists of a total of four motivic fields that each deal directly with their own individual form of altered perception. Noé's basic intention was to use cinematic means to reproduce, as intimately as possible, the states of human consciousness formed by exhaustion and drug-induced highs, memory, phantom disembodiment, and hallucination/transgression. What is important to note is that, in doing so, it is not only about the representational depiction of the respective changes in consciousness, but also about an intimate, in other words, a cinematic mimesis, very closely oriented to the somatic and psychological model, that is achieved with special effects. Thus, Noé is not trying to simply copy reality, but to generate a melding of the audience's perception with that of Oscar through immersive strategies. In this way, the film experience is intended to converge exactly with (fastidiously researched) modes of drug-induced, hallucinatory, and death-like experiences. Film should act like a drug, and in an extremely offensive way at that. If one believes the numerous critics who have described the film as a real 'trip', then Noé was successful in his endeavor.

The first layer of immersion sets in at the beginning of the film: the camera lens assumes the exactly same physical position, with regard to height and range of motion, as Oscar's eyes; it meticulously imitates the protagonist's visual perception, from spatial changes in his field of vision to blurred vision, suggestive of his level of exhaustion and intoxication, to regularly occurring blackouts that imitate blinking. In a way, the viewer looks around at the surroundings through Oscar's eyes – and hears through his ears or, more specifically, his auditory channels. Oscar's verbal utterances are different from the reproduction of his thoughts. The latter are unfiltered, causing the former to sound dull and modified, just like the altered acoustic perception of one's own speaking voice caused by bone conduction through the skull.

Illustration 3: Film still from Enter the Void *(dir. Gaspar Noé, France/ Germany/Italy 2009).*

In view of the utter lack of alternative camera angles that could provide orientation and stabilization, such as establishing or master shots, the mercilessly consequential blueprint of seeing and hearing results in the audience's surrendering their perception to Oscar's field of vision. The effect of this exact correlation between the movement of the camera lens and the protagonist's perspective is that the viewer is virtually pulled into Oscar's head. This immersive illusion is so strong that it is almost unavoidable: after going into the bathroom, Oscar looks into the mirror; his glance, imitated by the camera, leads from the sink upward; and, through Oscar's eyes, we briefly see the young man's reflection (see *Illustration 3*). Yet, there is no camera visible in the mirror, which, by now, however, seems completely natural to the viewer; the intimate liaison between the eye and the camera is, by now, too far gone for the viewer to still notice this paradox. The convergence of the perceptions is already too self-evident. Usually, when a mirror is shown in a film, it is considered a self-reflexive moment, whereby the reflection metaphorically represents the camera's objectifying gaze and reveals it to be a foreign, medially reshaped view (cf. Engell 2011: 106).

From a film-phenomenological perspective, the mirror scene should bring to mind what Vivian Sobchack calls the "film's body" (1992: 219f.). She divides the act of seeing in the movie theater into two different modes of viewing: firstly, the audience's view of the screen, and then the view of the camera lens, a second personified subject of perception, which 'sees' what the viewer is shown. From this, a third seeing results, whereby the viewer can relate to or, rather, take on the view of the film's body. Thus we do not just see things and people, but we watch the camera see. 'This process', as Michael

Islinger writes, 'is very important, because, within it, the existential structure of seeing multiplies itself and, in doing so, the existence of the film's body *appears* as the subject of this perception'[5]. Both Islinger and Sobchack emphasize that the film's body, located between the camera's view and that of the audience, facilitates a (critical) reflection of one's own immersive processes of reception. Sobchack, however, above all, points out that viewing oneself manifests itself as a deeply physical mode of action (see 2004).

Noé's immersive aesthetic begins, in fact, at precisely this intimate liaison between the media-based view and the audience's view. However, due to the fact that it melds the camera's view, Oscar's view, and the audience's view together, it constantly works against the creation of any kind of distance and, for this reason, against the viewer's ability to reflect upon it. To a certain extent, the adoption of the camera's gaze, through its synonymity with Oscar's field of vision, generates a psycho-sensory projection of one's own body image onto that of the main character – and vice versa. The camera's gaze is no longer even noticeable as a prosthetic extension, but disappears completely – after a brief period of astonishment at the very beginning, that is – into the dynamic of the audio-visual gestalt. Noé explicitly works toward creating self-evident physical involvement, an existential unquestionability that transcends both the opposition between realism and visual legerdemain, and the one between analogically and digitally processed images; this is how quick, how alluringly subtle he is in employing his effects. The sole purpose of this process is to increase the level of corporeal-visual identification on the part of the audience and to thereby cement their somatic connection with the film as a medium of 'authentic' experience. As Noé said, it is about letting the audience experience things beyond the range of everyday experience – be that in a positive or negative way – by evoking 'real' emotions in them through all the means at his disposal.

In this mimetic identification, the medium's 'magical' power is clearly celebrated and not denounced. It is a veritable seduction – as Jean Baudrillard understood it (see Stiglegger 2006) – and an artistic affirmation of the powerful mechanisms of post-cinematic film: the

5 "Dieser Akt ist von großer Bedeutung, weil sich in ihm die existenzielle Struktur des Sehens verdoppelt und damit die Existenz des Filmleibes als Subjekt dieser Wahrnehmung *erscheint*" (Islinger 2002: 36 [my emphasis]).

creation of immersive worlds in which, from the perspective of what the viewer feels, there is no longer any real contrast between empirical and technically produced images and sounds.

4. Intensities on the Film's Body/the Drugged Body

The question that arises, however, is which film body is produced in this fragmentation in the first place. Because this immersion also binds the viewer to the inferred body of the protagonist, it, in fact, creates a liminal state of 'betwixt and between', characterized by an oscillation between one's feeling for one's own body and the affinity for the exteriority of the protagonist's body. In reality, however, Noé goes beyond this kind of liaison, or more precisely, he circumvents it from the inside out: with the exception of the mirror scene, there is, in fact, no liaison with a complete image of the 'hero's' body. The only stabilizing forces that the mimetic passage into his body offers are the active gaze, sounds, and Oscar's hand, visible from a first-person perspective. Together these evoke Oscar's body, or at least the impression that that is what we are dealing with. Because the tactile and olfactory dimensions are also completely absent, the physical identification that occurs only affects parts of the viewer's body. Although it is brief, the mirror scene establishes, for a few moments, a certain identification with Oscar as an individual. First and foremost, however, it is about a purely physical, in other words, impersonal affinity between the viewer's eye and the eye of the camera, between the viewer's ear and the microphone, and between the movement of the viewer's eye and the tracking shot. Instead of congruence, this yields a complex network of individual positions. The vacant (empty) spaces between these positions leave room for the imaginary constitution of a shared body, primarily composed of internal movement. In other words, it is the way the film circumvents offering a complete pictorial representation of a body, its negation of a harmonious imago, that produces various passages for the flow of affects, emotions, and partial identifications, without ever making them complete. I interpret this as Noé's attempt to evoke the impression of a 'drugged body', which Gilles Deleuze and Félix Guattari describe as a (bad, in that it is sclerotic) kind of "Body without Organs", i. e., a body that is no longer integrated into or subject to the hierarchy of an organism. Accordingly, drug use is about the creation of a "*field of immanence of desire*, [...] with desire defined as a process

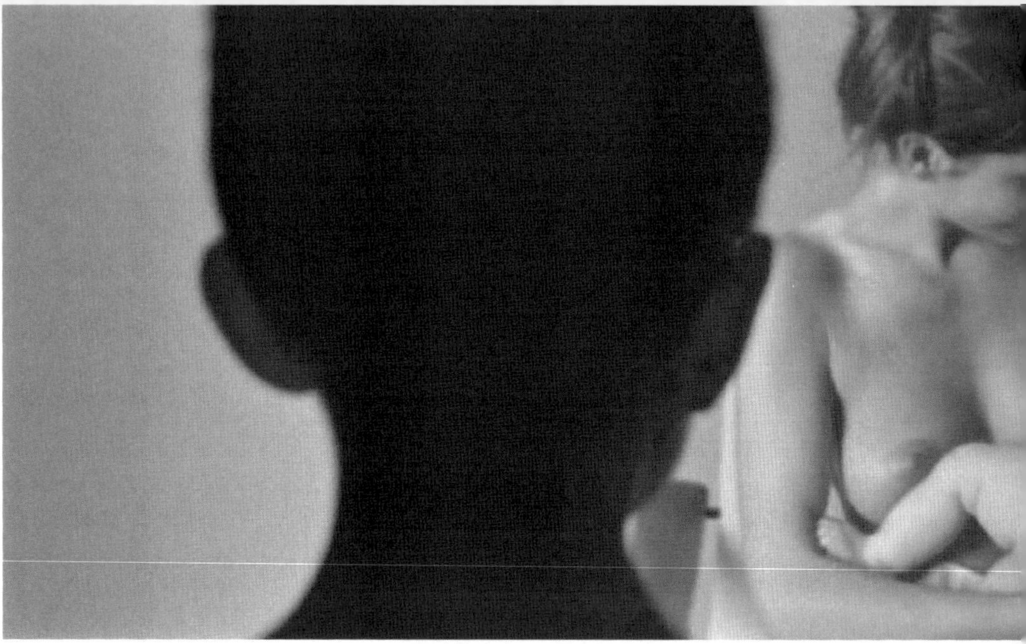

Illustration 4:
Film still from Enter the Void *(dir. Gaspar Noé, France/Germany/ Italy 2009).*

of production without reference to any exterior agency" (1987: 170)[6]. In fact, by separating a pictorially represented character's seeing and hearing processes from an entity securely established in the image, perception becomes a similarly liquid process of creating connections between all the individual impressions delivered by the video and sound tracks. The exterior movement of the lens brings movement into what is presented and opens it up for internal connections beyond the reception economy represented by the logic of perception of a representable individual. The course of the rest of the film, which consists of the increasing destruction of the perceptive individual on both sides of the screen, is already announced at the film's first level of immersion through the illusion that the viewer has taken on the perception of a junkie.

It is important to note that, in Noé's film, this drugged body – if we think in terms of a combination of Deleuze/Guattari and Sobchack – which opens itself up to other things, is one and the same with the film's body. The viewer's identification with the camera and sound dynamics, in a way, erodes his or her body, reduces it to just a few channels and, in doing so, creates empty cracks and passages through which pure imaginative powers circulate. The entire film represents a

6 "[…] *le champ d'immanence* du désir, […] sans reference à aucune instance extérieure" (Deleuze/Guattari 1980: 191 [emphasis in the original]).

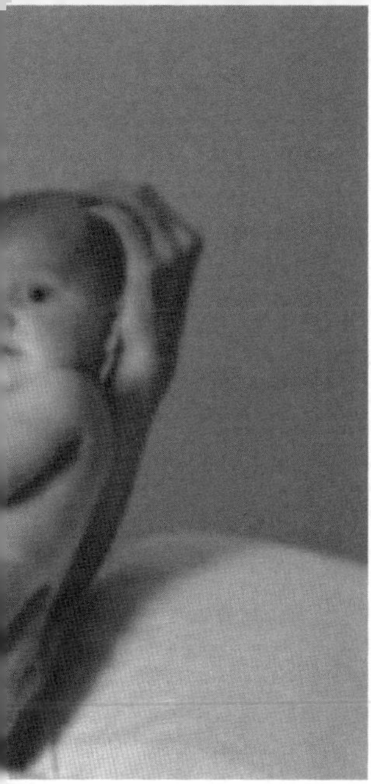

gradual eroding of the body's image and its transformation into pure, circulating signals. Thus it covers the entire spectrum of possible forms of immersion, from physical to mental and even to metaphysical immersion.

5. The Tragedy of the Flashback

After Oscar's death, his life up to that point is reviewed. The flashbacks begin with the birth of his sister, include scenes of loving affection between his mother and him and his sister as children (see *Illustration 4*), and end with a shockingly sudden shot of their parents' death in the accident. The following scenes show Oscar wandering around with friends in Tokyo, looking for drugs to sell. Similar to Lars von Trier, Noé deconstructs the film image by breaking up the flashbacks. He accomplishes this, for example, by using a high number of cuts, which cut out fractions of a second of a scene, or through unexplained pans and fast jumps forward and backward. The one constant we always have, however, is a close-up, frontal view of the back of Oscar's head and shoulders in the center of the image (see *Illustration 1*). It is like a dark anchor amid the motion we see from a frontal view evoked by the subjective camerawork and the editing, which itself resembles a film playing on a flat screen. Noé explains this uninteresting, shadowy perspective that prohibits the viewer from seeing any of the actor's mimetic expressions as follows:

> Well for the flashback sequences I shot it all from just behind Oscar's head because when I think of my own past, or when I dream or when I go back to my room and think of this interview, I will reframe it and the camera will go back and I will put myself inside the frame. That's how I experience memories, it's from a different perspective, so I have Oscar as this void shadow inside the frame during those sequences. (Qtd. Marsh 2010)

Memory thus represents *one* further mode of immersion, which, however, is weaker and tainted by tragic hidden past experiences. In a way, it places the subject who experienced the memories at a certain distance from the actual events; in other words, it places the subject in the third person. Along with Oscar's shadow – which, to a certain extent, is a kind of empty question mark between the image content and the viewer – the flashbacks create a reflexive zone. In this zone, the viewer is allowed to reflect upon his or her own conventional involvement in image narratives: a very passive kind of involvement that is anchored to the act of pure observation. Each time the view of Oscar's back, robbed of any complex expression, is shown, the viewers recognize their own position as mere film viewers, or better yet: they remind themselves of it. An indication of this is the shift to static camerawork in the scenes in which Oscar, immobile and unconscious, observes what is going on around him. He is as much in as he is out. While this staging positions the subject as a viewer in the middle of the image, he is still nothing more than a bodiless outline, incapable of perceiving himself as a total person or a feeling individual connected to a body. Noé fittingly stages this tragic lack of subjectivity and subjective agency in the form of observed flashbacks that can no longer be altered by the one remembering them. As such, this part of *Enter the Void* can be seen as a reflection of the precarious edges of involvement: wherever it is synonymous with pure visual observation, the act of witnessing becomes a tragic fate of excluded, and ultimately defenseless, observation. In the worst cases, it lacks even the slightest bit of physical affectation or affective identification, for we no longer see through Oscar's eyes, but are looking at the protagonist, who has been reduced to a view of his back, through the unforgiving, objectifying eye of the mechanical film apparatus. We are right up against his body but never in it, like a voyeuristic ghost that follows him around, trapped in a gap between the inner-cinematic level and the surface of the film image. We are a disembodied ghost, fatally transparent to itself, pressing up against the fourth wall on the transparent inner side of the screen. For Noé, seeing and visual recognition, however, do not seem at all to be the fundamental – or, better yet, exclusive – modes in which authentic film experiences find expression; on the contrary.

6. Phantom Ride

After the flashback marathon, Oscar's consciousness departs from any kind of personalized perception. From this point on, the rest of the film is carried by the movement of the camera, which, itself invisible, no longer stands for a physical subject as it did in the first part of the film. In what seems to be real time, a totally disembodied view races and staggers through Tokyo, glides through the urban canyon, goes through walls, creeps into apartments, circling around the people in

Illustration 5: Film still from Enter the Void *(dir. Gaspar Noé, France/Germany/ Italy 2009).*

them from a bird's-eye view (see *Illustration 5*). From this impersonal 'looking down', no real identification with the other characters' world is established; there is no longer any agency, just an audio-visual registry of actions and conversations – a view damned to objectivity. Although this disembodied seeing seems to be attracted again and again to physical details – for example, the warm neck of Oscar's sleeping sister – Noé will suddenly rip the miniature digital camera, twisting and turning, into a drain, an ashtray, a fireplace, only to let the disembodied gaze reemerge somewhere else out of a similar opening. This gaze also enters into the heads and bodies of those left behind, searching, feeling around, on an unconscious hunt for an opportunity to, once again, regain the stability of a body. It is the unconscious yearning of an ambling soul, lost in the big city, which contradicts the seeing process because, in a way, it is blind. What is critical here is that, from this point on, Noé no longer uses any recognizable cuts: the soul's flight is a masterpiece of special effects, creating sequence shots that turn the sky over Tokyo, the skyscrapers, streetcars, and rooms into the playground of the all-penetrating, restlessly wandering soul. The perspective of this soul, at the cost of becoming completely detached from actual goings-on, has achieved mobile ubiquity.

Here, Noé draws on the aesthetic of the phantom ride, a film genre that became very popular between 1896 and 1907 (see Gunning 2009). To create such a phantom ride, the camera was attached to the front of a locomotive not visible to the viewer. The camera recorded its forward and backward movement on the track, which was then viewed by an audience. Watching a phantom-ride film, the viewer cannot align his or her gaze with a figural entity. The camera represents the gaze of a phantom that manifests itself purely in the effect of motion: "Since it remains off-screen and invisible, the locomotive takes on a characteristic of a phantom, a presence evident in its effects, while remaining unseen" (ibid.: 170).

According to Huhtamo, the phantom-ride film, which has recently become popular in the form of simulated rides, is by no means to be misunderstood as 'nothing more than a primitive translation of a common experience in a new medium' but can be seen 'more so as an *alternative model* for a cinema spectacle'[7]. The alternative here clearly lies in physical involvement. The effect of phantom rides is surprisingly somatic: the viewer's body, immobilized in front of the screen, internally experiences the camera's movements. It is about a proprioceptive form of perception. It is not about communicating external impressions to the brain and processing stimuli into knowledge, but about forming physical attitudes, verves, and rhythms that precede any representational categorization. The viewer-body unknowingly absorbs the camera's momentum and dynamic and adapts to its movement as if it were a roller-coaster ride (cf. Huhtamo 2008: 54). In this process, the viewer's corporeality itself, stimulated through the act of viewing, becomes a dynamic component within a variety of relationships. To a certain extent, it enters into a psycho-sensory relationship with the image on the screen, which allows the viewer to physically settle into the visual density created by the movement of the camera; this then leads to a dizzying or reeling sensation of the internal faculties as well.

In his theory of aesthetics, Theodor Lipps develops the theory of the spatial mind, which, as he emphasizes, is not a subjective matter and is not dependent upon the individual's personal mood, nor, however, is it dependent on the clearly recognizable forms of objects in space. Rather, it is connected to the atmospheric experience of space itself. It is brought about by the 'endlessly diverse, inexpressible backward and forward weaving of energies through space, […] through vastness, how the objects are arranged in space and, in a way, *converse* with one another, *dialog* amongst themselves or with air and light, in any case, in space or through it'[8]. Using Dziga Vertov's film aesthetic

7 "[…] der phantom-ride-Film [lässt] sich mehr als *alternatives Modell* für ein Kinospektakel betrachten denn als lediglich primitive Umsetzung einer vertrauten Erfahrung in ein neues Medium" (Huhtamo 2008: 54 [emphasis in the original]).

8 "[…] das unendlich vielgestaltige unsagbare Hin- und Herweben der Kräfte durch den Raum, […] durch die Weise, wie die Gegenstände im Raume *zusammen* sind und

as an example, Gilles Deleuze describes a similarly extensive relationality as an attempt to evoke an objective way "'to see without boundaries or distances'. Thus in this respect all procedures are legitimate, they are no longer trick shots" (1986/1997: 81)[9]. Whereas Vertov employs montage extensively, Noé replaces this with manipulated sequence shots. However, he, too, tends to create "a correlation of two images which are distant (and incommensurable from the viewpoint of our human perception)" (ibid.: 82)[10]. Naturally, this is not about replacing the human gaze with the extra-human perspective of, for example, a bird or one's own personal spirit. Instead, Deleuze speaks of the inhuman "eye of the matter, the eye in the matter, not subject to time, which has 'conquered' time, which reaches the 'negative of time', and which knows no other whole than the material universe and its extensions" (ibid.: 81)[11].

Within this concept of an "eye of the matter", sight and filmic movement coincide, become identical. There is no longer a unit of temporal measurement that the gaze can use to divide the perceived movements into a linear perspective of before and after – no chronological order of events. There is also no longer an actual narrative that functions according to sensorimotor patterns, in other words, one that would create a causal relationship between individual movements. Instead of an organic chronology of events, time is shifted into movement and the moving picture itself. Everything is placed in relationship to everything else within the movement of the phantom eye, just as the film, as a whole, combines levels of time, and places hallucinations, memories, and the present alongside one another and mixes them up. It is not a truly cognitive seeing of the definite contours of the individual people and things, but more of an observing and looking through them that seems to stagger and reel around their movements.

---

sozusagen innerlich *Zwiesprache* halten; Zwiesprache unter sich oder mit Luft und Licht, in jedem Fall im Raume oder durch ihn hindurch" (Lipps 1906: 189f. [emphases in the original]).

9 "[…] 'voir sans frontières ni distances'. A cet égard donc, tous les procédés seront permis, ce ne sont plus des truquages" (Deleuze 1983: 117f.).

10 "[…] une mise en correlation de deux images lointaines (incommensurable du point de vue de notre perception humaine)" (ibid.: 118).

11 "[…] l'œil de la matière, l'œil dans la matière, qui n'est pas soumis au temps, qui a 'vaincu' le temps, qui accède au 'négative du temps', et ne connaît d'autre l'univers matériel et son extension" (ibid.).

In this way, the individual people, actions, and objects seen by the eye seem to increasingly converge into a two-dimensional, overall context, a field of immanence of seeing that is only divided into intervals of movement and perception. The effect of this is that, after a while, the viewer actually loses his or her sense of time and begins to passively float along a stream of images with the movement of his or her eyes. If we follow Deleuze, the soul journey, in fact, corresponds to an aspect of the drug experience: "drugs are supposed to *stop the world*, to release the perception of 'doing'" (ibid.: 85)[12]. This is also the purpose of the increased use of blurred and swirling images that begins in this part of the film. These are intended to fatigue the viewer and limit him or her to pure seeing and hearing, free of any interest in what is going on – which, again, is closely related to the pure perception resulting from a drug trip.

This form of absolute immersion, which creates close relationships between the movement of the camera and the internal movement of the viewer, makes *Enter the Void* a psycho-sensory event that powerfully asserts its similarity to the experiences of fatigue, death, and being stoned: a real death trip. The soundtrack, which, along with the recurring theme of Johann Sebastian Bach's "Air", combines droning sounds and deep heartbeat frequencies, also contributes to this effect. In this way, the filmic space expands equally through the eyes and ears into the viewer's body, allowing him or her to sink into the film's rhythm.

Without question, this detachment from reality comes at a tragic price: not only does the phantom eye rip holes into the concrete facts of life by effortlessly permeating the solid boundaries of things (buildings, road surfaces, bodies), but, in Noé's film, there is a constant hunt for holes (spouts, drains, fireplaces) to dive into, driven by a desire to find a stable and secure place. In fact, the camera's constant staggering motion around the bodies of the other characters represents the phantom gaze blindly 'feeling around' for something to hold on to, in order to, once again, establish itself within the realm of empirical reality. Because it is not successful in this attempt, it repeatedly disappears into holes, going down below to where the soul began its immaterial journey, in a drain hole, in a material location full of filth, born of Oscar's blood: "Instead of holes in the world allowing the world lines themselves to run off, the lines of flight coil and start to

12 "[…] la drogue est supposée *stopper le monde*, délier la perception du 'faire'" (ibid.: 123 [emphasis in the original]).

swirl in black holes; to each addict a hole, group or individual, like a snail. Down instead of high" (Deleuze/Guattari 1987: 314)[13]. As Deleuze and Guattari write, the drug user is constantly on a path of destruction, of death. At the same time, however, in his state of delirium, he runs the risk of restoring to "forms and subjects every instant, like so many phantoms or doubles" (ibid.)[14]. Here, Deleuze and Guattari criticize 'normal' drug experiences from the elevated perspective of transhuman concepts, which see the actual desired end result of a drug-induced transgression in the creation of a molecular plain of immanence that is no longer connected to the reality populated by everyday experiences. However, a drug experience that tries to escape the delirium in the finiteness of a refuge, which Noé stages by diving into holes and circling around bodies, can thus be interpreted as a tragic failure of the remnants of a consciousness.

According to Deleuze, however, the main aspect of drugs is "to substitute pure auditory and optical perceptions for motor-sensory perceptions: *to make one see the molecular intervals*, the holes in sound, in forms [...]; but also, in this stopped world, *to make lines of speed pass through* these holes in the world. [...] This is the programme of the [...] gaseous image, beyond the solid and the liquid: to reach 'another' perception" (1986/1997: 85)[15]. Here Deleuze closely correlates modern film and pictorial culture with the development of absolute boundary-eliminating modalities of perception – from the standpoint of everyday experience, a heterogeneous form of perception, which no longer abides by the diktat of stabile form that usually stabilizes human life.

13 "Au lieu que des trous dans le monde permettent aux lignes du monde de fuir elles-même, les lignes de fuite s'enroulent et se mettent à tournoyer dans des trous noirs, chaque drogué dans son trou, groupe ou individu, comme un bigorneau. Enfoncé plutôt que défoncé" (Deleuze/Guattari 1980: 348).

14 "[...] à chaque instant des formes et des sujets, comme autant de fantômes ou de doubles" (ibid.: 349).

15 "[...] c'est-à-dire substituer aux perceptions sensori-motrices des perceptions optiques et sonores pures; *faire voir les intervalles moléculaires*, les trous dans les sons, dans les formes [...]; mais aussi, dans ce monde stoppé et par ces trous dans le monde, *faire passer des lignes de vitesse*. [...] C'est le programme du [...] l'image gazeuse, au-delà du solide et du liquide: atteindre à une 'autre' perception" (Deleuze 1983: 123 [emphases in the original]).

7. Molecular Intervals
Film Experience as Drug Experience

Noé, however, goes one considerable step further when he integrates digitally created color patterns in 3-D as hallucinations into his film, the shapes of which are reminiscent of nerve pathways, synapses, and vascular structures (see *Illustration 6*). These deeply immersive scenes, like moving sculptures, begin with Oscar's first high at the beginning of the film. His consciousness leaves his body, circles above him in the form of a bodiless view, and is then sucked – along with the viewer's gaze – into a gossamer of tentacles of light. At the same time, the digital effects draw the phantom gaze toward the center of the constantly winding and morphing web, which seems to move toward and around the viewer. It is like a phantom ride into the mouth of a wonderful deep-sea kraken, which one cannot approach with hesitation, but only passive surrender, even at the price of delirium. These images, based on detailed research, are pictorial equivalents of the internal visual impressions caused by the consumption of drugs, in particular DMT. In these scenes, the film almost completely abandons representational depiction, creating instead purely audio-visual phenomena, which, due to their tactile character and their effect on the senses and the psyche, take possession of, fascinate, and unsettle the minds of those watching. While the act of taking the viewer through Oscar's eyes and through the restless eye of his soul evokes immersion in the traditional sense, Noé, through his light-objects, oversteps the boundary between film and viewer in the other direction. The light sculptures, entirely devoid of a narrative foundation, are shown for a considerable length of time; the more one watches them swirl and transform, the more they seem to emerge, expand, and – like a cloud of gas – move into the viewer's space. The structure of these kaleidoscope-like moving forms, which has neither a clearly identifiable beginning nor end and seems to be endless, is explicitly 'molecular': it is composed not of moles, in other words, firmly outlined individual entities, but of countless points and strands that, because they are angled toward each other, constantly vary but never congeal into a stabile form.

Technically speaking, all that is left here are image differences created by the self-movement of the objects, a perpetual transformation that, in a way, is the principle of visual movement itself. We are no longer dealing with a movement represented by an identifiable object, thus with an action-image, but with a movement-image in its purest form: an image composed of movement that passes this movement onto the viewer's body via his or her gaze in the form of psycho-sensory stimulation. Noé veritably rips open these "*molecular intervals*, the holes in sound, in forms", namely in the relationship between the viewer and the screen. The flatness and frontality of the latter, in a way, rotates itself 180 degrees, squeezes its way into the stereoscopic psycho-sensory space, and image and sound pour themselves directly into the viewer's intimate physical and psychological sphere[16].

The film's affinity for drugs mentioned here is not a metaphor: Noé outlines the intimate nexus of drugs and the exploitation of human potential in the image of Tokyo's semi-underworldly and underworldly experience industry, made up of bars, drug dens, and brothels. One could interpret this as a critique. However, by gearing the film's aesthetic toward the effect of drugs, he affirms its cinematic potential to create experiences in which something plants itself in the consumer's body and, under these hubristic conditions, expands his or her world. Furthermore, the film is a completely exhausting 156 minutes long, an aspect for which Noé has often been criticized. However, it is this length that embodies a considerable aspect of the drug experience: the film gives viewers a lasting high and is exhausting not only to their eyes but also to their backsides. As such, it is also soma-related. The result is an increasingly intense weakening of the viewer's reaction – a delayed recognition. This kind of a gap between perception and reaction would have been described by Deleuze and, later, above all, Brian Massumi (cf. 2002: 23–45) – while relying on Henri Bergson's law – with the term 'affect', or, more specifically, the cinematic 'affect-image'. This inability to involve oneself in the image content through mental action and categorization, to stabilize oneself on the depiction of understandable action, results in a constant physical tension that has an equal effect on the somatic, intellectual, and emotional spheres, in the sense of "a kind of motor tendency on a sensible nerve" (Deleuze

16 The fact that this assault is intended is proof of Noé's penchant for stroboscopic effects: both the opening credits and sequences during the actual film erupt, again and again, into blinding frenzies of flashing light. Stroboscopic effects break the film's understanding of illusion. Due to the quality of their sensory frequency, they attack the viewer directly on a physical-somatic level; they burn themselves into the retina.

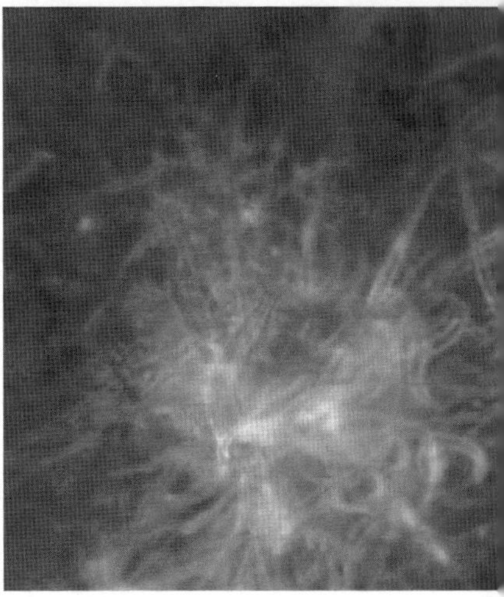

1986/1997: 66)[17]. Consequently, the viewer falls first into a purely passive position that then, however, coalesces with what was viewed, beyond all symbolic meaning and all outward-pointing narration, to form a cohesive occurrence ruled by currents of intensity – an affect block. At the same time, the following is true: "The affect is like the expressed of the state of things, but this expressed does not refer to the state of things, it only refers to the faces which express it and, coming together or separating, give it its proper moving context" (ibid. 106)[18].

Ultimately, the film itself goes from being a representation of the surrounding world to being part of the viewer's world of experience. The film itself becomes an affect in the sense that it functions like a material fact with intrinsic value, which appears before the eyes and ears – like the film's body. In its materiality, it virtually connects itself with the viewer's body and fills it with intensity. Noé, who, besides his films, also produced a TV experiment on the hypnotic powers of television, touches upon exactly this connection – his film is a drug, a dangerously attractive drug, that creeps into our bodies and, from there, minimizes the distance we keep between ourselves and the screen.

What is crucial here is that the drug experience, in connection with the topos of the soul journey, brings a premodern, almost archaic element into the context of the highly technologized, post-capitalistic world represented here by Tokyo. However, by making his film – itself highly technologized and riddled with special effects – the bargaining room for this relationship, Noé presents the drug experience and the noise of the post-capitalist environment as entirely compatible modes of experience. The supposed rationality of technology and capitalism and the irrationality of the drug experience do not contradict one another, but form a field of immanence in which one constantly merges into the other. In his interview, Noé mentions that Tokyo is like a giant pinball machine (see ZAK/Kaghado 2011).

17 "[…] une espèce de tendance motrice sur un nerf sensible" (Deleuze 1983: 96).

18 "L'affect est comme l'exprimé de l'état de choses, mais cet exprimé ne renvoie pas à l'état de choses, il ne renvoie qu'aux visages qui l'expriment et, se composant ou se séparant, lui donnent une matière propre mouvante" (ibid.: 151).

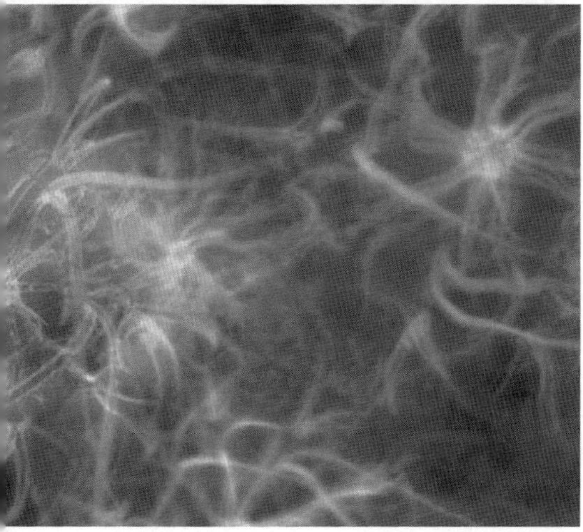

Illustration 6: Film still from Enter the Void *(dir. Gaspar Noé, France/Germany/Italy 2009).*

The main implication of this image, of this extreme dynamic, which evokes a playful-tactile relationship with reality and a certain frenzy of entertainment, is the elimination of the contradiction between true and false, or, more specifically, between empirical and virtual. If one chooses to believe the writings of Michel Foucault, also known to have consumed drugs, then this elimination is also the most significant benefit of a drug experience, which rises above traditional dichotomies (cf. Miller 1993/2000: 248). The authentic experience that immersion delivers, outlined at the beginning, namely that which disregards the opposition between technologically created virtuality and actual experience, shapes this dimension of the experience of being high. Not only does this experience transcend this opposition, it is evoked in the viewer as a real experience. In his writings on film, Deleuze mentions that, after the "big system" has fallen away, the drug experience could become a community-building factor. At the same time, he emphasizes that it is about letting the experimental perception that drugs can evoke take place through entirely different means (cf. Deleuze/Guattari 1987: 183). Noé's film is proof of the fact that, wherever it is concerned with immersion, experimental-film culture offers a form of perception that is, in fact, capable of imitating the main characteristics of drug-induced highs, minus the sclerosis of the human body that actual drug use entails. If we follow this entrance into the void, immersion, as Noé depicts it, is a cinematic dimension of experience complementary to the modern experience of the world. At the same time, it represents an alternative to drug-induced highs and intoxication that evokes "an unfilled sense of internal union with unrealizable breadth" (Nechvatal 2011: 60). The drug film is the community-building factor between us and the world around us; it is the generator of a techno-cultural community based on physical and psycho-sensory interconnectedness. Gaspar Noé is one of its eminent shamans.

References

Blanchet, Robert (2003). *Blockbuster: Ästhetik, Ökonomie und Geschichte des postklassischen Hollywoodkinos*. Marburg: Schüren.

Curtis, Robin (2008). "Immersion und Einfühlung: Zwischen Repräsentationalität und Materialität bewegter Bilder". *montage AV* 17/2: 89–107.

Deleuze, Gilles, Félix Guattari (1980). *Mille plateaux: Capitalisme et schizophrénie*. Vol. 2. Paris: Editions de Minuit.

— (1987). *A Thousand Plateaus: Capitalism and Schizophrenia*. Transl. Brian Massumi. London: Continuum.

Deleuze, Gilles (1983). *Cinéma 1: L'image-mouvement*. Paris: Editions de Minuit.

— (1986/1997). *Cinema 1: The Movement-Image*. 5th ed. Transl. Hugh Tomlinson. Minneapolis, MN: University of Minnesota Press.

Engell, Lorenz (2011). "Blicke, Dinge, Wiederholungen: Über die Genese einer Filmszene in Abbas Kiarostamis *Quer durch den Olivenhain*". Josef Bairlein et al., eds. *Netzkulturen: kollektiv. kreativ. performativ*. Munich: epodium. 95–120.

Grau, Oliver (2001). *Virtuelle Kunst in Geschichte und Gegenwart: Visuelle Strategien*. Berlin: Reimer.

— (2003). *Virtual Art: From Illusion to Immersion*. Transl. Gloria Custance. Cambridge, MA/London: MIT Press.

Griffiths, Alison (2008). *Shivers Down Your Spine: Cinema, Museums, and the Immersive View*. New York, NY: Columbia UP.

Gunning, Tom (2009). "The Attraction of Motion: Modern Representation and the Image of Movement". Klaus Kreimeier, Annemone Ligensa, eds. *Film 1900: Technology, Perception, Culture*. New Barnet: Libbey. 165–174.

Huhtamo, Erkki (2008). "Unterwegs in der Kapsel: Simulatoren und das Bedürfnis nach totaler Immersion". *montage AV* 17/2: 41–68.

Islinger, Michael A. (2002). "Phänomene des Gegenwärtigens und Vergegenwärtigens: Die Wahrnehmung von Videobildern im Film". Ralf Adelmann, Hilde Hoffmann, Rolf F. Nohr, eds. *REC – Video als mediales Phänomen*. Weimar: VDG. 30–43.

Lazzarato, Maurizio (2004). "From Capital-Labour to Capital-Life". *ephemera* 4/3: 187–204.

Lipps, Theodor (1906). *Ästhetik: Psychologie des Schönen und der Kunst.* Vol. 2: *Die ästhetische Betrachtung und die bildende Kunst.* Hamburg/Leipzig: Leopold Voss.

Marsh, James (2010: online). "HKIFF 2010: Gaspar Noé Talks *Enter The Void*". *Twitch Film.* http://twitchfilm.com/2010/03/hkiff-2010-gaspar-noe-talks-enter-the-void.html. [10/08/2012].

Massumi, Brian (2002). *Movement, Affect, Sensation: Parables for the Virtual.* Durham, NC: Duke UP.

Mersch, Dieter (2011). "Fraktale Räume und multiple Aktionen: Überlegungen zur Orientierung in komplexen medialen Umgebungen". Gertrud Lehnert, ed. *Raum und Gefühl: Der Spatial Turn und die neue Emotionsforschung.* Bielefeld: transcript. 49–62.

Miller, James (1993/2000). *The Passion of Michel Foucault.* Cambridge, MA: Harvard UP.

Murray, Janet H. (1997/1999). *Hamlet on the Holodeck: The Future of Narrative in Cyberspace.* 2nd ed. Cambridge, MA/London: MIT Press.

Nechvatal, Joseph (2011). *Immersion into Noise.* Ann Arbor, MI: Open Humanities Press.

Peters, Harald (2010: online). "Soll man ins Kino oder in Deckung gehen?" *Die Welt online.* http://www.welt.de/kultur/article9218613/Soll-man-ins-Kino-oder-in-Deckung-gehen.html. [10/8/2012].

Smith, Nigel M. (2010: online). "Gaspar Noé: 'Making movies to me is like constructing a roller-coaster'". *Indiewire.* http://www.indiewire.com/article/gaspar_noe_answers_to_indiewire_and_you. [10/08/2012].

Sobchack, Vivian (1992). *The Address of the Eye: A Phenomenology of Film Experience.* Princeton, NJ: Princeton UP.

— (2004). *Carnal Thoughts: Embodiment and Moving Image Culture.* Berkeley/Los Angeles, CA: University of California Press.

Stiglegger, Marcus (2006). *Ritual & Verführung: Schaulust, Spektakel & Sinnlichkeit im Film.* Berlin: Bertz + Fischer.

ZAK, Ja'bagh Kaghado (2011: online). "Gaspar Noé: Interview & Photos". *Unleash 2* (Autumn 2011). http://unleashpdf.com/downloads/unleash02.pdf. [10/08/2012].

Part 2:
Archaeologies and Technologies of Immersion

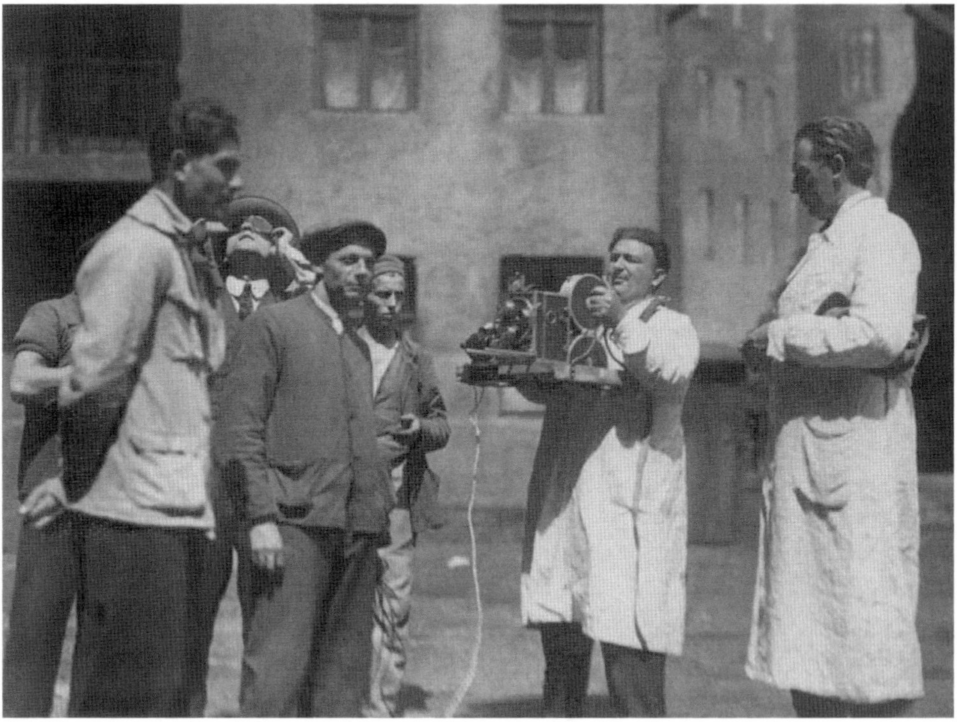

Illustration 1:
Production still from the set of The Last Laugh *with Karl Freud and F. W. Murnau. Photograph by Hans Natge. Deutsche Kinemathek, Berlin.*

From the Unchained to the Ubiquitous Motion-Picture Camera
Camera Innovations and Immersive Effects

Karl Prümm

In cinema, immersive effects are strongly dependent on the use of the camera, allowing for the viewer to enter into the image. This essay focuses on immersion from the perspective of production by considering three major innovations in the history of camera technology: the unchained camera ('entfesselte Kamera') that freed the gaze from the tripod in the 1920s; the Steadicam that fused the camera with the operator's body with its introduction in the 1970s; and the amateur technology of handheld cameras that has given rise to an era of digital presence since the turn of the millennium. In discussing F. W. Murnau's *The Last Laugh* (Germany 1924), Niklaus Schilling's *The Willi Busch Report* (Federal Republic of Germany 1979), and Susanne Bier's *Open Hearts* (Denmark 2002) as prominent examples of these historical innovations, the essay considers the camera's impact on the viewer's immersion into the film.

1. On the History of the Idea and the Media of Immersion

The term 'immersion', insofar as it is used for media phenomena, essentially encompasses two aspects. Firstly, 'immersion' can be defined as an extreme agenda of the representative – the mimetic – arts. Images or visual installations are constructed and arranged in such a way that special forms of energy radiate from them, so that they practically devour their users. These kinds of exceptional standards justify a special status among artifacts; the polarities of image and viewer, of inside and outside, are completely reversed. Immersive art objects count on viewers who allow themselves to be pulled, as if by a vortex, into a pictorial world, who immerse themselves entirely in it; viewers who want to be absorbed in the artificial until their awareness of the media is finally suspended and their own experience of time and space is completely absorbed by the illusory image. For this reason, in media studies' discourse, 'presence' is used as a complementary term to 'immersion' (cf. Neuendorf/Lieberman 2010: 10)[1] in order to denote the dimension of

1 Here, 'presence' is defined as a "perceptual illusion of nonmediation".

time, the absoluteness of the present, and the resulting abnegation of mediality as central components of immersive strategies.

The extreme agenda of immersion that is inscribed in media apparatuses certainly corresponds to a collective desire to be wrapped up in illusionistic, artificial worlds and to dive into new realities; accordingly, it can legitimate itself as a realization of a dream. The dimensions of immersion extend far beyond a pronounced addressing of the viewer – beyond his or her participation and involvement. This, however, also complicates the operative use of this category, which easily slips into the realm of the nebulous, the fantastic, and the speculative. Immersion belongs to the sphere of the imaginary – this much has been established. On the side of the maker, it is project, plan, idea, and intention; on the side of the audience, it is wish, dream, concept, and projection. It can hardly be established whether the intended totality and the jump into another world are achieved or if the barriers and obstacles are indeed bigger – if considerable limits to immersion are set. There is every indication that even an exaggerated illusionism cannot overcome the media user's perceptive distance or make his or her subjective disposition, concrete physicality, and 'in-the-worldness' disappear. Immersion's agenda to overwhelm remains utopian and fictional.

In addition, there are other difficulties in making immersion tangible and describable. Immersion is, first and foremost, a phenomenon of reception and is supposed to manifest directly in the act of reception; this is the term's second central aspect. Immersion targets receivers' consciousness and, above all, their bodies. The strong physical and massive somatic effects that are striven for, however, can only be measured with empirical methods of examination. In order to arrive at valid assertions, more elaborate physiological measuring techniques and more complex interviews of consumers are required. These requirements alone categorically exclude the study of historical objects. On a textual level, immersion can only vaguely be defined. The immersive has no set formal repertoire; the media-related initial conditions and material facts are simply too different. One can completely rule out a smooth transfer of immersive structures between media. Although building blocks and textual elements that are intended to have an immersive effect can be found – even cross-medially – they do not allow themselves to be reduced to this function in the respective media framework and are simultaneously integrated into other contexts. This is particularly the case with narrative cinema. Every discourse on media immersion must be aware of these limitations and the problems associated with the term.

It seems logical to locate this agenda of immersion in the industrial modern era. Firstly, this period brought forth the techniques and instrument-based media necessary for a perfect creation of illusion. Secondly, it created, especially in the big cities, a heightened and relieving expectation of immersion among the public as a counterpart to the ubiquitous, capitalistic working world, which had command over the human subject. The art historian Ulrich Pfisterer, however, justifiably points out a tradition of immersion that developed in the premodern era: image concepts in painting and graphic art from the early modern era that are geared toward a heightened illusion of space and an awareness of presence[2]. It was, without a doubt, central perspective that first sparked immersive fantasies. The epoch-making experiment with which architect Filippo Brunelleschi astounded his contemporaries between 1410 and 1415 can be described as the first immersive visual installation. He combined a mathematically precisely calculated viewpoint – a view of the front exterior of the church San Giovanni in Florence – with a perspectively painted spatial image to prove the interchangeability of artifact and perceptual image. With the help of mirrors that reflected the sky and clouds, he was even able to dissolve the boundaries of the image and bring it to life. In this perfect visual illusion, the viewer, to whose eye the entire construction of this 'optical machinery' ("optischen Maschinerie"; Busch 1989/1995: 65)[3] was directed, was completely integrated – a remarkable anticipation of the 'dispositifs' of photography and film.

Subsequently, however, the iconographic program of immersion disappeared from high culture. Through its strong accentuation of distance, alienation, shock, and deconstruction, of reflexivity and self-reflexivity, the classical modernism of the early 20th century almost banned immersive effects entirely and practically elevated their disavowal and avoidance to a moral demand. This, on the other hand, was a reaction to the undisputed dominance of immersive concepts in the popular media of the 19th century and in the early days of film (1895–1915). In a text from 1946 about the then recently published

2 In his unpublished lecture "Immersions/Emersions: Connection and Distance in the Image Concepts of the Renaissance" at the Munich Conference on Immersion in 2011, Ulrich Pfisterer explained this idea by referring to the graphic works of Hans Baldung Grien.

3 Unless otherwise indicated, all translations are mine.

first volume of Georges Sadoul's *Histoire générale du cinéma*, André Bazin speaks of the "myth of total cinema" (1967/2005: 17) ("le mythe du cinéma total"; 1958: 21), which he defines as a "total and complete representation of reality", as the "reconstruction of a perfect illusion of the outside world in sound, color, and relief" (1967/2005: 20) ("une représentation totale et intégrale de la réalité"; "la restitution d'une illusion parfaite du monde extérieur avec le son, la couleur et le relief"; 1958: 24). He grants this myth so much power that he goes so far as to declare film an "idealistic phenomenon" (1967/2005: 17) ("un phénomène idéaliste"; 1958: 21).

To a far greater extent than the material aspect of the apparatuses and inventions, according to Bazin, this idea advanced the development of the cinematograph. Long before the actual invention, the "concept" existed "fully armed" in the "minds" of the cinematic pioneers as well as of the public "as if in some platonic heaven" (1967/2005: 17)[4]. Consequently, film is the logical product of a myth that cast a spell over the entire 19th century – the myth of an "integral realism, a recreation of the world in its own image, an image unburdened by the freedom of interpretation of the artist or the irreversibility of time" (1967/2005: 21)[5]. The term 'immersion' is not mentioned in Bazin's text. He concentrates solely on the object level, on the process of representation. The text revolves around the aspirations of realism, which is already the key category of his film theory. The way he characterizes this myth, however, how he emphasizes the aspect of force and totality (although, in 1946, the political dimension of totalizing linguistic gestures naturally resonated), how he emphasizes the overwriting of the subject and pure presence as primary idealistic goals of "total cinema" – these factors all support the compelling conclusion that, here, immersion's agenda of effect was silently implied.

One can substantiate Bazin's provocative thesis of the idealistic origin of modern instrument-based media with countless pieces of evidence. In fact, in the 19th century, illusionism – the utopia of a complete reproduction of reality – was a kind of productive force that brought about an entire chain of illusion-creating media that spread

4 "L'idée que les hommes s'en sont faite existait tout armée dans leur cerveau, comme au ciel platonicien" (Bazin 1958: 21).

5 "C'est celui du réalisme intégral, d'une recréation du monde à son image, une image sur laquelle ne pèserait pas l'hypothèque de la liberté d'interprétation de l'artiste ni l'irréversibilité du temps" (ibid.: 25).

immersive energies. The panorama – which was invented at the end of the 18th century and, with its monumental architecture, had a determining influence on the image of metropolises up to the beginning of the 20th century – was probably the most spectacular expression of a then widespread longing to allow oneself to be enchanted by pictorial and optical illusions. The mechanisms used to surround visitors with another world and another time were of an impressive order. Visitors entered the panorama through a dark, subterranean corridor, which was intended to function as a boundary to the everyday reality they had just left and as a floodgate leading into the beaming, light-filled artificial world of the image (see Oettermann 1980 and 1997)[6]. By way of a spiral staircase, visitors climbed up to a viewing platform that presented a 360-degree view of a cityscape, a landscape, or the tumult of a battle. The viewer was completely surrounded by the giant circular image; the entire installation, down to the smallest detail, was geared toward his or her eye. The observing subject was totally integrated into the moment frozen in a painting, which presented itself in an infinity of space. A canvas hung above the platform blocked the view upwards so that the visitor could not see the glass cupola and was forced to believe that he or she was standing under the open sky. The lower edge of the painting was hidden by seamless transitions into three-dimensional landscape sceneries called 'faux terrains'. In the panorama, the eye could not escape the artificial world. In the diorama, which came into fashion after 1830, visitors in a darkened viewing room gazed through a black, rounded viewing tunnel at 'tableaux vivants': landscapes with three-dimensional buildings populated by humans and animals. A change in lighting – nightfall or sunrise – which took place in real time before the viewers' eyes, was *the* fundamental element of immersion. It was here that the dark viewing room in Richard Wagner's Festspielhaus and the blackness of the cinema were prefigured.

Photography satisfied an expectation of illusion of an entirely different nature. In the 19th century, it was celebrated as a subjectless, purely instrument-based view – a view that, as such, was free from falsehood and deception. Photography's impression of reality, indexical nature, and intended authenticity set a new cartography of the world in motion. It afforded viewers who had internalized these attri-

6 Oettermann's already classical study introduces a rediscovery of the panorama as an early mass medium.

butions the direct presence of that which was distant and absent. The stereoscope, patented in 1855, added a spatial effect to photography and, in this way, raised the immersive potential of photographic images. The early German magazine *Die Gartenlaube*, in which even the most bizarre media installations were explained in depth, announced the invention of the stereoscope – the "first domestic 'machine of vision'" (Huhtamo 1995: 161) – with the following prediction:

> It is believed that, one day, the time will come when man is no longer satisfied with paintings and statues, which are more or less termed dead and figments of artists' imaginations; that the stereoscope and daguerreotype will then go hand in hand to offer our eyes everything as it truly is. We already dream of galleries that authentically render the lively expression of faces we want to immortalize; of museums that present all the old and modern works of art "in the flesh", so to speak; of collections that show vaunted and famous places, buildings, and ruins as they really are, so that they awake in us the same feelings as if we were looking at them with our own eyes – a challenge at which even brilliant artists fail. One can already envision even portraits, the memorial signs of our loved ones, in connection with the stereoscope. (Ibid.)[7]

In the mid-19th century, the idea of total immersion was still completely fixed on the single image and on the illusion of space. It still originated from the traditional art medium, from the basic model of the gallery, which, however – as is shown by the *Gartenlaube*'s phantasmagoria – had already been broken down into an accessible world, a simulacrum of real landscapes, and deceptively similar replicas of well-known places of interest. With a quote such as this one, one can appreciate just how fully the moving image, the cinematograph, fulfilled the hopes of immersion and even exceeded them. The condensed image sequences of chronophotography, in combination with the time machine that was the phonograph, already gave rise to the dream of cinematographic docu-

7 "Man glaubt, dass einst der Tag kommen werde, wo man sich nicht mehr mit Gemälden und Statuen, die man mehr oder weniger todt und Phantasiegebilde der Künstler nennt, begnügen werde; daß dann Stereoskop und Daguerreotyp Hand in Hand gehen werden, um unseren Augen alles so darzubieten, wie es wirklich ist. Man träumt schon von Gallerien, die den lebendigen Ausdruck der Köpfe, die man verewigen will, getreu wiedergeben, von Museen, die alle alten und modernen Kunstwerke so zu sagen in Natur vorführen, von Sammlungen, die gerühmte und berühmte Gegenden, Bauwerke und Ruinen so zur Anschauung bringen, wie sie wirklich sind, so daß sie in uns dieselben Gefühle erregen, als wenn wir sie mit eigenen Augen schauten, – eine Forderung, an der selbst ausgezeichnete Künstler scheitern. Und selbst Porträts, die Gedenkzeichen unserer Lieben, sieht man schon mit dem Stereoskop vereint." (N. N. 1855: 172)

mentation and the continuous filmstrip. In 1887, the photographer Nadar remarked: "My dream is to see the photograph register the bodily movements and the facial expressions of a speaker while the phonograph is recording his speech" (qtd. Bazin 1967/2005: 20)[8].

There is no doubt that, with the cinematograph, a new and intensified phase in the history of immersive media began. This miniscule, easily transportable, and multifunctional machine enabled the linking of illusionistic spatial installation and 'living photographs'. With the sliding, flexible celluloid strips, moving images could be projected into sets that reconstructed real sceneries and concrete places. In this way, static things could be set into imaginary motion. Around the cinematograph – at fairs, amusement parks, and variety shows – a wealth of new immersive installations cropped up that used cinematic 'software'. The early cinema of attractions also excessively exhibited the immersive potential of the cinematic image. At the Paris World's Fair of 1900, two "ultrarealistic film attractions" (Fielding 1970: 36) were presented. Raoul Grimoin-Sanson's Cinéorama presented to an audience assembled on a platform the illusion of being on a hot-air-balloon ride. Above visitors' heads blew a giant gas-filled balloon, while ten projectors attached around the entire underside of the platform projected shots of a real ascent onto an enormous circular screen. The Lumière brothers' Maréorama simulated a seafaring journey across the Mediterranean Sea as seen from the bridge of a steamship traveling at full speed. Film sequences were projected into the open horizon, and the pitching and rolling of the ship was imitated with the use of mechanical tricks. Once again, both installations paid homage to the panorama.

Between 1905 and 1912, Hale's Tours caused a fury in the United States: in countless cities across the country, they offered train rides one could experience as a screen projection through the front window of a stationary, authentically furnished train car. Double projectors enabled seamless transitions from one film reel to another so that the duration of the 'trip' could be extended accordingly. The 'passenger train' could be tilted and rocked back and forth, and a sound mechanism could be synchronized exactly with the projected images. During these 'trips', which went all over the world, comedy films were interspersed to entertain the audience (cf. ibid.: 35–38). Starting in

8 "Mon rêve est de voir la photographie enregistrer les attitudes et les changements de physionomie d'un orateur au fur et à mesure que le phonographe enregistre ses paroles" (Nadar, qtd. Bazin 1958: 24).

1898, the phantom ride, a different kind of travel film shot from the very front of a train traveling into a landscape, became quite common in the short-film programs in England (cf. ibid.: 37). Even today, phantom rides still have an appreciative audience: the immersive pull deep into the image is still effective, as is evidenced by the many railway and commuter train rides one can tune into on the nighttime programs of certain television stations.

The perfection of the cinematic narrative, which took place in the 1910s in all the important national cinematographies, decisively weakened the effect of immersive installations that worked with the cinematic moving image. Ventures such as Hale's Tours suddenly lost their popularity and became unprofitable. Technically and structurally advanced, full-length 'cinema dramas' could now easily incorporate immersive effects in their design repertoire. In doing so, they fulfilled the widespread desire for immersion while simultaneously reducing it. Even if the cinematic fiction presents itself with the utmost directorial refinement as an alternative world, in the act of reception, the viewer never loses his or her awareness of the fact that it is a fictitious reality and of the insurmountable gap between it and one's own being. Christiane Voss justifiably notes that, in a cinematic fiction, immersion can only ever be episodal (cf. 2008: 71). Narrative films prefer vagaries and ambiguities; they work with different structural elements, narrative approaches, and gestures; they consistently switch between nearness and distance, between reflective and identificatory passages. As a result, the streamlined alignment with perfectly functioning, all-encompassing immersion can in no way be achieved. Immersive radicalism only occurs in the particulars, in individual sequences and shots, in episodes and interjections. Consequently, the phantom rides of the early days – the depersonalized view of a train ride from the very front of a locomotive, which, along its frantic journey, seemed to devour the tracks – go down in the genre of the train film as an exciting frame and an indispensable subcomponent.

The film *The Lady in the Lake* (dir. Robert Montgomery, USA 1947), based on a novel by Raymond Chandler, represents a miserably failed attempt to create an immersive full-length film that consistently operates with a subjective camera from the first to the last shot, thereby involving the viewer in the cinematic text to the furthest extent possible. It turned out, however, that the monocular camera differed from the human gaze (the perception of one's own body, which is always experienced as a unit although it is only particularly visible). Claude

Lelouch, in a departure from his celebrated melodramas, dared to make an immersive short film just for the fun of it: *C'était un rendez-vous* (France 1976). At the break of dawn, a car races through the streets of awakening Paris: the uncut, nonstop ride – despite red traffic lights and a number of obstacles – goes from the fast lanes of the Boulevard Périphérique to the boulevards surrounding the Opéra, through the narrow streets of Montmartre all the way up to the viewing platform in front of Sacré Coeur. The viewers' gaze merges with the car-turned-weapon; it is enclosed in a projectile capsule. Suspense and fear are transferred directly to the viewers, who, while watching the film, reach with their feet for the break, swerve to avoid the obstacles, and follow the abrupt turns with their entire bodies. With the final shot, Lelouch brings the elaborate immersive construction to an end in one fell swoop, turning thrill into irony. The driver exits the vehicle; a young, attractive woman approaches and greets him tenderly, thereby fulfilling the title of this immersive étude. Krzysztof Kieślowski and Leos Carax each briefly apply this impressive immersive view – as if the racing automobiles suddenly had eyes – in *Three Colors: Blue* (*Trois Couleurs: Bleu*, France/Poland/Switzerland 1993) and *The Lovers on the Bridge* (*Les amants du Pont-Neuf*, France 1991), respectively.

The integration of immersive strategies in narrative cinema has, by no means, satiated the longing for total cinema – for all-encompassing immersion. The media historian and media theorist Erkki Huhtamo terms the "quest for immersion" a "cultural topos" (1995: 160) and calls for immersion to be viewed as a "historical and ideological construction" that has manifested "in different times and places" (ibid.: 161). The expectation of immersion was and continues to be triggered and retriggered by technical innovations. The emergence of color films in the 1930s; Cinerama and CinemaScope in the 1950s; the sound revolution beginning in 1970; cyberspace, head-mounted displays, and virtuality beginning in 1990; and finally the renaissance of 3-D technology in the most recent millennium – all of these new technical developments also constantly brought the ancient topic of 'immersion' into the present. Last but not least, revolutionary camera technologies are radically changing the gaze regime of the cinema and, as a result, awaking new hopes for immersion. Every new filming technique spurs a renegotiation of the viewer's involvement and opens new fields of immersive narration. In the following, this will be explained using the example of three dramatic developments in camera technology, which span a period of nearly eight decades.

2. "We are Right in the Middle!" Immersive Effects of the Unchained Camera

Around 1925, the narrative style in European and American film underwent a decisive transformation. The tripod-mounted static shot was no longer the norm – the fundamental unit of pictorial discourse. The camera itself joined in on the action, was set in motion, opening new dimensions of spatial experience. In his book *The Spirit of Film* from 1930, the film critic, screenplay writer, and film theorist Béla Balázs amended and adapted his first film-theoretical draft, *Visible Man*, from 1924. He did this in view of both the sound film, whose unstoppable triumph can no longer be denied, and the fantastic mobility of the recording device, which has long since established itself. Among the factors that make up the "absolutely innovative" (2010: 98) ("das absolut Neue"; 1930/2001: 14) in film art, Balázs mentions – on the very first pages – the constant movement of the camera. The radical change brought on by the unchained camera ('entfesselte Kamera') seems, to him, to be far weightier than the widely hyped sound revolution. Under the headline "We are Right in the Middle!" (2010: 98) ("Wir sind mitten drin!"; 1930/2001: 14), Balázs puts a fundamental new aesthetic experience on record:

> But film has not just brought new material into view in the course of its development. It has achieved something else that is absolutely crucial. It has eliminated the spectator's position of fixed distance: a distance that hitherto has been an essential feature of the visual arts. The spectator no longer stands outside a hermetic world of art, which is framed within an image or by the stage. Here, the work of art is no insulated space, manifesting itself as a microcosm and metaphor and subsisting in a different space to which there is no access. (2010: 99)[9]

Balázs's enthusiasm knows no bounds. The immersive effect he ascribes film is a *total* one; it encompasses the viewer's spatial deploy-

9 "Aber der Film hat nicht nur Stofflich-Neues gebracht im Laufe seiner Entwicklung. Er hat etwas Entscheidendes getan. *Er hat die fixierte Distanz des Zuschauers aufgehoben; jene Distanz, die bisher zum Wesen der sichbaren Künste gehört hat.* Der Zuschauer steht nicht mehr außerhalb einer in sich geschlossenen Welt der Kunst, die im Bild oder auf der Bühne umrahmt ist. Das Kunstwerk ist hier keine abgesonderte Welt, die als Mikrokosmos und Gleichnis erscheint, in einem anderen Raum ohne Zugang." (Balázs 1930/2001: 15 [emphasis in the German original])

ment as well as his or her journey into a foreign consciousness – the unrestricted adoption of a foreign gaze. In describing immersion, he even points far beyond film and anticipates simulation rooms and cyberspace: "The camera takes my eye along with it. Into the very heart of the image. I see the world from within the filmic space. I am surrounded by the figures within the film and involved in the action, which I see from all sides" (ibid.)[10].

Georg Otto Stindt did not want to go as far as this when he formulated the effects of the unchained camera in 1927. He refers to the monumental film *Ben-Hur: A Tale of the Christ* (dir. Fred Niblo, USA 1925), which, at the time, was drawing viewers into movie theaters in flocks, and sees the artfully applied use of the moving film camera as contributing to a more enjoyable viewing experience. He finds the way it darts around the main character's gait appealing, in that, at times, it follows him, at others, it hurries ahead of him, so that 'the spectator sees both the form and movement of this beautiful youth'[11]. He acknowledges immersive effects, at most, in individual moments. He goes on to write that, in viewing the scene in which Ramon Novarro rides into the arena on his chariot, it is as if the spectator himself were riding in (cf. Stindt 1927: 38).

In August 1924, Guido Seeber – the sought-after cinematographer who knew his way around Studio Babelsberg and always had his ear to the ground – observed a sweeping movement in current film productions, a noticeable demand for a flexible filming technique that freed the camera from the tripod: 'There is a desire to transform the film camera into a handheld camera, that is to say a desire to handle it like a snapshot camera in photography and to be completely free from a fixed standpoint.'[12] Seeber calls the neighboring medium of photography an initiator of the unchained camera. Snapshot photography was also a challenge for film; the miniaturization of the devices that came with it stimulated the further development of film cameras as

10 "Die Kamera nimmt mein Auge mit. Mitten ins Bild hinein. Ich sehe die Dinge aus dem Raum des Films. Ich bin umzingelt von den Gestalten des Films und verwickelt in seine Handlung, die ich von allen Seiten sehe" (ibid.).

11 "[…] der Zuschauer Gestalt und Bewegung dieses schönen Jünglings zugleich sieht" (Stindt 1927: 37).

12 "Man will die Kino-Kamera zu einer Handkamera umgestalten, d. h. man will sie handhaben können wie in der Fotografie eine Momentkamera und völlig unabhängig sein von einem festen Standpunkt" (Seeber 1924: 246).

well. In 1925, the Leica was introduced as an easily accessible, extremely manageable 35 mm high-performance camera that could fit in a jacket pocket. Much loved by many photographers, the Leica ushered in a new era of photojournalism. What was vital to the rapid popularization of the unchained camera, however, was most likely the fact that the static shots of early film no longer met the current demands in cinematic depiction. In the mid-1920s, there was a demand for a new dynamic vividness. The clumsy, unruly tripod, without which film cameras, until then, had been unthinkable, was increasingly found to be burdensome, an obstacle to impressive images, a *shackle* that could finally be cast off. Initially, the, in all respects, freely moving camera was a vision, a notion in the minds of directors, screenplay writers, camera operators, and film critics. They formulated the discourse of the unchained camera, came up with the striking term, and established the new mobility of the camera among viewers.

Elaborate concepts of camera movement are a spectacular characteristic of the films of Abel Gance, Carl Theodor Dreyer, Jean Renoir, and Dziga Vertov. The unchained camera, however, remained by no means reserved for the ambitious art film. Around 1929, it even became natural in popular studio productions. This is why new equipment designed to perfect camera movement was also often praised in trade journals. At first, the instruments necessary for movement were produced by hand for one-time use. Camera dollies, camera cranes, drive motors, and battery systems that do not hamper the camera's freedom of movement were, however, quickly produced on an industrial level as well. A new market had emerged. Miniature cameras with spring balancers, such as the Kinamo or the Debrie Cine Sept, which had actually been developed for amateurs, began to be used in narrative films. Aerial shots also came into fashion in film.

With the extremely mobile, ubiquitous camera, a turn was made toward modern cinema. Innovative movement devices and the willingness to take risks on the part of directors and camera operators gives viewers a new experience of movement, a suggestive gliding into a three-dimensional space in a single, uncut motion, from framing, unframing, and reframing. The experience of time also becomes richer. Traveling time is a time of intoxicating viewing full of discovery – a time that is free from narrative calculations. The phantom rides of the early days were still bound to the train; their terrific speed was only borrowed. The movement devices developed specifically for the camera, however, made the principle of cinematic immersion freely accessible: the vertical movement of the camera deep into space and toward an imaginary vanishing point.

With this, film had finally freed itself completely from the traditional 'dispositifs' and their influence. The image was no longer a stage and even the photographic studio, with its painted backdrops and limited points of view, was no longer its point of reference. New studio architectures and production concepts became necessary. The key film of this heightened experience of movement made possible by the unchained camera is the *The Last Laugh* (*Der letzte Mann*, Germany 1924), which premiered in Berlin around Christmastime. The main players – the director, Friedrich Wilhelm Murnau; the screenplay writer, Carl Mayer; and the director of cinematography, Karl Freund – were all explicit advocates of a film of increased movement, of a pure, strictly visual imagery (see *Illustration 1*). The opening sequence even has a demonstrative air and celebrates the potential for movement of the apparatus now free of the tripod. With the elevator, the camera floats down into the lobby of a noble luxury hotel, crosses the reception area, is reverently greeted by the bellhops, purposefully heads for the massive revolving door, and passes through it to the outside as if the giant glass panels were no obstacle at all. It is unmistakable that an emphasis is being placed on immersive effects. The viewer should be able to feel the energetic power of the focalized narrative machine, which approximates a personal perspective – a human view; he or she should feel swept along in the frantic movement into the film space.

In the key sequence in which the old porter, played by Emil Jannings, is fired on account of his old age and violently stripped of his uniform, this movement takes place in reverse: from outside in the hotel foyer, which is accessible to everyone, to the inside, into the center of power: the hotel manager's office. Here, too, a closed glass door cannot impede the camera, which seems to possess magical powers (see *Illustration 2*). What is special about this sequence is that the gliding camera crosses yet another boundary: the adventurous movement concludes in the body – in the porter's mind. The camera offers a close-up of the porter and steps into a microcosm. On top of the notice of dismissal, which the porter arduously deciphers, a vision is inserted that is also significant to the narrative: the restroom attendant, for whom the porter is to take over, is seen handing over his uniform, namely, his jacket. In this scene, the subsequent dramatic divestment and humiliation of the old porter is prefigured. Ultimately, the all-per-

vading camera captures the porter's thoughts and feelings, the shock of his degradation, his attempts at repression and escape. Twice, the camera hesitantly reveals the word "Altersschwäche" (decrepitude), the letters growing more and more menacing, larger and blurrier, until they become completely indistinct. The mobile camera had now arrived at (and made plausible) a position from which it could naturally slip into the inner world of dreams and delirium.

While observing filming of *The Last Laugh* in July 1924, the film critic Willy Haas wrote that it had been the moving camera, the 'running, dancing, pirouetting, tumbling apparatus'[13], that had made depicting the 'continuity of the living, suffering, feeling, seeing subject in the film'[14] possible at all. In *The Last Laugh*, the journey to the inside, into the thoughts and feelings of a character, is integrated in a wealth of paradigms of movement of the camera: in the interpretation of space through the extremely long sequence shot in the fairy-tale epilogue; in the dramatizing parallel tracking shot as the doorman steals the uniform from the hotel at night; in the floating camera shot, which substitutes speech and sound as the rumor of the doorman's dismissal spreads throughout the tenements, from mouth to mouth, window to window, courtyard to courtyard. *The Last Laugh* shows the collapse of the old world – the shining uniforms and the belief in authority – with brutal clarity while simultaneously lamenting this collapse. Perhaps this is why it is so vividly apparent that the unchained camera was an impetus of modernization for narrative film. New requirements for images and new image practices make themselves known.

13 "[...] rennende, tanzende, pirouettierende, turnende Apparat" (Haas 1991: 109).

14 "[...] Kontinuität des lebenden, leidenden, fühlenden, sehenden Subjektes innerhalb des Filmes" (ibid.: 110).

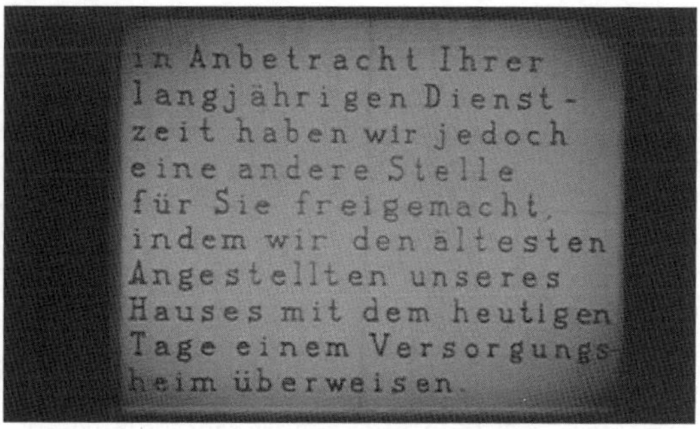

Illustration 2:
Film stills from The Last Laugh
(dir. F. W. Murnau, Germany 1924).

Without a doubt, the moving camera is integrated in the experience of movement in the modern era. It incorporates the liquid dynamic of big cities and metropolises, and reflects the acceleration of society, the frenzied rising and falling motion of recently overcome inflation, the ambivalence of the experience of movement, the rush of gliding and floating, and the fear of falling; the descent alludes to swirling and whirling, to the dominant immersive metaphors of the time. As a spectacular cinematic form, the unchained camera must certainly be seen in connection with the various discourses about movement in the 1920s, including the political semantics and the movement euphoria of the political parties. At that time, movement alone was already a promise of the future. The strict monitoring of movement and movement efficiency, which, at the same time, was rigidly enforced in the working world through Taylorism, describe the other pole of this extensive scenery of movement.

Already on a purely technical level, the moving camera was considered a sign of modernity. It unleashed a radical changing of all values. On the other hand, however, Guido Seeber, who enthusiastically announced the movement 'away from the tripod' ("Los vom Stativ"), complained that, under the banner of the mobile camera, the old visual ideals were no longer valid. Until then, all of the cinematographer's efforts, 'all the expended precision' ("alle aufgewandte Präzision"), had been aimed at making the image 'steadier, sharper, clearer' ("ruhiger, schärfer, klarer"). The beautiful 'steady image' ("Bildruhe"), however, was now gone for good (1998: 86).

All of these aspects overlie the immersive effects of the unchained camera, which Béla Balázs had so extensively emphasized and, in his enthusiasm, absolutized and superelevated to the realm of the fantastic. Balázs underestimates the other side of the moving camera, the technomorphic and self-reflexive component of expansive camera movements – the counterpart of the anthropomorphic dimension of the camera, which can align itself with the human body and human gaze so suggestively, almost to the point of becoming an organ[15]. The moving camera is also always film's expressive discourse about itself. In this enhanced movement, the camera becomes perceptible as a technical instrument; it reveals its technicity and, in doing so, emphatically points out the medium and its materiality. The flowing, gliding, and flying camera exhibits *technologies* of movement, shows its technical potential, how advanced it is, as if in an exhibition at a trade show. With this, it breaks the strong somatic effect of immersion, which is doubtlessly connected to the systematic moving camera. Somehow, this thrilling way of seeing 'sobers up'. The unchained camera also creates distance, represents a reflexive element, develops a counterbalance to the alluring attraction, total illuding, and disappearance of the viewer in the image. In a film as rich as *The Last Laugh*, immersive gestures are only one design element among many. The narrative has so many temporal levels and moves across such a variance of spatial strategies and levels of consciousness that it works against an immersive mono-structure, an all-consuming totality. The viewers are constantly being ripped out of their empathic witnessing of the story. They not only see with the eyes of the laid-off porter – the victim of the modern era – but also look distraughtly at a foolish, sappy, and dull-witted old man who makes them laugh. Laughter, however, is foreign to immersion.

3. Between Body and Machine The Steadicam Recording System

Many things resemble the unchained camera. Steadicam shots are a variation of the tripodless image; they too want to eliminate all static elements of the image, all obstacles to movement, and achieve a new visual expressiveness. The camera system emerged in the 1970s during a transformative period in post-classical cinema when directors

15 Here, I am drawing a connection to the terminology coined by Christine N. Brinckmann with regard to this characteristic of the film camera (cf. 1997: 277f.).

and camera operators were open to new technical possibilities of cinematic narration. Steadicam was developed by the American cinematographer and producer Garrett Brown and introduced to the public in 1976. The system initially remained a kind of secret knowledge, controlled like a monopoly, while rumors of its fabulous effect circulated. It quickly spread, however, to all important film countries; it clearly struck a nerve and met obvious needs. Today, it dominates the audiovisual sector throughout the entire world and is an everyday fixture of televised reports and live broadcasts. Steadicam images are in such high demand that 'Steadicam operator' has long since been established as a job description.

The basic idea of the apparatus is simple, the construction, however, highly complex. The operator wears the camera attached to a vest directly on his or her body, in front of the chest; the camera's weight is distributed evenly to the operator's shoulders, upper body, and hips (cf. Schernikau 2006: 317). What is striking is its anthropomorphic design; a support arm attached to the vest is equipped with joints modeled after the human anatomy. Together with the enclosed weights and stabilizers, this arm absorbs the body movement of the camera operator, reduces shocks and bouncing, and translates impulses from the body into a kind of steady glide. In addition, a small monitor is situated next to the batteries, which allows the operator to constantly check the image and gives Steadicam the character of an autonomous production unit.

In the interplay of all the elements, a new cinematographic view emerges out of the combination of the handheld or shoulder-mounted camera – which directly transfers body movements as physical inscriptions to the film material – with the mechanical perfection that is the geometrizing effect of a tracking or dolly shot. On the one hand, this results in a disembodiment and a de-individualization of the camera's gaze; on the other hand, the camera is more or less glued to the body of the operator, whose maneuverability and agility are exploited. The camera can get to all those places in which tracks can no longer be used. It can function in the narrowest of spaces: stairways, uneven surfaces, and difficult terrains pose no obstacles. The Steadicam facilitates simple, gliding, floating lines of movement of an 'impressive lightness' ("beeindruckender Leichtigkeit"; ibid.). Because the Steadicam itself can also be moved in three directions, additional gliding changes go into the image, creating a 'subtly breathing state' ("leicht atmenden Zustand"; ibid.: 330). The operator's body remains present in the image. The immersive effect of these operations of movement is enormous. The Steadicam manages to carry viewers into the scene: 'It snakes its way past the people, sees them approaching from a distance and looks closely at their faces.'[16] The Steadicam system is so variable that it can align itself directly with everyday behavior, conventions of perception, and gaze desires. Béla Balázs's dream appears to be coming true: the viewer is now really 'right in the middle' of the fiction. He or she slips into the roll of companion, involved eyewitness, partner of the actors – almost of co-actor. A kind of visual 'chumminess' emerges. The viewer is so close to the action that he or she receives the glances, gestures, and words that are actually directed at the characters in the film.

Narrative films, however, cannot be composed solely of these kinds of direct, purely presentist sequences that are close to everyday life and completely envelop viewers; this impedes an immersive program from the very start. Narrative framing, long-distance views, the organizing total picture, summarizing narration, and complex temporality are required. For this reason, the Steadicam is usually only used as one particular element – as a special effect. The Steadicam achieved a certain classicism in the famous Copacabana sequence in *Goodfellas* (dir. Martin Scorsese, USA 1990, cinematography: Michael Ballhaus), an almost self-contained episode, which, at the same time, is the film's climax. In an attempt to impress his girlfriend, the young hero (Ray Liotta), who has devoted himself to the Mafia, shows her the Copacabana nightclub, which serves as a meeting place for the world of organized crime. They are accompanied on this tour by the Steadicam. A four-minute-long, uncut Steadicam journey leads through the underground floors and backrooms, through the 'bowels' of the club, the kitchen. Everywhere, obsequiously smiling, servile, bowing people line the way. This visual condensing of Mafia structures of power and dependence and, at the same time, the climax of the hero's career as a gangster, his self-intoxication and self-stylizing, are additionally underscored by the first-person narrative and voice-over. Everything is compressed into this flowing, almost endless, careering yet floating movement. At the same time, the four-minute sequence radically distances itself from the fable and the characters. Everything is geared toward the gaze of the camera penetrating the

16 "Sie schlängelt sich an den Menschen vorbei, sieht sie von weitem ankommen und blickt nah in ihre Gesichter" (Schernikau 2006: 318).

labyrinthine space. In the way it glides uncut at eye level, it mimics a guest entering this locale for the very first time – diving into the club's totally distinct sphere. The viewer experiences the space intensely; the objects, in their overwhelming abundance, are given an almost haptic presence; the passing time is a time of pure seeing and experiencing. It is freed from narrative calculation. Like no other camera technology, the Steadicam system is capable of making this kind of 'episodic immersion' – which must suffice for the filmic fiction – a sensory experience and, for the most part, suppressing the awareness of technicity. Here, involving the viewer in the cinematic image is accomplished to the furthest extent possible.

In Stanley Kubrick's *The Shining* (UK/USA 1980), the Steadicam sensualizes the gigantic spatial dimensions of the deserted mountain inn as it follows the little boy riding through the endless hallways on his tricycle. The terror that emerges from the emptiness is made tangible in images that burn themselves deep into viewers' minds. With sprawling horizontal movements, the Steadicam in Bertrand Tavernier's *Coup de torchon* (France 1981) follows a bad cop, played by Philippe Noiret, as he runs amok through the tumultuous and desolate, cruel and disinhibited, colonial world of West Africa in the 1930s.

Niklaus Schilling was the first director to use the Steadicam in a West German narrative film. He was so impressed by the new means of visual representation that he decided to shoot an entire film using only this camera system (cf. Prümm 2014: 97–118). In *The Willi Busch Report* (*Der Willi-Busch-Report*, Federal Republic of Germany 1979), only one shot was created with a conventional camera. With his cinematographer, Wolfgang Dickmann, Schilling agreed to implement the Steadicam 'as if Willi the journalist were accompanied or at least constantly observed by a photographer'[17]. The camera is thus always by the side of the quirky local reporter. Willi (Tilo Prückner) works for an ailing small-time newspaper in a small town directly on the inner German border that is cut off from the rest of the world. The nervous, hectic nature of the main character, who intends to escape deadly boredom by creating sensational events himself, spreads to the camera that walks and breathes along with him. The frantic reporter uses a Messerschmitt Cabin Roller to arrive on site quickly. The Steadicam captures the drive in the archaic vehicle in such a way that it appears as if the

17 "So als würde der Journalist Willi von einem Fotografen begleitet oder zumindest konstant beobachtet" (Schilling 2008: 40).

Illustration 3:
Film stills from The Willi Busch Report
(dir. Niklaus Schilling, Federal Republic of Germany 1979).

'pilot's' longings were being fulfilled, and he could lift off at any moment, leaving provincial misery far behind him (see *Illustration 3*). Above all, the tracking camera, however, manages to make an observation within an observation and becomes a medium of journalism criticism. We watch Willi Busch, who, like his namesake, usually speaks in a kind of doggerel verse, from over his shoulder as he himself renders the telephone booths useless so he can then report on the 'telephone vandal'. We are there when, in a conspiracy with the police, he takes close-up photographs of a drowned body. Beyond analytical observation, the camera encircles, swirls around, and ensnares all of the characters. In its universality, it lets viewers feel the small-town world. In motion, it focuses the gaze, smoothly changes the perspectives, and makes cuts unnecessary. At the end, the film takes a turn toward the fantastic. Willi's scribblings become real. The small town attains distinction, actually becoming a nest of spies and a pilgrimage site as the scene of gruesome murders. Willi loses his mind and wafts away in the final scene in a rescue helicopter. In his film dedicated entirely to the

Steadicam technique, Niklaus Schilling clearly favors critical observation, playful distance, and irony over immersive effects.

4. New Body Images
Digital Video in the Narrative Film

Around the turn of the millennium, small, cheap digital cameras equipped with autofocus, which were actually intended for the consumer market, made their way into narrative film productions. Particularly in the wake of Dogme 95, countless theatrical films emerged with this amateur technology; Lars von Trier and Thomas Vinterberg were the pioneers. At the time, the uproar was considerable: many camera operators and critics complained about a decline of image culture and a loss of aesthetic standards. Today, the discussion has become markedly calmer. By now, it has become clear that the unassuming cameras have revolutionized film production, expanded the spectrum of visual modes of expression, and, in doing so, enriched cinematic narrative. With the miniature cameras, the movement 'away from the tripod' seems to have reached its goal. The featherweight instruments can easily be controlled by hand – practically with one's pinky finger. No obstacles stand in the way of filming. The space these disembodied cameras take up is next to nothing and is second only to the camera sensors used in medical research. The miniature cameras are now truly ubiquitous and can be used everywhere and at any time. They liberate filmmakers from the material strain of the celluloid era.

The extensive memory capacity of the chips allows for almost boundless experimentation and discarding of unwanted material, open-ended improvisation and waiting for the right moment – everything the many generations of the cinematic avant-garde dreamt of. But is the longing for immersion also fulfilled? Have new creative opportunities emerged for the agenda of immersion? These questions will be examined using the example of Susanne Bier's *Elsker dig for evigt* (*Open Hearts*, Denmark 2002, cinematography: Morten Søborg). What is special about this film, which presents the Dogme seal in the opening sequence, is that it redefines the relationship between body and image and attempts to find new body images with the means provided by DV cameras. The plot is like that of a chamber play and focuses on two couples. Niels (Mads Mikkelsen), a doctor working in a

Illustration 4:
Film stills from Open Hearts
(dir. Susanne Bier, Denmark 2002).

hospital, and Marie (Paprika Steen) are around forty years old, have three children, are established, and live in seemingly secure and stable circumstances. Cecilie (Sonja Richter) and Joachim (Nikolaj Lie Kaas) are a younger couple in their twenties. They want to get married but are facing a temporary separation because Joachim wants to go on a mountain-climbing trip to South America. The two couples become inextricably linked by a car accident in which Marie is involved and Joachim is seriously injured; after falling into a coma, he is left a paraplegic. Both are at fault: Marie was driving too fast, and Joachim unmindfully got out of his car, paying no regard to oncoming traffic. The terrible accident changes all their lives in a single blow. At Marie's behest, Niels takes care of Cecilie, whom Joachim, embittered and filled with hate, has turned away from. What begins as a professional task quickly turns into a mutual attraction and ultimately into a passionate relationship, which Niels keeps from Marie for a long time. He leaves his family, but also loses Cecilie, who returns to Joachim. At the end, it remains unclear what becomes of the two couples.

The film conveys these entangled events from an extremely close perspective – one that is only made possible by miniaturized cameras. Even in the young couple's carefree show of affection at the beginning of the film, the camera does not depict; rather, it gets involved in the tender play of their hands. The camera is so close to their bodies and faces that it itself is touched, shoved, and pushed away. Moments of physical intimacy such as these – a way of seeing that is akin to touch – go a step further than the close views of the Steadicam. *Open Hearts* begins and ends with street scenes shot using a thermal imaging camera. These serve as an apt, logical, and plausible metaphor. At the same time, with this framing, the narrative camera is defined, its imaging technique identified: the narrative camera does nothing other than register body wavelengths, body energies, and body emanations and gives them a visual expression. It works like a highly sensitive instrument through closeness and touch alone. It makes the destructive energies of the paralyzed body, which block out all tenderness, visible (see *Illustration 4*). It shows the energies of attraction and the power of desire that sweep up Joachim and Cecilie, as well as the alienation of the body and the cooling of feelings between Joachim and Marie. It is in this way that profoundly radical body images come about – drastic images of the sickly body; wonderfully illuminated images of the young, perfect bodies.

Here, one can also see – as in other examples from the Dogme series – that the mini-DV cameras allow traditional gaze and narrative systems to work together. It is this aspect that constitutes the disconcerting and unsettling character of these films. Each of the camera's views is unique and unrepeatable, like reality, to refer once again to Bazin. A reference system of points of view and fixed camera positions, of connections and reprises, cannot be constructed. This, in turn, accentuates the effect of authenticity, the closeness to the unique event, the physical immersion of the viewer in the body image. This, however, is confronted with the nervous, unsteady, imperfect, interference-prone, flat, shallow video image, in which space often disappears. All of this resists the illusory effect. By interspersing extremely grainy, short, flash-like shots recorded with a Super 8 camera – highlighted, condensed moments, glances, fragmented gestures, ideal and mental images – throughout the body sequences, *Open Hearts* dissociates itself one step further from representational realism. This switching of the support material creates more distance and self-reflexivity. The one-time and irretrievable nature of reality appears as a highly artificial image. Similar situations can be seen in *Festen* (*The Celebration*, dir. Thomas Vinterberg, Denmark 1998, cinematography: Anthony Dod Mantle), in which the video image is taken to the limits of disappearing and fading away, and in *Der Felsen* (dir. Dominik Graf, Germany 2008, cinematography: Benedict Neuenfels), in which, through editing and format transfers, a multilayered, almost painterly image is created. Thus, the range and the simultaneity of radical immersion and distancing repeat themselves in the most diverse innovative scenarios in camera technology.

References

Balázs, Béla (1924/2001). *Der sichtbare Mensch oder die Kultur des Films*. Frankfurt am Main: Suhrkamp.

— (1930/2001). *Der Geist des Films*. Frankfurt am Main: Suhrkamp.

— (2010). *Béla Balázs: Early Film Theory:* Visible Man *and* The Spirit of Film. Ed. Erica Carter. Transl. Rodney Livingstone. New York, NY: Berghahn Books.

Bazin, André (1958). "Le mythe du cinéma total" [1946]. *Qu'est-ce que le cinéma?* Vol. 1: *Ontologie et langage*. Paris: Editions du Cerf. 21–27.

— (1967/2005). "The Myth of Total Cinema". *What Is Cinema?* Vol. 1. Ed. and transl. Hugh Gray. Berkeley, CA/Los Angeles, CA/ London: University of California Press. 17–22.

Brinckmann, Christine N. (1997). "Die anthropomorphe Kamera". *Die anthropomorphe Kamera und andere Schriften zur filmischen Narration*. Eds. Mariann Lewinsky, Alexandra Schneider. Zurich: Chronos. 277–301.

Busch, Bernd (1989/1995). *Belichtete Welt: Eine Wahrnehmungsgeschichte der Fotografie*. Frankfurt am Main: Fischer.

Fielding, Raymond (1970). "Hale's Tours: Ultrarealism in the Pre-1910 Motion Picture". *Cinema Journal* 10/1: 34–47.

Haas, Willy (1991). "Was wird gearbeitet? Ein Besuch im Ufa-Gelände Neubabelsberg" [1924]. Wolfgang Jacobsen, Karl Prümm, Benno Wenz, eds. *Willy Haas: Der Kritiker als Mitproduzent. Texte zum Film 1920–1933*. Berlin: Edition Hentrich. 109–113.

Huhtamo, Erkki (1995). "Encapsulated Bodies in Motion: Simulators and the Quest for Total Immersion". Simon Penny, ed. *Critical Issues in Electronic Media*. New York, NY: State University of New York Press. 159–186.

N. N. (1855). "Das Stereoskop: Einrichtung und Geschichte". *Die Gartenlaube* 13: 170–172.

Neuendorf, Kimberly A., Evan A. Lieberman (2010). "Film: The Original Immersive Medium". Cheryl Campanella Bracken, Paul

Skalski, eds. *Immersed in Media: Telepresence in Everyday Life*. New York, NY/London: Routledge. 9–38.

Oettermann, Stephan (1980). *Das Panorama: Die Geschichte eines Massenmediums*. Frankfurt am Main/Vienna: Syndikat.

— (1997). *The Panorama: History of a Mass Medium*. Transl. Deborah Lucas Schneider. New York, NY: Zone Books.

Prümm, Karl (2014). *Ein notorischer Grenzverletzer: Niklaus Schilling und seine Filme*. Berlin: Verbrecher Verlag.

Sadoul, Georges (1946–1975). *Histoire générale du cinéma*. 6 Vols. Paris: Denoël.

Schernikau, Mirko (2006). "In Bewegung – der schwebende Blick der Steadicam". Thomas Koebner, Thomas Meder, eds. *Bildtheorie und Film*. Munich: edition text+kritik. 316–334.

Schilling, Niklaus (2008). "Wie die Stasi mich mit Antonioni zusammenbrachte: Rückblenden in die Wendezeit der Filmtechnik". Andreas Kirchner, Karl Prümm, Martin Richling, eds. *Abschied vom Zelluloid: Beiträge zur Geschichte und Poetik des Videobildes*. Marburg: Schüren. 39–52.

Seeber, Guido (1924). "Über Kraftantrieb von kinematographischen Aufnahme-Apparaten". *Die Kinotechnik: Halbmonatsschrift für die gesamte Wissenschaft und Technik der theoretischen und praktischen Kinematographie* 6/15: 245–249.

— (1998). "Die taumelnde Kamera" [1925]. Rolf Aurich, Wolfgang Jacobsen, eds. *Werkstatt Film: Selbstverständnis und Visionen von Filmleuten der zwanziger Jahre*. Munich: edition text+kritik. 84–87.

Stindt, Georg Otto (1927). "Die entfesselte Kamera". *Der Kinematograph* 1044: 37–38.

Voss, Christiane (2008). "Fiktionale Immersion". *montage AV* 17/2: 69–86.

Illustration 1:
Player of the VR game Wild Skies,
designed for Project Holodeck,
USC School of Cinematic Arts and
Viterbi School of Engeneering,
2012.

From Analog to Digital Image Space
Toward a Historical Theory of Immersion[1]

Gundolf S. Freyermuth

Coming to terms with immersion in digital culture seems to require, above all else, a historical and transmedial point of view. So far, aesthetic immersion – whether seen as a utopia or a dystopia of art and entertainment – has been perceived predominantly under media-specific and normative perspectives. Concentrating on just one central aspect of immersion, my essay follows the transformations of the modern image space. The starting point is an overview of the status quo of (audio-)visual imagery, which is characterized by three constitutive elements: hyperrealism in 2-D/3-D, multi-/non-linearity, and interaction/interfaces. In a second step I cast a look back at the media-technological and media-aesthetic construction of the analog image space between the Renaissance and postmodernism, based on the principle of separation, and then describe its being called into question since the mid-20th century. In a third step, I venture to explore the ongoing construction of a new digital image space, based on the principle of fusion. It seems to be characterized by three trends: transmediality, augmentation, and new modes of immersion. In a final outlook, a historical theory of immersion is charted that discerns four modes of immersion according to four modes of mediality.

1. Introduction

These days the perspectival image space as it has evolved since the Renaissance seems to be imploding and exploding at the same time. The experience of explosion is, of course, created by digital 3-D. Its audio-visions, sounds and images, cross the boundaries of the screen and jump right out at the audience. Complementary to this, the introduction of so-called natural user interfaces (NUIs) – touch screens as well as gesture and voice control – has caused a sensory implosion: the collapse of the perspectival space that analog media technology, on the one hand, evokes through distance and, on the other hand, installs through physical separation both in front of and behind the image.

1 This text resumes, combines, and continues observations I have previously made in German publications; see Freyermuth 2007; 2010; 2013.

The present Big Bang of digital audio-visuality, however, appears to be only one significant element of a broader and deeper change: the deconstruction of the familiar industrial media 'dispositif' and the emergence of a new digital media 'dispositif'. So far, its defining characteristic has been the transformation of analog media into one digital transmedium, namely software, which has thus effected a media-technological convergence. "[T]he media-specific distinctions between cinematic, televisual and computer media", for example, as Anne Friedberg states in *The Virtual Window*, "have been eroded beyond recognition by the digital technologies that have transformed them" (2006: 3). Central to this techno-cultural process of transmedialization is the surmised potential to increase immersion.

Immersion as Utopia and Dystopia

In her pioneering study *Hamlet on the Holodeck*, Janet H. Murray starts her reflection on the aesthetics of the developing digital medium by analyzing the "enchantment of immersion" (1997: 125) that computer-mediated experiences can offer like no other media has before. Two years later, in a paper Murray co-wrote with Henry Jenkins, both describe immersion as one of the two "aesthetic pleasures that emerge most immediately from the intrinsic properties of the computer medium" (Murray/Jenkins 1999: 36)[2]. Since then the question of immersion has gained even greater prominence in the discourse on digital culture. In his popular report *The Art of Immersion*, Frank Rose, for example, after interviewing dozens of leading filmmakers and game designers, claims that immersion is the longing of the age and that the wish to be immersed will be a central factor in the forming of new digital ways of telling stories: "We can see the outlines of a new art form, but its grammar is as tenuous and elusive as the grammar of cinema a century ago. We know this much: people want to be immersed. They want to get involved in a story, to carve out a role for themselves, to make it their own" (2011: 166).

While, as Marie-Laure Ryan maintained, the "history of Western art has seen the rise and fall of immersive ideals" (2001: 2), the last decades brought – after the strong anti-immersion stance of postmodern art and literature as well as poststructuralist theory in the 1960s and 1970s – an amazing popularization of immersive ideals. It seems no coincidence that this turn toward immersion originated in popular en-

2 The other aesthetic pleasure being interactivity.

tertainment itself. "Encounter at Farpoint" (dir. Corey Allen, USA 1987), the pilot of the sci-fi series *Star Trek: The Next Generation* (creator Gene Roddenberry, USA 1987–1998), introduced a totally immersive holographic entertainment environment called a holodeck as part of its fictional world. It quickly became a popular utopian model for the digital future of art and entertainment – not only among millions of *Star Trek* fans, but also for leading scientists, audio-visual artists such as filmmakers and game designers, and media theorists.

Its undiminished influence as a central point of reference can be demonstrated by three recent examples. In 2011 Stevie Bathiche, research director of Microsoft's Edison Lab, stated that the lab strives "to create a holodeck-like experience" (qtd. Sottek 2011). Since 2012 a Project Holodeck at the School of Cinematic Arts of the University of Southern California in Los Angeles has been using John Carmack's Kickstarter-financed Oculus Rift visor to experiment with interactive-immersive audio-visual experiences (see Stevens 2012). And Jeff Norris from NASA's Jet Propulsion Laboratory announced – fittingly, at the March 2013 Game Developers Conference in San Francisco – that the space agency is planning to allow millions of earthlings to experience space travel via an illusionistic system "of shared immersive exploration. Everyone exploring the universe through robotic avatars, not just peering at numbers or pictures on a screen, but stepping inside a holodeck and standing on those distant worlds" (qtd. Claiborn 2013). Not surprisingly, the power or rather promise of digitally induced immersion – Timothy Leary famously spoke of computers and immersive virtual-reality systems as "electronic LSD" (qtd. Kirby 2011: 224) – inspired as much anguish as it did hope. Counteracting the positive holodeck fantasy of the *Star Trek* series, there have been, for example, several dozen dystopic Hollywood movies that have painted the potentially enslaving dangers of immersion into virtual worlds in crude colors, among them *Tron* (dir. Steven Lisberger, USA 1982), *Arcade* (dir. Albert Pyun, USA 1993), *Strange Days* (dir. Kathryn Bigelow, USA 1995), *The Thirteenth Floor* (dir. Josef Rusnak, USA 1999), *eXistenZ* (dir. David Cronenberg, USA 1999), *The Matrix* (dir. Andy and Lana Wachowski, USA/Australia 1999), *Gamer* (dir. Mark Neveldine and Brian Taylor, USA 2009), and *Inception* (dir. Christopher Nolan, USA 2010).

A theoretical complement to these fictional warnings and rejections of immersion can be found in Katie Salen and Eric Zimmerman's influential game-design handbook *Rules of Play*. Analyzing the seemingly contradictory attitudes and efforts of those in game design who are proponents of digitally mediated immersion, Salen and Zimmerman diagnose the existence of a widespread "immersive fallacy" that confuses immersion with visual realism: "the idea that the pleasure of a media experience lies in its ability to sensually transport the participant into an illusory, simulated reality" (2004: 450). This overemphasis on world building and sensory sensations would be an underestimation of the extensive aesthetic means that games as a medium have to offer beyond holodeck-like immersion (see *Illustration 1*), above all immersion through 'meaning'. "To play a game is to take part in a complex interplay of meaning. But this kind of immersion is quite different from the sensory transport promised by the immersive fallacy" (ibid.: 452). The fallacy would thus be "a stumbling block to advances in game design, as it represents an overly romantic and antiquated model for how media operate" (ibid.: 455).

As We May Think of Immersion

Comparable examples of critical examinations of immersion focusing on just one medium – as Salen and Zimmerman did on games – could be cited from other disciplines, namely literature, film, and the arts (see Ryan 2001; Rose 2011). While such research has provided many insights – as immersion is obviously produced and experienced very differently in media such as text, still or moving pictures, linear or not-so-linear audio-visuality – all in all, these isolated approaches, oriented on the analog order of media, fail in the context of the ongoing process of virtualization and transmedialization. To come to terms with immersion in digital culture seems to require, above all else, a comparative and transmedial perspective transcending the disciplinary borders of, among others, aesthetics and art history, photo and radio theory, and literary, film, television, and game studies (cf. Freyermuth 2007: 15f.).

A second flaw in the prevalent discussion of immersion can be demonstrated, once again, by the example of game-design theory and game studies. For almost two decades, researchers have tried to define immersion with respect to games. In 2004, Ernest Adams, for example, differentiated tactical immersion, resulting from skilled tactile interactions; strategic immersion, resulting from responding to mental challenges; and narrative immersion, resulting from losing oneself in a story (see 2004). A year later Laura Ermi and Frans Mäyrä categorized immersion into sensory, challenged-based, and imaginative variants (see 2005). Quite similarly, Staffan Björk and Jussi Holopainen discerned sensory-motoric, cognitive, and emotional immersion, but added to the mix spatial immersion, the feeling of really being there (see 2005). These attempts, along with several others, to theoretically grasp the phenomenon of immersion are both instructive and arbitrary, as they share the same flaw: they all struggle to deliver a systematic definition tending toward the prescriptive and normative.

Thereby they fall short of a central insight of modern aesthetics dating back to the Enlightenment and specifically G. W. F. Hegel: that artistic production is constantly adapting to social and cultural developments – while at the same time documenting and expressing these changes. Since then and despite many other differences, advanced aesthetic thinking – from Marx and Engels in the 19th century to Lukács, Benjamin, and Adorno to McLuhan, Foucault, Barthes, and Baudrillard in the 20th century – has preserved this basic insight: in order to be able to comprehend – to come to terms with – the continuous development of creative production and the complexity and fluidity of individual artifacts theoretic reflection has to abandon all inherently normative taxonomies. Aesthetic products and processes from different times and places cannot be understood in ahistorical systematics – at least not adequately and sufficiently. Rather they have to be judged on their own terms and the terms of the time and the places they originated from.

Consequently, I will attempt to assume not only a transmedial, but also a historical perspective on immersion while concentrating on just one central aspect: the image space. Over the course of three sections, I will analyze, contextualize, and summarize its transformation – from the construction of the modern image space in the Renaissance to its deconstruction in the second half of the 20th century and the current emergence of a new digital image space. In the interest of brevity, I will do this in twelve rather simple, and probably even oversimplified, assumptions.

The starting point will be an overview of the status quo of (audio-) visual imagery, which is characterized by three constitutive elements: hyperrealism in 2-D/3-D, multi-/non-linearity, and interaction/interfaces (*Looking Around: A Preliminary Inventory of Digital Audio-visuality*). The next section casts a look back at the media-technological and media-aesthetic construction of the analog image space between the Renaissance and postmodernism against strong countercurrents and then describes its being called into question since the mid-20th century (*Looking Back: The Analog Image Space and the Principle of Separation*). The last of these sections ventures to explore the ongoing construction of a new digital image space, which is so far characterized by three trends: transmediality, augmentation, and new modes of immersion. In an outlook the emerging digital media 'dispositif' and a historical theory of immersion will be charted (*Looking Forward: The Digital Image Space and the Principle of Fusion*).

2. Looking Around
A Preliminary Inventory of Digital Audio-visuality

In the context of media history, the Big Bang of digital visuality currently under way involves the third phase of digital (audio-)visuality. It indicates the growing maturity of the digital transmedium, as, in modern times, the establishment of new media has always relied on three – of course, partly overlapping – phases: once the experimental development of key technological and aesthetic elements has taken place (phase one), a rationalization process sets in whereby traditional media practices are replaced with new and more effective ones (phase two), until finally in the third phase it becomes possible to tap into the full aesthetic potential of the new medium.

An example of such a course of events can be found at the beginning of modern times, when, alongside the printing press, perspective oil painting on panel or canvas began to prevail. In the first phase, a number of innovative basic elements were developed, such as mechanical methods for the production of canvas and oil paints; the specific mathematical formulae for perspective construction; a variety of craft techniques to improve perspective illusion; and, last but not least, mechanical drawing machines. With prerequisites for the new media 'dispositif' in place, the transition from wood panel and fresco to canvas panel as the defining visual medium initiated the rationalization of image production. In the beginning, this mainly meant faster, cheaper, simpler, and thereby more reliable production of the traditional, primarily Christian and mythological motifs. The new medium's special qualities, which greatly exceeded those offered by the older forms of media, both technically and aesthetically, could only be realized in the third phase. The fact that, compared to frescoes, for example, paintings on canvas panels were far cheaper to produce and also transportable brought about a blossoming of bourgeois-secular painting with new motifs and conventions as well as art's gradual transfer to the market; in other words, this change initiated processes of privatization and personalization.

Digital Aesthetics

Comparable triadic developments shaped, centuries later, the establishment of industrial media, of photography, film, and television. This suggests that today's digitalization might be following a pattern similar to the one seen before in the mechanization and industrialization of media. And indeed, between the middle and the end of the 20th century, necessary technological and artistic elements were designed and experimented with, ranging from John von Neumann's (see 1945) and Claude E. Shannon's (see 1948) complementary concepts of the separation of hardware and software to George Lucas's long-standing efforts to digitally create photo-realistic images, which finally led to the first digital master (see Vaz/Duignan 1996; Freyermuth 1999a; 2002). During the last two decades – and partially in parallel to the first phase – rationalization took place, a continuing replacement of traditional analog media practices by digital ones. The production of movies and television shows became cheaper, faster, and simpler, not least of all due to the popularization of digital cameras and the affordances of digital postproduction. The same applies to the disruptive practices of virtual distribution, their foundation being the establishment of both stationary and mobile broadband networking over the last decade.

This second phase is now approaching its end. "For all the talk of 'new media', it functioned as little more than a new delivery mechanism for old media – newspapers, magazines, music", Frank Rose writes in *The Art of Immersion*, "as disruptive as the Net has been to media businesses, only now is it having an impact on media forms" (2011: 97). As the title of Rose's study already suggests, this impact works toward new forms of immersion.

My first assumption therefore is: *Currently, digitalization is entering its third and artistically most exciting phase. With it comes the realization of the genuine potential of digital audio-visuality on the agenda, a long-term aesthetic transformation, which includes the emergence of a digital media 'dispositif' and a new digital aesthetics that deals particularly with the creation and experience of immersion.*

The further course of this phase seems to be framed by three preeminent conditions that have only recently come into place.

Hyperrealism in 2-D/3-D

First, a new technological form of picture production evolves: digital imaging fuses manual imitation, i. e., perspectival realism as it was developed in the mechanical age, and semi-automatic reproduction by analog machinery, i. e., 2-D and 3-D photo-realism as it was developed in the industrial age. The aesthetic result is a new, third form of realistic representation: hyperrealism, 'photo-realistic' imagery beyond photographic indexicality[3]. While analog photos and movies are obviously limited to showing what once happened, somewhere, sometime, hyperrealistic pictures and audio-visions – like realistic paintings – can show whatever their creators were able to imagine and to skillfully produce or program.

Right now, three different modes of producing non-indexical hyperrealistic audio-visuals coexist:

- *virtual creation*, in the tradition of analog animation, i. e., digital generation ex nihilo;
- *hybrid creation*, in the tradition of analog feature-film production, i. e., hyperrealistic modifications of previously captured live-action footage or the blending of such footage with computer-generated images; and
- *procedural creation*, in the tradition of digital games, i. e., image generation through game engines in real time depending on user interaction.

With hyperrealism, the way audio-visual content is produced changes dramatically. Starting in the 1980s, analog special effects and animation were gradually replaced by virtual creation, and movies and television shows became hybrids of photo-realistic and hyperrealistic imagery, with the hyperrealistic proportion steadily increasing. Only recently, however, the third variant of hyperrealism, developed in game design, won influence on linear audio-visuality as well. David Jones, responsible for *Grand Theft Auto* (GTA), one of the best and most successful series of games striving for hyperrealism, wrote: "*Grand Theft Auto* was not designed as *Grand Theft Auto*. It was designed as a medium. It was designed to be a living, breathing city that was fun to play" (qtd. Schell 2008: 90). Only after the 'game-scape', the hyperrealistic audio-visual world, had been designed was the story developed in many iterations – by playtesting possibilities and limitations of the virtual world. Once movies leave the analog realm, they

3 In retrospect, the painterly hyperrealism of the 1960s and 1970s, as well as an important part of special-effect practices in analog cinema, can be understood as aesthetic anticipations of digital media technology and their effects. For painterly hyperrealism, see Chase 1973/1975; for anticipation of cinematic hyperrealism, see Brinkemper 2012; for the historical and aesthetical origins of realism, photo-realism, and hyperrealism, and their differentiation, see Freyermuth 2007.

can, of course, be designed in almost the same way. Industrial processes that follow the model of assembly-line production – writing a story, building sets, shooting scenes non-chronologically, editing, and final montage – give way to digital processes that follow the game-design model of iterative prototyping and generative procedures. In the last decade, the potential of virtual 3-D design has attracted producers of hyperrealistic blockbuster movies, for example the makers of *Watchmen* (dir. Zack Snyder, USA 2009) or *Avatar* (dir. James Cameron, USA 2009). "Constructing worlds is the main idea", remembers *Watchmen* production designer Alex McDowell: "By creating a 3-D virtual production space, you can work with your fellow filmmakers in a very descriptive, data-rich, virtual representation of the film before you even start making it" (qtd. Hart 2009). In a similar way, James Cameron describes the hyperrealistic 'movie-scape' of *Avatar*: "It's like a big, powerful game engine. If I want to fly through space, or change my perspective, I can. I can turn the whole scene into a living miniature" (qtd. Chatfield 2010: 623f.).

Once, the constraints and affordances of photo-realism led the development of audio-visual content from mechanical production methods, as they were standard to the theater, toward industrial production methods, which became standard to the movie industry in the analog age. Now, it seems, the constraints and affordances of hyperrealism are leading the development of audio-visual content away from these industrial methods, if not analog production methods in general – specifically writing – and toward virtual 3-D design and its central method of iterative incremental prototyping. By producing linear audio-visions, filmmakers – like game designers and players – begin to experience the kind of immersion that only interactive 3-D game worlds offer, from real-time change in perspective to virtual cameras that can go where no real camera could. It can be expected that movies that are designed this way will, sooner rather than later, develop new aesthetics, particularly new and more immersive ways of constructing worlds and telling stories.

My second assumption therefore is: *One central element of the emerging digital media 'dispositif' is hyperrealism, a non-indexical form of realistic audio-visuality. In its most advanced procedural variant, hyperrealism allows for the virtual design of 3-D worlds that can be realized in real time, interactively manipulated, and arbitrarily navigated, thereby increasing immersion in production and the usage of non-linear and linear audio-visions.*

Multi-/Non-linearity

A second key element in the realization of the new, genuine potential of digital audio-visuality is clearly wedded to hyperrealism: the forming of non-linear – or rather multi-linear – ways of audio-visual storytelling, which are mostly, not quite accurately, subsumed under the term 'games'. Their rise poses a competitive threat to traditional narrative forms, both commercially and aesthetically, as they seem to be becoming the defining medium of the age, i. e., the cultural basis for the audio-visual construction of reality and its perception (see Freyermuth 2012). Once, theater represented the mentality of the mechanical age: "All the world's a stage." For contemporaries, the unity and sequentiality of the action adequately, if not perfectly, expressed the pre-industrial way of life, its perception of space and time, its conception of what it meant to be human. Later, in the early 20th century, cinema became the defining medium. Its audio-visual narratives were no longer played out live, but prerecorded in a Tayloristic manner, edited together in a final assembly – the so-called final cut – and then distributed in identical copies by physical transport. Specifically, movies' new way of manipulating space and time expressed like no other medium the industrial way of life, its mentality, its conception of what it means – or rather, meant – to be human (see Benjamin 2008).

Now games are assuming that role. While motion pictures tell of realized actions in fictitious worlds, games – as the German philosopher Hans-Georg Gadamer suggested long before digital games even existed – open up fictitious, rule-controlled worlds for possible action (see 1974/1993). Their hyperrealistic worlds enable players – the users formerly known as the audience – to interactively explore, experience, and co-create narratives in a non-linear or at least multilinear fashion. The aesthetic effect is two-fold: a virtualization of space and time and a spatialization and temporalization of virtuality. It is in this new virtual space-time continuum that the unique aesthetic experience of games emerges – through a fusion of the qualities of their malleable audio-visual worlds and their inherent narrative potential with the many individual choices, reactions, and interactions of their users. As a result, writes Tom Chatfield, games offer "a portal to a new destination in human experience, a space where people could interact in real time within an entirely simulated environment – as if a work of fiction had suddenly become real" (2010: 321f.).

My third assumption, therefore, is: *Another central element of the emerging digital media 'dispositif' is multi- and non-linearity. By realizing what hyperrealism affords for the first time – the interactive manipulation of audio-visual story worlds in real time – not-so-linear audio-visuality seems poised to become the defining audio-visual medium of digital culture, the basis for the social construction of reality and its aesthetic perception.*

Interaction/Interfaces

The technological basis of any non-linear experience in the digital trans-medium is, of course, the existence of interfaces that make feedback channels available to users so that they can control and manipulate the different elements of virtual story worlds. The relationship between interaction and immersion, however, has been debated for some time. Henry Jenkins and Janet Murray, for example, have asserted, "immersion and interactive agency reinforce each other" (1999: 37)[4]. Marie-Laure Ryan, on the other hand, has argued that interactivity conflicts with immersion, claiming the displacement of the immersive ideal "by an aesthetics of play and self-reflexivity that eventually produced the ideal of an active participation of the appreciator – reader, spectator, user – in the production of the text" (2001: 2). Neither position seems to take into account the historical transformation of digital interactivity over the decades, from hardly interactive punch cards to hard-to-learn command-line interfaces to easier to handle, but still abstract, graphical user interfaces (GUIs) to more natural user interfaces (NUIs), which seem to promise, finally, a convergence of interactivity and immersion.

A third key element in the realization of the new potential of digital audio-visuality thus is the current shift from hardware-based interfaces (different multi-key controllers in combination with GUIs) to more immersive and more intuitive software-based NUIs. This paradigm change dates back to artistic mixed-reality experiments, conducted in the 1980s and 1990s, with tracing visual, acoustic, tactile, gestural, and spatial data (gaze, speech, touch, balance, motion, position) (see Fleischmann

4 "The more we feel we are surrounded by another enticing environment, the more we want to manipulate it. The more the environment responds to our manipulations, the stronger our involvement with it, and the more persuasive the illusion of being there" (Murray/Jenkins 1999: 37).

2001)[5]. The broader popularization of physical immersion in transmedia data worlds was then initiated a decade ago by the movie *Minority Report* (dir. Steven Spielberg, USA 2002) – a clear-sighted anticipation of the current post-PC era (see *Illustration 2*). On the one hand, its futuristic scenes were inspired by cutting-edge webcam-based game controllers, which already existed at the time. On the other hand, the movie considerably influenced the further technical and commercial development and social adoption of the current generation of NUI controllers, particularly of Microsoft's Kinect[6]. Whether in the fields of science, the arts, or film, these early attempts to use natural human behavior to control digital hard- and software – to establish synesthetic-kinetic interaction between the real and the virtual – paved the way for NUIs to become industry standards, starting with Nintendo's Wii (2006), Apple's iOS (2007), Google's Android (2008), Sony's Move (2009), and Microsoft's Kinect (2010)[7].

It has only been within the past few years that NUIs have begun changing how we work and play, how we create, how we learn, how we express and entertain ourselves. This ability to physically interact with digital data complements – and advances – the transformation that images undergo with their digitalization. Kevin Kelly was probably one of the first to recognize that, once we can interact with them naturally, screens and what they show – still and moving digital images – turn into 'portals': "Don't think of them as tablets. Think of them as windows that you carry. […] This portable portal will peer into anything visible. You'll be able to see into movies, pictures, rooms, Web pages, places, and books seamlessly" (Kelly 2010). Writing about the young daughter of friends, Thomas Elsaesser put this shift in the view and perception of perspectival images in more concrete terms:

5 Parallel to this, software and website design went from UID (user interface design) to UXD (user experience design), in an effort to include the development of new interfaces and the experiences they afford. I have to thank Leon S. Freyermuth for pointing this out to me.

6 "So how does all this technology feel? Like a scene from *Minority Report* or some other sci-fi film set in the future" (Molina 2010; see also Savov 2010; Wong 2012).

7 Systematically a distinction should be made between gesture control (e. g., Nintendo's Wii, Sony's Move, Microsoft's Kinect), touch control (e. g., Apple's iOS, Google's Android), and voice control (e. g., Apple's Siri as part of later iOS versions).

Illustration 2:
Film still from Minority Report *(dir. Steven Spielberg, USA 2002).*

> [...] for her generation, pictures on a computer screen are not something to look at, but to click at – in the expectation of some action or movement taking place, of being taken to another place or to another picture space. The idea of a digital photo as a window to a view (to contemplate or be a witness to) had for her been replaced by the notion of an image as a passage or a portal, an interface or part of a sequential process – in short, as a cue for action. (2013: 241)

Thus, my fourth assumption is: *Another central element of the emerging digital media 'dispositif' is the NUI, which allows for direct physical interaction with digital data and thereby initiates a fundamental metamorphosis of digital images and audio-visions: from something that has to be watched from a certain distance to something that can be experienced immersively.*

Excursion: Touch and Tablet
The paradigm shift shows itself most clearly in the popularization of touch tablet PCs[8]. What appears to be a radically new technology is in fact quite traditional in its media form: the tablet as a portable storage medium for images and text can be found at the very beginning of me-

8 Smartphones like Apple's iPhone (2007) or Google's Android (2008) and tablet PCs like Amazon's Kindle (2007) and Apple's iPad (2010) as well as many follow-on products (see Freyermuth 2010).

dia culture. The 'biological naturalness' of the user interface that touch tablets offer thus correlates to the cultural familiarity of their physical form. For thousands of years, the typical tablet, whether made of stone, clay, wood, wax, papyrus, or parchment, was shaped like a modern hardcover or coffee-table book. Single tablets or sets of tablets – pads – were something you held in your hands as a means of holding on to something you would otherwise forget. The tablet form is a media 'analogatum princeps', the paradigm and thereby the measure of all subsequent media: a model prototype, an 'ur-medium'. With the touch tablet, it found its digital gestalt[9].

In the Renaissance, however, a departure from this form took place and with it the construction of the modern image space began. Thus, in the field of (audio-)visuality, the current return to the tablet form is less a sign of continuity than a sign of radical change.

3. Looking Back
The Analog Image Space and the Principle of Separation

In order to be perceived as images and not as objects, images require a specific space on which they appear[10]. Thus the development of visual culture leads from image spaces that are found in nature – for

9 Tablet PCs initiate a revival of the generic tablet form at a higher technological level. While regular PCs emulate the tablet form only in their software – e. g., the page view of word-processing programs – tablet PCs realize the tablet gestalt and its central functions as a digital hardware artifact, particularly when they offer touch screens. Thus digital technology, in a haptic sense, is directly linked to the analog and tablet-shaped media that preceded it, the single print, the pad, the photo album, the picture book, or the illustrated magazine, which, like image tablets, have always been held between hands and viewed at will. In the specific combination of innovative touch-screen hardware and a gesture-controlled NUI, tablet computers surpass their analog predecessors and may, for the first time, succeed in realizing the potential of digital visuality: the intimate, personalized, and interactive use of linear and non-linear audio-visions.

10 'The clear graphic presentation of immaterial objects only comes about on the perceived location of the material image area. Those who want to comprehend the pure visibility of pictorial objects have to pay attention to the tangible plane of their appearance as well.' Unless otherwise indicated, all translations are mine. ("Die anschauliche Präsentation immaterieller Objekte kommt nur auf dem wahrgenommenen Schauplatz der materiellen Bildfläche zustande. Die pure Sichtbarkeit von Bildobjekten kann nur erfassen, wer zugleich auf die handfeste Fläche ihres Erscheinens achtet"; Seel 2001). I have to thank Lisa Gotto for pointing me to this source.

example, cave walls for drawings – to image spaces that are found in architecture – for example, walls and ceilings for frescoes – to specifically manufactured image spaces – for example, ivory or wood tablets. As both image and text tablets were crafted using similar methods and materials, images and text coexisted largely in equal importance from antiquity all the way to the Middle Ages. It was only in the Renaissance – as a result of the mechanical media revolution and its new media technologies, the printing press and perspective painting – that image and text parted ways[11].

The Principle of Separation

The modern book, with its printed and bound pages made from linen and, later, wood, adopted the former tablet or codex format. Though its text space was intimate and personal, it also remained largely image-free until the early 20th century due to constraints in printing technology[12]. The image tablet gave way to larger panels and canvases as the dominant form of portable visual representation. Their – largely text-free – image space was characterized for one by the mathematically established representation of the dimension of depth: the adequate transfer from 3-D spatial relations to 2-D proportions. The aesthetic origin of this new concept of realism can be traced back to the invention and popularization of the glass mirror, which began in the 12th century. It introduced (photo-)realism avant la lettre. The intent to permanently save these realistic mirror images soon became the aesthetic reference point, a painterly ideal[13].

This modern transition from the visual conventions of the Middle Ages – the representation of spiritual meaning, social relevance, and cultural importance rather than the emulation of real-world relations and ratios – to an increasingly lifelike perspectival realism transformed aesthetic apperception by enabling a hitherto unattainable degree of purely visual immersion. As Marie-Laure Ryan points out: while the pre-Re-

11 With this separation, the modern history of media divergence began (cf. Faßler 2001: 185).

12 Major inventions that led to the industrial recombination of text and picture resulting in the illustrated press of the early 20th century were lithography (1796), the glass gravure screen (1881), and offset printing (1904). Furthermore, new variants of tablet and pad were invented, for example, the blackboard in the 18th century and the industrially produced legal pad in the 19th century.

13 Beginning in 1425 with Filippo Brunelleschi's mirror experiments (see Steadman 2001; Hockney 2001/2006).

naissance image space "was a strictly two-dimensional surface from which the body of the spectator was excluded, since bodies are three-dimensional objects", post-Renaissance "high realism" in painting, on the stage, or in the novel turned the spectator, viewer, reader "into the direct witness of events, both mental and physical, that seemed to be telling themselves" (2001: 9f.). This effect was, of course, intensified by industrial media's quest to achieve ever more perfect lifelikeness – first by the daguerreotype, which finally fixed the mirror image, then by photography, cinema, and television, progressing gradually to color pictures, stereo sound, and the live transmission of audio-visual events.

A second key element that shaped the emerging modern image space was the introduction of the canvas stretched on a frame. This innovation was modeled after another everyday experience: as the mirror mediated the private self-image of the modern individual, the window mediated the picture of the world – of public life, watched from the privacy of one's own home. The transition from fresco to framed panel painting followed the model of the window view, as Leon Battista Alberti famously stated in 1436: "una finestra aperta" (1436/1970: 52; 56). Constitutive for the modern image space was thus not only the separation of media – image and text – but also distancing, the separation of image and spectator: "the self becomes a spectator ensconced behind his or her window on the world [...] and the world, as a matter for his detached and observing eye, becomes a spectacle" (Romanyshyn 1989/2005: 32). In the course of mechanization, while windows became larger and larger – thanks to improved methods for producing glass – canvases grew as well and crossed by far the boundaries of the tablet format, thereby creating depersonalization and distancing in viewing.

The third element, which again was window-like, had a comparable effect: the clear separation of the image space from the environment – wall and room – through framing and, occasionally, covering the framed image with a curtain. The format in which (audio-)visual content is presented, as Jacob Burckhardt writes, provides 'the separation of the beautiful from all the rest of the room. [...] The format is not the work of art, but a condition of its existence.'[14] Modes of separation initiate and condition modes of reception. In the 19th and 20th centuries, these long-term processes finally led to, as Gernot Böhme explains, a praxis of 'not

14 "Das Format ist die Abgrenzung des Schönen gegenüber dem ganzen übrigen Raum. [...] Das Format ist nicht das Kunstwerk, aber eine Lebensbedingung desselben" (Burckhardt 1886/1918: 254).

handling' ("Nichtumgang"): 'this means the isolation of images from the context of everyday life, the forbiddance of touching images or physically handling or altering them further in any way, and the establishment and obeyance of a contemplative distance'[15]. *The modern image space* – this is my fifth assumption – *is based on the principle of separation.* Constructed between the Renaissance and postmodernism by decontextualization in production and a distancing in reception, the modern 2-D image was based on a threefold separation:

- first, the separation of media – of one medium from another – in particular, the separation of the image space from the textual space;
- second, the separation from the audience, through means of distancing, through spatial distance as well as physical concealment, e. g., curtains, doors, and glass panes; and
- third, the separation from the environment or reality, particularly through hardware framing.

Anti-Immersion

A similarly framed and distanced perspectival perception was commenced by the audio-visual adaptations of the perspective view, which began with the picture-frame stage. Its control of the viewer's gaze relied on a combination of 2-D perspectival painting and the material recreation of illusionary depth. In the industrial age, cinema continued the tradition of the window view. The framed screen, originally also covered by a curtain, processed aesthetically, as Anne Friedberg argued, the industrial experience of the mobilized gaze through the mostly closed – glass windows of different means of transportation moving faster and faster through the natural as well as the urban landscape (cf. 1993: 3)[16]. Later, in the second half of the 20th century, this everyday experience of transparent distance from moving images found its mediated correspondent in the framed glass screens of televisions (and then computers).

With regard to the degree of immersion that pre-digital audio-visual media – the stage, the cinema, the television – allow for, the

15 "[...] d. h. Isolierung der Bilder aus dem Lebenskontext, das Verbot, Bilder zu berühren oder in irgendeiner Weise konkret zu behandeln und weiterzubearbeiten und die Setzung und Einübung einer Betrachterdistanz" (Böhme 1999: 86).

16 In the preface to *The Virtual Window*, Anne Friedberg quotes her then five-year-old son, who enthusiastically answers the question of what he likes about riding a train: "It's all the moving pictures" (2006: xi).

impact of omnipresent framing needs to be taken into consideration (see Wolf 2006)[17]. During the Enlightenment, the very early days of the industrial age – that is, before photography – Immanuel Kant thought of the physical frame as a 'parergon', an extra or even exterior element securing the integrity of the picture (cf. 1790/1922: 65). A century later, however, when film was emerging as a new visual medium founded, like photography, on innovative ways of framing the picture content, Georg Simmel held that the physical frame was constitutive for the experience of the image space. 'It separates the work of art from its entire environment and thus the viewer as well and, in doing so, places it at a distance necessary for its aesthetic reception.'[18] Once again, another half a century later, in the age of television – the framed and glass-covered cathode-ray tube – Jacques Derrida found the frame not to be something that is exterior to images, securing their integrity, but something intrusive that questions them from within (cf. 1987: 80).

Their differences notwithstanding, Simmel and Derrida – in contradistinction to Kant – both thought of the frame as a constitutive part of the image space. Another approach, more informed by media theory, could lead to the conclusion that the physical frame – around paintings, the stage, photographs, the cinema, television, and computer screens – belongs neither to the images nor to the environment, but rather signifies a third state. From this point of view, the frame is a medium, something that separates two spaces – the space of representation and the space of the spectator, the viewer, the user. The first to understand this function of the frame as an 'isolator' might have been José Ortega y Gasset: "In order to isolate one thing from another, a third thing is needed which must be neither like the first nor the second – a neutral object. Now, the frame is not the wall, a merely utilitarian fragment of the real world; but neither is it quite the enchanted surface of the painting" (1990: 189). From a more digital point of view – and, as it seems, independently from Ortega y Gasset – Lev Manovich comes to a similar conclusion:

17 This article deals exclusively with the frame as a hardware and software medium between the image and its environment, but it does not elaborate on the transmedial function of the frame that is discussed in Wolf 2006.

18 "Er [der Rahmen] schließt alle Umgebung und also auch den Betrachter vom Kunstwerk aus und hilft dadurch, es in die Distanz zu stellen, in der allein es ästhetisch genießbar wird" (Simmel 1902/1998: 111).

> Visual culture of the modern period, from painting to cinema, is characterized by an intriguing phenomenon: the existence of another virtual space, another three-dimensional world enclosed by a frame and situated inside our normal space. The frame separates two absolutely different spaces that somehow coexist. [...] Defined in this way, a screen describes equally well a Renaissance painting (recall Alberti) and a modern computer display. (1995)

Against this background, it becomes evident how central a role the cathode-ray tube and its central medium, the glass screen, plays in media history. The invention of flat glass in the 17th century shaped not only the window view but also the perception of paintings, photographs, and audio-visions. Like the curtain, it protected the image space, yet now by leaving it visible. The glass frame not only prevented tactile access to the image but also distanced it visually. The first analog television screens enhanced this effect. With the television turned off, their thick curved glass panels covering the cathode-ray tube looked like a protective shield. That contemporaries of early television tended to hide their sets when not in use behind the doors of special television cabinets does not contradict this but rather proves the strength of the cultural habit of de-contextualizing image spaces. Once the television was turned on, its moving images appeared in deep distance behind the curved glass screen seemingly within reach – and yet remained in every sense untouchable.

The transparency of the glass frame, combined with the physical separation it created, thus emphasized the visuality of the image: the fact that what is being depicted, by allowing itself to be seen but not touched, is both there and not there. Regardless of how close they came, the spectators observed visual distance. For this arrangement there were – and are – good media-technological reasons. If you want to experience the full effect of perspectival 2-D pictures, whether they are hanging in a museum or running on cinema or television screens, you must maintain a certain – physical and psychological – distance in order to be able to translate their 2-D perspective into a 3-D view. The final consequence of all this framing and covering up, however, is, if not the prevention, then the impairment of immersion.

My sixth assumption, therefore, is: *The principle of separation on which the modern image space is based originates equally from media-practical interests – to increase perspectival illusion – and from media-theoretical and media-pedagogical interests: to separate art and life. With respect to this, the different methods of separation – from other media, from the environment, and from the spectator (viewer, user) –*

can be contextualized as efforts to ward off that which under the provisions of mechanical and industrial culture was considered improper or even dangerous: too deep an immersion.

Compensatory Cravings
That children tend to press their noses against screens (including shop windows and display cases) attests not only to the effectiveness of the decontextualization of the analog image space, but also to a fundamental dissatisfaction with it. Consequently, with the popularization of mechanical media compensatory desires, visions and experiments with more immersive media evolved. In the 17th and 18th centuries, endeavors as diverse as the utopian concept of the total work of art, cabinets of curiosities, trompe l'oeil frescoes, and the panorama tried to overcome the limitations of representation within the analog image space (see Stafford/Terpak 2001; Oettermann 1997). In the 19th century, the same was attempted with techno-aesthetic experiments like the diorama and particularly the booming stereoscopy. It effected on contemporaries "a dreamlike exaltation of the faculties, a kind of clairvoyance, in which we seem to leave the body behind us and sail away into one strange scene after another" (Wendell Holmes in 1859, qtd. Lane 2010) – words that, as Anthony Lane stated, anticipated current hymns to 3-D movies like *Avatar*. The longing for 3-D – for a higher degree of immersion – he concluded, "predated the arrival of the movies" (ibid.).

It seems only too consistent that parallel to the rise of cinema as the defining medium, the efforts to transcend the limitations of analog (audio-)visuality increased. Around 1900, the visual arts were seized with the desire to transcend the boundaries of the traditional image space. In the first decades of the 20th century, countless artistic experiments and art installations called the mono-medial purity of painting, its two-dimensional flatness and framed composition, into question. Avant-garde artists like Kurt Schwitters and Oskar Schlemmer, for example, started in various ways to overcome framing by painting over frames, through the integration of painted frames and 3-D objects etc. (cf. Maerker 1997: 1; 9). Around the middle of the century, art theory caught up with these avant-garde practices. In 1948, Clement Greenberg famously declared "The Crisis of the Easel Picture" and described the escalating deconstruction of the framed window-like panel painting: "cutting the illusion of a boxlike cavity into the wall behind it and organizing within this cavity the illusion of forms, light and space, all more or less according to the current rules of verisimilitude" (Greenberg 1986:

221)[19]. Its place, Clement Greenberg proclaimed, would be taken by "the 'decentralized', 'polyphonic', all-over picture [...] with a surface knit together of a multiplicity of identical or similar elements" (ibid.: 222). A few years later Werner Hofmann declared this change an aesthetic reaction to a new view of the world: 'The "framed" world lies behind us. Its experience of the world is not ours anymore.'[20]

These attempts to overcome the detached window view within post-realistic – abstract – art correlated with continuous, though very different, experiments to accomplish the same in cinema. Hardly a decade went by without the development of technical and aesthetic experiments to expand the two-dimensional image space: Lumière's 3-D *L'Arrivée d'un train en gare de La Ciotat* (France 1895) at the start of the 20th century, the Televiews and Plastigrams in the 1920s, the Audioscopiks in the 1930s, or the 3-D blockbusters and the Sensorama prototype of the 1950s. They all failed, however, due to the limitations and deficiencies of analog technology[21]. Long-term success was only seen in the many efforts – at once regressive and anticipatory – to move beyond the boundaries of the modern image space by converting 2-D images back into 3-D physical objects. This was particularly evident in the new medium of theme parks, beginning in the 1950s. Its creation was fed by a feeling Walt Disney had harbored for decades: that his studio's animated movies offered an inadequate degree of immersion (see Marling 1997). Since the early 1930s, he had aspired to blur the boundaries of the medium and to cross the border between the diegetic and the non-diegetic, between the fictional world of audio-visual representation and the real world of thc audience. Disneyland, which opened its doors in 1955, was thus planned as an immersive, photo-realistic 3-D fiction that viewers – now called guests – could enter and navigate. By doing away with the categorical separation that put distance between cinema – as just another window-view medium – and its patrons, who were forced to watch passively, Disney's goal was no less than to create "a cartoon that immerses the audience" (Thomas 1994: 11; cf. also Pine/Gilmore 1999: 47).

19 First published in *The Nation*, April 17, 1948.

20 "Die 'gerahmte' Welt liegt hinter uns. Ihr Welterlebnis ist nicht mehr das unsrige" (Hofmann 1952/2004: 19).

21 For the history of 3-D cinema, see Zone 2012.

Whereas Disney tried to augment the experience of audio-visual fiction through architectural means (and set design), at the same time, the founders of neighboring Las Vegas attempted the reverse: the phantasmatic and immersive augmentation of sparse, concrete, modern architecture through audio-visual media (see Freyermuth 2000). In a first phase, lasting from the mid-1950s to the mid-1960s, Las Vegas's reality, at night, was semiotically enhanced and enchanted by the narratively as well as pictorially moving magic of neon décor (see Venturi/Scott Brown/Izenour 1977/1997). The second phase, which peaked in the 1990s, set the global standard for entertainment architecture. Major casinos and in the end the whole Las Vegas strip and also Glitter Gulch metamorphosed – from the inside out and following the model of the theme park – into themed transmedia playgrounds (see Gottdiener 1997; Gottdiener/Collins/Dickens, eds. 1999)[22]. In a third phase, starting in the early 1990s and lasting hardly two decades, casinos heightened their immersive offerings by installing hybrid movie rides. "[T]wo-dimensional motion picture stories and spaces", Erkki Huhtamo writes, "were reconstructed in three-dimensional space and transformed into amusement park rides" (1995: 162). On the one hand, these attractions carried on the tradition of the panorama and diorama. On the other hand, they tried to emulate the most popular entertainment ideal of total immersion: the holodeck (see Freyermuth 1999b; 2001).

My seventh assumption, therefore, is: *Since the 17th century, a latent discontent with the limitations of the analog image space, specifically its separation of art and life, fiction and reality, initiated a steady stream of theoretical visions and practical experiments that tried again and again to deconstruct the principle of separation and to anticipate, within the confines of analog technology, more immersive aesthetic practices and experiences.*

4. Looking Forward
The Digital Image Space and the Principle of Fusion

Another challenge to the traditional image space originated with electronization in the 1970s when Teletext was introduced on analog television. The process of appropriating cathode-ray monitors, designed as

22 For a history and critique of entertainment architecture, see Sorkin 1992; Huxtable 1997; Venturi/Scott Brown/Izenour 1977/1997.

spaces for moving images, to display as well as manipulate other media escalated in the 1980s with the onset of cultural digitalization and especially the success of the GUI. The separation of text and image was abolished. This, of course, was the beginning of a development that, eventually, should end all separation of media. The century-old desire to create a total work of art, which couldn't really be fulfilled as long as art had to be materialized – as long as it had to become hardware – seems to find its fulfillment now in software, the digital transmedium. Technologically at least, we are experiencing a convergence of media – of visual and textual, auditive and audio-visual media.

Transmediality

In principle, transmedialization stems from the basic innovation of digital technology, the adequate transfer of analog qualities and functions into mathematical values, resulting in the separation of hard- and software as it was conceived for tools/programs by John von Neumann in 1945 and for materials/files by Claude Elwood Shannon in 1948. To practically realize the theoretically conceived virtualization of the different media, of course, took decades. Only since the turn of the 21st century has it been possible to call software the fourth medium for regular audio-visual production created in modern times – after the mechanical medium of the picture frame or proscenium stage and the industrial media of film and video. As text, sound, photos, and graphics had already been virtualized earlier, software thereby became a universal medium able to contain multiple analog and digital forms of expression. This long path to present transmedia culture, which spans over half a century, was anticipated fairly early on from three different perspectives: media technology, media art, and media theory. In 1977, when the Apple II computer gave just a faint notion of personal processing power, computer scientist Alan Kay praised software as a "metamedium" (Kay/Goldberg 2003: 394)[23]: "Although digital computers were originally designed to do arithmetic computation, the ability to simulate the details of any descriptive model means that the computer, viewed as a medium itself, can be all other media" (ibid.: 393). Twelve years later, when the overwhelming majority of PCs were still controlled by command-line interfaces and Timothy Berners-Lee had just started to toy with the idea of a graphical interface for global networking, telematics artist Roy Ascott wrote:

23 First published 1977 in *Computer* 10/3: 31–41.

> Increasingly, as artists we are impatient with single modes of operation in dataspace. We search for synthesis of image, sound, text. We wish to incorporate human and artificial movements, environmental dynamics, ambient transformations, altogether into a more seamless whole. We search, in short, for the Gesamtdatenwerk. [...] The computer industry is slow in releasing those technologies which will facilitate a seamless interface [...]. (1989/1999: 89)

Another decade later, when George Lucas was preparing the first digital master of a major feature film, media theorist Lev Manovich identified the aspect of arbitrary aesthetic construction that characterizes the transition into digital media and transmediality: "Cinema becomes a particular branch of painting – painting in time. No longer a kino-eye, but a kino-brush" (2000: 308).

Since then radically new transmedia options and artistic choices have opened up, particularly in the area of non-linear audio-visual narration. So far, advanced hyperrealistic games, such as *Heavy Rain* (Quantic Dream 2010, creator David Cage; see *Illustration 3*), *Alan*

Illustration 3:
Still from the hyperrealistic game Heavy Rain *(Quantic Dream 2010, creator David Cage).*

Wake (Microsoft 2010, creator Remedy Entertainment), *L.A. Noire* (Rockstar 2011, creator Team Bondi), or *Beyond: Two Souls* (Quantic Dream 2013, creator David Cage), seem to give only a foretaste of transmedia art and entertainment. Nonetheless, game designer Jesse Schell claimed, as early as 2008, that digital games would become a pivotal platform for transmedia storytelling:

> As technology advances, more and more aspects of human life and expression will be integrated into games. There is nothing that cannot be part of a game. You can put a painting, a radio broadcast, or a movie into a game, but you cannot put a game into these other things. [...] At their technological limit, games will subsume all other media. (2008: 48)

In his statement, however, Schell concentrates on only one of two variants of transmedia: the design of fictional or non-fictional products that contain several different media and thus, within themselves – in their interior structure – transcend traditional media boundaries. For this first variant of media fusion, I propose the term 'intensive transmedia', in contradistinction to the second variant, 'extensive transmedia', which tries to tell the same story or parts of it distributed over several media[24]. The most popular examples of this second variant are, of course, 'global brand fictions', such as *Star Wars*, *James Bond*, *Pokémon*, and *Harry Potter*. Drew Davidson characterizes extensive transmediality as "integrated, interactive experiences that occur across multiple media, with multiple authors and have multiple styles" (2010: 36)[25].

Therefore, my eighth assumption is: *The digital deconstruction of the analog image space is characterized by the breaching and crossing of the traditional boundaries separating analog media toward either intensive or extensive transmediality.*

---

24 Extensive transmediality addresses cross-media storytelling. The term 'cross media', however, is no longer widely used in media production since the Producers Guild of America introduced the credit 'Transmedia Producer' in 2010 (see Jenkins 2010).

25 Davidson uses the term 'cross media', but considers 'cross media' and 'transmedia' to be synonyms. In principle, the practices of extensive transmediality and adaptation are similar. In analog media, adaptation was a successive process: first the original work was published; adaptations came later. Transmedia replaces this analog sequentiality – for example, from novel to movie to video game – with parallel production, thus enabling a higher degree of aesthetic exchange, particularly of narrative and visual assets. In the reception, parallel offerings of the same story or story world in different media increase the potential for immersion.

Augmentation

The introduction of the GUI in the 1980s, however, not only did away with the separation of media, it also virtualized the window view, the framed perspective on visual and other media content, at first through the windowed interface of Apple's Lisa OS and Mac OS, then through the aptly named Windows OS, and finally through the windows of various web browsers. These virtual windows, by definition, do not have to be visible, as long as they remain functional. Like any other software element, they can be hidden, so that the visual content may appear to be un-framed or frameless. Thus, with its virtualization of the frame, the GUI opened up the prospect of a hybrid fusion of media and environment and of the integration of both – the real and the virtual – into interactive-immersive 3-D augmented realities. This interactive layering of media and environment, which, for decades, has been tried out in artistic and technical experiments, is now finding its way into mainstream practices, from navigation to gaming[26]. "The real world is way too boring for many people", game designer Daniel Sánchez-Crespo claimed: "By making the real world a playground for the virtual world, we can make the real world much more interesting" (qtd. Berlin 2009). What, under analog conditions, could only be spoken of metaphorically – that media, such as the images of feature films or television, were reshaping and overlaying the perception of reality – can now literally happen: GPS navigators, smartphones, tablet PCs, and data glasses are superimposing images, sounds, and texts upon reality, or rather our perception of it (see Pogue 2012; Stevens 2012). In the context of mobile networking, PCs, which amplify human intelligence, as J. C. R. Licklider first stated over half a century ago (see 1960/1990), are also starting to enhance reality and our perception of it. Along with this development, the second element of the analog image space, the separation of media and environment, was canceled out.

Thus my ninth assumption is: *The virtualization of windows and frames initiated the fusion of media and environment toward informative and playful variants of augmented reality.*

26 The history of GPS-enabled geocaching starts in May 2000, a few days after the U.S. improved GPS accuracy for civil use. *The Beast* (Microsoft 2001, creators Sean Stewart, Elan Lee, and Pete Fenlon), part of the marketing efforts for *A.I.: Artificial Intelligence* (dir. Steven Spielberg, USA 2001), is considered to be the first alternate-reality game.

Immersion

While GUIs helped to fuse media, during their rather long reign digital images (and texts) continued to exist behind glass, in virtual worlds that could not be touched. Virtualization – the process of transforming hardware into software – enabled arbitrary manipulation, though not yet in the literal sense of using hands and speaking gestures. The curvature and depth stemming from television's cathode-ray tube reinforced the enduring distance. Its abolishment – the abolishment of detachment – was foreshadowed by the transition to ever thinner and flatter screens in the 1990s. By eliminating spatial depth, which, despite all differences, equally characterized the picture-frame stage, the cinema, and the cathode-ray monitor, digital flat screens laid the foundation for sublating the separation of images and audiences or users. The main change, however, concerned interactivity.

A simple glass pane that allows for viewing in just one direction corresponds to the qualities of analog single-channel media. The digital feedback medium, its most prominent form being the game, however, requires influence and control, in other words, transmedial interaction. The upgrading of the analog flat screen to a digital touch screen brought about a fundamental change of purpose: glass covers functioned no longer as a means of separation but evolved into a medium for tactile contact. Monitors, however, were not only outfitted with touch screens so that they could feel users' touch and react accordingly, they were also given cameras, so that they could watch and react to users' gestures, as well as microphones, so that they could listen and react to users' words.

Within a relatively short time – beginning around 2010 and driven by touch tablet PCs – this radically changed how audio-visual products are perceived, consumed, and controlled. For the first time ever, touch tablet PCs make it possible to have an intimate, physically close, direct, and multi-sensory interactive relationship with linear and non-linear audio-visual content. As a consequence, modernity's analog image space is imploding. The distance in reception and use that the stage, the screens of cinema and television, and analog computer monitors demanded is dwindling. Natural interaction is replacing the analog separation of media and audiences.

The complement to this deconstruction of depth and distance (from life) characteristic of the analog image space is the adoption of digital 3-D visuality. Now that images, a quarter century after sound, can also move through space toward the viewer, the invisible fourth wall separating analog sound film and its audience is crumbling. What digital visuality loses in spatial depth 'behind itself', it gains in visual depth 'in front of itself'. The moving images are closing in on their viewers, shooting right out at them, surrounding them. Increased physical proximity potentially increases psychological proximity, involvement, and identification, resulting in a degree of immersion that could not be achieved in analog 2-D. Thus, it seems within a certain logic of escalation to try next to progress from 3-D to 4-D cinema, to moving pictures that involve their audience or users physically. Such endeavors can be witnessed these days in commercial efforts to create a cinema of physical sensations – "movies that shake, rattle and roll viewers" (Hart 2011) – as well as in experimental audio-visual installations, such as *Scenario* (dir. Dennis Del Favero, Australia 2011) (see Zukerman 2011).

Thus, my tenth assumption states: *The digital deconstruction of the analog image space works toward a reversal of the spatial and physical separation between media and users in favor of interactive immersion.*

A Distinctive Feature of the Digital Media 'Dispositif'

The historical development of a new digital media 'dispositif' that we are witnessing as mere contemporaries – while probably being unable to fully understand its implications – can at least preliminarily be reflected upon from two different points of view. Looking inside the digital transmedium, we can discern distinct developments.

My eleventh assumption, therefore, is: *With the virtualization of audio-visual production and the implementation of the digital transmedium, a threefold transition is gradually taking place: first, analog realism, which is non-indexical, and analog photo-realism, which is indexical, are both being supplemented by a digital hyperrealism that is merging and integrating non-indexical and indexical audio-visual assets; secondly, linear storytelling is competing with multi- and non-linear storytelling; thirdly, passive reception is, in part, being replaced by interactive use, which is furthered by interfaces that are becoming more and more 'natural'.*

The second point of view looks at the digital transmedium from the outside, at its relation to other media, the environment, and the recipients, that is: spectators, viewers, users. My twelfth assumption is: *In transitioning to a digital media culture, the principle of separa-*

tion, which characterized the analog media cultures of the past, is seemingly being replaced by its opposite, namely the principle of connection or fusion. More specifically:

- the separation of media is giving way to a connection or fusion of different media with one another, that is to say, transmediality;
- the separation of audio-visual media from the environment, i. e., hardware framing, is giving way to a connection or fusion of media with the environment through software framing, resulting in the potential to not just decorate but augment reality; and
- the separation of media from the audience through distance and physical barriers is giving way to their intimate connection or fusion with the user, i. e., hands-on interaction and even physical immersion.

Elements of a Historical Theory of Immersion

In the early 1970s, in an attempt to marry historical perspectives with systematic ones, Harry Pross introduced a theory of mediality that categorized media by the – historically escalating – use of material technology (see 1972; for a comprehensive description cf. Ludes/Hörisch 1998/2003: 64f.). Pross called pre-technical aesthetic production and communication – for example, street theater or face-to-face discussions – 'primary media' ("primäre Medien"; ibid.: 128f.). In contrast, secondary mediality requires advanced technology for the production of material artifacts or technically enhanced processes that, however, can still be received 'naturally', by employing the regular sensorial and cultural facilities also required in contemporary everyday life, like watching, listening, and later reading. Secondary mediality has, of course, existed for thousands of years but received a major push in its development at the beginning of modern times with mechanical technology, specifically printing, perspective painting, and illusionistic theater. Tertiary mediality then, as a result of industrialization – which includes film, radio, and television – requires the use of advanced technology on both sides, in production as well as in reception.

Digitalization, the consequences of which Pross could hardly have envisioned in the 1970s, added one more media form. While industrial mass media are based on the push model – that is, a technical division of senders and receivers – digital mediality is founded on the pull model, the provision of a feedback channel that enables every receiver to be a potential transmitter and vice versa. This categorical difference constitutes quaternary mediality.

Illustration 4:
The 'military holodeck', an immersive training simulator at Camp Pendleton, California, 2007.

In that it is both historical and systematic, this model of mediality understands the history of media as a process not of replacement, but of progressive accumulation and differentiation. Thus, distinguishing between primary, secondary, tertiary, and quaternary mediality can help answer many media-theoretical questions at the intersection of the artistic (genesis) and the aesthetic (validity). When studying the different variants of realism, for example, we can relate the perception of the real to primary audio-visuality: real is what happens before our own eyes; the perception of the realistic to secondary audio-visuality: realistic is what has been created by manual or physical imitation; the perception of the photo-realistic to tertiary audio-visuality: photo-realistic is what has been captured by semi-automatic reproduction; the perception of the hyperrealistic to quaternary audio-visuality: hyperrealistic is what has been constructed from virtual assets, regardless of whether they were created or captured or whether the realization was achieved manually or procedurally.

In a similar manner, we can analyze the modes of reception. Primary mediality enables all who are physically present to participate interactively. Works of secondary mediality have to be received passively but in a relatively autonomous manner. Works of tertiary mediality require submission to a heteronomous regime insofar as 'remedial' technologies have not yet come into play. Finally, quaternary mediality seems to enable all three historically accumulated modes of reception so that, at least in principle, recipients can choose arbitrarily between the participatory, autonomous, or heteronomous use of media.

As a starting point for a historical theory of immersion, focusing, for the time being, on different audio-visual media, it seems thus equally helpful to discern four modes of immersion according to the four modes of mediality. Primary audio-visuality relates to immersion in the real: losing oneself in events – just happening or being staged – that allow participants to act like the one he or she can be (and would like to be more often). Secondary audio-visuality relates to immersion in the realistic: losing oneself at an autonomous pace in artifacts – paintings, plays etc. – that transport spectators to places where they are not (but would like to be) and where they can identify with people whom they are not (but might want to be). Tertiary mediality relates to immersion in the photo-realistic: losing oneself at a heteronomous pace in artifacts – movies, television shows etc. – that transport viewers to places where they are not (but would like to be) and where they can identify with people whom they are not (but might want to be). Quaternary mediality relates to immersion in the hyperrealistic: losing oneself at an autonomous or heteronomous pace in artifacts or programmed processes – games and other non-linear audio-visions – that enable users to experience places where they are not (but would like to be) and where they can act like people whom they might want to be (but are not).

5. Epilogue

In historical theory, even preliminary classifications like the ones above are, by definition, temporary and subject to change. In conclusion, it thus seems imperative to outline a possible course of further investigations. One next step toward a theory of immersion would be, of course, to broaden the transmedial perspective and to include, in addition to audio-visual media, purely auditive and visual and textual media as well. Another essential step would be to reflect on how, at any given time, established media advances under the influence of new media: for example, how theater, as a secondary medium, reacted to the rise of tertiary media, namely film and television, and how it is currently reacting to the rise of quaternary media, such as non-linear storytelling and the proliferation of mobile and digitally networked cameras and screens[27]. A third field of research should focus on the emerging future of immersion: how the evolution of quaternary media is bringing about different, particularly procedurally generated interactive modes of immersion.

The future of media, however, is hard to envision, though it is always "already here", as William Gibson famously stated: "It's just unevenly distributed" and therefore hard to spot (qtd. Gladstone 1999: 11 min., 55

27 The same applies, of course, to film and television: how television changed the movies and how both media are now being transformed under the influence of new digital media, specifically games.

sec.). According to Anthony Lane, "3-D will ravish our senses and take us on rides that no drug could match" but, "like so many blessings, it won't make us happy. It will make us want more" (2010). Whatever that might end up being, it appears that, strangely enough, it will involve some kind of physical immersion in audio-visions. After the Big Bang of digital audio-visuality – after the *implosion* of the modern image space initiated by the bottomless depth of the touch tablet and its *explosion* initiated by digital 3-D – there remains the enduring, and ever stronger, allure of tactile interaction with immersive 3-D narratives. The allure of something utopian like the *Star Trek* holodeck.

That, of course, to a large extent, is a fan perspective: the position of someone who enjoys immersive media and looks forward to new modes of digitally induced immersion. But even from a more detached view, the decisive function of utopian visions for the development of media should be obvious. In pre-industrial times, the ideal of the total work of art became a central reference point for audio-visual production, only to be finally realized, not with mechanical technology on a stage – though Richard Wagner, in his time, certainly tried – but with industrial technology on celluloid. In a similar way, the holodeck, the industrial-mass-media utopia of holographic-haptic immersion, seems to point to the future of digital media (see *Illustration 4*), a future that might be realized first – before the next technological jump, in a preliminary 'Wagner opera' kind of way – as virtually accessible hyperrealistic story worlds, populated with procedurally generated non-player characters (NPCs) that are endowed with some artificial intelligence. Jesse Schell, at least, thinks this should and could lie in the near future of games: as film only became a match for the theater once the medium progressed from silent movies to talkies, games will become much more meaningful and immersive many times over once they progress from NPCs that can merely talk to AI characters that can actually watch, listen, and understand what we are trying to say[28].

28 Personal notes from Jesse Schell's talk "The Future of Storytelling: How Medium Shapes Story", Game Developers Conference, San Francisco, March 26, 2013: "According to Schell, these narrative weaknesses were best summed up by USC Games Institute's Chris Swain: 'Film wasn't taken seriously as a medium until it learned to talk. Games are waiting to learn to listen. I suspect he is dead-on right.' […] Schell then ran through a series of technologies that he thought could offer games the chance to 'learn to listen', from using player facial-tracking features to read a player's emotional state, voice recognition and natural language parsing tech for conversations" (Miller 2013).

References

Adams, Ernest (2004: online). "The Designer's Notebook: Postmodernism and the 3 Types of Immersion". *Gamasutra*. http://www.gamasutra.com/view/feature/2118/the_designers_notebook_.php. [15/01/2014].

Alberti, Leon Battista (1436/1950). *Della pittura*. Ed. Luigi Mallé. Florence: Sansoni.

— (1956/1970). *On Painting*. Transl. John R. Spencer. New Haven, CT: Yale UP.

Ascott, Roy (1989/1999). "Gesamtdatenwerk: Connectivity, Transformation and Transcendence". Timothey Druckey, ed. *Ars Electronica: Facing the Future*. Cambridge, MA/London: MIT Press. 86–89.

Benjamin, Walter (1935/1991). "Das Kunstwerk im Zeitalter seiner technischen Reproduzierbarkeit (Erste Fassung)". *Gesammelte Schriften*. Vol. I/2. Eds. Rolf Tiedemann, Hermann Schweppenhäuser. Frankfurt am Main: Suhrkamp. 431–508.

— (2008). *The Work of Art in the Age of Its Technological Reproducibility, and Other Writings on Media*. Eds. Michael W. Jennings, Brigid Doherty, Thomas Y. Levin. Transl. Edmund Jephcott et al. Cambridge, MA: Belknap Press of Harvard UP.

Berlin, Leslie (2009: online). "Kicking Reality Up a Notch". *The New York Times*. http://www.nytimes.com/2009/07/12/business/12proto.html?_r=1&partner=rss&cmc=rss. [15/01/2014].

Björk, Staffan, Jussi Holopainen (2005). *Patterns in Game Design*. Boston, MA: Charles River Media.

Böhme, Gernot (1999). *Theorie des Bildes*. Munich: Fink.

Brinkemper, Peter V. (2012: online). "Paradoxien der Enträumlichung: Zur Philosophie des 3-D-Films". *Glanz & Elend*. http://www.glanzundelend.de/Artikel/abc/s/starwars.htm. [15/01/2014].

Burckhardt, Jacob (1886/1918). "Format und Bild (2. Februar 1886)". *Vorträge 1844–1887*. Ed. Emil Dürr. 2nd ed. Basel: Schwabe. 252–260.

Chase, Linda (1973/1975). *Hyperrealism*. Introd. Salvador Dalí. London: Academy Editions.

Chatfield, Tom (2010). *Fun Inc.: Why Games Are the 21st Century's Most Serious Business*. London: Virgin.

Claiborn, Samuel (2013: online). "NASA Wants to Design a Holodeck". *IGN*. http://www.ign.com/articles/2013/03/28/nasa-wants-to-design-a-holodeck. [15/01/2014].

Davidson, Drew (2010). *Cross-Media Communications: An Introduction to the Art of Creating Integrated Media Experiences*. Pittsburgh, PA: ETC Press.

Derrida, Jacques (1978). *La Vérité en peinture*. Paris: Flammarion.

— (1987). *The Truth in Painting*. Transl. Geoffrey Bennington. Chicago, IL: University of Chicago Press.

Elsaesser, Thomas (2013). "The 'Return' of 3-D: On Some of the Logics and Genealogies of the Image in the Twenty-First Century". *Critical Inquiry* 39/2: 217–246.

Ermi, Laura, Frans Mäyrä (2005). "Fundamental Components of the Gameplay Experience: Analysing Immersion". Suzanne de Castell, Jennifer Jenson, eds. *Changing Views – Worlds in Play: Selected Papers of the 2005 Digital Games Research Association's Second International Conference*. Tampere: DiGRA. (Online: http://www.digra.org/wp-content/uploads/digital-library/06276.41516.pdf. [15/01/2014]).

Faßler, Manfred (2001). "Sind künstlerische und wissenschaftliche Bildungswege 'machbar'?" Weibel, ed. 180–193.

Fleischmann, Monika (2001). "Die Spur des Betrachters im Bild". Weibel, ed. 138–149.

Freyermuth, Gundolf S. (1999a). "Digitale Magie". *c't – magazin für computertechnik* May 25: 74–75; 78–81. (Reprint online: http://www.freyermuth.com/dl/digitalemagie.pdf. [15/01/2014]).

— (1999b). "Holodeck heute". *c't – magazin für computertechnik* August 30: 72–77. (Reprint online: http://freyermuth.com/reprints/archiv2008/reprintJMar2008/Holodeck_heute.html. [15/01/2014]).

— (2000: online). "Vegas, virtuelle Stadt". *Telepolis*. http://www.heise.de/tp/artikel/3/3488/1.html. [15/01/2014].

— (2001). "Von A nach D: Zwischen Hype und Utopie: Am Horizont der Digitalisierung von Kunst und Unterhaltung lockt das Holodeck". Rudolf Maresch, Florian Rötzer, eds. *Cyberhypes: Möglichkeiten und Grenzen des Internet*. Frankfurt am Main: Suhrkamp. 213–232.

— (2002). "Timeline: Digitales Kino". Joachim Polzer, ed. *Aufstieg und Untergang des Tonfilms: Die Zukunft des Kinos: 24p*? Potsdam: Polzer. 17M–33M.

— (2007). "Cinema Revisited: Vor und nach dem Kino: Audiovisualität in der Neuzeit". Daniela Kloock, ed. *Zukunft Kino*. Marburg: Schüren. 15–40.

— (2010). "Die Rückkehr zur Tafel". *swissfuture* 2: 3–8.

— (2012). "Movies and Games: Audiovisual Storytelling in the Digital Age". Ildiko Enyedi, ed. *New Skills for New Jobs / New Skills for Old Jobs: Film and Media Schools in the Digital Revolution*. Budapest: University of Theatre and Film Art. 21–39.

— (2013). "Der Big Bang digitaler Bildlichkeit: Zwölf Thesen und zwei Fragen". Gundolf S. Freyermuth, Lisa Gotto, eds. *Bildwerte: Visualität in der digitalen Medienkultur*. Bielefeld: transcript. 287–328.

Friedberg, Anne (1993). *Window Shopping: Cinema and the Postmodern*. Berkeley, CA: University of California Press.

— (2006). *The Virtual Window: From Alberti to Microsoft*. Cambridge, MA/London: MIT Press.

Gadamer, Hans-Georg (1974/1993). "Die Aktualität des Schönen: Kunst als Spiel, Symbol und Fest". *Gesammelte Werke*. Vol. 8: *Ästhetik und Poetik I: Kunst als Aussage*. Tübingen: Mohr. 94–142.

Gladstone, Brooke (1999: online). "The Science in Science Fiction (audiocast)". *NPR*. http://www.npr.org/templates/story/story.php?storyId=1067220. [15/01/2014].

Gottdiener, Mark (1997). *The Theming of America: Dreams, Visions, and Commercial Spaces*. Boulder, CO: Westview Press.

—, Claudia C. Collins, David R. Dickens, eds. (1999). *Las Vegas: The Social Production of an All-American City*. Malden, MA: Blackwell.

Greenberg, Clement (1986). "The Crisis of the Easel Picture" [1948]. *The Collected Essays and Criticism*. Vol. 2: *Arrogant Purpose, 1945–1949*. Ed. John O'Brien. Chicago, IL: University of Chicago Press. 221–228.

Hart, Hugh (2009: online). "Virtual Sets Move Hollywood Closer to Holodeck". *Wired*. http://www.wired.com/2009/03/filmmakers-use/. [15/01/2014].

— (2011: online). "4-D Cinema Explores Shake, Rattle and Sniff Options". *Wired*. http://www.wired.com/2011/07/4-d-movies/. [15/01/2014].

Hockney, David (2001/2006). *Secret Knowledge: Retracing Six Centuries of Western Art*. 2nd ed. New York, NY: Viking Studio.

Hofmann, Werner (1952/2004). "Das Bild nicht mehr Ausschnitt der Welt: Versuch über den Rahmen". Werner Hofmann, ed. *Die ge-*

spaltene Moderne. Munich: C. H. Beck. 19–20.

Huhtamo, Erkki (1995). “Encapsulated Bodies in Motion: Simulators and the Quest for Total Immersion”. Simon Penny, ed. *Critical Issues in Electronic Media*. Albany, NY: State University of New York Press. 159–186.

Huxtable, Ada Louise (1997). *The Unreal America: Architecture and Illusion*. New York, NY: New Press.

Jenkins, Henry (2010: online). “Hollywood Goes ‘Transmedia’”. *Confessions of an Aca-Fan: The Official Weblog of Henry Jenkins*. http://henryjenkins.org/2010/04/hollywood_goes_transmedia.html. [15/01/2014].

Kant, Immanuel (1790/1922). *Kritik der Urteilskraft*. 5th ed. Leipzig: Meiner.

Kay, Alan, Adele Goldberg (2003). “Personal Dynamic Media” [1977]. Noah Wardrip-Fruin, Nick Montfort, eds. *The New Media Reader*. Cambridge, MA/London: MIT Press. 393–404.

Kelly, Kevin (2010: online). “13 of the Brightest Tech Minds Sound Off on the Rise of the Tablet: Window on the World”. *Wired*. http://www.wired.com/2010/03/ff_tablet_essays/all/1. [15/01/2014].

Kirby, David A. (2011). “Creating a Techno-Mythology for a New Age: The Production History of *The Lawnmower Man*”. David L. Ferro, Eric Gottfried Swedin, eds. *Science Fiction and Computing: Essays on Interlinked Domains*. Jefferson, NC: McFarland & Co. 214–229.

Lane, Anthony (2010: online). “Third Way: The Rise of 3-D”. *The New Yorker*. http://www.newyorker.com/arts/critics/atlarge/2010/03/08/100308crat_atlarge_lane. [15/01/2014].

Licklider, J. C. R. (1960/1990). “Man-Computer Symbiosis”. *IRE Transactions on Human Factors in Electronics* HFE-1: 4–11. (Online: http://worrydream.com/refs/Licklider%20-%20Man-Computer%20Symbiosis.pdf. [15/01/2014]).

Ludes, Peter, Jochen Hörisch (1998/2003). *Einführung in die Medienwissenschaft: Entwicklungen und Theorien*. 2nd rev. ed. Berlin: Erich Schmidt.

Maerker, Daniela (1997). *Die Entgrenzung des Bildfeldes im ersten Viertel des 20. Jahrhunderts*. Munich: Utz.

Manovich, Lev (1995). “An Archeology of a Computer Screen”. *NewMediaTopia*. Moscow: Soros Center for the Contemporary Art. (Online: http://manovich.net/TEXT/digital_nature.html. [15/01/2014]).

— (2000). *The Language of New Media*. Cambridge, MA/London: MIT Press.

Marling, Karal Ann, ed. (1997). *Designing Disney's Theme Parks: The Architecture of Reassurance*. Exh. cat. Montreal: Canadian Center for Architecture, 17 June – 28 September 1997. Paris/New York, NY: Flammarion.

Miller, Patrick (2013: online). "Jesse Schell's Search for the Shakespeare of Video Games". *Gamasutra*. http://www.gamasutra.com/view/news/189370/Jesse_Schells_search_for_the_Shakespeare_of_video_games.php. [15/01/2014].

Molina, Brett (2010: online). "Review: Microsoft Kinect Marks Big Leap for Motion Gaming". *USA Today*. http://content.usatoday.com/communities/gamehunters/post/2010/11/review-microsoft-kinect-marks-big-leap-for-motion-gaming/1#.U3h_Gy-5Tak. [15/01/2014].

Murray, Janet H. (1997). *Hamlet on the Holodeck: The Future of Narrative in Cyberspace*. New York, NY: Free Press.

—, Henry Jenkins (1999). "Before the Holodeck: Translating *Star Trek* into Digital Media". Greg M. Smith, ed. *On a Silver Platter: CD-ROMs and the Promises of a New Technology*. New York, NY: New York UP. 35–57.

Neumann, John von (1945: online). "First Draft of a Report on the EDVAC". Copy of the original typescript draft, University of Pennsylvania Moore School Library. http://www.virtualtravelog.net/wp/wp-content/media/2003-08-TheFirstDraft.pdf. [15/01/2014].

Oettermann, Stephan (1980). *Das Panorama: Die Geschichte eines Massenmediums*. Frankfurt am Main: Syndikat.

— (1997). *The Panorama: History of a Mass Medium*. Transl. Deborah L. Schneider. New York, NY: Zone Books.

Ortega y Gasset, José (1943). "Meditacion del Marco". *Obras de José Ortega y Gasset*. Vol. 1. 3rd ed. Madrid: Espasa-Calpe. 369–375.

— (1990). "Meditations on the Frame". Transl. Andrea L. Bell. *Perspecta* 26: 185–190.

Pine, B. Joseph, James H. Gilmore (1999). *The Experience Economy: Work Is Theatre & Every Business a Stage*. Boston, MA: Harvard Business School Press.

Pogue, David (2012: online). "Google Glass and the Future of Technology". *The New York Times*. http://pogue.blogs.nytimes.com/2012/09/13/google-glass-and-the-future-of-technology/?_php=true&_type=blogs&_r=0. [15/01/2014].

Pross, Harry (1972). *Medienforschung: Film, Funk, Presse, Fernsehen*. Darmstadt: Habel.

Romanyshyn, Robert D. (1989/2005). *Technology as Symptom and Dream*. New York, NY/London: Routledge.

Rose, Frank (2011). *The Art of Immersion: How the Digital Generation Is Remaking Hollywood, Madison Avenue, and the Way We Tell Stories*. New York, NY: W. W. Norton & Co.

Ryan, Marie-Laure (2001). *Narrative as Virtual Reality: Immersion and Interactivity in Literature and Electronic Media*. Baltimore, MD: Johns Hopkins UP.

Salen, Katie, Eric Zimmerman (2004). *Rules of Play: Game Design Fundamentals*. Cambridge, MA/London: MIT Press.

Savov, Vlad (2010: online). "Kinect Finally Fulfills Its Minority Report Destiny (video)". *Engadget*. http://www.engadget.com/2010/12/09/kinect-finally-fulfills-its-minority-report-destiny-video/. [15/01/2014].

Schell, Jesse (2008). *The Art of Game Design: A Book of Lenses*. Amsterdam/Boston, MA: Elsevier/Morgan Kaufmann.

Seel, Martin (2001: online). "Eine Vorstufe des Cyberspace". *Die Zeit*. http://www.zeit.de/2001/06/Eine_Vorstufe_des_Cyberspace. [15/01/2014].

Shannon, Claude Elwood (1948). "A Mathematical Theory of Communication". *The Bell System Technical Journal* 27/3: 379–423; 623–656. (Online: http://cm.bell-labs.com/cm/ms/what/shannonday/shannon1948.pdf. [15/01/2014]).

Simmel, Georg (1902/1998). "Der Bildrahmen: Ein ästhetischer Versuch". *Soziologische Ästhetik*. Ed. Klaus Lichtblau. Bodenheim: Philo. 111–117.

Sorkin, Michael (1992). "Introduction: Variations on a Theme Park". Michael Sorkin, ed. *Variations on a Theme Park: The New American City and the End of Public Space*. New York, NY: Hill and Wang. xi–xv.

Sottek, T. C. (2011: online). "To Build a Holodeck: An Exclusive Look at Microsoft's Edison Lab". *The Verge*. http://www.theverge.com/2011/12/28/2665794/microsoft-edison-lab-holodeck-tour. [15/01/2014].

Stafford, Barbara Maria, Frances Terpak (2001). *Devices of Wonder: From the World in a Box to Images on a Screen*. Exh. cat. Los Angeles: J. Paul Getty Museum, 13 November 2001 – 3 February 2002. Los Angeles, CA: Getty Research Institute.

Steadman, Philip (2001). *Vermeer's Camera: Uncovering the Truth Behind the Masterpieces*. Oxford/New York, NY: Oxford UP.

Stevens, Tim (2012: online). "Project Holodeck and Oculus Rift Hope to Kickstart Every Gamers' VR Dream for $500 (video)". *Engadget*. http://www.engadget.com/2012/07/23/project-holodeck-and-oculus-rift/. [15/01/2014].

Thomas, Bob (1994). *Walt Disney: An American Original*. New York, NY: Hyperion.

Vaz, Mark Cotta, Patricia Rose Duignan (1996). *Industrial Light & Magic: Into the Digital Realm*. New York, NY: Ballantine Books.

Venturi, Robert, Denise Scott Brown, Steven Izenour (1977/1997). *Learning from Las Vegas: The Forgotten Symbolism of Architectural Form*. Cambridge, MA/London: MIT Press.

Weibel, Peter, ed. (2001). *Vom Tafelbild zum globalen Datenraum: Neue Möglichkeiten der Bildproduktion und bildgebenden Verfahren*. Ostfildern-Ruit: Hatje Cantz.

Wolf, Werner (2006). "Introduction: Frames, Framings and Framing Borders in Literature and Other Media". Werner Wolf, Walter Bernhart, eds. *Framing Borders in Literature and Other Media*. Amsterdam/New York, NY: Rodopi. 1–40.

Wong, Raymond (2012: online). "Hacker Improves Kinect Accuracy with *Minority Report*-inspired 'Power Glove' (video)". *BGR*. http://bgr.com/2012/09/19/kinect-hack-power-glove-xbox-360/. [15/01/2014].

Zone, Ray (2012). *3-D Revolution: The History of Modern Stereoscopic Cinema*. Lexington, KY: UP of Kentucky.

Zukerman, Wendy (2011: online). "Where's My Holodeck? The Latest Interactive Movie News". *New Scientist*. http://www.newscientist.com/blogs/culturelab/2011/06/wheres-my-holodeck-the-latest-interactive-movie-news.html. [15/01/2014].

Illustration 1:
Film still from a demonstration of
Ivan Sutherland's Sketchpad (1963).

On the Spot
The Double Immersion of Virtual Reality

Martin Warnke

Since its invention, virtual reality has promised strictly localized and simultaneously boundless mobility: it gives the user the impression of being in a whole new world while remaining in the same place and time. This paradox strips distant and simulated locations of their sense of danger and their exclusiveness, while eliminating the user's need to actually travel to reach them. You can practice flying a fighter jet or driving a tank without putting passengers and equipment at risk; you can engage in combat without actually risking your life; you can relax in a tropical paradise without having to fly to get there; you can fly through buildings without running the risk of falling – and all this while staying put. The cybernauts chase their phantasms from within a cube with an edge length of one meter, as if they were figures in a painting by Francis Bacon. Virtual reality is the only technologically possible method of immersing into computer worlds that remains thoroughly paradoxical. How this is possible and where this leads are the focus of this essay.

1. Immersion as Illusion
The Technology of Virtual Reality

Virtual reality, a highly sophisticated, technological, and extremely complex informatic illusion-producing machine, has, since its invention by Ivan Sutherland in 1968, been beset by a significant paradox. The striking contradiction between the freedom of movement it promises and the physical 'dispositif' of its users seems to be at its phantasmic core. While cybernauts effortlessly travel through an endless virtual world, they are in a kind of iron maiden that encloses them on the spot. Immobile freedom, or local boundlessness – this seems to be the paradox of virtual reality as a technology of immersion and is the subject of this article.

We will see that the materiality of virtual reality, as described by Ivan Sutherland in the mid-1960s, was the cause of this phantasmic charge. Newer technologies that, in principle, have the same function, though in entirely other forms, appear completely different, or at least do not give rise to comparable paradoxes. Classical virtual reality is thereby historicized as a maximally invasive technology of immersion.

Ivan Sutherland, the founder of virtual and augmented reality, became famous as an engineer of graphic machines. In 1963, he introduced Sketchpad to the public, a man-machine graphical communication system that was to become the precursor to all interactive computer graphics and computer-aided design programs (see 1963). With a light pen, one could draw figures on the screen that would then be manipulated, as needed, by geometric operations in industrial design processes. This device created the basis for all subsequent computer-graphic systems and ultimately for virtual reality as well (see *Illustration 1*).

Two years later, Sutherland described what could be called an engineer's vision, namely a display that could depict not only thin line graphics but anything you wanted: "A display connected to a digital computer gives us a chance to gain familiarity with concepts not realizable in the physical world. It is a looking glass into a mathematical wonderland" (1965: 506). We have to bear in mind that at this time punch cards were still high-tech, as can be seen in the film *Caprice* (dir. Frank Tashlin, USA 1967) starring Doris Day (see *Illustration 2*). Multi-medial, multi-colored, and fast-moving scenes were still far beyond anything that could be displayed by computer graphics. Thus, the wonderland that Sutherland envisioned was more abstract in mathematical-physical terms, a sphere that was normally invisible or unknown in nature like negative mass. But Sutherland, as an engineer, also rigorously embraced fantasies of an improved technology that would equate simulation and reality in a way that the French philosopher Jean Baudrillard evoked a decade later (see 1981). Sutherland's first virtual room definitely bears traits of a fantasy of omnipotence:

> The ultimate display would, of course, be a room within which the computer can control the existence of matter. A chair displayed in such a room would be good enough to sit in. Handcuffs displayed in such a room would be confining, and a bullet displayed in such a room would be fatal. With appropriate programming such a display could literally be the Wonderland into which Alice walked. (Ibid.: 508)

Here, virtual reality is the wonderland of wishful fantasy. What Sutherland fails to consider, however, is who exactly would want to sit handcuffed to this chair in a room where a shooting will take place.

His ideas become more explicit in 1968, the year Sutherland published a paper describing an actual technological invention: the head-mounted display as the core display technology of virtual reality (see 1968). This device allowed for an immersion in the terms of informa-

Illustration 2:
Film still from Caprice *(dir. Frank Tashlin, USA 1967).*

tion theory because it was capable of displaying spaces and actions in 3-D and in real time as if the participant were really there. It required a complex system of sensorics, computing, and display and can be considered a masterpiece of technological artistry (see *Illustration 3*). The cybernaut, whose eyes were not bound but rather equipped with two mini televisions, could turn, lift, and lower his head. An apparatus then measured his movement, while both eyes were offered a section of a virtual scene rendered by the computer, which corresponded exactly to the movement of the head. Whenever the user, for example, turned his head to the left, a part of the field of vision on the right would disappear, while on the left, a new section of the scene would slide into view. The apparatus was constructed on the basis of psychological research, which suggested that spatial-visual impressions are related to the perceiver's movement in space. Heinz von Foerster expresses this idea in the words of Humberto Maturana when he says: 'We see with our legs' ("Wir sehen mit den Beinen"; 1995: 242). NASA further developed the technology in the 1980s by adding stereoscopic graphics and stereo sound and by giving it a boost toward photo-realism.

This is the prehistory of virtual reality as a technology of immersion into imaginary computer-generated spaces.

2. The Paralyzed Cybernaut

Without any real-life experience of spatial vision, of the feedback loop between movement and perception, it would be impossible to acquire 3-D vision while navigating through a virtual environment. This is the case because the cybernaut is more or less tied to the pole of the technological device and his movements are restricted to an area of roughly one cubic meter, as any further movement would exceed the capacities of the sensorics that continually determine his precise

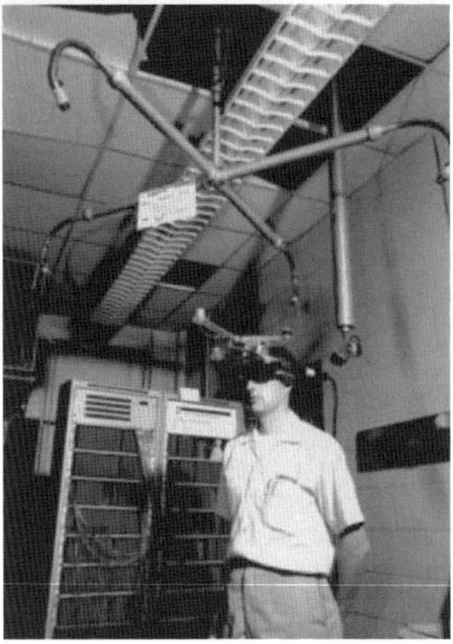

Illustration 3: Illustration from Ivan Sutherland, "A Head-Mounted Three Dimensional Display" (1968).

location in space. Curiously, all fictional versions of virtual reality assume spatial immobility during visits to virtual worlds as if they were all subject to the same technological restrictions of engineering design. Without exception, all of the cybernauts portrayed by Stanisław Lem and Oswald Wiener, by the Wachowskis and James Cameron, have some kind of walking disability.

In 1964, at the same time as Ivan Sutherland, Stanisław Lem developed the idea of virtual reality, which in his *Summa Technologiae* he calls 'phantomology'. He envisions a technological setting in which the nerve impulses of a person – for example, a man sitting on his veranda and smelling a rose – are recorded first. (That in itself would, in fact, lead to the death of the volunteer, as not only his nerves but also his brain would have to be tapped in order to record all of the impulses.) The recorded nerve impulses would then have to be inserted back into the nervous system of someone lying in lukewarm water in an isolation tank, thus constituting the actual 'phantomology':

> And thus when our man is resting in the dark, while a series of impulses are traveling along all of his nerves into his brain – impulses that are exactly the same as those that traveled along his nerves when he was sitting on a veranda with a rose in his hand – he will subjectively find himself in that situation again. He will see the sky, a rose in his hand, a garden in the background behind the veranda, grass, children playing, and so on. (Lem 1964/2013: 198)

So far, this sounds idyllic, but then he continues:

> A somewhat similar experiment has already been conducted on a dog. First, the impulses traveling along the dog's motor nerves while it was running were recorded, after which the dog's spinal cord was cut. Its hind legs thus became paralyzed. When the electric recording was inserted into the nerves of the paralyzed limbs, the hind part of the dog that has been paralyzed "came back to life," performing the same movements that are performed by a normal dog while running. (Ibid.)

Furthermore, at roughly the same time as Lem and Sutherland, Oswald Wiener – a member of Viennese Actionism who participated in the *Uni-Ferkelei* action, an obscene performance at the University of Vienna, and was a comrade-in-arms of the not-at-all-squeamish artists Otto Mühl and Hermann Nitsch – described, in his 1969 novel *Die Verbesserung von Mitteleuropa* ('The Improvement of Central Europe'), a virtual reality that considered the body of the cybernaut somewhat dispensable, and bloodily did away with it piece by piece. Wiener does not leave it at paralyzing the legs but, fictionally, proceeds to amputate body parts of the travelers in virtual worlds, whom he calls 'bio-modules' ("bio-module"; 1969/1985: CLXXXI):

> […] while, for example, the leg of a bio-module is being amputated, he is perhaps enjoying a refreshing walk through a scenic Hungarian landscape. The adapter simulates the complex interplay of the efferent nerves with kinesthetic and proprioceptive fibers, and a look at his leg tells the bio-module, at most, that the pleasure he is taking in physical activity is doing more and more good for the muscles in his extremities.[1]

Here, the double immersion of virtual reality becomes apparent. Not only does the cybernaut invade artificial worlds, the virtual-reality machine, at the same time, invades the cybernaut's body.

In *The Matrix* (dir. Andy and Lana Wachowski, USA/Australia 1999), the passage into virtual reality, similar to Sutherland's engineering vision, is staged like an execution (see *Illustration 4*): the props of the 'last walk' range from the nervous prisoner's shaved head and prison clothing to the reassuring gestures of the executioner, who even closes the condemned's eyelids before pushing the spike into his neck. *The Matrix* is a collection of nearly every cinematic stereotype about virtual reality that portrays it as being only accessible to those rendered absolutely immobile – those bound on the spot.

In the virtual-reality epic *Avatar* (dir. James Cameron, USA/UK 2009), the paradox of the freedom of the incarcerated is portrayed in a similarly striking manner. The opening sequence shows, quite sin-

1 "[…] während z. b. gerade ein bein des bio-moduls amputiert wird, genießt derselbe vielleicht einen erfrischenden fussmarsch durch reizvolle ungarische landschaften. der adapter simuliert das komplexe wechselspiel der efferenten nerven mit kinästhetischen und propriozeptiven fasern und ein blick auf seine beine belehrt den bio-modul höchstens über die tatsache, dass seine bewegungsfreude dem muskelspiel seiner extremitäten immer besser bekomme." (Wiener 1969/1985: CLXXXI) Unless otherwise indicated, all translations are mine.

isterly, the hero on a six-year-long trip in a kind of 'space morgue' (see *Illustration 5*) and the burial of his twin brother in a cardboard box. The hero himself is already disabled, a paraplegic like Stanisław Lem's laboratory dog. Before his legs can 'come back to life', however, he must enter what looks like an iron maiden. His passage into virtual reality is staged as his being buried alive. There follows the apotheosis: in the body of his avatar, the resurrected Jake can once again feel his legs; he childishly and recklessly indulges in his artificial dream of running, just like Oswald Wiener's bio-module.

3. The Structure of the Immersion Machine

Virtual reality is an established fictional topos, triggered and manifested by a technology that, through data helmets, tracking systems, and other equipment, encloses and immobilizes cybernauts' bodies in order to illusorily invade unlimited virtual worlds. The main motive is a wish machine that confines, straps, impales, and mutilates the test subject, accompanied by the fantasies of the narrator. Fictional virtual reality is a wish fulfiller, much like a dream, dependent on a more or less sadomasochistic author.

The submission to a dominant machine frames this wish fulfillment and creates a phantasmic setting, which, depending on the psychological disposition of the operator or narrator, can range from an authoritarian-technocratic to a mildly violent or even a manifestly sadomasochistic fantasy. Oswald Wiener's fantasies of the 'bio-adapter' and David Cronenberg's fantasies of the 'Videodrome'[2] (*Videodrome*,

2 I kindly thank Lisa Gotto for drawing this to my attention.

Illustration 4: Film still from The Matrix *(dir. Andy and Lana Wachowski, USA/Australia 1999).*

Canada 1983) are the sadistic consequences of the virtual reality described by Ivan Sutherland, whose vision in "The Ultimate Display", as we recall, is reminiscent of a mafia-style execution scene, including a chair, handcuffs, and bullets.

In retrospect, technological developments point out the fact that the violent streak in virtual reality arises from a clearly visible relationship between body and machine: a fetish. By contrast, today's technologies – playing on the most microscopic computers that are completely in our power and already part of our bodies: smartphones – no longer require a painful or pleasurable act of submission. An example of this is the iPhone pet, a pet that lives in the augmented reality of the smartphone. In his film *World on a Wire* (*Welt am Draht*, West Germany 1973), Rainer Werner Fassbinder already envisions a virtual word in which an apparatus of physical submission is no longer required: here, the world is 'on a wire' and not under the 'coffin lid' of virtual reality. The film thus relegates virtual reality as a topos to history, claiming that it belongs to the mainframe computer of the 1940s and 1950s, and not to today's networked world (see Warnke 2011). This is what makes *World on a Wire* avant-garde and *The Matrix* and *Avatar* kitsch: the latter make use of a concept of immersion that dates back to the 1960s and relies on an outdated 'dispositif' of localization.

Since then, however, the virtual has become inseparably interwoven with the real; it has become ubiquitous. It has also become much more confusing, because one no longer has to enter into an 'iron maiden' in order to be part of a computed world. As is shown in *World on a Wire*, there is no longer a staged passage into an artificial fantasy world. Our orientation is lost, because we don't know whether we ourselves are observing or are being observed, whether we are in the so-called real or in the so-called virtual world: the apparatus disappears in the palms of our hands, in our clothing, in our bodies, in the air. An interface that, in an emergency, could be rejected no longer exists. Even the wire that Fassbinder's world is still attached to and that, in ex-

Illustration 5:
Film still from Avatar *(dir. James Cameron, USA/UK 2009).*

treme cases, could be cut off no longer exists. With it, the spot where the singularity of a defined passage could still be localized has disappeared as well. This dreadful spot, a terrifying place, can no longer be banished, severed, or avoided by a dream with a happy ending.

The existence of such a spot or place has itself become a desire and a fantasy, a set piece in an irrecoverable techno-romanticism, as shown in *The Matrix* and *Avatar*. In reality, its time has passed once and for all.

References

Baudrillard, Jean (1981). *Simulacres et simulation*. Paris: Editions Galilée.

— (1994). *Simulacra and Simulation*. Transl. Sheila Faria Glaser. Ann Arbor, MI: University of Michigan Press.

Foerster, Heinz von (1995). "Worte". Klaus Peter Dencker, ed. *Interface II: Weltbilder Bildwelten – computergestützte Visionen*. Hamburg: Hans-Bredow-Institut. 236–246.

Lem, Stanisław (1964/2013). *Summa Technologiae*. Transl. Joanna Zylinska. Minneapolis, MN/London: University of Minnesota Press.

Sutherland, Ivan E. (1963). "Sketchpad: A Man-Machine Graphical Communication System". *AFIPS Conference Proceedings*. Vol. 23: *1963 Spring Joint Computer Conference, Detroit, May 1963*. Washington, DC: Spartan Books. 329–346.

— (1965). "The Ultimate Display". Wayne A. Kalenich, ed. *Information Processing 1965: Proceedings of IFIP Congress 65. New York City, May 24 – 29, 1965*. Washington, DC: Spartan Books. 506–508.

— (1968). "A Head-Mounted Three Dimensional Display". *AFIPS Conference Proceedings*. Vol. 33, Part 1: *1968 Fall Joint Computer Conference, December 9 – 11, 1968, San Francisco, California*. Washington, DC: Thompson Books. 757–764.

Warnke, Martin (2011). *Theorien des Internet zur Einführung*. Hamburg: Junius.

Wiener, Oswald (1969/1985). "Appendix A: der bio-adapter". *Die Verbesserung von Mitteleuropa*. Reinbek bei Hamburg: Rowohlt.

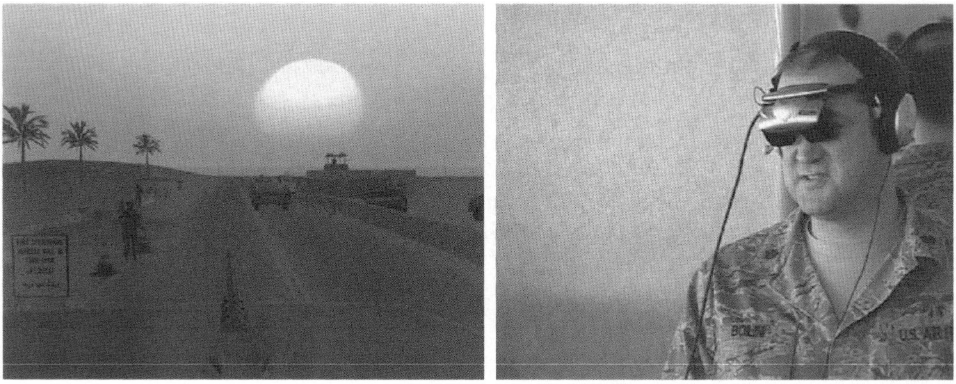

Illustration 1:
Film still from Immersion *(dir. Harun Farocki, Germany 2009). Video projection, double screen, 20 min. (loop). Copyright Harun Farocki.*

Expansion of the Immersion Zone
Military Simulacra between Strategic Training and Trauma

Ursula Frohne

Since the mid-1990s, military strategists have used so-called Military Operations in Urban Terrain (MOUT) scenarios as virtual training grounds to prepare soldiers for military operations. Here, model towns and buildings serve as a topographical infrastructure for training related to military emergencies. At the same time, computer animations of these ghost towns are utilized in the ludic practice of making contact with the enemy in the same way immersive 3-D visualizations combined with role-playing are employed in the therapeutic treatment of those traumatized by military service. The constitutive factors of these kinds of 'military dispositifs' are the focus of Harun Farocki's film *Immersion* (Germany 2009, as part of the series *Serious Games*). He makes the unsuspecting viewer a witness to a simulated experiment in which a visibly shaken test subject reconstructs a life-threatening conflict, which is simultaneously played as an animated film before his eyes. The photo series *personal kill* (2007) by Beate Geissler and Oliver Sann also refers to the constitutive efficacy of virtual combat scenes by capturing the ubiquitous analog military model towns as dystopian parallel worlds on the edges of our civilized living environments. Both artistic approaches address the fact that immersive combat simulations are not limited to restricted military areas or to the preparation for possible peacekeeping missions. Rather, their game format contributes to the implicit totalization of a culture of hostility. To the extent that they tend to reduce encounters with the foreign to a stereotypical friend/enemy polarity, they potentially naturalize the concept of a world order that appears to be only defensible by war.

1. Preliminary Thoughts

> A missionary of the Middle Ages even tells us that, in one of his voyages in search of the terrestrial paradise, he reached the horizon where the Earth and the heavens met, and that he discovered a certain point where they were not joined together, and where, by stooping, he passed under the roof of the heavens. (Flammarion 1873: 101f.)

An imaginary dip into virtual reality, whether in the cinema, at a computer screen, in an art installation, at a concert, or while reading a novel, is usually grasped as a transition into an 'other' sphere or world, one mobilized by an idea. Entrance into a fictional space removed from empirical reality occurs via the process of reception of a dramaturgy that is as metaphorical as it is participatory. In her study on the immersive experience of space, Laura Bieger describes it as a space in which 'the reality of the world and the reality of the image consolidate in the immediate reality of physical experience'[1]. Immersion, to sum up the current state of discourse on the subject, occurs in a perceptual act that leads into a superimposition of levels of reality in one's perception. As a consequence of "a shift of attention to [...] the media content" (Thon 2008: 31)[2], immersion is often accompanied by a psychological movement.

The concepts of immersion that have been discussed since the 1970s, initially in the context of film, and that have experienced a new dimension of sociocultural relevance with the rise of electronic and interactive visual technologies since the 1990s, all share a basic structure that marks a discrepancy between the artificially created realities of aesthetic fictions and the empirical world in which we live. In such approaches, immersion is coupled, as it were, with an experience of the beyond in which the continuum of normative coordinates of space and time seems to be eliminated in favor of a sensing of the moment and a heightened experience of the present. If the interests of media theorists and sociologists have focused on immersion effects primarily in relation to bodies and senses of interface and interaction modalities mobilized by visual technologies in the media or, respectively, on their sociocultural resonances, art historians associate immersive phenomena with the dispositive framework of certain orders of the gaze and of images that influence the viewers in an audio-visual space of illusion (cf. Blümlinger 2011: 37f.). From a historical-genealogical perspective, technologies of immersion, such as the panorama and its cinematographic descendants – from the IMAX cinema to the stereoscopic surround displays of 3-D vision systems – are now increasingly fused with the everyday actions of our online society, most visibly by means of mobile screen technologies. In view of the intensity of linkages between virtual experiences of presence and everyday

1 "[...] die Wirklichkeit der Welt und die Wirklichkeit des Bildes in der unmittelbaren Wirklichkeit körperlichen Erlebens konsolidieren" (Bieger 2011: 75). Unless otherwise indicated, all translations are mine.

2 Following Matthew Lombard and Theresa Ditton (see 1997), Jan-Noël Thon distinguishes between "perceptual and psychological immersion" (2008: 31), which, with a view to the immersion aesthetic of computer games, he subjects to a further distinction between the four levels of "spatial, ludic, narrative and social structure" (ibid.: 34f.).

performances, the general understanding of immersion technologies seems to fall short, if only with regard to components of media operation and perceptual aesthetics. Apart from the semantic vagueness of the term, which has yet to obtain any definitional contours[3], we can observe, in the applications and social embedding of current media practices, a tendency to expand the potential of immersive scenarios in the direction of controlling specific thought processes and sequences of events.

The idea of a binary order in which the immersive effects of fictional scenarios are part of the empirical world and its cultural manifestations but ultimately separate from or subordinate to the rational reality of life is scarcely viable any longer in an age in which entire generations navigate and communicate large parts of their lives in online forums, while gigantic financial transactions can trigger crises of global proportions in a fraction of a second by mouse click. Phenomena of immersion are by no means limited to hermetic spaces separated from reality. Rather, the contemporary subject is constituted by the internalization of a diversity of immersive apparatuses that function not so much as hideouts for attempts to escape temporarily but rather to adjust the mind of the modern world to a logic of potential omnipresence. Max Weber's dictum of the modern era's "shell as hard as steel" (1930: 181) ("stahlhartes Gehäuse"; 1920: 77; see also Baehr 2001) anticipated the idea of a mental state that constitutes the reality of life and that, in an age drowned with communication and information overload, has become a constant experience of immersion. The fictional worlds we frequent temporarily in the cinema, in novels, and on television that were considered the classical apparatus of immersion in the 20th century now offer niches for escaping the usurping attention regimes of ubiquitous screen technologies, the reactive metering of which is aimed at a protective fusing that branches into all realms of life. The Platonic model of 'another' space, depicted symbolically in Camille Flammarion's famous wood engraving that illustrates the limitedness of the medieval subject's world view, is being overtaken by the overwhelming pull of hypermodern scenarios of simulation that are interwoven into everyday actions.

3 Neither in the *Wörterbuch für Ästhetische Grundbegriffe* (see Barck, ed. 2010) nor in the *Encyclopedia of Aesthetics* (see Kelly, ed. 1998) is there a separate entry for the term 'immersion'. It is addressed in the latter in the 'virtual reality' entry.

The firmament of appearance whose illusionary nature the subject must break through in an act of cognition in order to achieve sovereignty (see Wolf 2013) can scarcely be applied any longer to today's phenomena of immersion, which have moved away from the metaphor of parallel models of space. Rather, the intensity of the fusing of the subject with today's communication technologies points to an internalization of neoliberal economics that is achieved as a global phenomenon in a culture of immersion by presuming the constant willingness to interact. Unlike under the conditions of the disciplinary society of the 20th century, contemporary efficiency-oriented 'performing subjects' voluntarily submit themselves to the excess of communication and multitasking. According to Byung-Chul Han, it is no longer the negativity of prohibition and the imperative of 'should' that shape the subject; rather, the positive schema of 'can' and the paradigm of obligation to performance, quotas, innovation, generation of attention, and profit maximization dominate with an immersive pull the modalities of contemporary life (cf. 2010: 17f.)[4]. This dictate of positivity supersedes the negativity of pausing and avoids any interruption of technologically motivated hyperactivity that could facilitate a cognitive process with critical distance. Instead, the primacy of unconditional productivity that is politically and socially invoked and its measurability essentially function by voluntary internalization of economic and strategic principles of thinking and acting.

Both of these perspectives on modern technologies of immersion – media-operational and sociocultural – intersect at a historically anchored point of convergence on which the following discussion will center. Following Johan Frederik Hartle, I call this point of convergence the 'military dispositif' ("militärisches Dispositiv"; 2010c: 8), the strategic thought processes of which influence the tactical orientation of all everyday practices. Goal-oriented action that obeys the purposeful logic of the 'in order to' without hesitation or interruption is not only found in specific everyday actions but is particularly in-

4 The philosopher Byung-Chul Han discusses the transition from Michel Foucault's model of the disciplinary society to the performance society of the 21st century: 'The positivity of "can" is much more efficient than the negativity of "should". The performing subject is faster and more productive than the obedient subject.' ("Die Positivität des Könnens ist viel effizienter als die Negativität des Sollens. Das Leistungssubjekt ist schneller und produktiver als das Gehorsamssubjekt"; 2010: 19). 'The performing subject is at war with himself or herself.' ("Das Leistungssubjekt befindet sich mit sich selbst im Krieg"; ibid.: 22).

volved in the production of subjects (cf. ibid.). Harun Farocki explores this process in his film *Immersion* (Germany 2009) by means of a disturbingly uncommented observation of the aesthetic potential and diversity of today's immersion techniques in the service of political ideology. As Farocki demonstrated in earlier works, immersive scenarios offer a set of instruments with which the perspective of war can be rehearsed. Through playing games, subjects can train in virtual scenarios of threat to prepare to regulate states of exception[5]. Computer-generated simulated scenarios of military operations, disguised as the user interface of a game, are based on reaction schemas that feed back into the real world. But the uncanny quality results from a matter-of-fact recording aesthetic in Farocki's study of the treatment of traumatized American soldiers who are subjected to simulation therapy after their deployment in Iraq.

In a similar way, *personal kill* (2007; see Hartle, ed. 2010a), a photographic work by Beate Geissler and Oliver Sann, shows American training areas in Upper Bavaria the sole purpose of which is to put as realistic a face as possible on a series of worst-case scenarios of confrontation with another person who has been declared the enemy. Whereas Farocki's film examines the deceptive nature of an immersion aesthetic intended to suggest safety, the abandoned buildings in the photographs of Geissler and Sann turn out, despite their seemingly real existence, to be the mock architecture of Potemkin villages to the extent that their design details mark them as enemy terrain. Just like Farocki's film, the photographs of *personal kill*[6] testify to an insidious process of smoothing out all distinctions between digital and analog spaces of simulation. More than that, they blur any point of stability between civilian spheres and those of actual military zones of conflict. With the extension of an all-embracing strategic logic that proliferates in both urban security technologies and the economization of all aspects of life, the boundaries between civil spheres and militarized zones of conflict become fluid. According to Hartle, these

5 With reference to Carl Schmitt's political theory, the philosopher Giorgio Agamben (see 2005) has elaborated on the alarming effects of shifts in political developments in which the law is displaced by a declaration of a state of emergency and legal status is withdrawn from subjects sequestered to extra-juridical zones.

6 The photographs show analog training grounds of American bases stationed around the world that function as physical companions to the digital computer scenarios that are also used to train for worst-case scenarios.

spheres fuse congruently 'in the attempted militarization of subjects' ("Militarisierung der Subjektivität"; 2010c: 10), which is expressly 'the fight against the communal forms of the metropolis' ("ein Kampf gegen die Vergesellschaftsformen der Metropolis"; ibid.).

The artistic images of training in and mastering techniques for potential wartime deployment discussed here suggest the basic dystopian tone, aside from all claims to military superiority, of the computer-generated and actually existing training scenarios and stylize them into zones of a state of exception. Farocki as well as Geissler and Sann characterize the latent combat logic inherent in such scenarios as traumatically repressed effects that influence civilian contexts, as is demonstrated not least by the debate over the oft-criticized violence that is distributed in popular computer games. As these works show, immersive strategies are part of a genealogy of tactical systems that are not limited to restricted military areas or to the simulation of conflicts. Rather, their 'game' formats have a specific influence on the implicit totalization of a culture of hostility. They not only demand the ability to efficiently eliminate competing Others but also compel a willingness to successfully suspend all disbelief about such an action – an aspect that is characteristic not least of immersion's response aesthetics (cf. Furtwängler 2006: 168).

2. Killing or Healing?[7]

The theme of war plays a special role in the spectrum of representational media. War has always been depicted as a genuine experience of immersion. The fact that battle scenes, as well as landscapes, were admired by audiences as one of the favorite subjects of the new attraction of the panorama in the 19th century underscores the fascination of war, the aesthetic representations of which mark the transition from an apocalyptic-archaic experience in the late 20th century to mass culture (see Holert/Terkessidis, eds. 2002; Holert 2003; Terkessidis 2003). The high-tech productions of Hollywood cinema, which aesthetically glorify war's modern transition to mass culture, are, af-

7 The words 'Tötung' (killing) and 'Heilung' (healing) can be identified on a photograph from 1926/1927 showing Warburg's art-historical image compilations as they were arranged on exhibition panels running along the wall of books in the Warburg Institute Library. For a reproduction of this photograph, cf. Fliedl 1992: 157.

ter all, part of a long tradition of immersive tactics of usurpation by war (see Holert/Terkessidis, eds. 2002). In parallel with deep-rooted change in the media, as the visual policies of military conflicts show, war itself is transforming and using the technological space of perception to press for its visual representations. Ernst Jünger's stylization in his wartime diaries (see 1932/1982) of the pull of destructive forces belongs to a longer historical tradition of epic war treatises from a wide variety of cultures. His dubious glorification of war's destructive excesses on an indescribable scale – horrors he stylizes in his diaries as a way to expand consciousness – culminate in the stylized figure of the worker. This is not intended to refer to an empirical person but is a figure for projection in which the modern fusing of technologies of perception with the military apparatus is manifested in a representative figuration. 'In total war', Jünger notes, 'every city, every factory is a fortified place, every merchant ship is a warship, all food is contraband, every active or passive measure has a military significance'[8]. The complete orientation around the 'military dispositif' addressed here radicalizes perception and its conditions to the point of dehumanization.

Pierre Robiquet comments on this process of complete decontextualization in the wake of the immersive forces of war in his discussion of French battle paintings from World War I, recognizing their aesthetic of naturalization as a war technology that has become autonomous. The associated transformation of the entire environment into a military scenario is ultimately aimed at humans, as Robiquet laconically points out: 'A battle is a landscape that is shooting at you' ("Eine Schlacht ist eine Landschaft, die auf Sie schießt"; qtd. Robichon 1994: 290). Under such conditions, technology can no longer be regarded as a tool; rather, it transforms into a medium of a specifically modern experience of the world. The adaptation of the apparatus of human perception to a catastrophic technology focuses the consciousness of the subject on the experience of a new 'media style of perception' ("mediale Wahrnehmungsstil"; Spangenberg 1991, qtd. Werneburg 1995) that formed on the battlefields of the early 20th century. Peter Sloterdijk also describes this effect of military immersion when

8 "Im totalen Kriege ist jede Stadt jede Fabrik ein befestigter Platz, jedes Handelsschiff, jedes Lebensmittel ist Konterbande, jede aktive oder passive Maßnahme hat kriegerischen Sinn" (Jünger 1932/1982: 149). For a discussion of Jünger's reflection on media, see Werneburg 1995.

he evokes the first use of gas in the Battle of Ypres in 1915 as a previously unknown fusing of atmosphere and war technology (cf. 2002: 12). The new (media) technology of war demanded images that expanded its representations into immersive experiences of space. The mediated dimension of experience increases its inherent value, since it is no longer limited to the functions of war but goes beyond the mode of immediate experience (see Werneburg 1995). The panorama was already such an attempt to totalize perception and dynamically heighten it by incorporating the viewer into the events. Viewers were placed in an elevated position around the battlefield and, despite carnage surrounding them, could follow all of the stages of the strategic conquest of the enemy undisturbed and in some cases even control it virtually via their physical movement in space[9].

Harun Farocki's film *Immersion*, the third part of a series titled *Ernste Spiele* (*Serious Games*, Germany 2010), addresses the potential usurpation of the living world and processes of agency by literally reducing them to a perspective of the dangers of terror and war. In a shocking simulated dramaturgy, the narrative shows how the factors of the 'military dispositif' that constitute the subject totalize language, the senses, and physical technologies into the paradigm of the deadly friend-foe categorization that Carl Schmitt proposed as a political theory conceived with war in mind (see 1963 and 2004). The unsuspecting viewer of the film witnesses training at the American base Fort Lewis near Seattle, Washington, in which civil therapists propose that a group of military therapists incorporate a computer program called *Virtual Iraq* into their role-playing (see *Illustrations 1* and *2*). This is simulation software developed to treat American soldiers suffering from trauma after deployment in a war. The test subjects wear data goggles that immerse them in a simulated battle scenario and navigate through the topographies of computer-generated images in order to find the places associated with their anxieties and come to terms with their trauma. At the same time, the therapists' questions mobilize memory by provoking a mental return to the repressed experiences in accordance with the classic method of psychoanalysis. The core scene in this twenty-minute, two-channel projection is a sequence in which a supposed veteran talks about his experience while on patrol in

9 The classic site of catastrophe combined with a distance from it that is ultimately established aesthetically is probably Lucretius' metaphor of the 'shipwreck with spectator'. On the history of the interpretation of this figure of speech, see Blumenberg 1997.

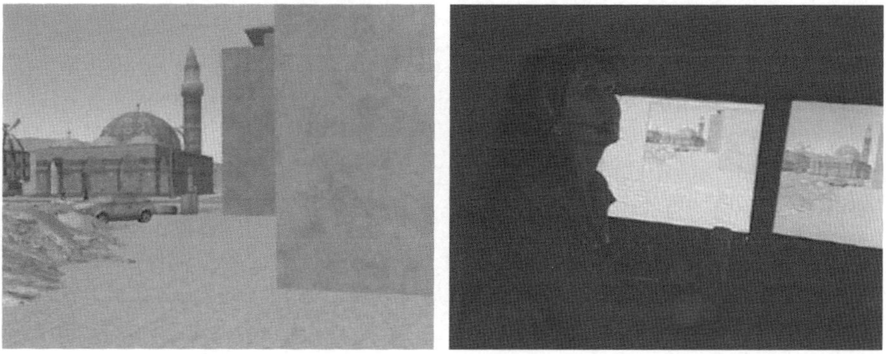

Illustration 2:
Film still from Immersion *(dir. Harun Farocki, Germany 2009).*
Video projection, double screen, 20 min. (loop). Copyright Harun Farocki.

Baghdad. He describes his first deployment, which ended terribly when a soldier under his command was killed in a horrifying way. On a computer screen, the therapist follows the images the test subject is seeing as a 3-D visualization via the head-mounted display. She repeatedly asks him to describe the course of events more precisely. Again and again, he digresses and protests that he is unable to confront the situation again. Even when he suffers a near breakdown, his requests to discontinue the session are not granted. The therapist encourages his efforts and at the same time insists that he continue the reenactment. Stammering and increasingly devastated by his physical reactions to being confronted with what he experienced, he approaches the site of the escalation in his computer-aided memory. At this cathartic point, at which the test subject recapitulates the attack and seems very credibly to be living through the experience of feeling completely abandoned in all its horror, Farocki's film culminates in the viewer's surprising disillusionment. This dramatic remembered experience, no doubt associated with the guilty feelings of a survivor – especially since, as troop leader, he considers himself responsible for the death of a comrade – becomes anticlimactic when it is suddenly revealed to the naïve viewer that the whole deeply moving scene was just a sham. The setting, as is clear from the equally shocking carefree demeanor of the actors when the 'performance' ends, was intended only to demonstrate the potential of the newly developed computer program *Virtual Iraq*. Just as the visual reactivation of the experience of war was simulated, the painful confrontation with the disaster the person supposedly lived through is based on the narrative pull of the performance. The test subject turns out to be another therapist involved in developing the program. He plays the role of the veteran so realistically that viewers are pulled in by the immersion techniques employed on various levels in the performative process of approaching the event associated with anxiety.

From earlier films and video essays by Farocki we know that computer-generated landscapes like those seen in the therapy sequences are used to prepare soldiers for unexpected challenges in war. It may seem cynical that these scenes are almost identical to those employed to treat the psychological damage caused by real experiences of war, but the pragmatism of this use merely confirms the polarizing logic of the 'military dispositif', which is programmed to colonize even the realms of the unconscious. Farocki investigates the circumstances of these techniques of immersion employed by the military and medical apparatuses. The same technologies used to control weapons at the front later serve to cure the resulting trauma. In Farocki's film, viewers' initial participation evaporates abruptly "after learning that the soldier and therapist are actually both employees of a software development firm, and their entire interaction was a scripted attempt to sell the firm's VR-therapy technology to the US military" (Weiner 2011: 79). Following Andrew Stefan Weiner, we might ask about the consequences that derive from the fact that the "therapeutic software shares the same platform as the battle-simulation programmes used to recruit and train soldiers" and "that the ostensible method of cure" (ibid.) employs the exact same immersive technologies of simulation that were developed as a training instrument to desensitize soldiers and prepare them for deployment in war.

Aby Warburg remarked on the antinomies of meaning that can either be inherent in the images themselves or result from the context in which they were created or presented. Without knowledge of the background of the story behind the images – that is, both a narrative, diegetic structure to which the image, as a reproduction of an event, specifically refers and a cultural and historical embedding in a visual tradition shaped by history – a depiction is often subject to contrary interpretations (see Fliedl 1992; Warnke 1980). This polyvalence of certain visual categories that Warburg addressed is tied not only to the history assigned to the level of representation but also to the history of perception and its logic of mediation and logistics of dissemination. Images, (spoken) text, and montage combine in the sequential series of images of a recording on film to create a complex corpus of sources that points beyond the level of statements that can be described visually to other qualitative constellations of meaning, which can include 'religious, ethnic, and social rituals, lifestyles, [and] habitual patterns of action' ("religiöse, ethnische wie soziale Rituale, Lebensstile, [und] habituelle Muster des Agierens"; Böhme 1997: 140) as well as ideological distinctions with regard to the function and meaning of images within a specific cultural context, as Warburg recognized.

The parallel projection and simulated character in Farocki's *Immersion* demonstrate that the meaning of images is *not* immanent to the subject matter of what they depict. Although the narrative of the sequences makes use of an immersive rhetoric, the discursive juxtaposition of visual levels – a method Farocki himself calls "soft montage" (cf. Silverman/Farocki 1998: 141–143) – results in a latitude for interpretation that the film scholar Thomas Elsaesser has characterized as part of Farocki's unmistakable style (see 2002; 2004). Farocki is thus employing one of the most important methods of art-historical analysis since the 19th century, in which two slides are shown in alternation and simultaneously in order to demonstrate a wide variety of relationships between images. Warburg's emphasis on the necessity to consider the field of discourse in which images are presented can also be traced back to this. As is confirmed in the revealing moment when it becomes apparent that this is just a simulated treatment of trauma, it becomes increasingly difficult in the immersive space of video games, military applications, and Hollywood genres to distinguish between 'killing' and 'healing' without first studying the historical, cultural, political, and social context and the dramaturgy of the event depicted (see Virilio 1989; 2006)[10]. Rather than calling for a distinction to be made, the simulation scenarios repress the actual destruction that occurs in war. 'They produce a symbolic space aimed at war' ("Sie modellieren einen symbolischen Raum, der auf den Krieg zugespitzt ist"; Hartle 2010a: 47). The ludic coding that camouflages a war in real time and its real destructive consequences as a purely visual spec-

10 The fiction of 'nonbloody' combative action becomes manifest not only as a visual phenomenon. Language, too, has adopted the notion of military operations as 'surgical interventions'. Campaigns like Operation Desert Storm legitimized war as a clinical concept, as the ultima ratio made necessary by the alleged failure of other political 'remedies'. This highly functionalized usage of language is reproduced on the visual plane.

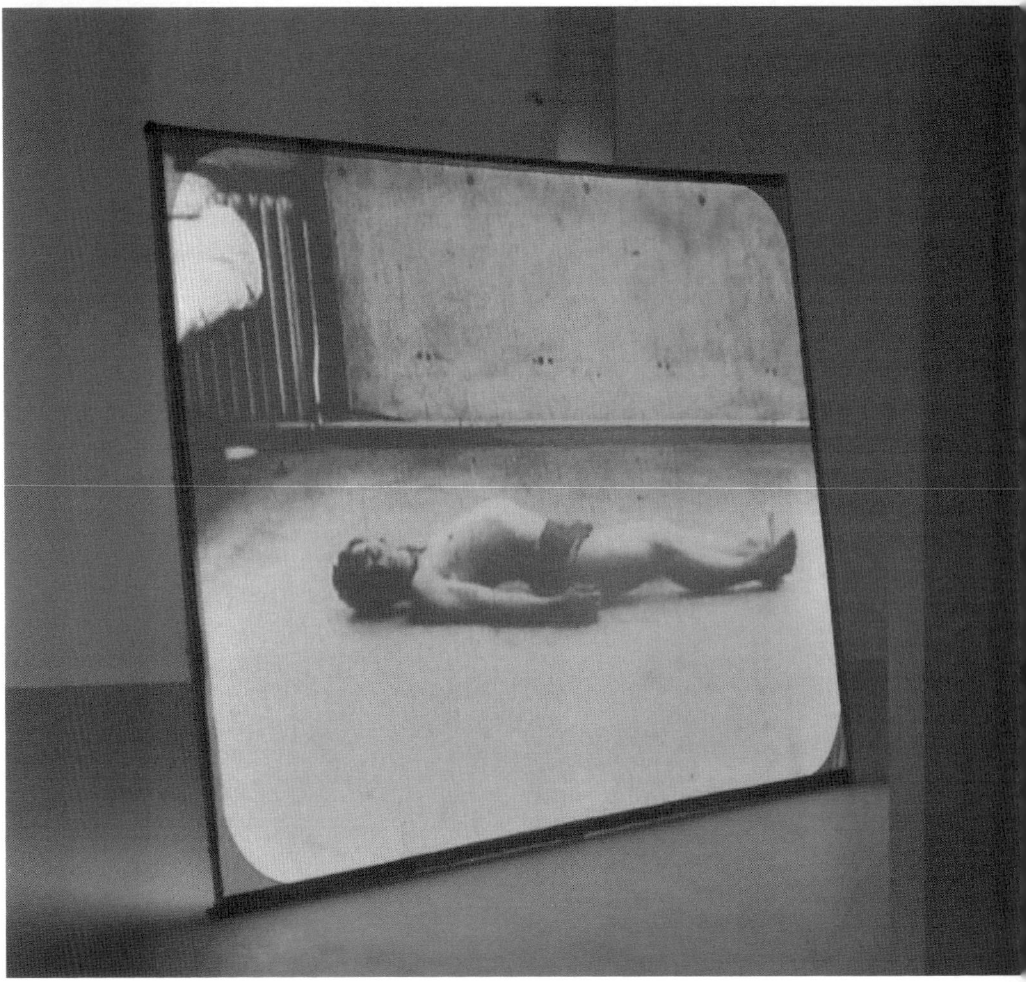

Illustration 3:
Douglas Gordon, 10 ms^{-1} *(1994). Video installation, single screen, 2 min. 10 sec. (loop). Stedelijk Van Abbemuseum, Eindhoven; Tate Gallery, London; British Council Collection, London.*

tacle undermines the taboo in civil society with regard to the fascination of an aesthetic of weapons and war. The fetishizing of computer games and hyperreal film scenarios in today's culture helps establish a visual politics that downplays their risks and claims to 'heal' rather than 'kill' by means of 'clinical' precision war tactics.

Already during the Gulf War in 1991, the distanced aerial recordings and computer animations documented the destruction of the foe as a schematic maneuver carried out by high-tech specialists in the media sphere. As the pilot inside the flight simulator casually remarks in Harun Farocki's film *Auge/Maschine II* (Germany 2002), the virtual theater of war lacks a form of depicting one's own annihilation. If you get hit, then the exercise is over. The monitor goes blank, and the 'game' starts from the beginning. Despite all the protection provided by the topography and the media, the damage resulting from the war has left clear traces that can even be followed back to the soldiers' homeland[11]. The numbers speak for themselves, if one considers that in the United States today one in four homeless persons is a Vietnam veteran, and the suicide rate among former soldiers increased 26 percent from 2005 to 2007. It becomes clear that targeted care for those harmed by war is increasingly important to maintaining domestic security. With the simulated visual scenarios of immersion therapy, however, the logic of war is perpetuated, since trauma awaits its symbolic (visual, narrative) representation. It returns in postwar society as a 'flashback, the compulsion to repeat and psychosomatic suffering' ("Flashback, Wiederholungszwang und psychosomatisches Leiden"; Hartle 2010b: 111). The repressed, dislocated reality of war penetrates the very heart of society, since, for those who have been traumatized, the war does not end in civil zones.

The trauma itself becomes an immersive reality that determines the lives of those affected. The first studies of these phenomena were done after World War I when a large number of veterans turned out to have not only physical wounds but also post-traumatic disorders such as shell shock and other compulsive motoric symptoms (see Bourke 1996; Kienitz 2001)[12]. In two video installations, the Scottish artist Douglas Gordon has addressed the flooding of the psyche with trauma that has been experienced, which in turn retroacts on civil society as the somatic suffering of those affected. Both works employ material from documentary films shot in British military hospitals around 1917

---

11 Post-traumatic stress disorder (PTSD) has been recognized by society as a consequential damage of war since 1980, when the American Psychiatric Association officially recognized traumatization by war as a syndrome. The International Classification of Diseases of the World Health Organization describes PTSD as "a delayed or protracted response to a stressful event or situation (of either brief or long duration) of an exceptionally threatening or catastrophic nature, which is likely to cause pervasive distress in almost anyone" (1992: 147).

12 On the historical development of the treatment of war neuroses, see Eissler 1986. Recent studies reveal that PTSD was already observed during war in early modern times (cf. Speckmann 2013: 3; see also Lorenz 2012).

and 1918. The freestanding projection *10 ms*$^{-1}$ (1994)[13] shows a man stretched out on the floor who tries again and again in vain, despite his athletic physique, to straighten up and rise (see *Illustration 3*). He is dressed only in a loincloth and exposed entirely to the gaze of the camera in the sparsely furnished room of a clinic as we witness his inexplicable failure. Projected at a slower playback speed, Gordon's presentation of the found film material decelerates the painful experience of incapacitation. Endlessly repeating the scene in a loop, Gordon's intervention underscores the compulsive character of the sequence of actions and at the same time transfers these to a symbolic figure. Viewers experience this Sisyphus motif as perplexing, since the physical stature of the man stands in a dramatic conflict with his obvious impairment.

Viewing the historical film from which it was excerpted reveals the narrative context of this enigmatic scene, which Gordon withheld. It is one of a set of medical film recordings archived at the Wellcome Collection in London under the title *War Neuroses: Netley Hospital, 1917, Seale Hayne Military Hospital, 1918* (see *Illustration 4*). These silent films were produced to explain to soldiers the symptoms of the war neuroses that were treated in British military hospitals during World War I. Unlike in Gordon's presentation, the scene is embedded in a highly suggestive 'before and after' dramaturgy that demonstrates the successful application of physiotherapy and psychotherapy to treat those traumatized by the war. Intertitles comment on the supposed healing and return to 'normality' of those who were seriously scarred but appear again in their uniforms after treatment. This does not simply allude to their readiness to be deployed again; the implied resumption of being familiar male role models also points to the return of the injured to their accustomed place within 'the social order of the societies at war' ("der sozialen Ordnungen der kriegführenden Gesellschaften"; Reimann 2008). As Aribert Reimann has emphasized, the experience of 'male invalidity' ("männlichen Invalidität"; ibid.) in and after World War I represented for contemporaries a 'spectacular "feminization" of men' ("spektakuläre 'Verweiblichung' der Männer"; ibid.): 'The application of the feminine-coded pre-war psychiatric discourse on "hysteria" and the syndrome of "neurasthenia" to the traumatized

13 According to Douglas Gordon, the title of the work *10 ms*$^{-1}$ refers to the rate at which an object falls when subject to Earth's gravity: 10 meters per second (cf. Brown 2004: 43).

Illustration 4:
Film still from War Neuroses: Netley Hospital, 1917, Seale Hayne Military Hospital, 1918 *(1918). Wellcome Film Collection, London.*

"shell-shocked" soldiers contributed substantially to uncertainty about male gender identity.'[14] By removing this fragment of film from its historically situated narrative, Gordon suppresses the discourse on 'forced' rehabilitation that is the goal of the montage of the documents filmed in 1917 and 1918. The repetitive circularity of its form of artistic de-familiarization essentializes, as it were, the experience of trauma and makes it a motif of the eternal return. It stylizes the immersive flooding of the man to a life-size form of presence. The cinematic logic of fragmenting the existing document can be read as a metaphor for the traumatized subject in that it negates the supposed healing of the trauma of war and literally 're-takes' what has been repressed (see Fritz 2010)[15].

In *Trigger Finger* (1994), a work produced the same year, Gordon intensifies the impotence and silent exposure of the protagonist in *10 ms*$^{-1}$ into an aggressive gesture. A hand appears in the visual field and seems to be pulling the trigger of a phantom weapon with a rhythmical movement of its index finger (see *Illustration 5*). Whereas the historical source is a demonstration of a treatment in which the therapist's manual intervention stops the compulsion to shoot (see *Illustration 6*), Gordon's film sequence isolates the symptom of the shell-shocked patient.

14 "Die Übertragung des weiblich codierten psychiatrischen Vorkriegsdiskurses der 'Hysterie' und des Krankheitsbildes der 'Neurasthenie' auf die traumatisierten 'Kriegszitterer' hat ein Übriges zur Verunsicherung der männlichen Geschlechteridentität beigetragen" (Reimann 2008).

15 The freestanding projection screen allows viewers to move around Gordon's installation. Viewers can not only identify with the character via the gaze but also enter into a spatial relationship with the work, so that, potentially, "perception turns into participation" (Frohne 2008: 357).

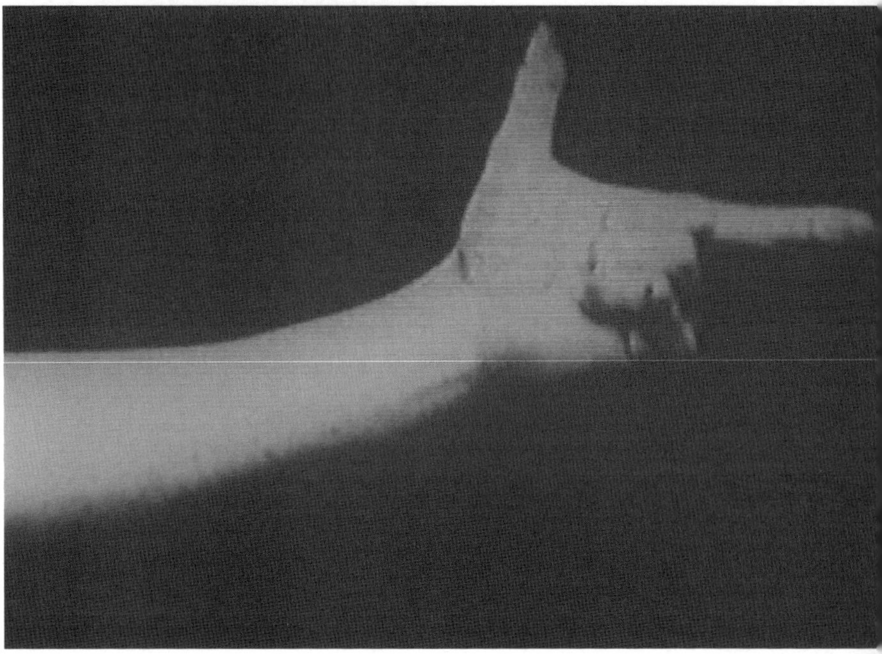

Illustration 5:
Douglas Gordon, Trigger Finger *(1994). Video installation, single screen, 10 min. 5 sec. (loop). Collection Museum für Gegenwartskunst, Zurich; Charley Szwajcer, Antwerp; Sammlung Goetz, Munich.*

In his metaphorical reading of the historical document, the uncontrollable gesture condenses into a symbolic figure for the psychological internalization of the traumatic experience, which can, at any moment, affect the civil society as a potential involuntary act or suicidal act of desperation[16]. In Gordon's alienated sequences, the rhetoric of a didactic film is turned against an objective that legitimizes war by drawing attention to the 'unfathomable and incomprehensible' quality of the psychological damage as the 'real' (see Fritz 2010). Like Farocki's film *Immersion*, they reveal the cynicism of the military apparatus, which makes the downplaying of the consequential damage of deploy-

16 Johan Frederik Hartle refers to soldiers traumatized by deployment in Iraq and Afghanistan as 'the ticking time bombs' ("die tickenden Zeitbomben"; 2010b: 111) that could explode at any time.

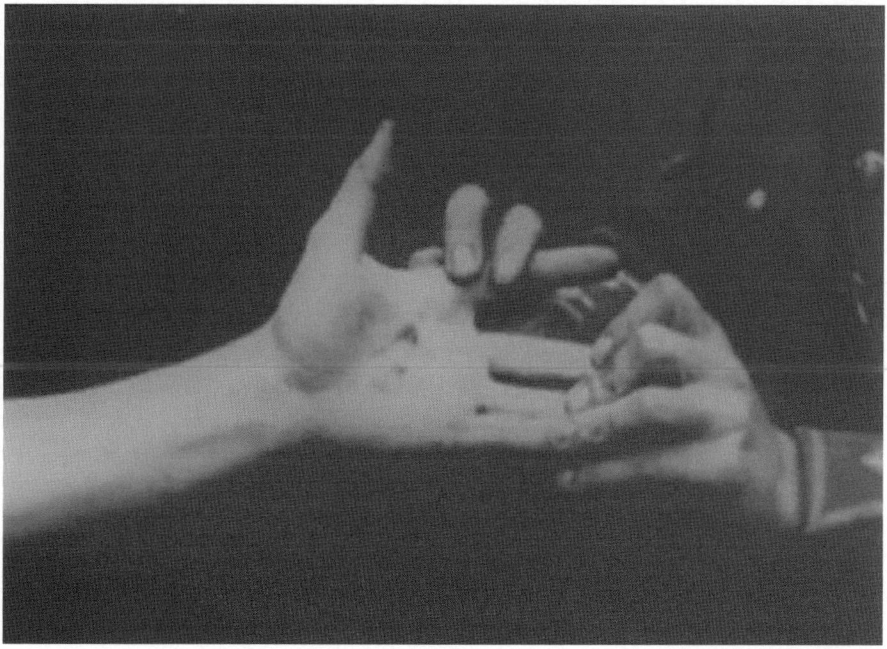

Illustration 6:
Film still from War Neuroses: Netley Hospital, 1917, Seale Hayne Military Hospital, 1918 *(1918). London, Wellcome Film Collection.*

ment in war plausible, while at the same time naturalizing the losses and traumatizations on the enemy's side as collateral damage.

Gordon's film *10 ms^{-1}* and Farocki's film *Immersion* both point to a genealogy of empirically and scientifically generated visual material that serves to propagate methods of supposed 'humanizing' of military deployments and situates itself in a context of overlapping discourse of media history, psychopathology, and war technology[17]. At the Salpêtrière in Paris in the late 19th century, Jean-Martin Charcot, Sigmund Freud's teacher, was already using drawings and photographs to document his experiments with female patients, who were, for their part, crucially

17 The evolution of media runs parallel to the automation of war. From Friedrich Kittler's approach to media archaeology we know how the history of war technology is continued in the chronology of the media (see 1999; 2010).

involved in the visual constructions of the symptoms he attributed to 'hysteria'. As Georges Didi-Huberman (see 2003) has shown, these clinical iconographies were, to a not insignificant degree, also the result of a dramatic competition among the female patients, who were trying to win Charcot's attention by emphatically reenacting the symptoms he described on the stage of the medical consultation. Gordon's alienation of the quotations from the pedagogical narrative of the film *War Neuroses* takes up the thread of this media discourse, as does Farocki's *Immersion*, which is about equating virtualized weapons systems with the overcoming of real war traumas by using a compatible training program called *Virtual Iraq*[18]. The dehumanizing attraction of this military apparatus is revealed in the contrary immersion effect of Farocki's film, which causes its viewers to be abruptly disappointed as soon as the scene is revealed to be nothing but a marketing maneuver to promote the allegedly therapeutic software.

Already in Farocki's earlier films, especially the *Auge/Maschine I–III* (*Eye/Machine I–III*) trilogy he produced between 2001 and 2003, the degree to which perception is modulated is clearly evident in the visual cone of the computer simulation of military operations. In a maneuver that is experienced as playful, enemy targets are perceived as electronically camouflaged chimeras. The look of such precision bombings, which were introduced during the first Gulf War in 1991 as a new form of clinical warfare, suggests the possibility of fighting without the direct participation of people. From the perspective of the pilot, this logic of distance applies to both sides participating in the conflict, since the enemy positions exist only as symbolic representations on the monitor. The monopoly on visual representation held by the United States military denied the world direct visual contact with the consequences of warfare: "At the same time, it was impossible to distinguish photographs from computer-simulated images. This loss of the 'authentic image' also rendered obsolete the role of the human eye as historical witness" (Farocki 2008).

The casualties or consequences of destruction were hidden from view. In his diary of the war, Farocki states: 'Here, the waging of war

18 This software was developed at the Institute for Creative Technologies, a research laboratory at the University of Southern California funded by the United States Army, and is based on the game *Full Spectrum Warrior*, which was also made available as a military recruitment tool in the early part of the first decade of the 21st century (see Halpern 2008; qtd. Weiner 2011: 84).

coincides with its reporting' ("Kriegs-Führung und -berichterstattung fallen hier zusammen"; 2003). In this new visual rhetoric, the eye becomes identical with the weapon, the bomb identical with the reporter. Seen through the visual cone of computer simulation, military operations have the appearance of ludic maneuvers. Enemy targets are fired on in the guise of electronic phantoms. The term 'precision bombing' suggests that combative action is taken without direct human involvement. Vision machines are produced with the aid of computer technology, yet we become blind to the devastation wreaked by such machines. In a process of autopoietic feedback, the machine exercises the same control over the viewing of successful strikes as it does over their execution. Military might takes on a new dimension in the form of digital weapons: the task of tracking down and destroying the enemy falls not to human beings but to intelligent machines ('smart bombs'), which are controlled remotely and literally blind to the opponent, whose location is identified not by the human eye but by an electronic tracking system. Of this computerized reference to the world Norbert Bolz says:

> Where the immaterial pixel configurations of computer simulations disintegrate the appearance of unchanging representation, the question of a reference becomes pointless. And nature, the most famous product of the reflections of humanist culture, becomes recognizable as a programmed environment under new media conditions.[19]

Targets, people, and weapons become of identical significance in the visual reference systems of the filtered, albeit immersive, space of augmented reality. "In this virtual world", the political scientist James Der Derian writes, "dying and killing becomes less plausible – and all the more possible" (2001: 8; qtd. Hartle 2010a: 49).

3. The Disillusionment of War

> It will be claimed that example breeds example, that if the attitude of cure induces cure, the attitude of murder will induce murder. Everything depends upon the manner and the purity with which the thing is done. [...] There is a risk in-

19 "Wo immaterielle Pixelkonfigurationen in Computersimulationen den Schein einer stabilen Gegenständlichkeit auflösen, wird die Frage nach einer Referenz sinnlos. Und Natur, das berühmteste Reflexionsprodukt der humanistischen Kultur, wird unter den neuen Medienbedingungen als programmierte Umwelt erkennbar." (Bolz 1994: 10)

> volved, but in the present circumstances I believe it is a risk worth running. (Artaud 1958: 82f.)

In his essay "Thoughts for the Times on War and Death" (see 1957), written in 1915 when confronted with World War I, Freud strips the reader of any hope that a pacifist attitude could result in wars being eliminated entirely in the future. Rather, he attributes the 'disillusioning' quality of war to the way in which the real comes back in a traumatic manner. The denial of one's own death is maintained by encouraging the idea that war only leads to the death of others, while the façade of civilization breaks down under the conditions of a state monopoly on injustice, and free rein is granted to the repressed drives of death[20].

The incomprehensible aspect of war is transformed into a phantasm, into the very vision that the title *Immersion* alludes to. Because Farocki evokes the crucial point of culmination of the event – the battle scene – indirectly, as if it were the visualized imagination of the test subject, he fundamentally calls into question the "powers of speech vis-à-vis the event" (Derrida 2007: 447) – contrary to the regime of representation of this genre of Hollywood films, in which this very moment is intensified into an immersive total experience in a crescendo of visual technology and visual aesthetics. Instead, by exposing the construction of the scene by actors, it becomes clear that it is impossible to ever grasp an event reliably (cf. ibid.). The simulation, which prevents direct visual contact with the events by means of the game's interface, is characterized as a performative appropriation of a remembered situation. Farocki's dramatization manifests the recognition that "what is shown to us live is already, not a saying or showing of the event, but its production" (ibid.). Farocki draws our attention to the fact that events, particularly those of existential dimension, can at most be visualized as a trace. As a wound, the event lives on in human experience and also in the film as a symbolic inscription that in turn

20 Freud's remarks can be applied to the modern experience of war in general when he writes: "Two things in this war have aroused our sense of disillusionment: the low morality shown externally by states which in their internal relations pose as the guardians of moral standards, and the brutality shown by individuals whom, as participants in the highest human civilization, one would not have thought capable of such behavior" (1957: 280). ("Zweierlei in diesem Kriege hat unsere Enttäuschung rege gemacht: die geringe Sittlichkeit der Staaten nach außen, die sich nach innen als die Wächter der sittlichen Normen gebärden, und die Brutalität im Benehmen der Einzelnen, denen man als Teilnehmer an der höchsten menschlichen Kultur ähnliches nicht zugetraut hat"; 1915/1924: 10).

testifies to the transience of the event. Farocki's perspective on the potential of simulation, which itself becomes an event of reenactment here, makes analogies between the violations of physical boundaries, the territorial and moral transgressions of war, and the methods of visual technology. These methods, for their part, tend to remove the boundaries of the frame. They create an immersive experience of visual space and radiate on the viewer by means of the dramaturgy of emotions. Farocki shows us that, just as the body can never remain within the contours of its biological demarcation, the space of simulation as a sphere of influence has an effect beyond itself both atmospherically and emotionally.

Through deferred presentation, which like an image in memory is enriched by fictional elements, the event emerges as a visionary one and, in Democritus' sense, a symbolic 'emanation' of something impossible. It is this hypertrophy of the ambiguous visual phenomenon that oscillates between realism and imagination that conditions the event-like character of the aesthetic experience produced by the image. Simulation is transformed here into the writing of history, which seems to produce post factum the very events it recapitulates – a practice of constitutive "deferred action" (1950: 356) that Freud attributes to the psyche itself.

This ambiguity between animating and alienating makes simulation a source of intellectual uncertainty, since it reveals the "deferred action" of denied traumatic history by means of the retroactive return of images, and hence it contributes to the "disillusionment of [...] war" (Freud 1957: 275) ("Die Enttäuschung des Krieges"; Freud 1915/1924: 1). The disembodied logic of simulation machines that Farocki addresses in his films returns in the therapy sessions of the traumatized as the flip side of a dehumanized war technology. Robbed of visual contact to one's real environment, one experiences the channeling of his or her perception into schematizations of the ethnically coded Other. In such immersion scenarios, the enemy appears as a phantasm of a menacing 'reality' lurking behind seemingly harmless surfaces. The invisible presence of something 'real' represents the vanishing point of omnipresent threat. It is the epitome of the immersion experience. Schematically, the simulation reproduced the type of the Arab as the inscrutable civilian. As the hidden Other in the garb of a foreigner, he embodies a hostility that fuses into unrecognizable paranoia and legitimizes the necessity of the military apparatus. In the simulation, the alien, as an instrument for sharpening reaction, breaks out strategically

Illustration 7:
Beate Geissler, Oliver Sann, Are you dead? Yes, I am. Living Room, Schwend *(2008). Photograph from the series* personal kill, *taken at the Joint Multinational Readiness Center of the U.S. Army in Hohenfels, Oberpfalz. Copyright Beate Geissler/Oliver Sann, courtesy ftc Berlin.*

in all directions as uncontrollable terror. The space of immersion becomes the field of the uncontrollable, which is to be eliminated.

Rather than creating simulation scenarios as spaces for reflection in which these schemata could be overcome by addressing trauma, the reactive matrix reinforces the reaction patterns that were pre-programmed in preparation for deployment in war. The encounter with the unfamiliar is experienced as a call to battle, thereby cementing the perspective of a world order that can only be defended by war. In this reactive schema, the trauma itself is stylized into the enemy who has to be controlled, since a perspective of war that has become engrained into everyday practice and is decisive for these simulation scenarios

Illustration 8:
Beate Geissler, Oliver Sann, Are you dead? Yes, I am. Kitchen II, Schwend *(2008). Photograph from the series* personal kill, *taken at the Joint Multinational Readiness Center of the U.S. Army in Hohenfels, Oberpfalz. Copyright Beate Geissler/Oliver Sann, courtesy ftc Berlin.*

has to mask the subject's existential dependence on a symbolic connection to others. Otherwise, this symbolic connection to others would penetrate the consciousness of the test subjects as a disturbance of their programmed perception, as Judith Butler has described with reference to Melanie Klein: "If I destroy the other, I destroy the one on whom I depend in order to survive, and so I threaten my own survival with my destructive act" (2009: 45; qtd. Hartle 2010b: 111). But when training soldiers for contact with the enemy, the military apparatus suppresses a culture of possible commonalities in forms of expression and encounter. With its friend-foe logic in the immersion space, the 'military dispositif' seeks to mask the real-world certainty

Illustration 9: Beate Geissler, Oliver Sann, Mutter Theresa, 90 *[nickname and pulse rate at the moment the photograph was shot] (2000). Photograph from the series* shooter. *Copyright Beate Geissler/ Oliver Sann, courtesy ftc Berlin.*

that, as Butler emphasizes elsewhere, we are existentially dependent on the Other.

Models for immersive role-playing in 3-D visualizations in virtual space to design analogous spaces in which militaries can develop training programs for hand-to-hand combat have been in use since the mid-1990s. In so-called Military Operations in Urban Terrain (MOUT) scenarios, locations, buildings, and interiors are modeled along with dislocated American bases and replicas of the real world of the cultural Other to serve as training areas for military deployment. They simulate the topographic infrastructure of the sites of war and the cultural features of living conditions there. Beate Geissler and Oliver Sann sought out such training grounds in Bavaria and the United States and documented the basic character of such training architecture for their series *personal kill* (see *Illustrations 7* and *8*). 'Personal kill', a term used in Vietnam and later in Iraq and Afghanistan, refers to the psychological situation of direct contact with the enemy in which the killing of an opponent is immediately experienced. It is such direct confrontation that leads to the greatest traumatization of soldiers. In order to minimize the vulnerability of the soldier's psyche, the U.S. Army relies on the success of targeted training in simulated MOUTs. Schematizations of the Other, simplistically imposed by the use of extras in costume for military training sessions, reproduce stereotypes of the Orient, which are staged as a clear antithesis to our own culture without fine distinctions.

The series *personal kill* identifies precisely the extreme military situations that occur in the computer simulations like maneuvers in a game with no further consequences but represent in reality the confrontation with a boundary of the symbolic and hence lead with great statistical probability to traumatization. In the virtual battle scenes, meanwhile, there is no visual representation of one's own elimination. If one is hit, the training simply ends. Injuries of those who are exercising the visual apparatus have no representation in the computer program. The visual transmission breaks off, and the 'game' begins again. Encoded as a game, in which a war is camouflaged and its real destructive consequences become a purely visual spectacle, the simulation undermines the taboo that applies in civil society to the fascination of an aesthetic of armed violence. The fetishizing of computer games and hyperreal film scenarios in our contemporary culture is thus not uninvolved in establishing a policy of the worst-case scenario and the constitution of a subject formed by immersive training for this logic of confrontation.

In conclusion, let us return again to the question of the immersive nature of the 'military dispositif': In "On the Advantage and Disadvantage of History for Life", Friedrich Nietzsche writes that it is not permitted to step out of the coordinate system of past and future, since only animals and obliviously playing children live in the 'lost paradise' that liberates human existence from the "never to be completed imperfect tense" (1980: 9) ("nie zu vollendendes Imperfectum"; 1874: 1). From the outset, a mythical dimension is attributed to those immersed in the present, in what is depicted as a happy state of exception, which also points to an archaic basic structure even in Nietzsche's representation of it. The animal stands for an instinctive and reflexive relationship to one's surroundings, which can also imply the struggle for survival, while the child's game as a topos of immersive absorption refers to the innocent character of a structure for agency free of purpose, a process borne by the pure flow of activity[21].

A look at the *shooter* series by Geissler and Sann can confirm that this immersive effect of the game, which is, no doubt, also charged with myth, is a force that shapes reality. In preparation for this series, the team of artists studied the expressions of video-game players during local area network (LAN) battle sessions they arranged in their studio. Their portrait photographs capture the exact moment when the participant is eliminated in the game (see *Illustration 9*). The idiosyn-

21 Thon bases his explanation of the concept of 'flow' on Mihály Csíkszentmihályi's study (see 1990). According to Thon, the state of flow is obtained "when the difficulty of an activity matches a person's abilities" (2008: 37). Ludic immersion occurs only "when the abilities of the player and the level of challenge of the game are balanced and could also be described using the concept of flow" (ibid.: 40).

Illustration 10:
Beate Geissler, Oliver Sann, High-frequency trading workspace 10, Willis Tower, Chicago *(2011). Photograph from the series* volatile smile. *Copyright Beate Geissler/Oliver Sann, courtesy ftc Berlin.*

crasies of their facial expressions show how the supposedly obsolete body is visually altered by such simulated cyber maneuvers in virtual space. The titles of these likenesses are composed of the pseudonyms the players have chosen for themselves and their respective pulse frequencies at the moment of virtual death, which coincides with the moment the picture was taken. The inscription of emotions into the physical presence of the players offer an impressive picture of the complex relationships between actions in virtual surroundings and their (de)formative effects in the material world. The *shooter* series is a portrait of a generation that has an intimate relationship to these gaming worlds, which are closely related genealogically to the 'military dispositif'. Contemporary alliances between the electronic entertainment industry and the military apparatus model a symbolic space centered on a polarizing perception of the self and others[22]. But as other series of photographs by Geissler and Sann surely make clear, immersion in the culture of games is a kind of preliminary socializing stage not just for deployment in the military but even more so for risky maneuvers in the virtual spaces of the global economic systems that are inhabited by their players. These coherent ways of life are based on self-contained references to the world, remote from civility and ethical considerations. Geissler and

22 Hartle, quoting Stephen Graham (see 2007), has remarked: "Since 2002, *America's Army* remains the most successful of all war games circulated by the Pentagon. *Full Spectrum Warrior* followed in 2003. The political coding of the virtual play space could not be clearer: 'Both games centre overwhelmingly on the task of occupying stylized Arab cities. Their immersive simulations work powerfully to equate these environments with "terrorism" and to stress that they need "pacification" or "cleansing" by military means.'" (2010a: 47)

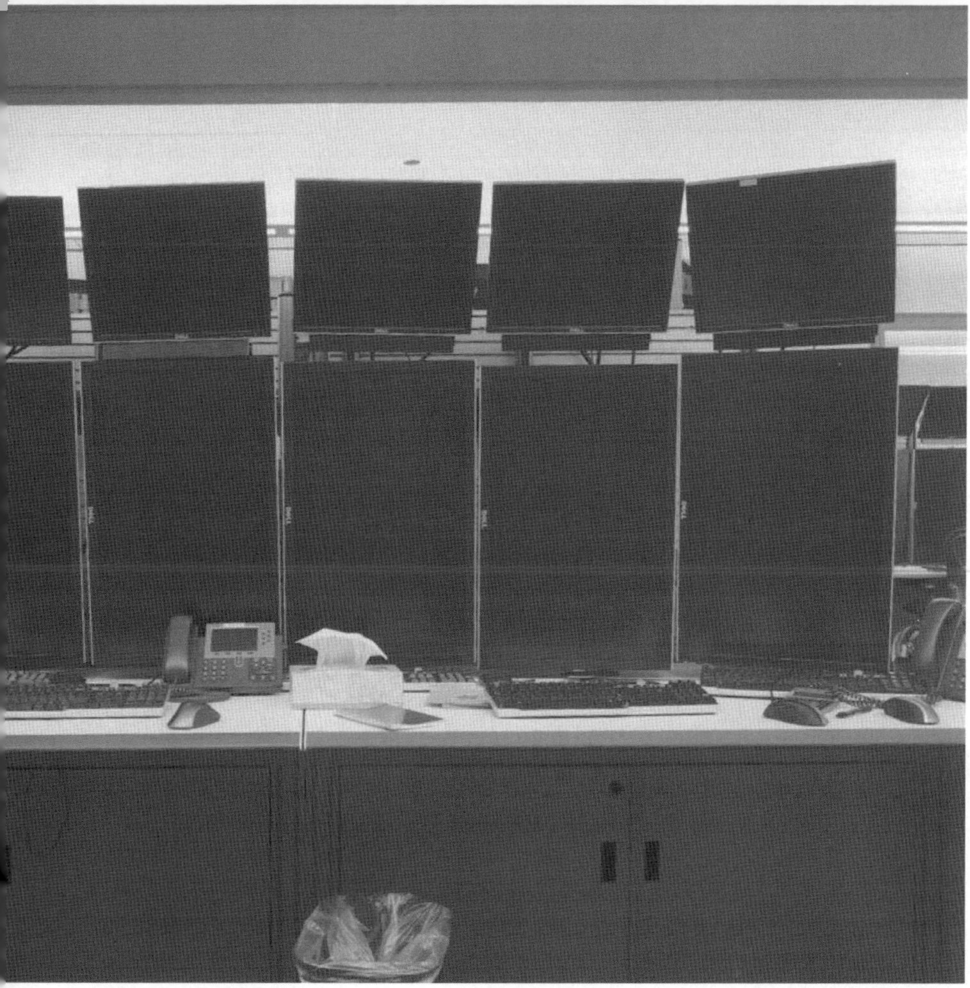

Sann's equally documentary and suggestive look at the sober workplaces of global trading companies in Chicago (see *Illustration 10*) suggests that navigating these crowded spheres of action is by no means limited to a playful, inherent phenomenon of the gaming interface; rather, real-world constellations are profoundly permeated by the strategic goals that are not merely practiced in immersion scenarios but leave psychological, physical, and social traces whose traumas are intertwined with all aspects of the living environment[23].

Farocki's films, Gordon's found-footage installations, and Geissler and Sann's photo series draw attention to immersive tactics that are embedded in the repertoire of today's reality effects. These immersive

23 The *shooter* series was followed by further cycles of photographs that address the effects of virtual actions – in the financial industry, for example – on private lives through the collapse of the real estate market in the United States and congruencies between technological and social systems. Geissler and Sann conducted extensive research before taking these photographs (see Holmes, ed. 2014).

tactics are attributed to the matrix of a visual culture that provides new forms of historical reconstruction and frameworks of meaning for every generation. By transferring the viewers' horizon of experience, these art works recast the historiography of immersive war technologies and their capacity to kill and heal by revealing that the alleged access to the 'real' is always a mediated action. As viewers suddenly become aware that they have been misled through immersion, it is only by disturbing the aesthetic order, namely by the "production of a liberating difference" (Mondzain 2009: 27), that they achieve an interpretive perspective on the event. Rather than employing immersion as a vehicle for fusing experience, the works by Farocki, Gordon, and Geissler and Sann discussed here open up the framework of the machinery of strategic effects only to include the moment of productive disillusionment[24]. Hence they are closer to insight into the actual 'disillusionment of war' than the deceptive mimesis of omnipresent simulation scenarios is able to suggest.

In memory of Harun Farocki.

References

Agamben, Giorgio (2003). *Stato di eccezione*. Turin: Bollati Boringhieri.

— (2005). *State of Exception*. Transl. Kevin Attell. Chicago, IL: University of Chicago Press.

Artaud, Antonin (1933/1985). "En finir avec les chefs-d'oeuvre". *Le Théâtre et son double*. Paris: Editions Gallimard. 115–129.

— (1958). "No More Masterpieces". *The Theatre and Its Double*. Transl. Mary Caroline Richards. New York, NY: Grove Press. 74–84.

Baehr, Peter (2001). "The 'Iron Cage' and the 'Shell as Hard as Steel':

24 An aesthetic of disillusionment is achieved by Harun Farocki's split-screen montages. He thereby claims the necessity of a discursive space that has to be defended against the politics of evidence and to secure, as Philippe-Alain Michaud writes, "the distance between the images, which tends to invert the parameters of time and space, produces tensions between the objects depicted and, inductively, between the levels of reality from which these objects proceed" (2004: 253; see also Frohne 2006).

Parsons, Weber, and the Stahlhartes Gehäuse Metaphor in *The Protestant Ethic and the Spirit of Capitalism*". *History and Theory* 40/2: 153–169.

Barck, Karlheinz, ed. (2010). *Ästhetische Grundbegriffe: Historisches Wörterbuch in sieben Bänden.* 7 Vols. Stuttgart: Metzler.

Bieger, Laura (2011). "Ästhetik der Immersion: Wenn Räume wollen. Immersives Erleben als Raumerleben". Gertrud Lehnert, ed. *Raum und Gefühl: Der Spatial Turn und die neue Emotionsforschung.* Bielefeld: transcript. 75–95.

Blumenberg, Hans (1979/1997). *Schiffbruch mit Zuschauer: Paradigma einer Daseinsmetapher.* Frankfurt am Main: Suhrkamp.

— (1997). *Shipwreck with Spectator: Paradigm of a Metaphor for Existence.* Transl. Steven Rendall. Cambridge, MA/London: MIT Press.

Blümlinger, Christa (2011). "Krieg als Herausforderung an den Realismus technischer Bilder / War as a Challenge to Digital Realism". Yilmaz Dziewior, ed. *Harun Farocki: Weiche Montagen / Soft Montages.* Transl. Toby Axelrod. Exh. cat. Bregenz: Kunsthaus Bregenz, 23 October 2010 – 9 January 2011. Cologne: König. 34–46.

Böhme, Hartmut (1997). "Aby M. Warburg (1866–1929)". Axel Michaels, ed. *Klassiker der Religionswissenschaft: Von Friedrich Schleiermacher bis Mircea Eliade.* Munich: C. H. Beck. 133–156.

Bolz, Norbert (1994). "Computer als Medium: Einleitung". Norbert Bolz, Friedrich Kittler, Christoph Tholen, eds. *Computer als Medium.* Munich: Fink. 9–16.

Bourke, Joanna (1996). *Dismembering the Male: Men's Bodies, Britain, and the Great War.* Chicago, IL: University of Chicago Press.

Brown, Katrina M. (2004). *DG: Douglas Gordon.* London: Tate Publishing.

Butler, Judith (2009). *Frames of War: When Is Life Grievable?* London: Verso.

Csíkszentmihályi, Mihály (1990). *Flow: The Psychology of Optimal Experience.* New York, NY: Harper & Row.

Der Derian, James (2001). *Virtuous War: Mapping the Military-Industrial-Media-Entertainment Network.* Boulder, CO: Westview Press.

Derrida, Jacques (2001). "Une certaine possibilité impossible de dire l'événement". *Dire l'événement, est-ce possible?* Paris: L'Harmattan. 79–112.

— (2007). "A Certain Impossible Possibility of Saying the Event".

Transl. Gila Walker. *Critical Inquiry* 33/2: 441–461.
Didi-Huberman, Georges (1982). *Invention d l'hystérie: Charcot et l'iconographie photographique de la Salpêtrière*. Paris: Macula.
— (2003). *Invention of Hysteria: Charcot and the Photographic Iconography of the Salpêtrière*. Transl. Alisa Hartz. Cambridge, MA/ London: MIT Press.
Eissler, Kurt R. (1986). *Freud as an Expert Witness: The Discussion of War Neuroses between Freud and Wagner-Jauregg*. Madison, CT: International UP.
Elsaesser, Thomas (2002: online). "Introduction: Harun Farocki". *Senses of Cinema* 21. http://sensesofcinema.com/2002/21/farocki_intro/. [01/06/2013].
—, ed. (2004). *Harun Farocki: Working on the Sightlines*. Amsterdam: Amsterdam UP.
Farocki, Harun (2003: online). "Kriegstagebuch (18.03.2003)". *new filmkritik*. http://newfilmkritik.de/archiv/2003/03/. [06/06/2013].
— (2008: online). "*Eye Machine 1, 2,* and *3* (2001–2003)". *Art Torrents*. http://arttorrents.blogspot.ch/2008/01/harun-farocki-eye-machine-1-2-and-3.html. [23/07/2014].
Flammarion, Camille (1871). *L'Atmosphère: Description des grands phénomènes de la nature*. Paris: Hachette.
— (1873). *The Atmosphere*. Ed. James Glaisher. Transl. C. B. Pitman. London: Sampson Low, Marston, Low & Searle.
Fliedl, Ilsebill Barta (1992). "'Vom Triumph zum Seelendrama. Suchen und Finden oder Die Abentheuer eines Denklustigen': Anmerkungen zu den gebärdensprachlichen Bilderreihen Aby Warburgs". Ilsebill Barta Fliedl, Christoph Geissmar, eds. *Die Beredsamkeit des Leibes: Zur Körpersprache in der Kunst*. Exh. cat. Vienna: Albertina, 13 May – 11 July 1992. Salzburg/Vienna: Residenz. 165–170.
Freud, Sigmund (1895/1987). "Entwurf einer Psychologie". *Nachtragsband: Texte aus den Jahren 1885 bis 1938*. Ed. Angela Richards. Frankfurt am Main: Fischer. 387–477.
— (1915/1924). *Zeitgemäßes über Krieg und Tod*. Leipzig/Vienna/Zurich: Internationaler Psychoanalytischer Verlag.
— (1950). "Project for a Scientific Psychology". *Pre-Psycho-Analytic Publications and Unpublished Drafts*. Ed. and transl. James Strachey. London: Hogarth Press. 281–397.
— (1957). "Thoughts for the Times on War and Death". *On the History of Psycho-Analytic Movement: Papers on Metapsychology and*

Other Works, 1914–1916. Ed. and transl. James Strachey. London: Hogarth Press. 273–300.

Fritz, Elisabeth (2010). “Das Reale wiederholen – Die Wirklichkeit zitieren: Überlegungen zum dokumentarischen Filmzitat am Beispiel von Douglas Gordons *10 ms*$^{-1}$ (1994)”. Unpublished manuscript from a lecture presented at the International Summer School “Um/Bruch”, Department of Art History at the University of Zurich, 13 – 16 September 2010.

Frohne, Ursula (2006). “Media Wars: Strategische Bilder des Krieges”. Annegret Jürgens-Kirchhoff, Agnes Matthias, eds. *Warshots: Krieg, Kunst & Medien*. Weimar: VDG. 161–186.

— (2008). “Dissolution of the Frame: Immersion and Participation in Video Installations”. Tanya Leighton, ed. *Art and the Moving Image: A Critical Reader*. London: Tate Publishing. 355–370.

Furtwängler, Frank (2006). “Computerspiele am Rande des metakommunikativen Zusammenbruchs”. Britta Neitzel, Rolf F. Nohr, eds. *Das Spiel mit dem Medium: Partizipation – Immersion – Interaktion*. Marburg: Schüren. 154–169.

Graham, Stephen (2007). “War and the City”. *New Left Review* 44: 121–132.

Halpern, Sue (2008: online). “Virtual Iraq: Using Simulation to Treat a New Generation of Veterans”. *The New Yorker*. http://www.newyorker.com/reporting/2008/05/19/080519fa_fact_halpern?currentPage=all. [11/04/2014].

Han, Byung-Chul (2010). *Müdigkeitsgesellschaft*. Berlin: Matthes & Seitz.

Hartle, Johan Frederik (2010a). “Simulation”. Hartle, ed. 47–49.

— (2010b). “Trauma”. Hartle, ed. 111–113.

— (2010c). “Warban Urfare”. Hartle, ed. 7–11.

— , ed. (2010). *Beate Geissler & Oliver Sann: personal kill*. Nürnberg: Verlag für Moderne Kunst.

Holert, Tom, Mark Terkessidis, eds. (2002). *Entsichert: Krieg als Massenkultur im 21. Jahrhundert*. Cologne: Kiepenheuer & Witsch.

— (2003). “Zwischen Ästhetisierung und Ikonografie: Zur Faszination von Kriegsbildern bei Simon Reynolds, Martha Rosler und Wolfgang Tillmans”. Weibel/Holler-Schuster, eds. 290–303.

Holmes, Brian, ed. (2014). *Volatile Smile*. Nuremberg: Verlag für Moderne Kunst.

Jünger, Ernst (1932/1982). *Der Arbeiter: Herrschaft und Gestalt*. Stuttgart: Klett-Cotta.

Kelly, Michael, ed. (1998). *Encyclopedia of Aesthetics*. 4 Vols. Oxford et al.: OUP.

Kienitz, Sabine (2001). "'Fleischgewordenes Elend': Kriegsinvalidität und Körperbilder als Teil einer Erfahrungsgeschichte des Ersten Weltkrieges". Nikolaus Buschmann, Horst Carl, eds. *Die Erfahrung des Krieges: Erfahrungsgeschichtliche Perspektiven von der Französischen Revolution bis zum Zweiten Weltkrieg*. Paderborn et al.: Schöningh. 215–238.

Kittler, Friedrich A. (1986). *Grammophon, Film, Typewriter*. Berlin: Brinkmann & Bose.

— (1999). *Gramophone, Film, Typewriter*. Transl. Geoffrey Winthrop-Young, Michael Wutz. Stanford, CA: Stanford UP.

— (2002). *Optische Medien: Berliner Vorlesung 1999*. Berlin: Merve.

— (2010). *Optical Media: Berlin Lectures 1999*. Cambridge: Polity Press.

Lombard, Matthew, Theresa Ditton (1997: online). "At the Heart of It All: The Concept of Presence". *Journal of Computer-Mediated Communication* 3/2. http://onlinelibrary.wiley.com/doi/10.1111/j.1083-6101.1997.tb00072.x/full. [15/04/2014].

Lorenz, Maren (2012). "Tiefe Wunden: Gewalterfahrung in den Kriegen der Frühen Neuzeit". Ulrich Bielefeld, Heinz Bude, Bern Greiner, eds. *Gesellschaft – Gewalt – Vertrauen: Jan Philipp Reemtsma zum 60. Geburtstag.* Hamburg: Hamburger Edition. 332–354.

Michaud, Philippe-Alain (2004). *Aby Warburg and the Image in Motion*. New York, NY: Zone Books.

Mondzain, Marie-José (2002). *L'Image peut-elle tuer?* Paris: Bayard.

— (2009). "Can Images Kill?" Transl. Sally Shafto. *Critical Inquiry* 36/1: 20–51.

Nietzsche, Friedrich (1874). *Vom Nutzen und Nachtheil der Historie für das Leben*. Leipzig: Fritzsch.

— (1980). *On the Advantage and Disadvantage of History for Life*. Transl. Peter Preuss. Indianapolis, IN: Hackett.

Reimann, Aribert (2008: online). "Der Erste Weltkrieg: Urkatastrophe oder Katalysator?" *Bundeszentrale für Politische Bildung*. http://www.bpb.de/apuz/28201/der-erste-weltkrieg-urkatastrophe-oder-katalysator?p=all. [01/06/2013].

Robichon, François (1994). "Ästhetik der Sublimierung: Die französische Kriegsmalerei". Rainer Rother, ed. *Die letzten Tage der Menschheit: Bilder des Ersten Weltkrieges*. Exh. cat. Berlin: Deutsches Historisches Museum, 10 June – 28 August 1994. Berlin: Ars Nicolai. 285–300.

Schmitt, Carl (1963). *Theorie des Partisanen: Zwischenbemerkung zum Begriff des Politischen.* Berlin: Duncker & Humblot.

— (2004). *The Theory of the Partisan: A Commentary/Remark on the Concept of the Political.* Transl. A. C. Goodson. East Lansing, MI: Michigan State UP.

Silverman, Katja, Harun Farocki (1998). *Speaking about Godard.* New York, NY/London: New York UP.

Sloterdijk, Peter (2002). *Luftbeben: An den Quellen des Terrors.* Frankfurt am Main: Suhrkamp.

Spangenberg, Peter M. (1991). "Mediale Kopplungen und die Konstruktivität des Bewusstseins". Hans Ulrich Gumbrecht, Karl Ludwig Pfeiffer, eds. *Paradoxien, Dissonanzen, Zusammenbrüche: Situationen offener Epistemologie.* Frankfurt am Main: Suhrkamp. 791–808.

Speckmann, Thomas (2013). "Früh traumatisierte Neuzeit: Folgen elementarer Gewalterfahrungen in Kriegen des siebzehnten Jahrhunderts". *Frankfurter Allgemeine Zeitung*, 12 June.

Terkessidis, Mark (2003). "Doku-Malerei und Simulations-Realismus: Über die Veränderungen im Verhältnis von Kriegsfotografie und Kriegsfilm". Weibel/Holler-Schuster, eds. 282–289.

Thon, Jan-Noël (2008). "Immersion Revisited: On the Value of a Contested Concept". Olli Leino, Hanna Wirman, Amyris Fernandez, eds. *Extending Experiences: Structure, Analysis and Design of Computer Game Player Experiences.* Rovaniemi: Lapland UP. 29–43.

Virilio, Paul (1977). *Vitesse et politique: Essai de dromologie.* Paris: Editions Gallimard.

— (1984). *Guerre et cinéma: Logistique de la perception.* Paris: Editions du Cahiers du Cinéma.

— (1989). *War and Cinema: The Logistics of Perception.* Transl. Patrick Camiller. London/New York, NY: Verso.

— (2006). *Speed and Politics: An Essay on Dromology.* Transl. Mark Polizzotti. Los Angeles, CA: Semiotext(e).

Warnke, Martin (1980). "Vier Stichworte: Ikonologie, Pathosformel, Polarität und Ausgleich, Schlagbilder und Bilderfahrzeuge". Werner Hofmann, Georg Syamken, Martin Warnke. *Die Menschenrechte des Auges: Über Aby Warburg.* Frankfurt am Main: Europäische Verlagsanstalt. 61–83.

Weber, Max (1920). "Die protestantische Ethik und der Geist des Kapitalismus". *Gesammelte Aufsätze zur Religionssoziologie.* Vol. 1.

Tübingen: Mohr. 1–206.
— (1930). *The Protestant Ethic and the Spirit of Capitalism*. Transl. Talcott Parsons. London: G. Allen & Unwin.

Weibel, Peter, Günther Holler-Schuster, eds. (2003). *M_ARS: Kunst und Krieg*. Exh. cat. Graz: Neue Galerie Graz am Landesmuseum Joanneum, 10 January – 26 March 2003. Ostfildern-Ruit: Hatje Cantz.

Weiner, Andrew Stefan (2011). "Pretexts: The Evidence of the Event". *Afterall* 26: 79–87.

Werneburg, Brigitte (1995: online). "Der Arbeiter und sein Bilderbuch: Der Wechsel des Mediums in Ernst Jüngers Fotobüchern". *Website of Brigitte Werneburg*. http://werneburg.nikha.org/?id=-499&sn=1. [23/05/2013].

Wolf, Werner (2013). "Aesthetic Illusion". Werner Wolf, Walter Bernhart, Andreas Mahler, eds. *Immersion and Distance: Aesthetic Illusion in Literature and Other Media*. Amsterdam/New York, NY: Rodopi. 1–63.

World Health Organization (1992). *The ICD-10 Classification of Mental and Behavioural Disorders: Clinical Descriptions and Diagnostic Guidelines*. Geneva: World Health Organization.

Illustration 1:
Protesters in Na'vi costume,
Bil'in, 2012. Photograph
by Oren Ziv, Activestills.org.

Immersion between Recursiveness and Reflexivity: *Avatar*

Thomas Elsaesser

This essay approaches the topic of immersion from the perspective of reflexivity and recursiveness. I consider different forms of reflexivity – commonly understood as the opposite of immersion and empathy – that 'bind' the spectator to the cinema as 'event' rather than 'text'. Contemporary Hollywood cinema creates immersion through forms of self-reference that reflect the film industry's situational contradictions as well as engage the recipients' cognitive dissonances. My case study is James Cameron's *Avatar*, a film that evokes the idea of self-forgetful immersion, but achieves this effect through layers of self-reference and feedback loops that generate intense but floating forms of identification.

1. Immersion and Recursiveness

My contribution is devoted to the topic of immersion from a perspective which at first may seem counterintuitive, namely, the self-applied forms of reflexivity and recursiveness in Hollywood movies and their production conditions. To this end, I will begin with a few explanations. Today, the term 'immersion' is broadly defined. As this collection shows, its meanings range from classical formulations of cinematic immersion such as plunging into an artificial world through the dissolution of spatial boundaries between the viewer and the image, to a full-body experience of space and time and the somatic-affective, proprioceptive, and identificatory involvement of the recipient, all the way to the interactive transition from bodily, physical reality to a media-based, fictional computer-game environment. The term also encompasses the creation of illusion and imaginary participation in general and takes into account the tendency to consider the cinematic experience to be body-based rather than merely ocular.

Béla Balázs, perhaps the first film theorist to formulate the basic idea of cinematic immersion, famously stated:

> The agile camera carries my eye and *thus my consciousness* along: into the heart of the picture, into the middle of the space where the action takes place. I don't see anything from the outside. I am seeing everything as the acting person must see it. I am surrounded by the figures of the film and thus entwined into its action.

> I am coming along, I am driving along, I am falling along – even though I physically remain seated on the same spot.[1]

Almost diametrically opposed to all of the definitions listed here stands the term 'reflexivity', as it is most commonly used to describe precisely the distance and medial techniques or aesthetic processes of distancing that are suspended by immersion. The Hollywood film of today, in particular, not only destroys Balász's self-contained composition of the work of art but also negates the ways in which any illusion of immediacy and transparency was broken by abstract images as used by the avant-garde filmmakers of the 1920s and the non-narrative sequences in the auteur films of the 1960s. At the same time, the concept of immersion provides us with a theoretical framework for the interactive role-playing games in virtual space, made popular through new media. It thereby also assigns a new function to cinema beyond the traditional illusionistic idea of film as a transparent 'window to the world' and the anti-illusionistic metaphor of film as 'mirror of the self and the viewer'. This new function accounts for the increasingly seamless transitions, even in everyday life, from the physical world of real things to augmented reality, i. e., to environments and objects that are enhanced by sensors, chips, and electronic information with which the user interacts. Therefore, after 'window' and 'mirror', film and cinema would be better described for the 21st century as a 'door' or 'portal', as far as their relationship to these media-related changes is concerned. This also points to the necessity to reevaluate the often negatively interpreted creation of illusion and to give immersion – understood as the delegation of agency, as well as its modes of interactivity and interpassivity – a new, possibly even normative, status.

Precisely the definition of the word 'portal', namely, 'entrance', 'access', 'passage', allows me to reintroduce reflexivity and recursiveness into the debate surrounding immersion. In contrast to 'window', with its transparent yet sealed entrance, and 'mirror', as a reflective

1 "Die bewegliche Kamera nimmt mein Auge, und *damit mein Bewußtsein*, mit: mitten in das Bild, mitten in den Spielraum der Handlung hinein. Ich sehe nichts von außen. Ich sehe alles so, wie die handelnden Personen es sehen müssen. Ich bin umzingelt von den Gestalten des Films und dadurch verwickelt in seine Handlung. Ich gehe mit, ich fahre mit, ich stürze mit – obwohl ich körperlich auf demselben Platz sitzen bleibe." (Balázs 1938/1995: 215 [emphasis in the original]) Unless otherwise indicated, all translations are mine.

yet impenetrable surface, 'door' and 'portal' refer to an opening accessible from both directions, which allows for various forms of entering and bypassing, but also suggests recursive and circular movement – think revolving door, feedback loop, and Moebius band.

The topic of immersion also gives rise to the question of self-reference. Let us take, for example, a different definition: 'Immersion is a state of consciousness in which the subject, as a result of an arresting and demanding (artificial) environment, experiences a decline in his or her self-perception.'[2] Although this sounds plausible, it contains an internal contradiction, for 'decline in his or her self-perception' is not a forgetting of the self but still a form of self-awareness and thus a form of self-reference. Self-reference, on the other hand, stands in direct relationship to recursion, particularly regarding system theory and cybernetics, wherever 'processes generating structure without rigid planning instances'[3], in other words, autogenerative systems, are concerned. Although these approaches have so far not had as much of an impact in the field of film theory as in that of media theory, it seems useful – even in the analysis of complex and interconnected systems that are reliant on permanent feedback, such as Hollywood cinema – to acknowledge the productivity of operations of reflexivity and self-reference, immersion and recursiveness, autopoiesis and self-regulation, in order to explore both epistemological and historiographical questions as they affect contemporary (Hollywood) cinema.

Here, I can offer only a few initial steps toward this ambitious program. They have, in part, been taken from a book I recently published, entitled *The Persistence of Hollywood* (2012b), in which I try to take stock, so to speak, of the changes from classical to post-classical and post-Fordist Hollywood. At the same time, I want to account for the parallel developments in film theory, which, over the past fifty years, has continually oscillated between approaching and distancing itself from its subject. Consider, for example, the auteur

2 "Immersion beschreibt die Überführung in einen Bewusstseinszustand (Eindruck), bei dem sich die Wahrnehmung der eigenen Person in der realen Welt vermindert und die Identifikation mit dem 'Ich' (dem Avatar) in der virtuellen Welt vergrößert" (*Wikipedia* 2013).

3 "[…] Selbstbezüglichkeit für Strukturbildungsprozesse ohne rigide planende Instanzen" (Vehlken 2010: 1).

theory and cinephilia of the 1950s and 1960s followed by the anti-Hollywood sentiment and cinephobia of the 1970s and the renewed change of direction in the 1980s and 1990s, which, thanks to Cultural Studies, with its interest in fan cultures and cult films, finally led to a new cinephilia that has come to embrace blockbusters, computer games, and horror, slasher, and trash movies with equal euphoria.

My aim is thus to reinterpret and expand reflexivity with regard to Hollywood in order to recognize different types of reflexivity that I believe are inherent in Hollywood as a creative industry and an institutional system. In this system, reflexivity and self-reference are tools of self-regulation – that is to say, instances and mechanisms of self-control – meant to act as a protective shield to ward off and preempt interference from the outside. Hollywood's audience address, on the other hand, is aimed at continually finding new modes of accessing and entering into films. The system as a whole, in other words, confirms the door metaphor in both directions: closing and opening are its two complementary modes. In turn, this double movement serves as a constant source of friction and tension, to the point of amounting to a constitutive contradiction inherent in Hollywood's dual function of both producing 'goods' (films) and providing 'services' (the cinema experience). One consequence for us as scholars is to accept that a Hollywood movie (when considered as product as well as service) does not have the status of a text but functions as a relay, in other words, as a dynamic and reversible circuit between the film and its viewers, which equally allows for glasslike transparency, mirrorlike reflection and duplication, and even immersive experiences.

Four such types of reflexivity can be identified: 'modernist' self-reference, associated with the director as auteur; the self-reference of the industry as a whole, which, on the one hand, manifests itself in a persistent concern with self-regulation and, on the other, with annual rituals of self-celebration; the self-reference of the individual studios in the form of intellectual-property-rights protection, logo management, and branding; and, finally, the self-reference and recursiveness established through the circuits of promotion and audience research that bind producers to consumers and regulate reception of a given film as story, event, and experience (via poster, tag line, advertising, press coverage).

Despite their crucial differences, all of these forms of reflexivity and recursiveness can be read as manifestations of ongoing power struggles, both within the industry (in the early years, between editorial control on the part of the exhibitors versus editorial control by the producers; in later years, vertical integration – its loss in 1948 and reinstatement since the 1980s) and between the industry and its audiences (in the early years, disruption through censorship, followed by preemptive self-censorship via the Hays Code, to be replaced by more covert forms of self-regulation and more aggressive marketing techniques, as well as more sophisticated tools of audience research and technology-backed feedback loops). That the site of such struggles can be the film itself is what is fascinating about studying Hollywood's modes of address, because one of the means of address and control is reflexivity itself in the form of complicity and knowingness. It is in this way that the film implicates the viewer at the story level and a meta-level, enfolding the audience in cognitive dissonances and double binds, countering blasé indifference with immersive sensory overload, or acknowledging fan power through narrative complexity while also answering (by performing them within the film) the conspiratorial-paranoid readings of Hollywood that we, professional academics and critics, are so fond of.

My contribution, therefore, focuses on the forms, meanings, and possibilities of recursiveness – interpreted as broadly as I have tried to define it here – practiced by 'mainstream' cinema, that is, the Hollywood film of today. I would like to develop the theory that Hollywood cinema creates immersion through forms of self-reference that reflect the film industry's situational contradictions as well as the recipient's cognitive dissonances. To this end, I will call upon the example of digital 3-D cinema, in particular, James Cameron's *Avatar* (USA/UK 2009), thus precisely those kinds of films that specifically evoke the idea of immersion in its original sense: self-forgetful entanglement and absorption. In other words, within the framework of my analysis, 'immersion' is not an autonomous umbrella term but a special case within a series of forms of self-reference and feedback.

Here is a brief list of some of the more well-known forms of self-reference in the Hollywood movie:

The Trailer as an Example of Self-Reference

A few years ago, using John McTiernan's *Die Hard* (USA 1988) as an example, I tried to show that in 'classical' Hollywood cinema, the first scenes of a film or the pre-credit sequence serve as a sort of instruction manual for how to read the film as it is intended to be read (see Elsaesser 2002). In this way, along with their function as a condensation and mise en abyme of the film as a whole, these opening or pre-credit sequences also function as a kind of threshold, in that they facilitate, in an auto-referential way, the viewer's entry into the film, which Roger Odin has referred to as the "mise en phase", meaning attunement to the film (2000: chapter 7). At the same time, however, a Hollywood movie exhibits a great deal of redundancy and repetition, in other words, moments of recursiveness and reemployment, which serve to counteract interference, transmission errors, or distraction (much like the similar moments Claude Lévi-Strauss demonstrated in myths and Vladimir Propp in fairy tales). Computer scientists would call these feedback loops; Roman Jakobson, following Bronisław Malinowski, spoke of the 'phatic' aspect of communication (see 1960). The introduction provided by the trailer, often very condensed in its imagery and story line, is thus an integral part of the film and simultaneously a commentary on the film, thereby making our first contact with the film both immersive and reflexive. Noteworthy in this context is Britta Hartmann's extensive research on precisely these 'phatic' and recursive aspects of the beginnings of films (see 2009).

Recursiveness as Knowingness

In both classical and post-classical cinema – this is a further aspect of my theory – another dimension of recursiveness is present, in which the film, by signifying that it is aware of its own genre-related stereotypes and plot formats in the story line, constantly reassures the viewer by offering an ironic sort of complicity. It reveals a certain performative or self-deprecating knowingness along the lines of, 'I know that you know that I know'. The result is a kind of endless loop of reference or insinuation, with which a form of feedback between the film and the viewer based on foreknowledge is activated. The 'naïve' viewer only sees one dimension of the story line and its progression, while the knowing viewer, or 'fan', is provided with all kinds of clues and cues, thanks to which he or she is able to enter into a dialogue with the film.

The Internet forums and YouTube clips that deal with the endless number of possible interpretations of the films of Tarantino, for example, clearly attest to the ability of a cult film to enter into a dialogue, while inviting appropriation, identification, or interpretive 'work' in order to decode its many meanings. This mimetic-hermeneutic position, as both an affective and cognitive tie to the film as well as a guideline for making sense and enriching one's experience, can indeed be described as immersion.

The 'Mind-Game Film' as Immersion

An extreme example of this kind of reflexivity, which generates not only complicity but also deliberate, i. e., structured ambiguity, is what I have termed the genre or the tendency of the "mind-game film" (2009b). These are films that include the viewer in the fundamental principles of their construction while simultaneously blurring the usual lines between subjective involvement and objective distance. Generally, such films deal with epistemological problems that extend from the protagonists to the viewers: what is the relationship between seeing and knowing? How do we know what we know? How can we project ourselves into extreme situations? What exactly do we know about what is going on in the body and mind of someone else? Protagonists and viewers of mind-game films alike have to ask themselves: can I believe what I see? Can I trust my reflexes? Can I have faith in the world or are paranoia and skepticism more important to survival? Ideally, we observe the protagonists in these types of films as they gradually discover that things are drastically different from what they previously believed to be the case. Usually, however, the change or flip from one reality to another catches us by surprise as much as it does the on-screen heroes. What we experience with films such as David Fincher's *Fight Club* (USA/Germany 1999), Christopher Nolan's *Memento* (USA 2000) and *Inception* (USA/UK 2010), Richard Kelly's *Donnie Darko* (USA 2001), M. Night Shyamalan's *The Sixth Sense* (USA 1999), and Alejandro Amenábar's *The Others* (USA/Spain/France 2001), among many others, is the sense that alternative orders of being are also affecting ours: that the real and the virtual are not mutually exclusive but go hand in hand, and may even require each other. Mind-game films, therefore, can be considered meta-films about identification, empathy, and immersion, which teach the viewer to differentiate between different role assignments coded according to the level of immersion, between protagonists (autonomous characters within the work of fiction) and players (the character as instrument of manipulation in the fictional world), or between personas (the character as a split subject or internally divided and multiple) and avatars (the character as a representative of the viewer of the character in the fictional world).

In this sense, Cameron's *Avatar*, based on the title alone, could be considered a mind-game film, because the protagonist, in a complex form of recursiveness, is in a dialogue with himself. In other words, he exists simultaneously and sequentially in multiple forms and environments that do not merely mirror or duplicate one another but depend on one another in a counterflow feedback loop. Here conscious and unconscious, alive and dead, able-bodied and disabled, as conditions of the body and mind, are constantly pitted against and played off of one another. Therefore, while in game-design discourse, the term 'immersion' is used to describe a player's experience of existing in a virtual world, the motion picture is able to vary the epistemic level and experiential concentration of immersion and, as the case may be, make immersion itself the subject of the story. The latter is found in *Avatar*, which virtually becomes an allegory of the problem of how today's Hollywood can make its products equally compatible for the big screen and the small screen of the smartphone and game console. 'Allegory as a form of recursiveness' would thus be a further mode of Hollywood cinema, which, however, I have chosen to omit, despite the fact that it has regained a significant amount of attention from the film theorists still interested in hermeneutics. Examples of this can be seen in the works of Jerome Christensen (see 2012) and J. D. Connor (see 2000), but also among other scholars interested in typical franchise movies, Hollywood logos, and questions of branding and marketing such as Charles Acland (see 2003) and Paul Grainge (see 2008). Connor, for example, reads Mel Gibson's film *Braveheart* (USA 1995) not only as an allegory of the company merger between Universal Studios and Vivendi but as an examination of the fact that Hollywood has grown increasingly dependent upon its foreign viewers and, for this reason, enlists foreign directors as well (see 2000). With respect to Oliver Stone's *Alexander* (Germany/USA/Netherlands 2004), starring Colin Farrell and Anthony Hopkins, which tells the story of Alexander's campaign within a framing narrative, Connor observes:

> When Alexander or Achilles yells about "everlasting glory," the hearts of studio marketing executives beat a little faster: everlasting glory equals more downstream revenue [...]. (No wonder Anthony Hopkins, as the old general Ptolemy, narrates *Alexander* from the great library at Alexandria: Library rights are where it's at, and they're certainly why Sony recently bought MGM [...]). (2004)

Transfer via the Protagonist's Placeholder Function

Lastly, there is another kind of recursiveness – upon which *Avatar* draws and which it gives a new spin – that is also constitutive of Hollywood cinema. The male hero of a Hollywood movie is often an outsider or someone who is gradually included in the world of the story. He is often skeptical of this world, is a random witness to a fatal incident, or only becomes involved in the doings of others after much hesitation or even against his will. The fact that such a character usually serves as a kind of placeholder or substitute for the viewer is obvious. The use of this strategy can even be seen in characters such as Schindler in Steven Spielberg's *Schindler's List* (USA 1993). The spin that *Avatar* puts on this cliché – which is both structurally and ideologically necessary – is that it presents a protagonist bound to a wheelchair, who is literally transported to another world and whose telekinesis coincides with his 'tele-action'. He is thus not only a witness, but also an actor and even serves as a substitute for his brother in the story. He also follows orders – and is thus both passive and active – and can only become active by being passive. He also, however, goes over to the 'enemy' and, in doing so, goes against orders to restore his soul (in the film, his body). In this protagonist, it is not only easy to recognize the customary avatar of the viewer but, at the same time, the gamer, also bound to his chair or couch in front of his monitor. The allegory is that of the 3-D experience itself: transported through the plasticity of the images to the realm of an 'as-if' reality, the viewer/participant/fellow player can take on the role of action hero and savior and enjoy, by proxy, his own alienation and helplessness before the beauty of Pandora – a narcissistic figure par excellence. The title, *Avatar*, thus has a manifold recursive and mediating, but also immersive, function. This is highlighted by the fact that, on their planet, the Na'vi – or navigators – are just as reliant upon the avatar principle of transferring, mediating, and delegating when they communicate and interact with their means of transportation and flying animals.

2. From Recursiveness to 'Access for All'

This ambiguity and these multiple layers are evidence of perhaps the central form of recursiveness of a Hollywood movie, which – as suggested, for very practical, tangible-economic but also technological-industrial reasons – has to not only play on all screens, platforms, and devices but also be available in all media formats and on all media markets. For this reason, instead of aiming at self-reference directed at the author and creator (the classical form of reflexivity of avant-garde and auteur films), Hollywood tries to make its films accessible to as many viewers as possible, who differ in terms of nationality, language, occupation, skin color, gender, age, religious affiliation, culture, and political opinion. This means creating opportunities for viewers to empathize with the story and characters and to recognize in them their own concerns. I refer to this 'door' or 'portal' function as 'access for all'. With this, I mean to suggest that even the creators of blockbusters construct their images, materials, texts, and sounds in a way that leaves them open, ambivalent, or even duplicitous without thereby rendering the film incoherent or incomprehensible. In this regard, the advantage of the Hollywood film – in contrast to European auteur cinema – has always been that it is constructed in such a way that viewers can 'get into' or 'enter' the story at anytime and at any screening or broadcast. Therefore, while classical Hollywood cinema was, in the words of David Bordwell, "excessively obvious" (1985: 3), in the case of the mind-game film, it must be 'excessively enigmatic' or 'excessively self-contradicting', and this in such a way that it still teaches the viewers the 'rules of the game', which dictate how the film is to be read (cf. Elsaesser 2009a: 67–77). In this way, a control function is once again introduced, which ensures a certain level of self-regulation.

Avatar accomplished this 'access' and 'entry' but also 'passage for all' in a particularly remarkable way. I would like to call upon just a few examples of its reception in order to indicate their varied and contradictory nature before turning to the modalities, the logic, and various philosophical backgrounds of this strategy of immersive recursion, particularly regarding 3-D digital imaging technology.

In my opinion, one of the film's most surprising points of access was the approach taken by biologists. On January 18, 2010, the scientist Carol Kaesuk Yoon wrote in the *New York Times*:

> When watching a Hollywood movie that has robed itself in the themes and paraphernalia of science, a scientist expects to feel anything from annoyance to infuriation at facts misconstrued or processes misrepresented. What a scientist does not expect is to enter into a state of ecstatic wonderment, to have the urge to leap up and shout: "Yes! That's exactly what it's like!" So it is time for all the biologists who have not yet done so to shut their laptops and run from their laboratories directly to the movie theaters, put on 3-D glasses and watch the film *Avatar*. In fact, anyone who loves a biologist, or better yet, anyone who hates a biologist – and certainly everyone who has ever sneered at a tree-hugger – should do the same. Because the director […] has somehow managed to do what no other film has done. He has recreated what is the heart of biology: the naked, heart-stopping wonder of really seeing the living world. (2010)

Alongside this (and yet on an entirely different plane of reference) stand the countless YouTube clips in which girls – and boys – dress up as Na'vi and give tips on how one can quickly (and at little cost) transform oneself into a Na'vi – interpreted here more as 'native' than 'navigator'.

Furthermore, newspapers everywhere reported the story of how *Avatar* was received, manipulated, and eventually almost banned in China because of how it was interpreted in rural areas as a protest against the forced displacement of China's peasant population. Meanwhile, thousands of miles to the west, young Palestinians – for entirely different reasons and yet hardly different from the Chinese – immediately drew political parallels between their own situation and *Avatar*. They identified themselves with the blue creatures to the point of physical immersion, dressing up and painting themselves as Na'vi in order to march and protest against the security fence erected by the Israeli army in the small border town of Bil'in near Ramallah (see *Illustration 1*). It was in this way that, within a short period of time, the color blue had become the new 'green' (of the environmentalists) and simultaneously the new 'red' (of political protest).

The ideological ambiguity segues into the countless interpretations by cultural theorists and political commentators, who, before long, had interpreted the film from a radically left-wing perspective (Slavoj Žižek) and from a conservative viewpoint (David Brooks) and who, in doing so, despite their diverging ideologies, arrived at similar conclusions, namely, that under the fig leaf of anti-capitalism, the film is racist:

> *Avatar* is a racial fantasy par excellence. The hero is a white former Marine who is adrift in his civilization. He ends up working with a giant corporation and flies through space to help plunder the environment of a pristine planet and displace its peace-loving natives. The peace-loving natives – compiled from a mélange of Native American, African, Vietnamese, Iraqi and other cultural fragments – are like the peace-loving natives you've seen in a hundred other movies. They're tall, muscular and admirably slender. They walk around nearly naked. They are phenomenal athletes and pretty good singers and dancers. The white guy notices that the peace-loving natives are much cooler than the greedy corporate tools and the bloodthirsty U.S. military types he came over with. He goes to live with the natives, and, in short order, he's the most awesome member of their tribe. He has sex with their hottest babe. He learns to jump through the jungle and ride horses. It turns out that he has even got more guts and athletic prowess than they do. He flies the big red bird that no one in generations has been able to master. [...] Still, would it be totally annoying to point out that the whole White Messiah fable, especially as Cameron applies it, is kind of offensive? (Brooks 2010)

In contrast, followers of Gilles Deleuze wax almost as ecstatically about the film as the biologist in the *New York Times*, because in *Avatar*, they recognize almost all of the forms of becoming listed in *A Thousand Plateaus* by Deleuze and Guattari (see 1987): "becoming-woman", "becoming-animal", in short, the Spinozist 'Weltbild' of a multiple mutuality. For instance, the following passage provides probably one of the most lyrical and yet precise definitions of immersion:

> The movie downloads the viewer with such ferocity and such poetic space the film bends back cinema upon itself, and introduces its content – the question of Avatarship – into the very experience, pulling out from technological increase and its inherent relatability the buried question of sensitivity, connection and projected identification, in short, the implied organic mutuality in everything our machines have brought us. Cameron and his magicians in such a threshold defying 3D invade our bodies and throw out our affects into the arms and sinews of operators which defy all of our repeated attempts to take map of where we are. (Duuglas-Ittu 2009)

While Deleuzians are jubilant at the sight of the film and its boundary-expanding, deterritorializing sensory plenitude, there are others who find themselves 'in the depths of despair' after seeing the film, because life has become boring and stale. The so-called *Avatar* blues deprived them entirely of the will to live in the here and now. A user named Mike on the fan website Naviblue writes:

> Ever since I went to see *Avatar* I have been depressed. Watching the wonderful world of Pandora and all the Na'vi made me want to be one of them. I can't stop thinking about all the things that happened in the film and all of the tears and shivers I got from it [...]. I even contemplate suicide thinking that if I do it I will be rebirthed in a world similar to Pandora and the [sic] everything is the same as in *Avatar*. (Qtd. Piazza 2010)

If this is the case, then what is one to make of the response of Bolivia's president?

> Bolivian president Evo Morales went to the cinema for the third time in his life in order to view *Avatar* which he says is "a profound sign of resistance to capitalism and the struggle for the defense of nature". ¡Viva Pandora! One of the only other films he ever traveled to the cinema for was a biopic on Pelé. (Casares 2010)[4]

---

4 In the 'conversation' following this quotation, one blogger denounces Morales, writing, "Morales is an idiot who spouts platitudes, he is the 'brown guy' front for Álvaro García Linera. Álvaro is using Evo to trap the indigenous populations", while another one replies: "this movie *Avatar* has a lot of meanings for different people. Green peace

Without question, 'access for all', in the age of the Internet, has become a multifaceted, multicultural process of mediation and appropriation, which, in terms of plot, presupposes a calculated ambivalence within the film itself. Furthermore, it forces a director such as Cameron to construct his story using well-known elements of fairy tales and myths, which, however, are then linked together in a very synthetic or syncretic way. In his review, Jan Distelmeyer put it well when he wrote:

> *Avatar* works and, to this end, combines, along with a few interesting slights of hand of digital media, a host of cultural fragments from various parts of our planet. Jesus, sitting beneath the Tree of Knowledge, is having sex with Pocahontas and converts to Buddhism, whereupon he declares the "hereafter" to be the "here and now" and, as Tamer of the Dragon, restores harmony and equilibrium to a planet whose sole purpose is to serve as a giant data-storage space. You consider this gaga and a joke? It's what happens when a James Cameron blockbuster is seeking perfect balance and happily doesn't go for the lowest common denominator.[5]

The point of access is, in other words, a passage; that is to say, it does not function by way of the content or the message itself but rather via the way in which the content is encoded. This means that the ambiguity must be structurally anchored and this in such a way that it can sustain diametrically contradicting ("gaga") interpretations. The point here is not the film's controversial reception and that naïve and 'sophisticated' minds parted ways, as is the norm with Hollywood movies. Rather, the claim is that these contradictions were preprogrammed and hardwired into the film and are a part of its basic concept. Cameron, I believe, added another dimension to the 'constitutive ambiguity' of classical film – which characterized, for example, the bawdy double

activists would draw their own meanings, Iraqis who feel they were invaded for their vast oil resources, would have their own. What Evo Morales drew out of this movie, is relevant to most of us on this planet earth. Capitalism will eat us away, if we don't do something in time."

5 "Genau dort, weltweit, muss und will *Avatar* funktionieren und vereint darum neben ein paar interessanten Volten zu digitalen Medien vor allem jede Menge Kulturbrocken aus unterschiedlichsten Teilen unseres Planeten. Jesus hat unter dem Baum der Erkenntnis Sex mit Pocahontas und konvertiert zum Buddhismus, bevor er das Jenseits zum Diesseits erklärt und als Drachenreiter für das totale Gleichgewicht auf einem Mond sorgt, der eigentlich ein großer Datenspeicher ist. Sie finden das gaga? Das kommt dabei heraus, wenn ein Blockbuster von James Camaron das Gleichgewicht sucht und zum Glück nicht den kleinsten gemeinsamen Nenner will." (Distelmeyer 2010: 34)

entendres in films made under the Hays Code, that is to say, strategically self-censoring films (a prime example being the sexual innuendos in *Casablanca*, USA 1942) – which, earlier, I termed "cognitive dissonance". My argument is that the director of *Avatar* added a further twist and adopted a strategy of conceptual double binds, or what Karl-Otto Apel calls 'performative self-contradiction' ("performativer Selbstwiderspruch"; 1987: 165f.)[6].

If we take the ideological message of the film, it is clear that it has been precisely calibrated. This can be seen, for instance, in the degree of anti-Americanism the film allows itself; the manner in which ecological motifs are incorporated; and how, within the matrix of the 'White Messiah' referred to by Brooks (see 2010) as politically offensive and Žižek (see 2010) as brutally racist, there is still enough ideological leeway for the indigenous peoples and tribes fighting for their rights to have their say through the film: whether in China or Australia, in the Middle East or Latin America. Cameron – regardless of his own political opinions (though it is safe to assume that he belongs to Hollywood's liberal wing) – was well aware of how deeply controversial the United States' role in the world had become under Bush, in the midst of two wars of aggression, but how this perception had become complicated by the nation being led, for the first time, by a black president.

Avatar's anti-Americanism is thus calibrated in such a way that it flatters Hollywood's vast international market while not coming off as so 'in your face' that Americans, at least those in the relevant demographic (viewers between 12 and 32 years of age), feel repelled or insulted by it (in contrast to Michael Moore's explicit Leftism). The anti-military-industrial-complex message was, therefore, structurally necessary: it responded to the fact that today, up to 70 percent of a Hollywood blockbuster movie's earnings come from viewers residing outside of the United States[7]. Well-dosed anti-Americanism is thereby

6 'The narrow definition is that I find myself in a performative self-contradiction then, when I claim to be doing something (or claim not to be doing something) that, with my claim, I am actually not doing at that moment (or am actually doing).' ("Die enge Definition wäre die, daß ich mich in einem performativen Selbstwiderspruch genau dann befinde, wenn ich etwas zu tun behaupte [bzw. nicht zu tun behaupte], was ich mit der Behauptung gerade nicht tue [bzw. tue]"; Steinhoff 1993: 293).

7 According to Box Office Mojo, by early 2011, *Avatar* had grossed $760 million in the U.S. and Canada, but $2,022 billion in other territories, bringing the world-

also an instrument in Hollywood's arsenal used to maintain its dominance in the world market and thus another example of exercising power and keeping control under conditions Deleuze would call 'modulation': by giving America's ideological 'enemies' – who are also its ideal customers – a 'voice' or a 'stake', Cameron actually searches for balance, though perhaps not quite in the way Distelmeyer meant it. And yet it is very much a sign of a level of (self-)reflexivity, with which the film invites one to read it as an allegory of its own conditions of possibility. Although the reviews that accuse *Avatar* of ideological mystification are not exactly wrong, they miss the point. They overlook the fact that false consciousness is the design principle of the film, for with it, the film stages the conditions that allow the USA to assert both its military superiority and its cultural hegemony on a meta-level. These elements not only reinforce one another but actually become even more effective when they seem to contradict each other.

3. Keeping Control through Performative Self-Presentation

Hence it is important to remember that 'access for all' is a strategy that must always maintain a balance between opening a door and keeping the key. Yet how does this double priority manifest itself for the director? How does he retain control, not only internally – by having final-cut privilege included in his contract or by serving as his own producer, as is the case with directors such as, among others, Cameron, Spielberg, Lucas, and Scorsese – but also over the image that the public or the fans create for themselves? One of the most important means is the director's interview, which today, along with the DVD bonus package, is an indispensable component of an advertising campaign. With this, the director can exert control by performatively staging his own self-presentation.

Cameron delivered this self-presentation in the form of an autobiographical narrative at his March 2010 TED talk (see Cameron 2010). It is not only notably different from Francis Ford Coppola's cinephile persona as an heir of Alfred Hitchcock and Orson Welles, or Steven Spielberg's World War II/Holocaust identity, but it also has little in common with, say, Martin Scorsese's ethnically distinct New York/Little

wide total to over $2,780 billion, meaning that nearly 75 percent of the film's income was foreign-earned.

Italy narrative or Quentin Tarantino's identity as fatherless 'poor white trash', brought up by the Blockbuster video store. The core of the Cameron legend is that of the 'curious boy', who, from a young age, was drawn not only to biology, natural history, and conducting scientific experiments, but also to drawing, painting, and making up stories. Cameron thereby establishes a clear link between science and technology, on the one hand, and images from literature and the visual arts, on the other, as the twin motivations of both his biographical and his artistic life. In the same talk, he confirmed that it was the deep-sea explorations of Jacques Cousteau that had always shaped and influenced him more than moon landings or any other kinds of outer-space research and adventures (despite what *Avatar* might suggest). Cameron even claims that his only reason for making *Titanic* (USA 1997) was to get his hands on a budget and a topic that would allow him to live out his fervent childhood dream of one day seeing and exploring the actual wreck of the *Titanic* on the floor of the Atlantic Ocean.

What is perhaps most fascinating about this story is that the strongest echo of the topics and personal motivations most typical to Cameron's work in *Avatar* is actually the ubiquitousness of water, even though it never actually appears in the film as such. In this respect, I am not only thinking of the amniotic fluid in which Jake Sully's avatar is cultivated and develops (see *Illustration 2*), although it is naturally the most direct reference to immersion, but of all the other forms of metamorphosis, of flowing, floating, and undulating, present in the film (see *Illustration 3*).

If, therefore, the Latin word 'immersio' refers to the physical experience of being immersed in a liquid, it appears, at first, as though Cameron too were building upon the metaphorically extended interpretation of immersion and derived its effects from spatial envelopment and the way the images panoramically guide the viewer's gaze. This, however, means overlooking an element that, in my opinion, places the aforementioned cognitive dissonance within the viewer's physical experience itself. For *Avatar* is able to cause the viewer to feel empathy and experience immersion thanks in part to its subtle but crucial change in register in the physiological experience on which the images are based. Here, the sensations of movement we usually associate with being in the ocean and deep-sea diving have been metaphorically and kinetically displaced into a rain forest or outer-space setting, the hybridization of which makes for the beauty of the planet Pandora. The gravity-free universe, in which the power-

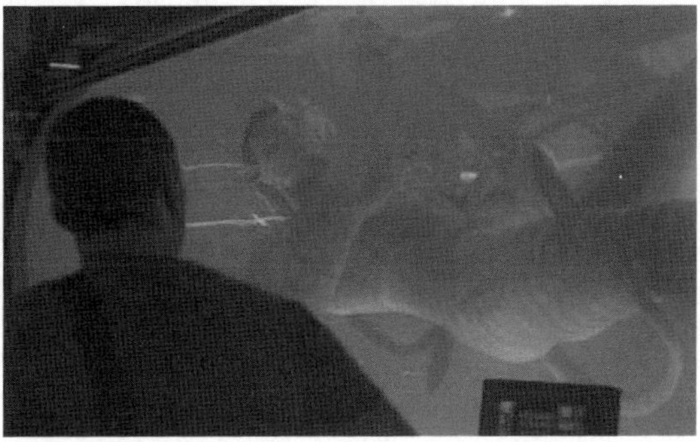

Illustration 2:
Film still from Avatar *(dir. James Cameron, USA/UK 2009).*

ful leaps, swoops, and flights would obviously not be possible (no more than they would be possible in the thicket and undergrowth of the tropical rain forest), is associated with the freedom of diving and the state of floating deep under water – where gravity is suspended rather than abolished. It is this property that grants aquatic creatures the freedom to move in all directions as well as agility and speed of propulsion – elements that *Avatar* knows so well how to employ.

This dissolution of registers, the merging of elements or the exchange of associations from one habitat to another is particularly emphasized in the depiction of flora: the plants, trees, bushes, grasses, and even rocks; in short, the macro- and micro-organisms experience a completely new vitalization and appearance, which is the most likely explanation for the biologists' excitement (see *Illustration 4*). Here, not only did a new digital visualization technology, which was specially developed for Cameron – the qualitative leap from motion capture to performance capture – give animals, birds, protozoans, and the human-animal Na'vi new dimensions of affective expression and sensory movement, but even the original meaning of the term 'animation' itself was revitalized, given a breath of life, reminding one of the first days of creation.

This connection between technology and nature, between soul ('anima') and artificial life ('animation') leads in yet a further direction, in which the term 'immersion' is given renewed importance: not only does it provide the grounds on which people can discuss – under distinctly different circumstances – their rediscovered enthusiasm for 3-D movies, but, in the same breath, it also causes a mixing and blending of various spheres of life and knowledge, namely a new convergence between technology, entertainment, and education. It was, therefore, more than just a coincidence when James Cameron presented his shortest and yet most complete self-presentation to date to the TED community, as TED stands for Technology, Entertainment, Design.

Illustration 3:
Film still from Avatar *(dir. James Cameron, USA/UK 2009).*

At the same time, however, I would connect this tendency toward convergence with the three main actors in a paradigm change. With this, I do not mean Spielberg, Cameron, and Katzenberg, the three generals of the 3-D revolution, as Katzenberg likes to call it, but *Hollywood*, the *avant-garde*, and the *software industry*: Hollywood, as a multifunctional network, represented, as previously mentioned, in all forums, media, and markets; the avant-garde as memory and reinvention of the technical or the scientific obsolete; and the software industry – the former military-industrial complex – which covers the full range of simulation technology and formats in the same way it makes use of the newest 3-D imaging and measurement technologies in the areas of construction, tourism, architecture, land surveying, rescue, discovering natural resources, et cetera. This is what led someone like Tim Lenoir and Henry Lowood to speak of the "military-entertainment complex" (2005: 428f.), chiming in with the theorists of the logics of war and cinema, such as Paul Virilio (see 1989) and Friedrich Kittler (cf. 1999: 124f.).

It goes without saying that these three areas cannot be seen as convergent elements that seamlessly blend into one another but as existing in an interdependent relationship with one another, or put more strongly, in an antagonistic, reciprocal, or heteronymous one. On the one hand, this results in the frequently noticeable asymmetry of the force ratios of the various areas to one another (which is lost in the term 'convergence'). On the other hand, the term "antagonistic mutuality" (2012a: 706f.), which I have used in other contexts, takes into account the level of contradiction, which is the basis for the entire concept of *Avatar* – as a blockbuster and media event as well as in its textual-ideological form – and which I tried to describe earlier by quoting the term 'performative self-contradiction'.

In closing, I would like to further explain this term regarding its intrinsic recursiveness, particularly in the forms in which it manifests itself in *Avatar*. As my quotations show, it is not difficult to accuse Avatar of false consciousness or of ideological mystification. In doing so, however, critics overlook the already-mentioned fact that the film and

Cameron's project, on almost every level, systematize and normativize this false consciousness or ideological inconsistency. A philosophically more appropriate way to understand such strategic inversions would be to draw, besides Apel's term 'performative self-contradiction', on Jacques Derrida's term "pharmakon" (1981: 127f.).

The technology in *Avatar*, for example, is the pharmakon par excellence: nature can only be rescued by the technology that threatens it. Through the proper dosage and application, the 'bad' technology becomes 'good' technology. Sully, who turns the 'bad' technology into doing 'good', is thus – in relation to the scientists of the space station but also to the paramilitary corporation – the pharmakon that is supposed not so much to save Pandora as to rectify the bad system through his own good intentions; Slavoj Žižek would call it pure ideology. In this way, the film itself resembles the Cretan who claimed that all Cretans are liars and, in doing so, told the truth and yet contradicted himself at the same time – which is why his credibility rests on a performative self-contradiction.

In order to understand the underlying logic, one must once again bring the various conflict situations in *Avatar* to mind: for the most part, one finds exactly these kinds of antagonistic mutualities, which can also be described as parasite-host relationships, not only between Earth and Pandora but also between the big malevolent corporations and the well-meaning scientists. On the one hand, they exist in a relationship of antagonistic mutuality, because they are supposed to work together on

Illustration 4: Film still from Avatar *(dir. James Cameron, USA/UK 2009).*

this mission. On the other hand, there is the developing antagonism between the biologist Grace Augustine (Sigourney Weaver) and the RDA commissary Parker Selfridge (Giovanni Ribisi), a pseudo-conflict, for both parties are, as is yet to be shown, equally committed to the logic of exploitation (of foreign lands) and appropriation (of foreign knowledge).

With reference to *Avatar*, this means that, with the help of simulation technology, a virtual world has been created, which, while it possesses all of the characteristics of the real world, is constructed in such a way that it both compensates for and complements the flaws of the real world. In this way, the virtual world (of the avatar) is shown so realistically and consistently that an element of the real world, in this case the war-damaged ex-Marine Sully, can be transported and translated into it and develop within it. A complex system generates an even more complex system, which internalizes a part of the complex system and, in doing so, reverses the operational vector and power ratio, whereby the creature, in a way, rescues its creator (as opposed to the creatures in *The Sorcerer's Apprentice* or *Frankenstein*, who avenge themselves on their creators). The principle in effect here is akin to Daniel C. Dennett's pilloried "skyhooks" (1995: 73f.), whereby a complex biological process or living creature did not necessarily evolve from a simpler life form (as Stephen Jay Gould and Richard C. Lewontin argued when they spoke of heavenly "spandrels"; 1979: 582f.), but pulled itself up, so to speak, on a hook hanging from the sky. The hanging cliffs of Pandora can be seen as a powerful image of such skyhooks (see *Illustration 5*), as can the flexible extensions with which the Na'vi, thanks to their nerve fibers, connect themselves in order to telepathically steer their dragons – in a way, poetic skyhooks for the creation of an online community. At the same time, these fibers are a recursive mise en abyme of the 'avatar principle' of the remote control, whereby the virtual aspect of this control is translated back into physical contact and thus erotically charged: a clear sign of the extent to which the laws of unadulterated natural life on Pandora embody the idealized logic of the computer game and correspond with the self-image of the gamer when he or she logs on to a social network such as Facebook or Twitter.

The connections and involvements suggested here could also be approached from the standpoint of a system-theoretical analysis, in particular, via the principle of 'bootstrapping' as a widespread metaphor for processes that generate themselves without external influence or help. The metaphor itself comes from the story of Baron Münchhausen, who pulled himself out of a swamp by his own hair, which is often translated in English as 'pulling oneself up by the bootstraps'. Within the context of system theory, bootstrapping has the same meaning as recursion and is defined as a mathematical operation that rests on the repeated recall of a function by itself. According to Ofak/Hilgers, this self-referential auto-induction 'enables, step by step, the more elegant and compact derivation of solutions to a function'[8]. It increases the efficiency of computational power through a piece of programming whose algorithms are characterized by self-reflection and self-correction – an efficiency, which must be controlled through the corresponding anticipatory programming methods and termination conditions: 'time and calculable complexity are certainly its advantage'[9].

In this way, bootstrapping is also applied in computer jargon when referring to 'booting' up from a simple system to a more complex one ("the technique of starting with existing resources to create something more complex and effective"[10]), which reaffirms the fact that bootstrapping is a regenerative form of reflexivity. However, as is the case with every recursive loop, bootstrapping, too, needs the corresponding termination condition.

This termination condition would thus be the pharmakon or the performative self-contradiction, whereby technology changes into something else – in other words, into its very own other. In the film, this is explicitly laid out in the description of the object of the collective efforts of the scientists, corporate representatives, and military personnel on Pandora: everyone is searching for 'unobtainium', which Cameron uses to name the self-nullifying void around which the story revolves. The military is searching for a raw material by this name; the scientists are looking for knowledge, better edible plants, better medicine, better spirituality; however, both are, as has already been mentioned, entirely committed to the same logic of exploitation and appropriation. They conduct mining in the literal and

8 "[...] ermöglicht schrittweise die elegantere, kompaktere Lösungsherleitung einer Funktion" (Ofak/Hilgers 2010: 12).

9 "Zeit und berechenbare Komplexität sind dann freilich ihr Gewinn" (ibid.: 13).

10 The definition of "bootstrap" in the *Oxford Dictionaries*, http://www.oxforddictionaries.com/definition/english/bootstrap. [25/02/2014].

metaphorical senses, whether they are mining valuable metals or valuable 'data', with regard to the flora, fauna, culture, religion, and minds of the Na'vi. This common logic, shared by the military, scientists, and the entertainment industry, centered around the ground zero of unobtainium, gets to the heart of the matter regarding the previously mentioned antagonistic co-operation and Cameron's self-presentation in the TED program more than the charge that the film is fundamentally 'racist'.

The quest for unobtainium – a word that, by the way, actually exists – is intimately related to the use of 3-D technology outside the entertainment industry. The clumsy weapons with which the military attempts to conquer the Na'vi in the film hide what is right before our eyes, namely, that a more promising approach would have been to persuade the inhabitants of Pandora to relinquish their hidden treasures and their 'Tree of Life' through the use of beautiful images and feel-good sentiments. This would have been comparable to the way in which the film succeeded in being deemed 'anti-imperialist' and 'pro-environmentalist' by Evo Morales, the Chinese farmers, and the Palestinians, thanks to 3-D imaging technology, which today, particularly for the topographical measurements of natural resources and for remote-controlled weapons, is an economic priority and of strategic importance.

We thus have proof that the problem of 'access for all' and the conditions of 'immersion through feedback and recursion' (that is, the instruction manual the film itself provides on how to empathize, go along, and identify with the film) have become a sort of battleground for Hollywood. The effect of this is that one of the most effective skyhooks of contemporary Hollywood cinema is not to ensure an ideologically balanced message of some kind of middle-of-the-road liberalism, but rather – with regard to the increasingly heterogeneous, global yet internally divided target audiences – to engineer ever more subtle strategies of performative self-contradiction.

Simulators, test practices, crisis missions, humanitarian campaigns, and other paramilitary techniques, which should spell war but are declared as freedom missions, are part of these performative self-contradictions in the way they inform Hollywood and emulate politics. Here, the perfectly staged Abbottabad raid on Osama bin Laden's

Illustration 5: Film still from Avatar *(dir. James Cameron, USA/UK 2009).*

compound comes to mind, in which a shoot-to-kill mission was turned into a noble act of justice: after all, even President Obama has to address an entirely heterogeneous global public.

In this respect, Hollywood, in its efforts to introduce 3-D as the standard viewing method for motion pictures, delivers possibly the most fitting metaphor. Even 3-D is a physiologically based performative self-contradiction, inasmuch as the stereo effect is not based on any visual evidence or any form of ocular perception. Rather, it relies on the fact that the brain receives a precisely calibrated discrepancy or dissonance as perceptive input, which it compensates for by translating such an inconsistency into spatial categories, thereby reducing it to the lowest common denominator of coherence, namely, spatial depth. The brain thus tricks itself in order to regain balance, trading and short-circuiting cognitive dissonance for an increase in visual pleasure. With regard to our perception, 3-D could thus be considered the good conscience within the bad conscience or, in terms of the plot categories in *Avatar*, something like the ethics of the Na'vi within us. It is under this sign that the performative self-contradiction appears – a contradiction that is condensed and perfectly captured by the term 'unobtainium'. It appears not only as the cynical proof that Hollywood is at its most honest – as well as at its most immersive – when it openly admits that 'all Cretans are liars' (or, as Cameron so perceptively put it in the title of one of his other films, when Hollywood tells us 'True Lies'). It is also proof of the fact that the quest for total immersion is similar to the search for unobtainium, which is not meant to be sarcastic but could be a sign of hope, projected against a sky of *Avatar*'s self-suspending and thus seemingly gravity-defying rocks.

References

Acland, Charles R. (2003). *Screen Traffic: Movies, Multiplexes, and Global Culture*. Durham, NC: Duke UP.

Apel, Karl-Otto (1987). "Fallibilismus, Konsenstheorie der Wahrheit und Letztbegründung". Forum für Philosophie Bad Homburg, ed. *Philosophie und Begründung.* Frankfurt am Main: Suhrkamp. 116–211.

Balázs, Béla (1938/1995). "Zur Kunstphilosophie des Films". Franz-Josef Albersmeier, ed. *Texte zur Theorie des Films*. Stuttgart: Reclam. 204–226.

Bordwell, David (1985). "The Classical Hollywood Style, 1917–60". David Bordwell, Janet Staiger, Kristin Thompson, eds. *Classical Hollywood Cinema: Film Style and Mode of Production to 1960.* London: Routledge. 1–87.

Brooks, David (2010: online). "The Messiah Complex". *The New York Times*. http://www.nytimes.com/2010/01/08/opinion/08brooks.html. [10/09/2013].

Cameron, James (2010: online video). "Before *Avatar* ... a curious boy". *TED*. http://www.ted.com/talks/james_cameron_before_avatar_a_curious_boy. [10/09/2013].

Casares, Cindy (2010: online). "Evo Morales Loves *Avatar* Because 'It's a Story of Resistance from Capitalism'". *Guanabee*. http://guanabee.com/evo-morales-loves-avatar-because-its-a-story-of-resis-504433833. [27/01/2010].

Christensen, Jerome (2012). *America's Corporate Art: The Studio Authorship of Hollywood Motion Pictures*. Stanford, CA: Stanford UP.

Connor, J. D. (2000). "The Projections: Allegories of Industrial Crisis in Neoclassical Hollywood". *Representations* 71: 48–76.

— (2004: online). "The Anxious Epic". *The Boston Globe*. http://www.boston.com/news/globe/ideas/articles/2004/11/28/the_anxious_epic?pg=full. [25/10/2010].

Deleuze, Gilles, Félix Guattari (1980). *Mille plateaux: Capitalisme et schizophrénie*. Vol. 2. Paris: Editions de Minuit.

— (1987). *A Thousand Plateaus: Capitalism and Schizophrenia*. Transl. Brian Massumi. London: Continuum.

Dennett, Daniel C. (1995). *Darwin's Dangerous Idea: Evolution and the Meanings of Life.* New York, NY: Simon & Schuster.

Derrida, Jacques (1972). "La pharmacie de Plato". *La dissémination.* Paris: Editions du Seuil. 71–197.

— (1981). "Plato's Pharmacy". *Dissemination.* Transl. Barbara Johnson. Chicago, IL: University of Chicago Press. 61–171.

Distelmeyer, Jan (2010). "*Avatar – Aufbruch nach Pandora*". *epd-Film* 1: 34.

Duuglas-Ittu, Kevin (2009: online). "*Avatar*: The Density of Being". *Frames/sing.* http://kvond.wordpress.com/page/2/. [10/09/2013].

Elsaesser, Thomas (2002). "Classical/Post-classical Narrative (*Die Hard*)". Thomas Elsaesser, Warren Buckland, eds. *Studying Contemporary American Film: A Guide to Movie Analysis.* New York, NY: Oxford UP. 26–79.

— (2009a). *Hollywood heute: Geschichte, Gender und Nation im postklassischen Kino.* Berlin: Bertz + Fischer.

— (2009b). "The Mind-Game Film". Warren Buckland, ed. *Puzzle Films: Complex Storytelling in Contemporary Cinema.* Malden, MA: Wiley-Blackwell. 13–41.

— (2012a). "European Cinema and the Postheroic Narrative: Jean-Luc Nancy, Claire Denis, and *Beau Travail*". *New Literary History* 43/4: 703–725.

— (2012b). *The Persistence of Hollywood.* New York, NY/London: Routledge.

Gould, Stephen Jay, Richard C. Lewontin (1979). "The Spandrels of San Marco and the Panglossian Paradigm: A Critique of the Adaptationist Programme". *Proceedings of the Royal Society of London* 205/1161: 581–598.

Grainge, Paul (2008). *Brand Hollywood: Selling Entertainment in a Global Media Age.* New York, NY/London: Routledge.

Hartmann, Britta (2009). *Aller Anfang: Zur Initialphase des Spielfilms.* Marburg: Schüren.

Jakobson, Roman (1960). "Closing Statement: Linguistics and Poetics". Thomas A. Sebeok, ed. *Style in Language.* Cambridge, MA: MIT Press. 350–377.

Kittler, Friedrich (1986). *Grammophon, Film, Typewriter.* Berlin: Brinkmann & Bose.

— (1999). *Gramophone, Film, Typewriter.* Transl. Geoffrey Winthrop-Young, Michael Wutz. Stanford, CA: Stanford UP.

Lenoir, Timothy, Henry Lowood (2005). "Theaters of War: The Military-Entertainment Complex". Helmar Schramm, Ludger Schwarte, Jan Lazardzig, eds. *Collection, Laboratory, Theater: Scenes of*

Knowledge in the 17th Century. Berlin: de Gruyter. 427–456.
Odin, Roger (2000). *De la fiction*. Brussels: De Boeck.
Ofak, Ana, Philipp von Hilgers, eds. (2010). *Rekursionen: Von Faltungen des Wissens*. Munich: Fink.
Piazza, Jo (2010: online). "Audiences Experience *Avatar* Blues". CNN Online. http://articles.cnn.com/2010-01-11/entertainment/avatar.movie.blues_1_pandora-depressed-posts?_s=PM:SHOWBIZ. [10/09/2013].
Steinhoff, Uwe (1993). "Wahre performative Selbstwidersprüche". *Zeitschrift für philosophische Forschung* 47/2: 293–295.
Vehlken, Sebastian (2010: online). "Reviews: Ofak/von Hilgers, *Rekursionen*". *Zeitschrift für Medienwissenschaft* (ZfM). http://www.zfmedienwissenschaft.de/?TID=51. [10/09/2013].
Virilio, Paul (1984). *Guerre et cinéma: Logistique de la perception*. Paris: Editions du Cahiers du Cinéma.
— (1989). *War and Cinema: The Logistics of Perception*. Transl. Patrick Camiller. London/New York, NY: Verso.
Wikipedia (2013: online). "Immersion". http://de.wikipedia.org/wiki/Immersion_(virtuelle_Realit%C3%A4t). [10/09/2013].
Yoon, Carol Kaesuk (2010: online). "Luminous 3-D Jungle Is a Biologist's Dream". *New York Times*. http://www.nytimes.com/2010/01/19/science/19essay.html?_r=0. [10/09/2013].
Žižek, Slavoj (2010: online). "*Avatar:* Return of the Natives". *New Statesman*. http://www.newstatesman.com/film/2010/03/avatar-reality-love-couple-sex. [10/09/2013].

Part 3:
Landscapes and Architectures of Immersion

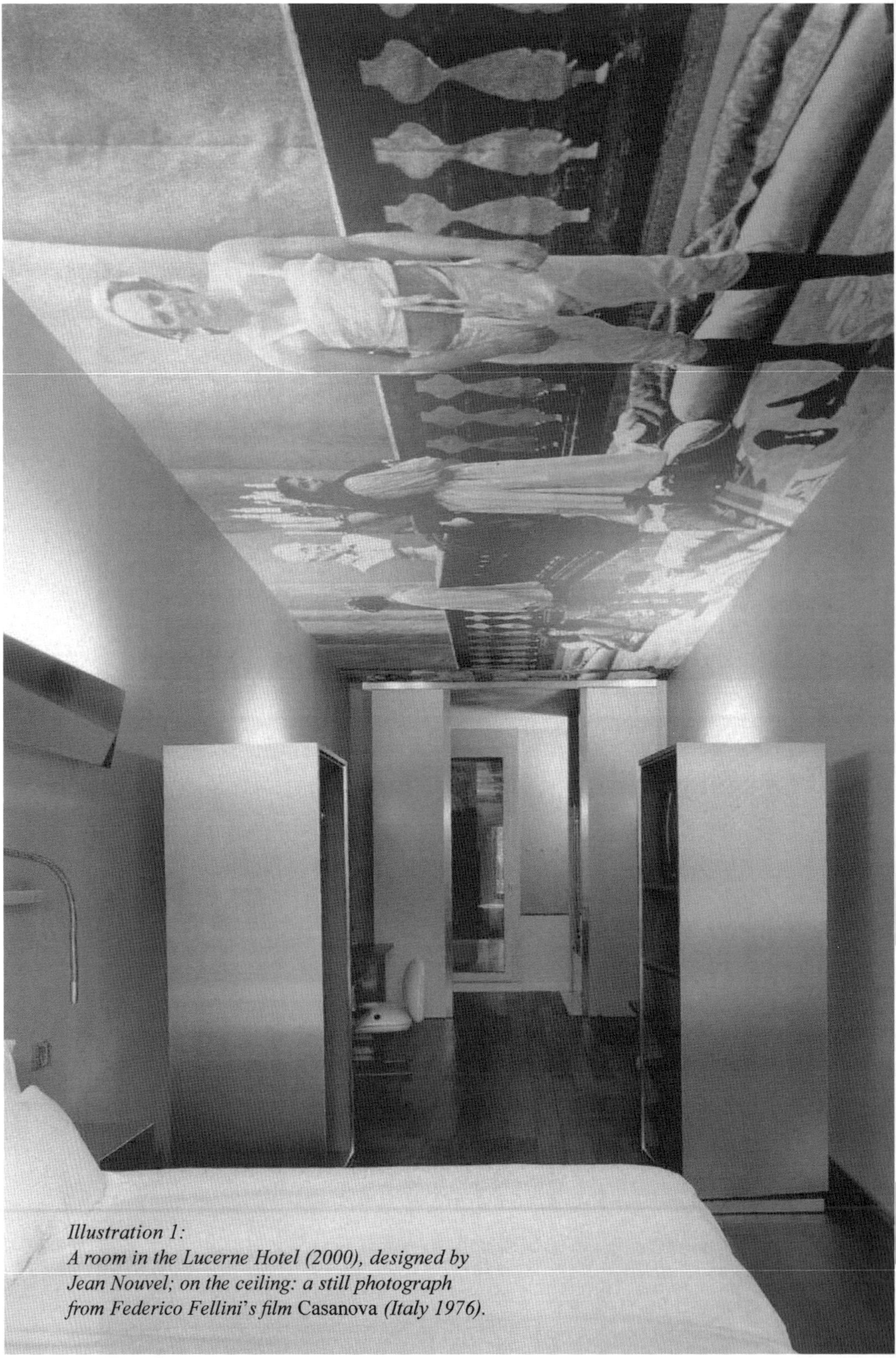

Illustration 1:
A room in the Lucerne Hotel (2000), designed by Jean Nouvel; on the ceiling: a still photograph from Federico Fellini's film Casanova *(Italy 1976).*

Projection Rooms
Film as an Immersive Medium in the Architecture of Jean Nouvel

Henry Keazor

In her contribution to the volume *Architecture and Film* from 2000, the architecture historian Joan Ockman wrote: "Film has been compared to architecture almost since its inception." The numerous parallels between the visual arts, film, and architecture listed there explain why contemporary architects such as Jean Nouvel increasingly refer to and rely on the aesthetic achievements of film in the conception and realization of their building projects. By discussing several projects and buildings by Nouvel I will show how he potentiates these insights via a repertory of further immersive means that are not at the disposal of the filmic medium (these means include spatially achieved 'montages' and 'cross-fading', techniques that create fluent passages between rooms as well as architectonically crafted narrative strategies that produce suspense). Moreover, in the case of Nouvel, film itself is often made a topic of these rooms.

It may seem paradoxical at first sight to examine the question of if and how architects and their buildings make recourse to the principle of immersion, since this principle is precisely defined (according to Béla Balázs's description in his text "Zur Kunstphilosophie des Films" from 1938) as a cinematic strategy used to involve and draw in a viewer situated at some distance from the action depicted on the screen. Balázs saw this quality as being proper to film in that it destroys a principle of the traditional special arts, namely 'the distance and the segregated closeness of the artwork' ("die Distanz und die abgesonderte Geschlossenheit des Kunstwerks"; 1938/2003: 212)[1]:

> The agile camera carries my eye and *thus my consciousness* along: into the heart of the picture, into the middle of the space where the action takes place. I don't see anything from the outside. I am seeing everything as the acting person must see it. I am surrounded by the figures of the film and thus entwined into its action. I am coming along, I am driving along, I am falling along – even though I physically remain seated on the same spot.[2]

1 Unless otherwise indicated, all translations are mine.

2 "Die bewegliche Kamera nimmt mein Auge, und *damit mein Bewußtsein*, mit: mitten in das Bild, mitten in den Spielraum der Handlung hinein. Ich sehe nichts von

In the case of constructed architecture, this dissolution of the lines between the image space and the viewer's space – this drawing-in, sucking-in, and diving-in – not only seems unnecessary, it does not even seem possible, since the image space and the viewer's space are one and the same. So why and how should the viewer be 'immersively' drawn into a space in which he or she already is?

If one considers this question further, however, it becomes clear that, on the one hand, immersive strategies have always been and still are relevant for architecture. On the other hand, it can be demonstrated that, in particular cases, such immersive strategies can even be apprehended as being especially necessary. This has to do with certain crises in the more recent phases of architectural history but also with building tasks, which are dictated by the specific functions some types of buildings are required to serve. The architecture of the 20th and 21st centuries has been reproached in various ways on the grounds that the creations developed and presented by their representatives focus primarily on concepts oriented toward an exterior effect. Consequently, they neglect the interior space in such a way that the recipients would not even feel invited to step into the building or, worse, would instead feel hindered, if not outright diverted or even repelled, from doing so (see Keazor 2010).

This – and with this we come to the above-mentioned building tasks – presents an even greater conflict with regard to the original destination and function of, in particular, public buildings (or buildings especially addressed to the public), such as theaters, concert halls, or cinemas, in which case the exterior appearance and the building should have a positive effect on the viewer.

One can thus already determine where architecture's interest in the principles of immersion and of its specific application might lie: at first sight, filmic space and the sense of immersion it creates may appear deficient in comparison with 'real' space, since filmic space only wants to make the viewers believe that here they can have experiences similar to those they would have in a real room (meaning: a personal experience of space) (cf. Agotai 2007: 15). But if we consider the means with which this is to be made possible more closely, the lesson architecture can learn from film becomes clear. Thus, in her doctoral thesis, *Architekturen in*

außen. Ich sehe alles so, wie die handelnden Personen es sehen müssen. Ich bin umzingelt von den Gestalten des Films und dadurch verwickelt in seine Handlung. Ich gehe mit, ich fahre mit, ich stürze mit – obwohl ich körperlich auf demselben Platz sitzen bleibe." (Balázs 1938/2003: 212 [emphasis in the original])

Zelluloid: Der filmische Blick auf den Raum, published in 2007, Doris Agotai writes:

> The filmic space is a two-dimensionally represented pictorial space, which, in the form of a projection of light, develops an illusionistic-immersive effect. [...] In contrast, the perception of architecture is tied to the movement and direct physical presence of the viewers. While film aims at directing the viewer's emotionality, architecture is predominantly determined by functional aspects.[3]

It is exactly this presumption – that architecture is mostly determined by 'functional aspects' – to which more and more positions in the 20th and 21st centuries have objected, referring occasionally to earlier architectural traditions while at the same time demanding the 'emotionality' usually claimed by film: rooms should not just 'function', but should also convey something, address the physically present visitors as they move through these spaces, involve them. In this light, the definition of 'immersion' as furnished by Agotai can also be applied to architecture:

> Immersion can be understood as a process that triggers a mental absorbance. Hereby the critical distance between work and viewer is reduced and an emotional involvement becomes the goal. The space [pictorial space] thus gains power of suggestion over the viewer [...].[4]

In order to gain this kind of power of suggestion over the viewers and to convey something to them, architecture has to develop strategies for designing rooms and staging the experiences emanating from them, for structuring the visitors' physical presence and movement in order to make them complete, and rounding them off via the viewers' mental as well as emotional involvement.

---

3 "Der filmische Raum ist ein zweidimensional dargestellter Bildraum, der als Lichtprojektion eine illusionistisch-immersive Wirkung entfaltet. [...] Die Wahrnehmung von Architektur dagegen ist an die Bewegung und direkte körperliche Präsenz des Betrachters gebunden. Während der Film die Emotionalität des Zuschauers zu steuern versucht, wird die Architektur weitgehend von funktionalen Gesichtspunkten bestimmt." (Agotai 2007: 19) Agotai takes the opposite approach to the procedure presented here: she considers filmic means of composition, such as editing and framing, from the perspective of architecture in order to understand their effects and how they are received in the context of film.

4 "Immersion kann als Prozess verstanden werden, der eine mentale Absorbierung auslöst. Dabei wird die kritische Betrachterdistanz gemindert und eine emotionale Involvierung angestrebt. Der Raum gewinnt so an Suggestionsmacht über den Betrachter [...]." (Ibid.: 19)

Agotai's statement that with the help of filmic means of design, directorial staging intentions are achieved (cf. ibid.: 43), could thus refer to architecture as well, which can also develop such directorial and staging intentions and recur to filmic means of design in order to achieve its aims.

The fact that such directorial intentions, which are aimed at the visitor's perception, are by no means new to architecture is shown not only by the recourses of directors such as Sergei Eisenstein to earlier architectural analyses but also by positions such as the one held by the psychologist and philosopher Theodor Lipps. Lipps began working and teaching in Munich in 1894 and (as Robin Curtis has emphasized; cf. 2008a: 12f.; 2008b: 100f.) examined architecture and its elements as objects of human empathy in his text *Raumästhetik und geometrisch-optische Täuschungen*, published in June 1897. Beginning with the observation that architecture is 'not just space in general, but shaped space' ("nicht nur Raum überhaupt, sondern geformter Raum"; Lipps 1897: 11)– and thus also encompasses formal elements that the human consciousness does not perceive neutrally but through interpretation and association – Lipps drew the conclusion that, essentially, architecture is also 'animation of space' ("Raumbelebung"; ibid.: 12). According to Lipps, this is because humans conceive the forms used by architecture involuntarily and spontaneously (and this means: beyond all conventions determined in the sense of symbolism) against the background of their experiences and, in an emphatic way, as expressions of interactions and reactions. Lipps's examination of the effect of the appearance of a Doric column has become famous in this context. According to him, the column erects itself in the perception of the viewer and thus triggers certain associations:

> The powerful concentration and raising of the Doric column is pleasant for me like my own powerful concentration and raising which I can remember and like the powerful concentration and raising which I perceive in others. I am thus in s y m p a t h y with the way the Doric column behaves or operates an inner vitality, since I recognize here a way of behavior, proper to nature, and at the same time also my own way of conduct that makes me cheerful. Thus, all joy about spatial forms – and we can add: all aesthetic joy in general – is an exhilarating feeling of sympathy [emphasis in the original].[5]

5 "Das kraftvolle sich Zusammenfassen und Aufrichten der dorischen Säule ist für mich erfreulich, wie das eigene kraftvolle Zusammenfassen und Aufrichten, dessen ich mich erinnere, und wie das kraftvolle Zusammenfassen und Aufrichten, das ich an einem Anderen wahrnehme, mir erfreulich ist. Ich s y m p a t h i s i r e mit dieser Weise der dorischen Säule

According to Lipps, the viewer is affected by such phenomena that shape a room and, in this way, is placed in relation to them in an affective way. By purposefully employing insights into such principles of the operation of forms, the architect is able to increasingly incorporate the viewer into his buildings. This is specifically achieved through the power of suggestion of the buildings' rooms and by isolating viewers in the sense of removing them from their distanced views and immersing them in a more emotional involvement with the structure.

At the time Lipps wrote his text, film, which had been introduced in 1895 in Berlin and Paris, was just two years old[6]. Therefore, at that time, one could not foresee the extent to which aspects as interesting as they are relevant to architecture would emerge from this new medium. Soon after, however, what Anthony Vidler described in 1993 came true:

> Since the late nineteenth century, film has provided a laboratory for the definition of modernism in theory and technique. As the modernist art par excellence, it has also served as a point of departure for the redefinition of the other arts, a paradigm by which the different practices of theater, photography, literature, and painting might be distinguished from each other. Of all the arts, however, it is architecture that has had the most privileged and difficult relationship to film. (1993: 45)

A brief look into their history shows that both art forms were actually, very early on and increasingly, associated with one another: "Film has been compared to architecture almost since its inception", as the architectural historian Joan Ockman opened her contribution to the volume *Architecture and Film* (2000: 171). In fact, in his manifesto on the seventh art from 1911, the Italian futurist and film theorist Ricciotto Canudo, who lived and worked in Paris, established a hierarchy according to which music and architecture are the closest to film among the other arts (cf. Weihsmann 1988: 45). This constellation was emphasized even more by the architect Le Corbusier in 1928 when he said:

---

sich zu verhalten oder eine innere Lebendigkeit zu bethätigen, weil ich darin eine naturgemässe und mich beglückende eigene Verhaltungsweise wiedererkenne. So ist alle Freude über räumliche Formen, und wir können hinzufügen, alle ästhetische Freude überhaupt, beglückendes Sympathiegefühl." (Lipps 1897: 7)

6 See the bioscope, presented by the Skladanowsky brothers in Berlin on November 1, 1895, or the cinematograph, publicly presented by the Lumière brothers on December 28, 1895, in Paris.

Illustration 2:
The 19th-century façade of the Lucerne Hotel from the outside, with glimpses of the different ceiling images inside.

"Architecture and the cinema are the only two arts of our time" (qtd. Cohen 1987/1992: 49)[7].

Possible reasons for this correlation are, firstly, the parallels regarding the conditions and processes in the production of film and architecture, as they are often stressed by directors as well as architects and architecture theorists: "The architect is a sort of theatrical producer, the man who plans the setting for our lives [...]. He sets the stage for a long, slow moving performance [...]" (Rasmussen 1959: 10f.). Furthermore, in both disciplines, directors and architects are subjected to financial, hierarchical, and organizational constraints, since they both have to take care not to exceed their budgets; both must work in a team; both have an authority to whom they have to answer, whether in the figure of a client or a producer; and both must try to realize their ideas in coordination with these authorities. Moreover, directors such as Vsevolod Pudovkin have voiced their view that a film is not shot but constructed like a house (see Pudovkin 1928/2003)[8]. Parallels between the two art forms, however, can also be drawn in light of the fact that both deal with the dimensions of time and space, the common means given to and used by architecture and film, and the results achieved therewith.

Or, to put it in the words of the French architect Jean Nouvel (born 1945): both art forms produce images (which is also why he considers himself an "architecte-créateur d'images"; 1987: 23). Nouvel himself

7 "Le cinéma et l'architecture sont les deux seuls arts de l'époque contemporaine" (qtd. Cohen 1987: 72). This quote is from an interview Le Corbusier gave during a visit to Moscow in 1928.

8 Rasmussen gives this idea yet another twist when he specifies: "The building is produced like a motion picture without star performers, a sort of documentary film with ordinary people playing all the parts" (1959: 14).

repeatedly stressed the fact that, in architecture, there is also a tendency toward two-dimensionality[9]. The way this is expressed in his work can be observed, for example, in the hotel he designed and built in Lucerne between 1998 and 2000 (cf. Nouvel 2008b: 419; 96–103 illustrations). Here, the architect has substituted the ceiling frescoes, often present in magnificent and representative early modern buildings, with huge film stills, hovering above the heads of the hotel guests inside (see *Illustration 1*), but at the same time still visible from the outside (see *Illustration 2*). In this way, these ceiling images also have the function of intriguing and teasing passersby in such a way that they begin to wonder what the interior rooms look like and are thus lured into the hotel.

Such references concerning film are frequent in Nouvel's work, from the use of aperture blinds, which frame the visible landscape in the case of the windows of the Institute du Monde Arabe, constructed between 1981 and 1987 (cf. 2008a: 396f.; 74–93 illustrations), to this recourse to, once again, film stills in the case of his building at the Anděl metro station in Prague, built between 1999 and 2000 (cf. 2008b: 411; 66–71 illustrations)[10]. As these examples show, these references to film are not merely quirky, isolated cases in the French architect's oeuvre, but are deeply grounded, on the one hand, in an enthusiasm for cinema – which, according to Nouvel himself, began in his early childhood[11] – and, on the other hand, in his fundamental examination of the possibilities and range of the filmic medium.

9 Jean Nouvel in a talk with Paul Virilio: 'I also pretend (and this always causes violent reactions) that there is, in architecture, a tendency towards two-dimensionality.' ("Je prétends aussi [et cela suscite toujours de violentes réactions] qu'existe, en architecture, une tendance à la bidimensionnalité"; qtd. Goulet 1987: 107).

10 For this building, cf. also Keazor 2011: 393f.

11 For the interview by Françoise Puaux with the architect, see Puaux 1995.

Thus, in 1990, Nouvel designed a projection hall for a planned but never realized competition entry to renovate the meanwhile too constricted and outdated Palazzo del Cinema in Venice, built by Luigi Quagliata in 1937/1938. This projection hall would have presented a kind of double immersion (cf. Nouvel 2008a: 420f.; 286–289 illustrations): during intermissions, the view of the Venetian landscape in front of the palazzo would have been brought into the projection hall through a giant panorama window located at the front of the room (see *Illustration 3a*). Due to the fact that this window would not have had a frame, which usually identifies a window as such, a perceptive-psychological amalgamation of interior and exterior would have facilitated a fusion of the limited, close-up view within the room with the unlimited, distant view to the outdoors, thus drawing the landscape into the hall

Illustration 3:
Jean Nouvel's design for the auditorium of the restructured Venice Palazzo del Cinema (1990) in its two states: a) before the projection of a film, b) during the projection.

while immersing the audience in the landscape[12]. During screenings, the window would have been covered with a screen onto which – after the architectural/scenic immersion – the films would have been projected, thereby creating the filmic immersion (see *Illustration 3b*).

However, in the context of his projects, Nouvel has especially and repeatedly referred to phenomena that are central to film, such as sequence, the succession of images, on the one hand, and, on the other hand, montage, "la succession des séquences" (Puaux 1995: 105)[13], which creates the illusion of a coherence of movement and action in a film in the first place. The architect has also referred to the fact that every image – and, in the case of narrative cinema, even the entire film – aims at making itself forgotten. The audience is made to believe that they are following a flow of observed events and not looking at single film scenes merely attached to each other: 'I like the film that makes me forget the camera as I like the architecture that makes me forget the constructive means.'[14]

With this kind of recourse to the procedures of sequencing and of montage, Nouvel positions himself at an almost classical intersection between architecture and film: in this respect, it is telling that, between 1920 and 1940, both the architect Le Corbusier and the film director Sergei Eisenstein referred to the principles stated in *Histoire de l'architecture*, by the architectural historian Auguste Choisy, in order to illustrate the principles they propagated. In his work, Choisy dem-

12 This concept has a precursor in an unexecuted idea by Gottfried Böhm, who planned such a building with his design for a theater in Bonn in 1959: the wall was to open behind the stage in such a way that not only could one look from the exterior into the room, but the exterior could be included in the action on stage, making it part of the set. The plan even involved the idea of opening up the wall behind the stage in such a way that inside and outside, stage and reality, would have been conflated. For more on this project, cf. Voigt 2006: 254, No. 103.

13 Cf. also the statement by Odile Fillion: "He no longer regarded architectural space as simple volume, or combinations of sets of images, but rather as a series of sequences" (1997: 119).

14 "J'aime le film qui me fait oublier la caméra, comme j'aime l'architecture qui me fait oublier les moyens constructifs" (Nouvel 1987: 24).

onstrates that the seemingly asymmetrical and non-axial layout of the Parthenon in Athens (a mysterious thorn in the sides of French Hellenists of the 19th century, who extolled symmetry and order as a commandment) could be explained by the fact that the whole complex of buildings constituting the Acropolis was conceived as a series of four main 'pittoresque' tableaus, composed of buildings and statues, to be experienced while approaching and perambulating the complex (cf. Choisy 1899: 413–422). According to Choisy, the Greeks would have regarded angular views as being 'plus pittoresque' than the more majestic frontal views. The visitor would have thus been guided on an oblique route through a series of tableaus, among which the seeming asymmetry of the whole complex would have been balanced and corrected by the lateral approach (see Etlin 1987). In order to show this concept, Choisy illustrates the different stops along this ideal approach in the form of a cinematic storyboard (cf. Bois/Glenny 1989: 114). It is exactly this series of views presented in words and images that Le Corbusier as well as Eisenstein adopted in their texts. In his series of articles written for the review *L'esprit nouveau* between 1920 and 1922, which were later published as a book in 1923 under the title *Vers une architecture*, Le Corbusier quotes Choisy's illustrations (see 1923/2007[15]) and, three years later, praises his *Histoire* as the most dignified work on architecture (cf. 1926: 116). Most importantly, however, this work inspired Le Corbusier to develop his own concept of a "promenade architecturale" as a central category of architecture (cf. Etlin 1987: 273). With reference to his own buildings, such as the Maison La Roche-Jeanneret (1923/1924) and the Villa Savoye (1928–1931), Le Corbusier demonstrated, in an exemplary way, the realization of these principles in the context of modern architecture: 'In this house, one encounters a true "promenade architecturale", offering constantly changing, unexpected, and sometimes baffling views.'[16] '[…] the architectural spectacle offers itself to one's eye bit by bit: one follows a route, and a great variety of prospects unfolds.'[17]

15 See, for example, the illustration to the chapter heading "Trois rappels à messieurs les architects – III: Le Plan".

16 "Dans cette maison-ci, il s'agit d'une véritable promenade architecturale, offrant des aspects constamment variés, inattendus, parfois étonnants" (Le Corbusier 1947/1929–1934: 24).

17 "[…] le spectacle architectural s'offre de suite au regard: on suit un itinéraire et les perspectives se développent avec une grande variété" (Le Corbusier 1948/1910–1929:

In the context of his *Entretien avec les étudiants des écoles d'architecture* in 1943, he finally expressed his sentiment that, by observing and following the courses prescribed by architecture, a specific frame of mind would be evoked[18]. The character this frame of mind can have becomes clear in a remark made by Nouvel, who, for his part, claims to convey to the viewer a specific emotion he has previously experienced himself. In this objective, he sees another parallel between the architect and the director:

> To experience a sensation – to be moved – to be aware of this – to have via one's own emotion the perversion to analyze this emotion – to remember it – to initiate a whole strategy in order to imitate this emotion, to enhance it in order to better convey it to others and to assure that it is made felt – for the joy of shared pleasure. All of this is what it means to be a director of film or of architecture.[19]

This precisely was also the objective of Eisenstein, who wanted to develop the cinematographic means to achieve this so that (as Yve-Alain Bois and Michael Glenny sum up) "the spectator will obtain an impression of the object or – moreover – the impression which the author wishes to induce in transforming the relationships of reality, that which he wants to inscribe for the perception" (1989: 111). The most efficient procedure in this respect was discovered by Eisenstein in the combined possibilities of the sequence and its 'juxtaposition' in the montage (cf. ibid.; Eisenstein 1938/1991: 66). For Eisenstein, Choisy's analysis of the Acropolis thus functions as evidence to the fact that these two procedures could have already been inscribed into architecture long before the invention of film: "[...] it is hard to imagine a montage sequence for an architectural ensemble more subtly composed, shot by shot, than the one our legs create by walking among the buildings of the Acropolis", Eisenstein states, before adding a long quote from Choisy's *Histoire* in word and image (1938/1991: 61–66), in his article "Montage and Architecture", written between 1937 and 1940.

60).

18 Cf. Le Corbusier 1943/1957, without pagination, chapter on architecture, no. 5.

19 "Éprouver une sensation – être ému – en être conscient – avoir la perversion à travers son émotion d'analyser cette émotion – s'en souvenir – mettre en œuvre toute une stratégie pour la simuler, l'amplifier, pour mieux la donner aux autres et, à coup sûr, la faire éprouver – pour le bonheur du plaisir partagé. C'est tout cela être réalisateur du cinéma ou d'architecture." (Nouvel 1987: 23)

In his 1971 study *Sur l'espace architectural*, Philippe Boudon emphasized that, ideally, built architecture is a kind of a projection of results developed in the imagination of the architect onto a defined space. Furthermore, according to Boudon, the perception of exactly this architecture, in particular, means to perceive and experience these thoughts and ideas, which have been developed in the mind of the architect: "The mental process that goes on in the mind of a person who observes a building in this way is very much like that which goes on in the mind of an architect when planning a building" (qtd. Rasmussen 1959: 44)[20].

In order to project his ideas concerning the desired perception of a room and the visitor's involvement onto the space as efficiently and clearly as possible, Nouvel enhances the potential already given to architecture through sequence and montage by potentiating these with other filmic means: not only should the viewer walk through his buildings and explore them in the context of a "promenade architecturale", but Nouvel also aims at extending the possibilities generally given to the architect when inscribing alternating and superimposing sequences onto the structure of a building and making the viewer experience certain aspects and views in order to convey related emotional sensations. Nouvel expanded this with the help of a very spe-

Illustration 4: Elevators in Jean Nouvel's Lyon Opera House (1993) carry the visitors toward the upper levels from where the huge volume of the black auditorium is looming.

20 Here, I am following the later German translation of Boudon's book, which was published under the title *Der architektonische Raum: Über das Verhältnis von Bauen und Erkennen*: 'Architecture is the projection of the architect's imagination of the concrete space.' ("Architektur ist die Projektion der Vorstellung des Architekten vom konkreten Raum"; 1991: 58). 'Perceiving architectonic space in a building means to perceive, at the same time, something that has been thought before.' ("Architektonischen Raum in einem Bauwerk wahrnehmen, heißt zugleich auch etwas zuvor Erdachtes darin wahrnehmen"; ibid.: 76).

Illustration 5:
After having to walk on loud metal grid floors, an acoustic lock, illuminated in bright red, awaits the visitors; through the lock they can enter the auditorium of the Lyon Opera House.

cific and targeted direction of light, sound, and color, which are also known in cinematic contexts.

Two examples illustrate this: in 1986, after winning the competition, Nouvel received permission to completely gut the building of the Lyon Opera, built in 1831 by Antoine-Marie Chenavard and Jean-Marie Pollet, and to extend its premises considerably through the addition of underground levels as well as a large glass dome roof (cf. Nouvel 2008a: 402–404; 158–179 illustrations).

The modernization of housing technology and the more efficient use of the building aside, this renovation, along with an extension completed in 1993, also gave the architect the chance to take the contrasts between the old, stony exterior and the new, modern interior as a starting point for a designed course. Together with the subtle color compositions, especially the lighting conditions, differences in dimensions (which address optical perception), surfaces (which address haptic perception), and greatly varying acoustic experiences interlace with the visitors' corporeal experiences as they move through the building, creating a dramatically structured sequence. Thus, when approaching the opera in the evening, visitors already encounter the chromatic triad of black, yellow, and red, which guides them toward the interior. Here inside the lounge, permeated by golden reflections, they then encounter the black, glistening skin of the voluminous auditorium looming above, placing the exterior walls of their destination before their eyes (see *Illustration 4*). Escalators guide them silently upward toward this destination, where, however, they then have to continue on their way by foot via a system of walkways, which, because of their metal grid floor, resonate loudly with the visitors' footsteps. A respective contrast then awaits the visitors at the entrance to the auditorium, where they must first pass through a soundproof lock, illuminated in red and lined with sound-deadening material (see *Illustration 5*), before the black auditorium, illuminated

Illustration 6: The long sequence of the passage, punctuated by lights and windows, which leads toward the auditorium of the KKL Lucerne (1998).

by small lights, finally opens up in front of them: 'a true "promenade architecturale", offering constantly changing, unexpected, and sometimes baffling views'.

This consequent use of a sequence consisting of different and sometimes contrasting impressions concerning color, sound, and physical experience works as a kind of strategy of abduction, which aims at carrying the visitors away from everyday life toward the anticipated pleasure of the art form of opera, while simultaneously time-sensitizing and preparing them for the acoustic as well as optical sensations which are paramount there. At the same time, such a dramaturgy of abduction and rapture refutes the main objection that is often voiced toward such a parallelization between architecture and film, according to which architecture does not have narration at its disposal. Even a fervent critic such as Kester Rattenbury, who normally argues against this parallel, had to admit the following in an article on the architecture of Jean Nouvel: "The architectural direction is undeniably potent: linking a filmic perception with personal experience of architecture" (1994: 35)[21].

Nouvel has designed similarly structured passages in which, each time, particular stations are assembled to form a homogenous 'course', in subsequent public buildings, such as in the Culture and Convention Center in Lucerne, the so-called KKL, a complex finished in 1998, which includes a concert hall, conference rooms, and exhibition spaces (cf. Nouvel 2008b: 404f.; 6–27 illustrations)[22]. In the 1998 documentary film *Jean Nouvel – Aesthetics of Wonder* by Beat Kuert, Brigitte Métra, the architect who cooperated with Nouvel on the KKL project, explains:

21 For the discussion of the "debated, if not contested" term 'narrative', cf. Koeck, who states that "film forms a dynamic space that is held together by a narrative" (2013: 21). This is something that can also be applied to architecture if one interprets the notion 'narrative' as a "series of events or actions" (ibid.: 19) that is perceived as somewhat structured and meaningful.

22 For this building, cf. Keazor 2011: 405f.

> Jean often uses film metaphors. That's because he creates sequences for his buildings. He wants the visitor to go through his buildings as though they were in a film, with different shooting sequences and emotions, accompanying every change of setting. His aim is to create emotions. You enter the buildings through sheets of glass, [...] so you pass from the exterior to the interior as if by magic, with no door as such. We tried to avoid anything that might serve as a reminder of the fact that this is a door. The function is forgotten. You are left with the emotion. The public [...] proceeds to the lower floor. Space is somewhat restricted in the basement as the ceilings are low. In fact, it's only as you approach the hall [the concert hall] that the space opens up. You now have a full vertical view – a round-angle perspective of the wooden shell of the concert hall. It resembles a musical instrument that stretches upward beyond the terrace. The way leading to the hall may almost be considered an initiation. In cooperation with Alain Bony, the artist who worked on the colors and painting, Jean also focused on the materials. As a result, we have shiny, polished surfaces alternating with matte surfaces. The length of this passage is emphasized by the punctuations of light – we've worked on every detail so that these small openings wouldn't look like windows. The idea was to conceal the window frames that are practically absorbed by the plasterwork so that all that is left is a glass-covered hole. Full focus is on the view. [...] This punctuated lighting leads us to the hall [see *Illustration 6*]. After the long sequence of light, you enter into a grey, pleated lock – another sequence, an intermediary buffer, and presto, you find yourself in a grey elephant-skin box. You can touch the wide, grey pleats[23]. You get the impression you are in a padded cocoon. It's an acoustic lock. Sound and light are dulled by the anthracite grey color of the carpet and the floor. So you pass through this area – this intermediate sequence between the large foyer and the long corridor and you find yourself in this small room. What next? The white hall! It's like in a script – we work as they do in the movies.[24]

23 In this respect, Nouvel's architecture also fulfills the claims voiced by the supporters of the so-called Phenomenology of Architecture movement, such as Steven Holl, Juhani Pallasmaa, and Alberto Pérez-Gómez, who, in their writings, have repeatedly asked for an architecture that challenges "ocularcentristic" or "retinal" conceptions (as Pallasmaa calls buildings exclusively addressed to the sense of vision) in favor of designs that also respond to the senses of hearing, smell, and taste, but most of all, touch. As Pallasmaa puts it: "All the senses, including vision, can be regarded as extensions of the sense of touch" (2005: 42). See also Holl/Pallasmaa/Pérez-Gómez 1994/2008.

24 The transcript follows the English translation of Métra's statements in the film *Jean Nouvel – Aesthetics of Wonder* (dir. Beat Kuert, Switzerland 1998).

References

Agotai, Doris (2007). *Architekturen in Zelluloid: Der filmische Blick auf den Raum.* Bielefeld: transcript.

Albersmeier, Franz-Josef, ed. (2003). *Texte zur Theorie des Films.* 5th ed. Stuttgart: Reclam.

Balázs, Béla (1938/2003). "Zur Kunstphilosophie des Films". Albersmeier, ed. 201–223.

Bois, Yve-Alain, Michael Glenny (1989). "Sergei M. Eisenstein: Montage and Architecture". *Assemblage* 10: 110–131.

Boudon, Philippe (1971). *Sur l'espace architectural: Essai d'épistemologie de l'architecture.* Paris: Dunod Editeur Bordas.

— (1991). *Der architektonische Raum: Über das Verhältnis von Bauen und Erkennen.* Basel/Berlin/Boston, MA: Birkhäuser.

Choisy, Auguste (1899). *Histoire de l'architecture.* Vol. 1. Paris: Gauthier-Villars.

Cohen, Jean-Louis (1987). *Le Corbusier et la mystique de l'USSR: Théories et projets pour Moscou: 1928–1936.* Brussels: Mardaga.

— (1987/1992). *Le Corbusier and the Mystique of the USSR: Theories and Projects for Moscow: 1928–1936.* Transl. Kenneth Hylton. Princeton, NJ: Princeton UP.

Curtis, Robin (2008a). "Einführung in die Einfühlung". Robin Curtis, Gertrud Koch, eds. *Einfühlung: Zu Geschichte und Gegenwart eines ästhetischen Konzepts.* Munich: Fink. 11–30.

— (2008b). "Immersion und Einfühlung: Zwischen Repräsentationalität und Materialität bewegter Bilder". *montage AV* 17/2: 89–107.

Eisenstein, Sergei M. (1938/1991). "Montage and Architecture". *Selected Works.* Vol. 2: *Towards a Theory of Montage.* Eds. Michael Glenny, Richard Taylor. London: British Film Institute. 59–81.

Etlin, Richard A. (1987). "Le Corbusier, Choisy, and French Hellenism: The Search for a New Architecture". *The Art Bulletin* 69/2: 264–278.

Fillion, Odile (1997). "Life Into Art, Art Into Life: Fusions in Film, Video and Architecture". François Penz, Maureen Thomas, eds. *Cinema and Architecture: Méliès, Mallet-Stevens, Multimedia.* London: British Film Institute. 118–121.

Goulet, Patrice (1987). *Jean Nouvel.* Milan: Electa.

Holl, Steven, Juhani Pallasmaa, Alberto Pérez-Gómez (1994/2008).

Questions of Perception: Phenomenology of Architecture. San Francisco, CA: William Stout Publishers.
Keazor, Henry (2010). "'Avis de recherche': Verlorene Zeit und gefundener Raum in Jean Nouvels INIST". Burcu Dogramaci, Simone Förster, eds. *Architektur im Buch.* Dresden: Thelem. 211–226.
— (2011). "'L'architecte fait son spectacle': Medienrekurse in der Architektur Jean Nouvels". Andreas Beyer, Matteo Burioni, Johannes Grave, eds. *Das Auge der Architektur.* Munich: Fink. 377–420.
Koeck, Richard (2013). *Cine | Scape: Cinematic Spaces in Architecture.* New York, NY/London: Routledge.
Le Corbusier (1923). *Vers une architecture.* Paris: Editions Crès.
— (1923/2007). *Toward an Architecture.* Introd. Jean-Louis Cohen. Transl. John Goodman. Los Angeles, CA: Getty Research Institute.
— (1926). *Almanach d'architecture moderne.* Paris: Editions Crès.
— (1943/1957). *Entretien avec les étudiants des écoles d'architecture.* Paris: Editions de Minuit.
— (1947). "Villa Savoy à Poissy". *Œuvre complète.* Vol. 2: *1929–1934.* Ed. Pierre Jeanneret. 4th ed. Zurich: Editions d'architecture. 23–31.
— (1948). "2 Hôtels particuliers à Auteuil (La Roche-Jeanneret)". *Œuvre complète.* Vol. 1: *1910–1929.* Ed. Pierre Jeanneret. 5th ed. Zurich: Editions d'architecture. 60–67.
Lipps, Theodor (1897). *Raumästhetik und geometrisch-optische Täuschungen.* Leipzig: Barth.
Nouvel, Jean (1987). "Cinéma, architecture: Une envie de deserter". *L'architecture d'aujourd'hui* 254: 23–28.
— (2008a). *Jean Nouvel by Jean Nouvel.* Vol. 1: *1970–1992.* Ed. Philip Jodidio. Hong Kong et al.: TASCHEN.
— (2008b): *Jean Nouvel by Jean Nouvel.* Vol. 2: *1992–2008.* Ed. Philip Jodidio. Hong Kong et al.: TASCHEN.
Ockman, Joan (2000). "Architecture in a Mode of Distraction: Eight Takes on Jacques Tati's *Playtime*". Mark Lamster, ed. *Architecture and Film.* New York, NY: Princeton Architectural Press. 171–195.
Pallasmaa, Juhani (2005). *The Eyes of the Skin: Architecture and the Senses.* Chichester: Wiley.
Puaux, Françoise (1995). "Entretien". *CinémAction* 75: 104–106.
Pudovkin, Vsevolod (1928/2003). "Filmregie und Filmmanuskript: Einführung zur ersten deutschen Ausgabe". Albersmeier, ed. 70–73.
Rasmussen, Steen Eiler (1959). *Experiencing Architecture.* Cambridge, MA/London: MIT Press.

Rattenbury, Kester (1994). "Echo and Narcissus". *Architectural Design Profile* 112: 35–37.
Vidler, Anthony (1993). "The Explosion of Space: Architecture and the Filmic Imaginary". *Assemblage* 21: 44–59.
Voigt, Wolfgang, ed. (2006). *Gottfried Böhm.* Exh. cat. Frankfurt am Main: Deutsches Architekturmuseum, 26 August – 5 November 2006. Berlin: Jovis.
Weihsmann, Helmut (1988). *Gebaute Illusionen: Architektur im Film.* Vienna: Promedia.

Picture Credits

Ills. 1, 2: Fernando Márquez Cecilia, Richard Levene, eds. (2002). *El Croquis* 112/113: *Jean Nouvel – 1994/2002.* Madrid: El Croquis Editorial. 150, 139; Ills. 3a, 3b: Jean Nouvel (1999). *Una lezione in Italia.* Milan: Skira. 57; Ill. 4: archive of the author; Ill. 5: Olivier Boissière (2001). *Jean Nouvel.* Paris: Editions Pierre Terrail. 78; Ill. 6: Philip Jodidio (2012). *Jean Nouvel 1945: Donneur de formes.* Hong Kong et al.: TASCHEN. 52.

Illustration 1:
Herzog & de Meuron, Tristan und Isolde,
Berlin State Opera, Act 3, April 8, 2006. Photograph by Monika Rittershaus.

"The Treachery of Images"
Architecture, Immersion, and the Digital Realm

Ole W. Fischer

In the mid-1930s, faced with the double threat to European culture posed by Fascism and Stalinism, Walter Benjamin attempted to reassess art on the basis of the popular, technically reproducible media of photography and film. To do so, he made use of their political advantage: the transformation of individual contemplation into a collective perception and thereby the transformation of society as a whole. And it seems no accident that he refers to architecture as the art form whose reception has always taken place in a state of dispersion and adaptation. With regard to the new media of today and their immersive potential, this text proposes a reassessment of Benjamin's concept of an 'optic unconsciousness' and a 'collective, dispersed, haptic perception', updated by the contemporary shift from mechanical to digital reproduction. If Benjamin set his political hopes on architecture and the city, on their function in everyday life and on their dispersed, unconscious reception by the masses, where then do the emancipatory, participatory, and critical potentials for the appreciation of digital reproductions and immersive environments lie today? Preliminary answers might be drawn from a case study of an atmospheric stage set by Herzog & de Meuron.

1. Dive into Immersion

The term 'immersion', literally 'diving into', has taken on two different meanings in contemporary aesthetic discourse: both denote a shift into another form of reality, the loss of the present here and now in favor of an alternative mental state. Both further underline the emotional participation of the observer by reducing the (critical) distance between him or her and the observed. The two notions, however, take diverse positions on the degree of absorption of the viewer: on one side, immersion is pictured as a total enclosure by a medium, as an illusionistic image space, which presents a seamless totality capable of capturing the viewer's perception, and which addresses primarily digital virtual realities (cf. Grau 2003: 13f.)[1]. While this strand of 'im-

1 "On the one hand, they [virtual immersive spaces] give form to the 'all-embracing' ambitions of the media makers, and on the other, they offer the observers, particularly through their totality, the option of fusing with the image medium, which affects the

mersion' focuses on the medium and reduces the viewer's role to passive receiver[2], it is the term's other interpretation that emphasizes its internal effect. Following this hypothesis, each medium has the potential to bring about an emphatic experience: books (for example, the effect of Johann Wolfgang von Goethe's *The Sorrows of Young Werther* on the readership of his time), music (from Richard Wagner to contemporary raves), opera, theater, and cinema but also games, works of art and architecture, and even nature. Here, 'immersion' describes emotional absorption in a medium, a state of mind that psychology has labeled 'flow'. Immersion in 3-D films, virtual reality, augmented reality, or computer games might be new variations on a recurring perceptual motif but do not come close to constituting a media revolution. While the various media show differences, of course, regarding the construction of absorption, all forms of immersion guided by reception underline the active role of the enwrapped viewer, who willingly dives into their world. In other words, immersion takes place in the mind.

Although, historically, immersion can be traced back to the 1930s – when Béla Balázs introduced the term in order to distinguish between the multi-sensual 'new' medium of sound film and the 'old', one-dimensional, framed media of theater and painting – there is another genealogy, which leads back to the origin of the arts in religious cult: shifts of awareness, transcendence, and transgression have accompanied the arts from their prehistoric beginnings. This heritage includes the emotional participation of the masses as well as enhanced physiological conditions: ecstasy, intoxication, drive, and fury. Traces of this genealogical background are still present in the aesthetics of contemplation of modern philosophy (Immanuel Kant, Theodor W.

sensory impressions and awareness. This is a great difference from the nonhermetic effects of illusionistic painting, such as trompe l'oeil, where the medium is readily recognizable, and from images or image spaces that are delimited by a frame that is apparent to the observer, such as the theater or, to a certain extent, the diorama, and particularly television. In their delineated form these image media stage symbolically the aspect of difference. They leave the observer outside and are thus unsuitable for communicating virtual realities in a way that overwhelms the senses. For this reason, they do not form part of this study" (Grau 2003: 13f.).

2 In this regard, Michael Fried takes an extreme position by differentiating between the 'theatricality' of overwhelming and spectacular media and a viewer's contemplative absorption into a work and by denying the former the status of a work of art (see Fried 1980; 2002).

Adorno): the term 'contemplation' derives from religious assumption and literally means self-absorption in a religious work[3]. It removes viewers from their surroundings and seduces them into passivity – at least this is the suspicion Walter Benjamin and Hannah Arendt hold against contemplation, to which we will return later. If media theorists today play off the so-called manipulative and passive nature of immersion, atmosphere, and (virtual) image spaces against the distanced, critical contemplation of the arts, this text suggests an alternative reading, wherein both states of aesthetic assumption appear as cultural refinements of a cultic ritual (religious ecstasy), and hence as immanently related.

But let us return for a moment to the role of media as instruments of absorption in immersive experiences: shouldn't we consider architecture, or more specifically, interior design, as immersive, per se, since (interior) architecture is an artifact that encloses the viewer completely and confronts him or her with a total, synesthetic, artificial environment? Or, rather than confronting, does it encase him or her and present a human inner world (and hence oneself), as previously noted by Paul Valéry (see 1923)? Or should interiors be thought of as ego-cells and self-containers along the lines of Peter Sloterdijk, who defines architecture as the 'explication of inhabitation' ("Explikation des Aufenthalts"; 2004: 523) and human dwelling as 'spatial immune system' ("räumliche[s] Immunsystem"; 2004: 534)[4], with obvious references to Heidegger as well as neo-phenomenology?

2. Architecture and the (Digital) Image

Today, as soon as we touch upon architecture and immersion, the question of the digital image comes to the fore. This happens for two reasons: first, since architecture is designed with digital-image software (CAD, rendering, Photoshop, etc.), following the theory that the tools determine the product (see Kittler 1986), one expects to find a different type of work. The second reason is that architecture today is primarily distributed and consumed via (digital) images. Yet what ex-

3 The term 'contemplation' comes from the Latin words 'con' ('together' or 'with') and 'templum' ('sacred place', 'room reserved for the Gods'). As a compound, it might be translated as 'assumption' or 'pure perception', 'immersive meditation'.

4 Unless otherwise indicated, all translations are mine.

Illustration 2:
Herzog & de Meuron, Tristan und Isolde, *Berlin State Opera, Act 1, April 8, 2006. Photograph by Monika Rittershaus.*

actly is an image – and what is the difference between an analog and a digital one? In English, the word 'image' derives from the Latin 'imago', which refers to 'picture', 'effigy', 'figure', 'portrait', but also 'representation' (for example, a waxen death mask of an ancestor). It is also connected with the terms 'shadow', 'appearance', and – a hint pointing to the long-lasting dialectic between 'real being' versus 'superficial illusion' in Western philosophy from Plato to Jean Baudrillard – 'mimesis', since 'imago' shares the same Latin root with 'imitor', which translates to 'copy' or 'simulation'.

According to contemporary visual studies, an image produces a perceptual phenomenon that often (though not always) establishes a similarity between an image object and a physical object: the icon, as a natural symbol of semiotics. The image consists of a physical carrier (medium), which is the perceptual stimulus, and a resulting mental effect (phenomenon). The medium exists as a material substrate, like pigment on canvas or pixels on a screen, and triggers an immaterial representation of the image object in the viewer's sensory perception (cf. Wiesing 2005: 30f.). Therefore, the medium has to remain transparent, that is, below the viewer's threshold of recognition, in order to refrain from interfering with the visibility of the image object. This differentiation between matter and imagination, between physical carrier and psychological effect, connects visual studies to semiotic theories and resonates in the proverb that an image makes visible something other than itself. This does not exclude the eventuality of the transparency of the medium becoming the very subject of an artwork or artistic practice – one of Clement Greenberg's central claims regarding modern painting.

Regarding the question of architecture and image, we face a fundamental problem: the reduction of a multi-sensual, three-dimensional work to a visual phenomenon. This act of reduction has, of course, a

long tradition within the discipline. Architecture is primarily analyzed, distributed, taught, and discussed on the basis of visual representation: plan, perspective, photography. Yet it seems necessary to differentiate between image and image object – an edifice can be the motif of an image (analog or digital) just as well as any other object. The representation should not be confused with the object itself, as René Magritte reminded us with his painting *The Treachery of Images* (1928–1929): the image of a pipe is just as little a pipe as the word 'pipe' is a pipe (or as is the painted image of the word). Magritte problematizes, as Michel Foucault argues (see 1973), the relationship between representation by apparent resemblance via image as well as by arbitrary reference via language – and hence, our habitual order of things.

If visual representations determine the proliferation of, discourse about, and reflection upon architecture today, this only means that architects, historians, and theoreticians have come to believe that images are able to transport specific aspects of architectural projects. Yet the images (analog or digital) remain an abstraction and a deficient approximation of a complex, three-dimensional cultural artifact, a mediation of architecture. Therefore, we should take the initiative by Rem Koolhaas as a reminder: the master himself did not cease to build but formed AMO, a special think tank to explore the production of ideas, images, logos, and content within his larger, conventional architectural office, OMA.

The lament about the power of images' seductive nature was raised early on in modern architecture: around 1900, critics such as Adolf Loos and Hermann Muthesius complained about the dominance of graphic devices derived from Art Nouveau and painter-architects, and called for a return to (archi-)tectonic discipline. The proliferation of digital media added another layer to this 'paragone': contemporary architectural production is inseparable from digital image media. During the 1990s, there was an experimental enthusiasm for digital architecture. Designers dreamt, for example, of the fusion of architecture and image space in media architecture (a few of these projects were actually realized, like the Kunsthaus Graz by Peter Cook in 2003), of liquefied spaces and the transgression between material and immaterial, as well as of digital cities (see Mitchell 1995). At the same time, CAD promised to make extravagant designs possible with the help of digital fabrication (such as the Guggenheim Museum Bilbao by Frank Gehry in 1997). Today, however, digital representation has completely penetrated everyday office work: beginning with data collection, almost all projects are designed, drawn, tested, optimized, presented, detailed, and constructed via digital models (BIM), including the operation and control of the erected buildings. This is also true for the decision-making process involved in design: from orthogonal projections to perspectives, renderings, and animations, including 3-D plotting, digital fabrication, and the application of robots in manufacturing – all steps are entirely based on digital representation. In addition, parametric design software is increasingly being used to script, calculate, and optimize complex design decisions.

Yet, does this omnipresence of digital media in the planning, execution, and reception of design sufficiently explain the shift in the relationship of architecture to image? Specifically, does it qualify as a digital style in architecture, as critics have argued with regard to the work of Zaha Hadid, UNStudio, F.O.A., Frank Gehry, Greg Lynn, and other contemporary offices? Or does the relationship between architecture and (digital) immersive media offer a more complex reading? Without questioning the impact of digital media on contemporary architecture, this essay scrutinizes digital technology's linear narration of determination and proposes an alternative, in which medium, practice, and reception are more dialectically intertwined, and which – in the footsteps of Walter Benjamin – discusses the effects of new media on the perception of time, space, place, and the city in the arts as well as in everyday life.

3. Learning from Benjamin
The Immersion of Architecture and the Architecture of Immersion

In the mid-1930s, in the face of the dual threat to European culture by Fascism and Stalinism, Walter Benjamin took on a revision of the arts on the basis of the popular, technically reproducible media of photograph and film (see 2008)[5]. He believed in the political advantage of these 'new' media, despite the widely lamented loss of the artwork's authenticity and autonomy: the replacement of "cult value" by "exhibition value" (ibid.: 25) ("Kultwert"; "Ausstellungswert"; 1936/1977: 21). Although in his preface, he relativized orthodox mantras of materialist Marxism in favor of a slower, more dialectical evolution between idealistic superstructure and material conditions of cultural production, this opposition between a mythological "cult value" and a visual/perceptive "exhibition value" appears to be a straight recourse to the pair 'exchange value' and 'use value' employed by Karl Marx to describe the fetishistic character of money (and surplus value) in the capitalist liberal market economy. According to Benjamin, this shift from "cult value" to "exhibition value" caused by the reproducible media of photography is shown in Eugène Atget's empty, ghostly images of deserted Parisian streets: he interprets them as a "scene of crime" and "evidence in the historical trial" (2008: 27) ("Tatort"; "Beweisstücke im historischen Prozess"; 1936/1977: 21). This homage to Atget, however, was already a regressive move in the mid-1930s, at the time when Benjamin conceived the artwork essay, in which he dives back into the short history of the then new medium of photography in very

Illustration 3: Herzog & de Meuron, Tristan und Isolde, *Berlin State Opera, Act 2, April 8, 2006. Photograph by Monika Rittershaus.*

5 Written during the years of his exile in Paris between 1934 and 1935, Walter Benjamin's essay "The Work of Art in the Age of Mechanical Reproduction" originally appeared in 1936 in a shortened French translation in *Zeitschrift für Sozialforschung* 5: 40–68.

much the same mode as his numerous references to silent movies, although they had been replaced by talkies by the early 1930s.

Therefore it is less the novelty of 'new' media than the conclusion drawn by Benjamin that is of interest for this discussion: from a shift in the value of art – that is, the accessibility and the use of artworks – he deduces a shift in human perception and, ultimately, a shift in the definition of art, with all its societal implications. The crisis and renewal of the arts – triggered by technical reproducibility and new means of mass distribution, which, for Benjamin, must necessarily lead to artworks that take these conditions into account conceptually – relate to the crisis and renewal of society at large and promise the destruction and liberation of traditional societal conditions.

The notion of the 'identical copy' that is inscribed into film and photography as mechanically reproduced images fundamentally differentiates them from a traditionally crafted work of art, whose authority relies on singularity, permanence, and historical evidence – or, as Benjamin defined the inapproachability of "aura", which he derives from the mythological origin of the arts in ritual, on "the unique apparition of a distance, however near it may be" (2008: 23) ("einmalige Erscheinung einer Ferne, so nah sie sein mag"; 1936/1977: 15). While in traditional art, the individual observer immerses him- or herself into the singular work (in a temple, museum, or private collection), the situation in the modern metropolis is reversed: the multitude of technically reproduced works is immersed in the distracted and dispersed urban masses[6]. Benjamin expects an emancipatory potential, a shift of perception from the individual contemplative to the collective tactile and unconscious. Not for nothing, he refers to architecture and urban space as precedent of an art form

6 "Distraction and concentration form an antithesis, which may be formulated as follows. A person who concentrates before a work of art is absorbed by it; he enters into the work, just as, according to the legend, a Chinese painter entered his completed painting while beholding it. By contrast, the distracted masses absorb the work of art into themselves. [...] This is most obvious with regard to buildings. Architecture has always offered the prototype of an artwork that is received in a state of distraction and through the collective" (2008: 39f.). ("Zerstreuung und Sammlung stehen in einem Gegensatz, der die Formulierung erlaubt: Der vor dem Kunstwerk sich Sammelnde versenkt sich darein; er geht in dieses Werk ein, wie die Legende es von einem chinesischen Maler beim Anblick seines vollendeten Bildes erzählt. Dagegen versenkt die zerstreute Masse ihrerseits das Kunstwerk in sich. Am sinnfälligsten die Bauten. Die Architektur bot von jeher den Prototyp eines Kunstwerks, dessen Rezeption in der Zerstreuung und durch das Kollektivum erfolgt"; 1936/1977: 40).

that has always been received in a state of dispersion, distraction, and habituation, as tactile art par excellence (cf. 1936/1977: 41).

Benjamin's analogy, however, also raises some questions: isn't architecture an art form of singularity (place, time, authorship, context, etc.), of permanence, of historic authority (monument, representation) and auratic distance? Doesn't architecture confront us with cultic-ritualism? Isn't it an expression of the ruling societal relations, even an instrument of power, surveillance, and control, as Foucault demonstrated in his study on the Panopticon? The last fortress of metaphysics, as suspected by Jacques Derrida? Therefore shouldn't we consider architecture as the remaining shelter of traditional art of "cult value"? Maybe we need to rethink Benjamin's comparison of technical media with architecture against the background of his *Arcades Project*: here he regards Haussmann's Paris of the 19th century as a homogenous ensemble of nearly anonymous buildings, as a collective piece of art or memory, which he approaches with Sigmund Freud's method of dream work, in order to excavate its unconscious modern traits. This perspective of architecture – and of the urban fabric – as a manifestation of latent collective memory, where the singular architectural element recedes behind common rules (or structures), experienced a renaissance during the second half of the 20th century with the morphologic-typological analysis of the European city as championed, for example, by Saverio Muratori or Aldo Rossi. Especially Rossi (see 1966) – with his poetic interpretation of archetypical forms, buildings, and spatial configurations – refers to the notion held by C. G. Jung as well as by Maurice Halbwachs (see 1939/1950) of the city as a 'collective memory', and hence closely parallels Benjamin's ideas from a prior generation. Or is Benjamin referring to the indeterminacy of architecture, its contaminated position between art and commerce, between cultural superstructure and infrastructural base, and hence its "use value", which he parallels with the distraction and dispersion of film? Here the term 'Zerstreuung' employed by Benjamin, meaning 'dispersion' or 'distraction', offers a twofold reading of, first, the spatial distribution of a work of art (series, reproduction, circulation) and, second, society's inattentive perception and enjoyment of an artwork and its overall popularity, as, for example, in the case of motion pictures. Hence, Benjamin underlines the aspect of "simultaneous collective reception" (2008: 36) ("simultane Kollektivrezeption"; 1936/1977: 33) in architecture and (formerly) the epic, which he recognizes in motion pictures, except here, film's specific means of expres-

Illustration 4:
Herzog & de Meuron, Tristan und Isolde, *Berlin State Opera, Act 2, April 8, 2006. Photograph by Monika Rittershaus.*

sion (close-up, slow motion, montage) provoke a change in the audience's spatial and temporal imagination.

If we understand the modern metropolis, on the one hand, as a historical product of political processes and, on the other, as a space of projection for prospective social, political, and cultural ways of life – as a field of activity that allows for, determines, and limits forms of political action – this raises the question of the interaction of experience and imagination, of the perception of the existing and the projection of alternative urban spaces, in short, of history and design. Therefore I would suggest a reconsideration of Benjamin's concepts of the "optical unconscious" (2008: 37) ("Optisch-Unbewussten"; 1936/1977: 36) and the collective, dispersed, distracted, tactile perception[7] of ar-

7 "Buildings are received in a twofold manner: by use and by perception. Or, better: tactilely and optically. Such reception cannot be understood in terms of the concentrated attention of a traveler before a famous building. On the tactile side, there is no counterpart to what contemplation is on the optical side. Tactile reception comes about not so much by way of attention as by way of habit. The latter largely determines even the optical reception of architecture, which spontaneously takes the form of casual noticing, rather than attentive observation. [...] The sort of distraction that is provided by art represents a covert measure of the extent to which it has become possible to perform new tasks of apperception" (2008: 40). ("Bauten werden auf doppelte Art rezipiert:

chitecture as starting points, in order to update them in light of the current shift from mechanical to digital reproduction.

4. The Profane Illuminations of Surrealism

The desire to lose oneself, to transgress into another reality, and for the intense emotional perception of immersive phenomena is entangled with dreams, intoxication, sexual or religious-cultic ecstasy – in short, with enhanced physiologic states. This insight is not new but is at the core of the writings of Friedrich Nietzsche (as in the oppositional pair Dionysian/Apollonian) and Henri Bergson, as well as the psychoanalysis of Sigmund Freud. In the arts, we can identify Surrealism as the most distinct manifestation of these enhanced physiologic states, which Benjamin recognized with a dialectical reading in 1929. He highlights its close connection to dreams, intoxication, and the unconscious, but without any prejudice: on the contrary, Benjamin sees the immersion in different realities of delirium, dreams, and drugs as a 'loosening of individuality' ("Lockerung des Ich"; 1929/2007: 146), as anarchic-communist forces, and hence scrutinizes the traditional differentiation between distanced, rational, critical art and, apparently, the uncritical, emotional surrender and dissolution into an immersive medium. Significantly, he gives an alternative meaning to the 'esoteric' nature of Surrealist novels: neither love story (André Breton's *Nadja*) nor rapture but proximity to everyday things (or should we say a presence 'in the things'?). This is because Benjamin ascribes to Surrealism the discovery of the 'revolutionary energies that appear in the "outmoded"' ("revolutionären Energien, die im 'Veralteten' erscheinen"; ibid.: 149), that is, the transformative forces that reside in the close observation and conscious use of – or immersion in and misuse of – everyday commodities of the past. This goes beyond

durch Gebrauch und deren Wahrnehmung. Oder besser gesagt: taktil und optisch. Es gibt von solcher Rezeption keinen Begriff, wenn sie sich nach Art der gesammelten vorstellt, wie sie z.B. Reisenden vor berühmten Bauten geläufig ist. Es besteht nämlich auf der taktilen Seite keinerlei Gegenstück zu dem, was auf der optischen die Kontemplation ist. Die taktile Rezeption erfolgt nicht sowohl auf dem Wege der Aufmerksamkeit als auf dem der Gewohnheit. Der Architektur gegenüber bestimmt diese letztere weitgehend sogar die optische Rezeption. Auch sie findet von Hause aus viel weniger in einem gespannten Aufmerken als in einem beiläufigen Bemerken statt. [...] Durch die Zerstreuung, wie die Kunst sie zu bieten hat, wird unter der Hand kontrolliert, wie weit neue Aufgaben der Apperzeption lösbar geworden sind"; 1936/1977: 40f.).

Illustration 5:
Herzog & de Meuron, Tristan und Isolde, *Berlin State Opera, Act 2, April 8, 2006. Photograph by Monika Rittershaus.*

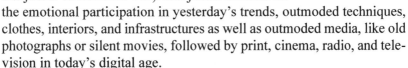

the contemplation of passed time, as in, for example, Alois Riegl's notion of emotional 'age value' (see 1903), but embraces the revolutionary experience that lies in the 'immense forces of "atmosphere"' ("gewaltigen Kräfte der 'Stimmung'"; Benjamin 1929/2007: 149). Benjamin touches on the emotional participation in yesterday's trends, outmoded techniques, clothes, interiors, and infrastructures as well as outmoded media, like old photographs or silent movies, followed by print, cinema, radio, and television in today's digital age.

According to Benjamin, Surrealism operates via the displacement of old things through dreams and intoxication – a de-contextualization and re-contextualization – which facilitates a 'substitution of a political for a historical view of the past' ("Auswechslung des historischen Blicks aufs Gewesene gegen den politischen"; ibid.). This is most obvious with the largest and most artificial object of all: the outdated city. The immersion of the protagonists in Surrealist novels (or art per se) in urban spaces and interiors (particularly, in a combination of the two in the form of Parisian arcades) uncovers the mechanism of the unconscious, of the process of historic evolution. Individual experiments with the personal unconscious of the past reveal society's unconscious, the 'transformation of a highly contemplative attitude into revolutionary opposition' ("Umwandlung einer extrem kontemplativen Haltung in die revolutionäre Opposition"; ibid.: 156). According to materialist dialectics, the projection of a different world is not possible – only a critique of the existing one is. Estrangement, dreams, intoxication, and Surrealism's deep-rooted pessimism induce 'profane illuminations' ("profane Erleuchtung"; ibid.: 157), which prepare the subject for different practices but (still) elude representation. Novels and the arts will exhaust themselves in neither contemplation nor optimism but will proceed to a critique of politics and its hegemonic image space[8] and bring about a change of attitude via a

8 "To win the energies of intoxication for the revolution – this is the project about which Surrealism circles in all its books and enterprises" (Benjamin 1986: 189). ("Die

change of perception[9]. Hence, in close analogy to his artwork essay, Benjamin underlines the revolutionary potential embedded within the appropriation of new aesthetic practices, in the transgression of the arts from the sacred grove of the museum or discourse into everyday life.

5. 'Dive in and go under' *Tristan*, from a Physiological Point of View

Let's return to the hypothesis of the artwork essay: what if digital technologies do not effect historical, political, and cultural evolution directly (via production process and form), but indirectly, via a change in the perception of the city, space, time, and body? A potential test case for a more nuanced 'digital architecture' might be the design and performance of immersive environments that aim for the production of apparent presence, for the staging of authenticity. As Benjamin noted, the realism and naturalness of motion pictures spring dialectically from the very artificial process of shooting disconnected, individual takes and later re-assembling these scenes into a montage as well as from the total

Kräfte des Rausches für die Revolution zu gewinnen, darum kreist der Sürrealismus in allen Büchern und Unternehmen"; Benjamin 1929/2007: 157).

9 "The collective is a body, too. And the *physis* that is being organized for it in technology can, through all its political and factual reality, only be produced in that image sphere to which profane illumination initiates us" (Benjamin 1986: 192). ("Auch das Kollektiv ist leibhaft. Und die Physis, die sich in der Technik ihm organisiert, ist nach ihrer ganzen politischen und sachlichen Wirklichkeit nur in jenem Bildraume [des politisch-öffentlichen] zu erzeugen, in welchem die profane Erleuchtung uns heimisch gemacht hat"; Benjamin 1929/2007: 158f.).

penetration of the mechanical image with the apparatus (cf. 1936/1977: 32). While in the theater, the stage actor plays a role (somebody else), for Benjamin, it is distinctive of the movie star (and the modern dictator) to be a product of a complex media construction, always acting as a fictitious personality – hence turning into a sort of prop. In parallel, atmospheric architecture could be regarded as a similarly complex construction of physical, haptic, and authentic stimuli, which result from the total penetration of techniques of digital reproduction.

One possible example is Herzog & de Meuron's stage design for Richard Wagner's music drama *Tristan und Isolde* at the Berlin State Opera in 2006 (see *Illustrations 1* and *2*): in accordance with the scenic director, Stephan Bachmann, and musical director, Daniel Barenboim, Jacques Herzog and Pierre de Meuron refrained from using screens, projections, sensor-driven digital interaction, and multi-media stage sets, as have been employed by other avant-gardist colleagues – such as Diller + Scofidio[10] – and instead aimed to stage the 'things' themselves. They used everyday 'things', not fragments or motifs taken from their own oeuvre, such as the Prada Aoyama Epicenter in Tokyo or the National Olympic Stadium, the *Bird's Nest*, in Beijing, the way some other famous architects did, such as Zaha Hadid, Frank Gehry, or Stephan Braunfels, who were asked to contribute to sets and delivered 'signature' elements of their buildings. Herzog & de Meuron presented these 'things' not in a naturalistic fashion but as impressions or casts of physical objects, which were then pushed from behind against a semi-transparent, off-white, concave rubber skin that took up large parts of the actual stage (see *Illustrations 3* to *6*). This mediatization is a trick used to bring out the haptic qualities of the physical objects in order to convey a visual tactility to the audience, seated the customary distance from the stage for a concert hall, similar to the close-up in cinema. Herzog & de Meuron employed this strategy not only to question digital mediatization and reproduction in architecture but also to criticize postmodern mimetic-picturesque theatricality, which was exemplified by the Strada Novissima exhibition at the 1980 Venice Biennale. Instead of semiotic references, the two Swiss architects played out the silent presence of materials (stones, rigging, stairs), which, although they are not presented, exist as quasi-tactile impressions translated into

10 See the stage designs of Diller + Scofidio for *Moving Target* (Charleroi, 1996) or *Rotary Notary and His Hot Plate* (Philadelphia, 1986), part of *The Bride/Bachelor Trilogy*.

the visual domain on the 'breathing skin' of the stage. Yet here, the design, construction, and operation of the membrane, which transformed the backstage into one large low-pressure chamber, relied completely on CAD and building IP: in the words of Benjamin, they have been totally penetrated by the apparatus of digital reproduction.

But for what effect? The flattening out of the entire stage, leaving only a small strip of the proscenium for the actors, and the reduction of the height of the stage opening to about 1/3 its original height led to a transformation of the stage into a wide, cinemascope format. Other perceptual manipulations related to the world of cinema as well: an equally distributed, indirect light dematerialized the actors, quite similar to the effect seen in Stanley Kubrick's *2001: A Space Odyssey* (USA/UK 1968). In this film, the glistening, indirect, white light suppresses shadows, the weight of objects, and their spatial depth, thereby reducing the filmed pictures to seemingly abstract, two-dimensional images and supporting the impression of zero gravity. The set of *Tristan und Isolde* introduced a peculiar contradiction between the haptic corporeality of the objects presented on stage and the apparent floating immateriality of the actors in front of them, which was underlined by Bachmann's instruction to give frozen, static performances. This might be a hint pointing to the pessimism of Wagner, who was an acknowledged adherent of Arthur Schopenhauer: the singers' posed, distanced, and stiff acting in slow motion as well as the visual tangibility of the casts of the physical objects on stage alluded to the 'veil of Maya', the illusionistic 'reality' of images, people, and things, while the 'truth' lay in the dramatic music. Furthermore, it is in the tradition of the young Nietzsche, who interpreted Wagner's *Tristan* as the genealogical successor of the ancient Greek tragedy, as an Apollonian appearance of Dionysian truth, as a collective 'vision' of something invisible, unspeakable, and unimaginable: will (cf. Nietzsche 1872/1999: 30f.).

Yet this would mean leaving the ground of modernity and regressing into some metaphysical romanticism, vitalism, or phenomenology, which Wagner, Schopenhauer, and Nietzsche stand for as much as Heidegger does. But this example raises the question of whether one has to understand the re-auratization of architecture in dialectical reaction to digital techniques of reproduction and visual simulation – as an anti-modern reflex. Doesn't even Benjamin's essay on the artwork contain regressive elements, such as his recourse to silent movies after their time had passed? And what about his take on Surrealism? Doesn't he express unashamed enthusiasm for intoxication, drug use, dreams, and esoteric

Illustration 6:
Herzog & de Meuron, Tristan und Isolde, *Berlin State Opera, Act 2, April 8, 2006. Photograph by Monika Rittershaus.*

truths? Isn't his reconsideration of architecture and the metropolis of the 19th century as well as his reflection on the epic rather a working through of cultural memory and trauma – a swan song for outdated media and urban environments at the time of their disappearance?

Especially Benjamin's term 'aura' is a hint in this direction, since, etymologically, it means 'breeze' or 'breath of air', and had already been deciphered, at the time he wrote the essay, as a reference to the mystic ideas of Kabbalah. The re-interpretation of 'aura' by Gernot Böhme, which bypasses the criticism and neo-phenomenological spin placed on the term by former authors, is part of a larger reconsideration of aesthetics – literally, a study of perception and sensory-emotional values – regarding nature, architecture, and the arts. Closely connected to 'aura' is the concept of 'atmosphere', which refers to a bodily relation of the recipient to the emanation of the artwork (or space in general) and his or her previous mental or, more specifically, emotional state (see Böhme 1995; 2006). While Böhme's concept of 'atmosphere' enjoyed growing popularity among architects parallel to the rise of (Swiss) minimalism and architecture's return to the experiential qualities of space, material, and site – echoing older strands of contextualism, regionalism, and phenomenology (see Zumthor 2006a/b) – this does not answer questions regarding its political content: for Benjamin, the loss of 'aura', of traditional forms of art (and their reception), was compensated for by an increase in availability, distribution, and popularity; hence he embraced technologically reproducible arts for their politically emancipatory effect. For him, immersion – in the twofold sense of everyday, habitual experience (of, for example, architecture or new media) and of the appropriation of new (revolutionary) forms of perception (induced by these media) – replaced the exhausted possibilities of critical works of art. Today, however, the relationship between techniques of digital reproduction, their effect on apperception, and political agency remains unclear. Is the politicization of the arts asked for by Benjamin still plausible today in the face of the widespread de-politicization, privatization, and commercialization of urban spaces as well as of the media? In particular, how can we understand architecture – structures fetishized as global brand events, staged as auratic works of art, styled by signature 'starchitects' – that wants to be consciously contemplated, experienced, and (virtually) consumed? Could the critical potential of architecture in the age of digital reproducibility lie within its tactility? Maybe theorists and critics should focus more on questions of everyday use, performance, appropriation, and sensual experience, in other words, approach architecture from the receptive framework of collective apperception rather than from the productive framework of technology and form. What conclusions could be drawn for architectural and urban design? A thorough evaluation of the political implications of the interaction between contemporary architecture, digital media, and collective apperception remains open, but here is a hint: it comes down to learning from Benjamin.

References

Benjamin, Walter (1929/2007). "Der Sürrealismus". *Passagen: Schriften zur französischen Literatur*. Ed. Gérard Raulet. Frankfurt am Main: Suhrkamp. 145–159.

— (1936/1977). *Das Kunstwerk im Zeitalter seiner technischen Reproduzierbarkeit: Drei Studien zur Kunstsoziologie*. Frankfurt am Main: Suhrkamp.

— (1986). "Surrealism: The Last Snapshot of the European Intelligentsia". *Reflections: Essays, Aphorisms, Autobiographical Writings*. Ed. Peter Demetz. New York, NY: Schocken. 177–192.

— (2008). *The Work of Art in the Age of Its Technological Reproducibility, and Other Writings on Media*. Eds. Michael W. Jennings, Brigid Doherty, Thomas Y. Levin. Transl. Edmund Jephcott et al. Cambridge, MA: Belknap Press of Harvard UP.

Böhme, Gernot (1995). *Atmosphäre: Essays zur neuen Ästhetik*. Frankfurt am Main: Suhrkamp.

— (2006). *Architektur und Atmosphäre*. Munich/Paderborn: Fink.

Foucault, Michel (1973). *Ceci n'est pas une pipe: 2 lettres et 4 dessins de René Magritte*. Paris: Fata Morgana.

— (1983). *This Is Not a Pipe: With Illustrations and Letters by René Magritte*. Ed. and transl. James Harkness. Berkeley, CA: University of California Press.

Fried, Michael (1980). *Absorption and Theatricality: Painting and Beholder in the Age of Diderot*. Berkeley, CA: University of California Press.
— (2002). *Menzel's Realism: Art and Embodiment in Nineteenth-Century Berlin*. New Haven, CT: Yale UP.
Grau, Oliver (2001). *Virtuelle Kunst in Geschichte und Gegenwart: Visuelle Strategien*. Berlin: Reimer.
— (2003). *Virtual Art: From Illusion to Immersion*. Transl. Gloria Custance. Cambridge, MA/London: MIT Press.
Halbwachs, Maurice (1939/1950). *La Mémoire collective*. Paris: Presses Universitaires de France.
— (1980). *The Collective Memory*. New York, NY: Harper & Row.
Kittler, Friedrich A. (1986). *Grammophon, Film, Typewriter*. Berlin: Brinkmann & Bose.
— (1999). *Gramophone, Film, Typewriter*. Transl. Geoffrey Winthrop-Young. Stanford, CA: Stanford UP.
Mitchell, William J. (1995). *City of Bits: Space, Place, and the Infobahn*. Cambridge, MA/London: MIT Press.
Nietzsche, Friedrich (1872/1999). "Die Geburt der Tragödie aus dem Geiste der Musik". *Sämtliche Werke: Kritische Studienausgabe in 15 Bänden (KSA)*. Vol. 1. Eds. Giorgio Colli, Mazzino Montinari. Munich/Berlin: dtv/de Gruyter. 9–156.
Riegl, Alois (1903). *Der moderne Denkmalkultus: Sein Wesen und seine Entstehung*. Vienna/Leipzig: Braumüller.
Rossi, Aldo (1966). *L'Architettura de la città*. Padova: Marsilio.
— (1982). *The Architecture of the City*. Introd. Peter Eisenman. Cambridge, MA/London: MIT Press.
Sloterdijk, Peter (2004). *Sphären*. Vol. 3: *Schäume: Plurale Sphärologie*. Frankfurt am Main: Suhrkamp.
Valéry, Paul (1923). *Eupalinos ou l'architecte, précédé de L'âme et la danse*. Paris: Nouvelle Revue française.
— (1932). *Eupalinos: Or, The Architect*. Transl. William McCausland Stewart. London: OUP.
Wiesing, Lambert (2005). *Artifizielle Präsenz: Studie zur Philosophie des Bildes*. Frankfurt am Main: Suhrkamp.
— (2010). *Artificial Presence: Philosophical Studies in Image Theory*. Stanford, CA: Stanford UP.
Zumthor, Peter (2006a). *Atmosphären: Architektonische Umgebungen – die Dinge um mich herum*. Basel/Berlin/Boston, MA: Birkhäuser.
— (2006b). *Atmospheres: Architectural Environments – Surrounding Objects*. Transl. Ian Galbraith. Basel/Berlin/Boston, MA: Birkhäuser.

Illustration 1:
Hans Thoma, Blick vom Pilatus
(1904). Oil on canvas, 161 x 132 cm.
Staatliche Kunsthalle Karlsruhe.

Painting Immersion
Hans Thoma's Landscapes

Matthias Krüger

This essay explores the landscape paintings by the German artist Hans Thoma. For Alois Riegl and other art theorists, the concept of 'Stimmung' that is demonstrated in Thoma's paintings is based on the experience of immersion in nature. In his seminal essay on this topic, Riegl names silence, peace, and distant vision as its necessary preconditions. Indeed, contemporary critics praised Thoma's landscape paintings for their immersive quality, often contrasting the serene atmosphere of his paintings with the unrest of modern life. The essay traces the lines of the argument that Thoma's paintings served as an antidote to modernity. In a historical perspective, it also shows that the German concept of 'Stimmung' was intrinsically bound to the experience of nature in the Industrial Age and, thus, is by no means identical with 'immersion' in the terms of recent media studies. On the contrary, the essay implicitly uses the concept of 'Stimmung' as a possible cross-check of the expansibility of the term 'immersion' by pointing to the importance of the historical discourse that gave this concept its decisive shape.

1. Riegl's Concept of 'Stimmung'

The German concept of 'Stimmung' is not casily explained. It can be translated into various English terms such as 'atmosphere', 'mood', 'sentiment', 'spirit', 'temper', 'tune', and 'vibe', but none of these terms seems to fully capture its meaning. Just as various are the results one receives when one enters the keyword 'Stimmung' into the search engine Google Images. Approximately half of the images that appear have something to do with landscape photography: a close-up of a stream rippling over a mossy crag, an evening atmosphere at a lake, or a sunset in the mountains. The other half are snapshots of people dancing and celebrating – photos which are meant to document the 'great atmosphere' prevailing at a party or concert[1]. The contrast could hardly be greater: on the one hand, deserted landscapes; on the other, dense throngs of people. This opposition can also be cap-

1 As of June 16, 2012.

tured onomatopoetically: in one picture, the peaceful natural setting allows us to almost hear the gurgling of the stream; in another picture, we 'hear' jubilation and loud music. We can, thus, speak of two contrary soundscapes[2]. Indeed, at all times, both examples of 'Stimmung' can be understood as soundscapes, because the German word has its origins in the specific vocabulary of music. It derives from the verb 'stimmen', meaning to tune (an instrument, for example). Where there is 'Stimmung', everything is accordingly attuned to one tone. Yet 'Stimmung' has its place not only in the outside world, but also within the subject (see Wellbery 2003)[3]. As such, the correlation between external and internal moods can be described in a variety of ways. The subject, for example, can project his or her internal mood onto the external world; he or she can also be influenced by external moods, indeed, plunge into these and then feel at one with his or her surroundings – regardless of whether these surroundings take the form of a secluded natural setting or a mass of humans.

In a broad sense, the experience of 'Stimmung' may be understood as a certain form of immersion defined as a process of "recentering" by which "consciousness relocates itself to another world" (Ryan 2001: 103). In a more specific understanding, however, the term has to be understood on the grounds of its own discursive history, which is the subject of this article. In this historical perspective, images belonging to the category of 'Stimmung' can not only be seen as proposals to immerse into the mood or atmosphere that is captured or represented therein (cf. Lübbren 2001: chapter 5)[4], they also offer the opportunity to reflect on the expansibility and limits of the concept of 'immersion' itself.

According to the definition established by Alois Riegl in his 1899 essay "Stimmung als Inhalt der modernen Kunst", only a selection of the aforementioned images could be said to have 'Stimmung' (see 1899/1929). Riegl names two necessary conditions that must be fulfilled for the subject to be able to 'tune in': peace ('Ruhe') and distant

2 On soundscapes in general, see Schafer 1977/1994; on the soundscapes of modernity, see Thompson 2002; on soundscapes in art, see Jøran, ed. 2011.

3 According to Wellbery, it is constitutive of the term 'Stimmung' that it resists a clear categorization as being subjective or objective (cf. 2003: 704).

4 According to Nina Lübbren, the concept of 'Stimmung' offered 19th-century landscape painters a way of thinking about and painting the experience of immersion (cf. 2001: chapter 5).

view ('Fernsicht'). The pictures of parties thus fall away, as does the close-up of the forest stream. In contrast, the photos of mountain landscapes would almost epitomize Riegl's demands.

His essay starts out with a description of an alpine atmosphere: 'I came to rest on a remote alpine mountaintop. The ground dropped directly in front of my feet so that no thing before me remained within reach to tease the organs of my tactile sense.'[5] The two motifs of 'peace' and 'distant view' already make themselves heard in this first sentence. On the one hand, the peak is described as remote – remoteness is a virtual guarantee of peace – and, on the other, the hillside drops away from him so steeply that his view can range unhindered and far afield without becoming snagged on the foreground. Distant view and peace are co-determinant. From a distance, it seems to Riegl's first-person narrator that nature has been submerged in an overarching peace: though the grazing cows do not remain still for a moment, from where he is looking, they seem to him to be no more than tiny white specks. When seen from the distant lookout he occupies, the awe-inspiring, angrily thundering waterfall metamorphoses into a bright band of silver. Surveying from a height, he perceives only the cloud of smoke rising from a house's chimney among all the to-and-fros of the valley dwellers. The distant view harmonizes and, at the same time, it also relieves Riegl of an oppressive feeling, namely the knowledge that the struggle for existence rules everywhere in nature (cf. 1899/1929: 28f.). 'Stimmung' is able to temporarily deactivate this knowledge, but nothing safeguards the sense of peace from being abruptly destroyed again at any time by the very incursion of the fight for survival. In Riegl's essay, exactly this befalls the first-person narrator. A mountain goat not only tears him out of his absorption but also wakens his hunting instinct and has him automatically reaching for his gun, which he mistakes for his walking stick. Riegl reasons from this experience:

> Such a subtle thing is this 'Stimmung' that a nearby sign of life is enough to cast it to the wind. [...] It is the cross-checking of those elements – peace and distant

5 "Auf einem einsamen Alpengipfel habe ich mich niedergelassen. Steil senkt sich das Erdreich unmittelbar zu meinen Füßen, so daß kein Ding vor mir in greifbarer Nähe bleibt und die Organe meines Tastsinns reizen könnte" (Riegl 1899/1929: 28). Unless otherwise indicated, all translations are mine.

> view – from which 'Stimmung' issues: movement and proximity have hurled me back into the struggle for existence.[6]

According to this, partaking in the nature of 'Stimmung' is no simple undertaking. First of all, anyone who seeks to become attuned must find as lonely a place as possible, such as a mountaintop or a bay (cf. ibid.: 30). The most minimal disturbance is enough to rip the viewer out of the state of absorption and to destroy the feeling of immersion. The value of capturing 'Stimmung' in painting must be seen precisely in the light of this problem. No peak has to be scaled for the viewer to be able to dive into the atmosphere that has been painted. What is more, the viewer can abandon him- or herself to it with fewer interruptions. Riegl even calls landscape painting 'the most expedient method of putting us in "Stimmung" […] often much more suitable than the landscape in nature itself, where one is distracted from the "*Stimmung*" by too many things [my emphasis]'[7]. Painting, at the same time, provides the perfect general conditions for the experience of 'Stimmung' – a view that Georg Simmel similarly represents in his 1913 article "Philosophie der Landschaft" (cf. 1913/2001: 482). Indeed, contemporary German art theory considered 'Stimmungsmalerei' (a branch of painting devoted to rendering mood and atmosphere) an important subgenre of landscape painting (see *Meyers Großes Konversationslexikon* 1905)[8].

2. Distant Views in Thoma's Landscapes

In what follows, I will cast a look through Riegl's lens at Hans Thoma's 'Stimmungsmalerei'. Thoma is explicitly counted as being

---

6 "Ein so subtiles Ding ist diese Stimmung, daß eine Lebensregung in der Nähe genügt, um sie hinwegzublasen. […] Es ist die Gegenprobe auf jene Elemente – Ruhe und Fernsicht –, aus denen die Stimmung hervorgeht: Bewegung und Nahsicht haben mich in den Kampf ums Dasein zurückgeschleudert." (ibid.: 29f.)

7 "[…] das geeignetste Mittel […], um uns in Stimmung zu versetzen […] oft viel geeigneter als die Landschaft selbst in Natur, wo man durch vielerlei von der Stimmung abgelenkt wird" (Riegl in a lecture from 1896, qtd. Olin 1992: 218, n. 28).

8 This encyclopedia entry divides landscape painting into the three subgenres of "Vedute" (veduta), "stilisierte Landschaft" (stylized landscape), and "Stimmungslandschaft" (landscape of 'Stimmung').

one of the modern painters of atmospheres in Riegl's essay, albeit in a surprising context. The Austrian art historian cites Thoma's satyrs alongside Böcklin's nixies as proof of the compatibility of 'Stimmungsmalerei' and 'free poetry' ("freier Dichtung"; Riegl 1899/1929: 36). We could argue that this extending of Riegl's notion to encompass mythological painting muddies rather than sharpens his concept of 'Stimmung'; certainly, Thoma's landscape paintings, which manage well without the addition of the mythological, are considerably better able to meet Riegl's requirements of distant view and peace.

Illustration 2:
Hans Thoma, Mein Heimattal *(1918).*
Oil on wood, 91 x 105 cm.
Staatliche Kunsthalle Karslruhe.

One of the most spectacular distant prospects in Thoma's oeuvre is surely the 1904 painting *Blick vom Pilatus* (see *Illustration 1*). The painting is also interesting from another perspective: almost two-thirds of the field of vision are barred by cloud vapor. Such meteorological phenomena had flourished in 'Stimmungsmalerei' since its beginnings in the age of Romanticism. Here, the depiction of atmospheric apparitions like the dawn and twilight, the rising and setting of the sun, light and air, wind, mist, gales, and rain assume the function of a medial veil, which unifies the depicted scenery, pitching it completely in the same key (cf. Krüger 2011: 254f.)[9].

Although a whole series of his paintings is based on such meteorological atmospheres, to his contemporaries, Thoma did not count as a 'painter of light and air in the strict sense' ("Licht- und Luftmaler in strengem Sinne"; Meissner 1899: 59); indeed, weather paintings only

9 In his essay on Jacob van Ruysdael, Riegl investigates the importance of air in the painting of mood (cf. 1902/1929: 134).

Illustration 3:
Hans Thoma, Taunuslandschaft *(1890).*
Oil on canvas, 113.3 x 88.8 cm.
Neue Pinakothek, Munich.

make up a relatively small proportion of his oeuvre[10]. Views down valleys from elevated standpoints are, however, a typical motif of Thoma's work. Dozens of his paintings show, for example, Bernau – the artist's birthplace – lying in a valley (see *Illustration 2*). Smoke climbing from a chimney can be read entirely in Riegl's sense, as a quiet witness to human activity. Many of Thoma's paintings even illustrate distant view quite directly in the form of an onlooker. For example, in *Taunuslandschaft* (1890) (see *Illustration 3*), a resting wanderer looks down a hill onto the valley opening out before him. The figure's inner peace is underlined by a slumbering dog. The animal might also function as a metaphor for the deactivation of the hunting instinct, which certainly seemed to Riegl to be inimical to 'Stimmung'. Distant view is suggested by both the strong repoussoir effect and the complete truncation of the picture's foreground. In other landscape paintings by Thoma the mediating figures of the onlookers are pushed so far into the middle ground that one almost believes them to be beyond calling distance.

3. 'Stimmung' as Soundscape

But what about peace, the second condition Riegl names for the existence of 'Stimmung'? Historically at least, peace can be understood as one of the constitutive characteristics of Thoma's paintings, for his contemporaries assigned this quality to his works almost unanimously. In so doing, the peace inherent in the paintings was often traced back to the landscapes Thoma depicted: few places seem as suited to illustrating peace as the Black Forest so loved by Thoma. As late as 1922, in Joseph August Beringer's biography of Thoma, the following was written about the valley from which the artist came:

> The area of this old glacial valley, almost entirely sealed off from the world, is home to an indigenous population of strange race and culture. No engine whistle can be heard for miles around. No factory chimney pierces the wide expanse of this deep valley. No roar of wheels or drivebelts interrupts the silence of the

10 See, for example, the paintings *Landschaft im Sturm* of 1892 (Sammlung Georg Schäfer, Schweinfurt), *Vor dem Sturm* of 1906 (Kaiser Wilhelm Museum, Krefeld), and *Gewitterregen am Oberrhein* of 1914 (private collection).

mountains. But a hurrying stream tinkles and winds its way delicately through the moraine rubble, driving the waterwheels of the local workshops.[11]

Beringer describes Thoma's paintings as soundscapes. He perceives the contrast between the Black Forest and modernity not so much in visual terms as in aural ones: instead of puffing locomotives and factory noise, only the tinkling of the stream that keeps the mill wheels of the local businesses in movement is heard (on the soundscape of the Industrial Revolution, cf. Schafer 1977/1994: 71–87). Other than this, mountain calm prevails.

Not unlike Beringer, Franz Meissner contrasted the world of sounds of the Black Forest and the wall of sounds of the disagreeable modern era in his 1899 book on Thoma, one of the first monographs on the artist:

[...] silent are the mountain ranges and a mysterious reflection weighs down upon this small world where the whistle and roar of an express train never blare; it seems to be forgotten by major traffic. An Alemannic race of bony and firm build, unhurried pulse, and pronounced features dwells here, a people with a stately walk, healthy in body and soul. The Aleman talks no more than necessary anyhow, and his countryman from the Bernau valley is of an even more conspicuous reticence [or reserve], which goes well with the temperate life of the surrounding landscape.[12]

Meissner conjures two different soundscapes when faced with Thoma's landscapes. Noisy modernity – symbolized here by the whistles and drone of a high-speed train – is juxtaposed with the quiet peace of the mountains and the taciturn inhabitants of Bernau. It is interesting that the place and

11 "Die fast völlig weltabgeschlossene Gegend dieses alten Gletschertales beherbergt eine urtümliche Bevölkerung von eigenartiger Rasse und Kultur. Kein Pfiff der Lokomotive ertönt auf Stundenweite. Kein Fabrikschornstein sticht in den weiten Raum dieses Hochtals. Kein Räder- und Riemengebraus unterbricht die schöne Bergstille. Aber ein eiliger Bach glöckelt in zierlichen Windungen zwischen den Moränengeröllen und treibt die Wasserräder der Heimwerkstätten." (Beringer 1922: 11)

12 "[...] schweigsam sind die Bergzüge und ein rätselhaftes Sinnen lastet auf dieser kleinen Welt, in die niemals das Pfeifen und Gedröhne eines Eilzugs hineingellt; sie scheint vom großen Verkehr vergessen zu sein. – Ein alemannischer Menschenschlag von knochiger und erdsicherer Gestalt, gemächlichem Pulsschlag und ausgeprägten Zügen haust hier, der stattlich einhergeht und gesund an Leib und Seele ist. Der Alemanne redet ohnehin nicht mehr als nötig ist, – sein Landmann aus dem Bernauer Thal ist sogar von einer auffälligen Schweigsamkeit, die mit dem verhaltenen Leben der Landschaft ringsum gut zusammengeht." (Meissner 1899: 24f.)

Illustration 4: Hans Thoma, Der Ziegenhirt *(1869). Oil on canvas, 104 x 80 cm. Landesmuseum, Mainz.*

its people speak 'one' language and are united in a common silence. Elsewhere Meissner conceives of this relationship with the help of a musical metaphor: 'For Thoma, the landscape is primordial sound itself and the first revelation; man, however, even in his most perfect state, is no more than a tuning fork, which merely reproduces the tone with unquestionable clarity.'[13] In Thoma's paintings, man is therefore not the most terrible foe of 'Stimmung', as he was designated by Riegl (cf. 1902/1929: 30), but

13 "Die Landschaft ist für Thoma der eigentliche Urlaut und die erste Offenbarung; der Mensch hingegen ist ihm in der Vollendung selbst nicht mehr als eine Stimmgabel, welche die Tonart nur eben unzweifelhaft klar wiedergibt" (ibid.: 78).

rather the 'tuning fork'. He finds himself in perfect harmony with the landscape that surrounds him: everything is tuned to one key.

With this musical metaphor, Meissner may have been thinking about the many paintings by Thoma in which the man in the landscape actually begins to sing or to play an instrument. Through music, even animals can be affected by and amicably incorporated into a landscape (see *Illustration 4*), which reminds us of the etymological roots of the term 'Stimmung'. However, Meissner's musical metaphor has yet another meaning: it sketches Thoma's Black Forest folk as people whose lives still proceed in 'harmony' with nature and the 'rhythm' of the seasons:

> They are curious people in their composed peace and simplemindedness – in their silent thoughtfulness and sometimes almost coarse sentiment. They are utterly dependent on the time of day and year and on the laws of nature; they only dance in spring, only work during the day, become tired with the onset of darkness. They never laugh or cry, and they only use language in short, rough mumbles, when pantomime is not enough [...].[14]

4. Deceleration

Groundedness and rootedness are seen by Meissner as values that have become rare in the era of progressive mobility. He even recognizes a type of fossil worthy of a cabinet of curiosities in Thoma's inhabitants of the Black Forest: for Meissner, Thoma's figures still show that 'quaint awe of the world' ("wunderliche Weltscheu von Menschen"; 1899: 80) that characterized people 'in the lost age of the post coach' ("aus der verschollenen Postkutschenzeit"; ibid.)[15].

14 "Sind das merkwürdige Menschen in ihrer nervenlosen Ruhe, Einfalt und Einfachheit – in ihrer schweigsamen Bedachtsamkeit und fast ungefügen Empfindung mitunter! Sie hängen völlig von der Tages- und Jahreszeit und den Naturgesetzen ab; sie tanzen nur im Frühling, arbeiten nur bei Tage, werden müde mit der Dunkelheit; sie lachen und weinen niemals und gebrauchen die Sprachen in kurzem, spröden Lallen nur, wo die Pantomime nicht ausreicht [...]." (ibid.: 78f.)

15 According to Anton Springer, the motif is shown in a very nationalistic light: 'In a time of haste and international hustle, of doubts and unrest, he [Thoma] seemed like a guardian of an old German inwardness and silent dreaminess that clings to the soil in everlasting love.' ("In einer Zeit des Hastens, und der internationalen Betriebsamkeit, des Zweifels und der Unruhe, erschien er wie ein Hüter alter deutscher Innerlichkeit und stiller Verträumtheit, die in unvergänglicher Liebe an der Scholle hängt"; 1909: 320).

For his contemporaries, the sense of peace was therefore based on the absence of modern modes of transport in Thoma's paintings – a view that Anna Spier takes in her Thoma monograph of 1900: 'He [Thoma] painted nature itself as it was, still untouched by new modes of transport; he did not paint the train tracks, the steamboat, horse-drawn trams, carriages, telegraph wires. Down his Main glide old-fashioned barges with white sails [...].'[16] Naturally the latter was said in a context in which quite different ships were already plying the river.

Unlike those of the approximately contemporary Impressionists, Thoma's paintings show no railway bridges, to say nothing of train stations. Yet peace is communicated in Thoma's pictorial world through more than just their absence; it is also suggested by motifs like the resting figures as well as the ramblers and day-trippers who go leisurely on their way[17]. Even those persons in the paintings who are mounted – many on horseback, but the donkey is preferred – tend to trot quite comfortably through the landscape[18]. Often the pace of work in them is dictated by the complacency of these beasts of burden and the roughness of the terrain.

But more effectively still than by the people who populate the paintings, a sense of peace is evoked by other pictorial elements, by the routes taken by the rivers, for example, which snake unhurriedly[19]. Something similar can be said of the paths and roads in Thoma's paintings: in the way their routes conform entirely to the contours of the landscape, their form adapts to nature. This is shown particularly nicely in the aforementioned painting of Thoma's home valley, where

16 "Er [Thoma] malte die Natur an sich, wie sie noch unberührt vom neuen Verkehre war, – die Schienenstränge, das Dampfboot, die Pferdebahnen, die Equipagen, die Telegraphendrähte malte er nicht. Auf seinem Maine fahren altmodische Kähne mit weissen Segeln" (Spier 1900: 75f.). There can be no doubt that Anna Spier is making a reference to Thoma's famous 1893 painting *Die Mainlandschaft* (private collection).

17 See, for example, Thoma's paintings *Der Wanderer im Schwarzwald* of 1891 (Niedersächsisches Landesmuseum, Hannover), *Das Silberhorn* of 1914 (private collection), and *Die Taunuslandschaft* of 1897 (Hessisches Landesmuseum, Darmstadt).

18 See, for example, Thoma's 1884 painting *Schwarzwaldlandschaft* (private collection) and the contemporary lithograph *Reiter auf einem Esel.*

19 See, for example, Thoma's paintings *Schwarzwaldbächlein* of 1885, *Das wandernde Bächlein* of 1906, and the *Campagnalandschaft (Aqua Certosa)* of 1880 (all in private collections).

the track and stream find their way into the vale with similarly playful sinuosity (see *Illustration 2*). While it was said of modern streets and waterways that their straightness had no regard for natural conditions varying from region to region (cf. Haushofer 1903: 110)[20], Thoma's paintings present a harmonious relationship between culture and nature.

5. The Idea of 'Stimmung' in the Age of Speed

Modern means of transport were charged not only with raping the landscape but also with interfering in the relationship between man and nature. Universal mobility was accused of bringing about increasing alienation from home and nature. For Meissner, the actual value of Thoma's landscape paintings lay in their function as correctives to this alienation. For him, the haunting element in Thoma's painting is 'powerful nature in her sacredness and depth of unspoiled conception, which, when we are peacefully absorbed, so rightly suggests to us epigones the distortedness of our relationship with nature, made shallow by the

20 In his monograph *Die Landschaft*, Max Haushofer, son of the Munich landscape painter of the same name and father of the geographer and founder of geopolitics Karl Haushofer, writes: 'The most modern designs of road construction, the railroads and telegraph wires, show the triumph of man over the unevenness of the earth's crust and over distance. Yet, they thus remove two of the greatest appeals of the landscape. Incisions, embankments, and railroad viaducts draw straight lines through the diversity of the ground's composition; and the telegraph wires spin their threads rather unattractively through the air.' ("Die modernsten Gestaltungen der Wegbaukunst, die Eisenbahnen und die Telegraphenleitungen, zeigen den vollendeten Sieg des Menschen über die Unebenheit der Erdrinde und über die Entfernungen. Aber damit beseitigen sie zwei der größten Reize der Landschaft. Einschnitte, Dämme und Viadukte der Bahnen ziehen gerade Linien durch die Mannigfaltigkeit der Bodengestaltung; und die Telegraphendrähte spinnen ihre Fäden meist recht unschön durch die Luft"; 1903: 110). Interestingly, Haushofer makes an exception when it comes to the unpainterly effect of modern means of transport and communication: 'Yet even these things can be made tolerable and graceful through the "Stimmung" of the landscape in which they appear. Indeed, so can the rolling locomotive with its smoke cloud and its fiery eyes.' ("Doch selbst diese Dinge können durch die Stimmung der Landschaft, in der sie erscheinen, erträglich und anmutig gemacht werden. Und sogar die rollende Lokomotive mit ihrer Rauchwolke und ihren Feueraugen"; ibid.). Here, 'Stimmung' functions simultaneously as an antidote to modernization. For Haushofer, noisy intrusions or those of movement do not necessarily destroy a mood. Rather, 'Stimmung' can neutralize noise and movement, indeed even make them appear charming.

Illustration 5: Hans Thoma, Die Berge von Carrara *(1881). Oil on canvas, 62 x 74 cm. Kunsthaus Bühler, Stuttgart.*

view from bar patios, train windows, and bicycles'[21].

What makes Meissner's statement about Thoma interesting is not so much the fact that he also ranks the bicycle, alongside the train, as a vehicle inimical to 'Stimmung' but more his interpretation of Thoma's paintings as counter-images to a relationship with nature that has been made shallow by modern transport – as paintings that call the distortedness of the modern viewer's outlook into consciousness by causing him or her to become absorbed in them. The experience to be had by one standing before a Thoma painting was, therefore, a compensating one.

The idea that trains and indeed all modern forms of transport nip any kind of 'Stimmung' in the bud is admittedly an art-theoretical topos of the time. We also find it, for example, in the collection of lectures on aesthetics published in 1898 by the philosopher Friedrich Theodor Vischer, who had died eleven years prior:

21 "[...] die mächtige Natur in ihrer Heiligkeit, Tiefe und Ursprünglichkeit der Auffassung, welch bei ruhiger Versenkung uns Epigonen so recht die Verzerrtheit unserer eigenen, von Lokalveranden, Eisenbahnwagenfenstern und Zweirad aus verflachten Naturverhältnisse nahe legt" (Meissner 1899: 80).

> It is quite bad how our times shatter the 'Stimmung' of quiet contemplation. Our life is ever more nervously drawn into the general hustle and bustle. Of course, I do not wish to fault the infinite progress which comes with the railways. But now that we fly in such a frenzied hurry that even a few minutes rest are too much, the soul gets into such a haste and rush that we can barely get into the 'Stimmung', for example, to quietly linger and behold a landscape.[22]

Hans Thoma enjoyed train travel. He availed of trains, for example, on his journey through Italy. And, quite unlike what is suggested by the passage in the Thoma monograph, he thoroughly enjoyed the view from their windows when traveling. He traversed Tuscany by rail in 1887 – an experience about which he excitedly wrote: 'Such a restless train journey drives image after image past us, one blurring the next – but on the whole, I enjoy this winging about, and some of the fleeting images linger strongly in my memory'[23]. In fact, according to Thoma, these fleeting images even inspired him when it came to the pictures he produced: 'Some of my landscapes actually came into being out of the fleeting impressions seen from the passing train.'[24] His 1881 painting *Die Berge von Carrara* (see *Illustration 5*), for example, was apparently created thanks to a five-minute stop at the train station in the small Tuscan town of Massa, during which Thoma captured the view in quick strokes in his sketchbook (cf. 1909: 74). The finished painting cannot, however, be described as an impression. In terms of painterly technique at least, the train journey and the view from it were without consequences; the high frequency with which the images flitted by him had no implications for the artist. The train made no Impressionist of Hans Thoma (cf. Wegmann 1989: 27f.). In fact, in Thoma's opinion, a painting had to be more than just an impression on the retina. He refused Impressionism with the justifica-

22 "Es ist arg, wie unsere Zeit die Stimmung seelenruhigen Betrachtens zerzaust. Unser Leben wird in das allgemeine Geläufe und Gedränge immer nervöser hineingerissen. Es ist ja selbstverständlich: ich will durchaus nicht den unendlichen Fortschritt bemäkeln, der in den Eisenbahnen liegt. Aber jetzt, wo wir in so rasender Eile fliegen, daß nur ein paar Minuten Aufenthalt schon zu viel sind, gerät die Seele in ein Jagen und Hetzen, daß wir kaum mehr in die Stimmung kommen, z.B. vor einer Landschaft ganz ruhig betrachtend zu verweilen." (Vischer 1898: 46)

23 "So eine rastlose Eisenbahnfahrt führt Bild an Bild an uns vorüber, eines verwischt das andere – aber im ganzen habe ich dieses Dahinfliegen gern und einzelne Flugbilder blieben mir stark in Erinnerung" (Thoma 1919: 95).

24 "Manche meiner Landschaften sind geradezu aus der Flucht der Eindrücke von der Eisenbahn entstanden" (ibid.).

tion: 'When a theory becomes fixated with the idea that an image should appear to be momentary, then [the image] must be passed before the eyes before the viewer has found time to perceive it as something fixed.'[25] Consequently, Thoma, as an artist, did not want to settle for the fleeting impressions to which he, as a train traveler, abandoned himself. Rather, a painting had to be something fixed that invites the viewer to immerse into it.

Thoma was therefore counting on an attentive viewer who would take the necessary time to relocate himself or herself in the painted landscape. For Meissner, it was exactly this persistence of looking that characterized Thoma, whom he styled as nature's child from the Black Forest: 'First he looked long and deep into nature, discovered many things that others did not see, and picked up "Stimmungen", which the city dweller is unable to comprehend [...].'[26]

6. The Black Forest
The Loneliness of the Mountains and Mass Tourism

In many of Thoma's paintings, the immersing of oneself in the image that is demanded of the viewer has its equivalent in the immersion within the image. This is true, on the one hand, for the already-discussed people whose gaze is absorbed in nature, which is assigned the function of a catalyst for the immersion the viewer has to achieve. But the same function is also fulfilled in Thoma's images by many other figures, whose attention is not turned over to nature but given to their own activities: figures picking flowers (see *Illustration 6*) or crouching in meadows making daisy chains. Obviously having stronger nerves than Alois Riegl, these figures do not allow themselves to be

25 "Wenn eine Theorie sich darauf versteift, daß ein Bild momentan wirken soll, so müßte es auch vor den Augen vorübergezogen werden, ehe der Beschauer Zeit gefunden hat, es als etwas Feststehendes aufzufassen" (Thoma 1909: 187).

26 "Er blickte erst lange in die Natur hinein, entdeckte Vieles, was Andere nicht sahen und raffte Stimmungen auf, die dem Stadtmenschen zu erfassen unmöglich ist" (Meissner 1899: 19).

Illustration 6:
Hans Thoma, Auf der Waldwiese *(1876).*
Oil on mahogany, 45.8 x 37.2 cm.
Hamburger Kunsthalle, Hamburg.

put off from what they are doing by the cows grazing in their immediate proximity[27], figures fishing[28], or losing themselves in love[29].

To be able to indulge in such pastimes with leisure – therein lies the attraction of the Black Forest. In particular, the desire to go rambling had brought a surging stream of tourists to the region since the end of the 19th century. Visitors to the Black Forest sought that which today's tourists still hope to find, namely, respite from the stress and hecticness of everyday life. In his book on 'social acceleration' dealing with the change of time structures in modernity, Hartmut Rosa speaks of the Black Forest as a 'deceleration oasis' ("Entschleunigungsoase"; 2005: 253). With this term, he denotes those spaces in which modern man, at least temporarily, seeks refuge from the increasing dynamics of acceleration in all areas of life (meaning, therefore, not only technical acceleration) (cf. ibid.: 143f.). For Rosa, and not by accident, the prime example of such oases of deceleration is represented by 'a late-modern weekend on a Black Forest farm *without* a car, phone, or Internet connection', for this 'promises time for going on walks, wood carving, star gazing etc.'[30].

Here I would like to propose the thesis that 'Stimmungsmalerei' can be understood as a painted oasis of deceleration – indeed, that it fulfils this function much better than the real Black Forest. For as backwoodsy as Thoma's biographers like to depict the region from which he came, in reality it was already a holiday destination approaching mass tourism that had long before arrived in the modern age. So it was, for instance, that Hermann Dischler – another painter from the Black Forest specializing in snow landscapes, who had painted the Feldberg, the highest rise in the Black Forest, approximately 350 times – observed with resignation in 1933: '[…] since the Feldberg became a mountain for all, thanks to the train and car, and

27 See Thoma's painting *Kühe im Schwarzwald* (whereabouts and date unknown).

28 See, for example, Thoma's painting *Der Angler* of 1878 (private collection).

29 See, for example, Thoma's painting *Sommerglück* of 1903 (Wallraf-Richartz-Museum, Cologne).

30 "Ein spätmodernes Wochenende auf einem Schwarzwaldbauernhof *ohne* Auto, Telefon, und Internetanschluss […] verspricht Zeit fürs Spazierengehen, Holzschnitzen, in die Sterne sehen etc." (Rosa 2005: 253 [emphasis in the original]).

everything echoes with skiers' salutes, I avoid it. The beautiful peace and virginity has disappeared for ever.'[31]

7. The Struggle for Existence

The peace that Riegl found on an alpine mountaintop had allowed him, at least temporarily, to shake off the onerous weight represented by modern people's knowledge of the struggle for existence, which prevails in nature[32]. Yet a mountain goat was sufficient to bring him hurtling back into that very battle. Interestingly, as a young man, Thoma had had quite a similar experience. In his autobiographical *Winter des Lebens*, published in 1919, Thoma quoted an entry from his diary of June 1861. It starts with a lyrical soar:

> How beautiful is my home valley. […] It is calm and peaceful […] in nature, when I lie on a mountain slope on a Sunday morning, looking down into the green valley, while the church bells peal, the sun shines on the beeches, the thrush sings, white clouds float over me, and a hawk circles the sky. Then I forget all my worries and the peace of nature encloses my soul too.[33]

Where this inner peace only developed in Riegl when he removed himself from everything, to Thoma, it seems to partake of its immediate surroundings:

31 "[…] seit der Feldberg durch Bahn und Auto ein Allerweltsberg geworden ist und alles von Skiheil widerhallt, meide ich ihn. Die schöne Ruhe und Unberührtheit ist für immer verschwunden" (Dischler 1933: 37, qtd. Graf 1992: 104).

32 Anna Spier's interpretation makes evident that Thoma's art can be understood utterly in the Rieglian sense as a temporary liberation from the struggle for survival: 'In the recent struggle for existence and public standing that even reaches decisively into the development of art, such a simple, natural, and true art, as that of Hans Thoma, seems like a gift of peace.' ("In dem gegenwärtigen Kampf um's Dasein und um's Dagelten, welcher selbst in die Kunstentwicklung bestimmend eingreift, wirkt eine so einfache, natürliche, wahrhaftige Kunst, wie die Hans Thoma's, wie eine Friedensgabe"; Spier 1900: 112).

33 "Wie schön ist doch mein Heimattal. […] Still und friedlich ist es […] in der Natur, wenn ich am Sonntagvormittag so auf einem Berghang liege und ins grüne Tal hinuntersehe, die Kirchenglocken rufen, die Sonne glänzt im Buchenwald, die Drossel singt, über mir schweben weiße Wolken und ein Habicht kreist. Da vergesse ich alle Sorgen und der Friede der Natur umschließt auch meine Seele." (Thoma 1919: 32)

> How beautiful it is by the little stream in the shady pine forest, by the golden brown creek enveloped in velvet green moss. The ants crawling in the moss and the lustrous dragonfly, floating over the brown water like a blue sunbeam, are friendly creatures to me. I understand the chaffinch singing his ditty, I share in the pleasure of the trout zooming down the clear stream. When I fall half asleep to the murmur of the water, it seems to me as if angels from a better world were floating around me.[34]

And, in fact, angels populate not only the daydreams of the young Thoma, but also a good number of his later paintings[35]. Yet while he imagines such 'angels from a better place', the fight for survival abruptly breaks into Thoma's idyll, and the harmony, which appeared to enfold everything, is suddenly destroyed:

> But then, what we humans call reality can appear all of a sudden. Then I see an ant dragging a worm away to be devoured, a shudder runs through me, an arcane terror drives me from the forest. I hurry home; I don't know what it is that I dread. Perhaps myself. In the parlor with my mother and sister, there is a very pleasant reality, and the phantasms flee.[36]

The analogies between Thoma's diary entry of 1861 and Riegl's episode with the mountain goat in his essay of 1899 are evident. Here the experience of 'Stimmung' is also brought to its end by a sudden confrontation with the struggle that is life. And here, as there, this happens due to something that takes place in immediate proximity to the author, who is lost in the contemplation of nature.

34 "Wie schön ist's am Bächlein im schattigen Tannenwald, am goldbraunen Bächlein von samtgrünem Moosufer umfaßt. Die Ameise, die im Moose kriecht, und die glänzende Libelle, die wie ein blauer Sonnenstrahl über das braune Wasser hinschwebt, sind mir befreundete Wesen. Ich verstehe den Buchfinken, der sein Liedchen singt, ich nehme teil an dem Wohlbehagen, mit dem die Forelle durch den klaren Bach dahinschnellt. Wenn ich beim Gemurmel des Wassers so halb einschlummere, so ist es mir, als ob Engel aus einer besseren Welt um mich schweben." (Ibid.) See, on this, Thoma's painting *Frühlingsreigen* of 1873 (Kunstmuseum Basel), which can be understood as the pictorial realization of a daydream.

35 See, for example, Thoma's painting *Frühlingsreigen* of 1873 (Kunstmuseum Basel).

36 "Dann kann aber auch plötzlich kommen, was wir Menschen Wirklichkeit nennen. Dann sehe ich, wie die Ameise einen Wurm mitschleppt zum Fraß, ein Schauer überläuft mich, ein geheimes Grauen treibt mich aus dem Walde fort. Ich eile heim; ich weiß nicht, wovor mir graut. Vielleicht vor mir selber. Im kleinen Stübchen bei Mutter und Schwester ist eine gar schöne Wirklichkeit, und die Wahngebilde fliehen." (Thoma 1919: 32)

The things that tear Riegl and Thoma from their trances appear curiously harmless. The fears that they project upon nature are more likely to have their actual cause in the culture of the modern era. Immersing oneself into nature thus could serve as a compensation for and temporary escape from modernity.

References

Beringer, Joseph August (1922). *Hans Thoma*. Munich: Bruckmann.

Dischler, Hermann (1933). "Hotzenwälder Eindrücke und Erinnerungen eines Malers". *Der Schwarzwald* 16: 37–39.

Graf, Heinrich (1992). "Hermann Dischler und die stürmische Entwicklung des Fremdenverkehrs". Margret Zimmermann, ed. *"O. Schwarzwald o. Heimat!" ... Verlust oder Anpassung: Hermann Dischler, Maler und Fotograf (1866–1935)*. Exh. cat. Freiburg im Breisgau: Augustinermuseum, 18 October 1992 – 6 December 1993. Freiburg im Breisgau: Rombach. 104–119.

Haushofer, Karl (1903). *Die Landschaft*. Bielefeld/Leipzig: Velhagen & Klasing.

Jøran, Rudi, ed. (2011). *Soundscape i kunsten: Soundscape in the Arts*. Oslo: NOTAM.

Krüger, Matthias (2011). "Die Farben der Luft: Lokalkolorit in der Malerei des deutschen Regionalismus". Jakob Steinbrenner, Christoph Wagner, Oliver Jehle, eds. *Farben in Kunst- und Geisteswissenschaften*. Regensburg: Schnell & Steiner. 247–260.

Lübbren, Nina (2001). *Rural Artists' Colonies in Europe, 1870–1910*. Manchester: Manchester UP.

Meissner, Franz Hermann (1899). *Hans Thoma*. Berlin/Leipzig: Schuster & Loeffler.

Meyers Großes Konversations-Lexikon (1905). "Landschaftsmalerei". 6th rev. and enl. ed. Vol. 12. Leipzig/Vienna: Bibliographisches Institut. 123–125.

Olin, Margaret (1992). *Forms of Representation in Alois Riegl's Theory of Art*. University Park, PA: Pennsylvania State UP.

Riegl, Alois (1899/1929). "Die Stimmung als Inhalt der modernen Kunst". *Gesammelte Aufsätze*. Ed. Karl Maria Swoboda. Augsburg/Vienna: Filser. 28–39.

— (1902/1929). "Jacob van Ruysdael". *Gesammelte Aufsätze*. Ed. Karl Maria Swoboda. Augsburg/Vienna: Filser. 129–138.

Rosa, Hartmut (2005). *Beschleunigung: Die Veränderung der Zeitstrukturen in der Moderne*. Frankfurt am Main: Suhrkamp.

Ryan, Marie-Laure (2001). *Narrative as Virtual Reality: Immersion and Interactivity in Literature and Electronic Media*. Baltimore, MD: Johns Hopkins UP.

Schafer, R. Murray (1977/1994). *The Soundscape: Our Sonic Environment and the Tuning of the World*. 2nd ed. Rochester, VT: Destiny Books.

Simmel, Georg (1913/2001). "Philosophie der Landschaft". *Aufsätze und Abhandlungen 1909–1918*. Vol. 1. Eds. Rüdiger Kramme, Angela Rammstedt. Frankfurt am Main: Suhrkamp. 471–483.

Spier, Anna (1900). "Hans Thoma". *Die Kunst unserer Zeit* 11: 61–112.

Springer, Anton (1909). *Handbuch der Kunstgeschichte: Das 19. Jahrhundert*. Ed. Max Osborn. 5th rev. and suppl. ed. Leipzig: Seemann.

Thoma, Hans (1909). *Im Herbste des Lebens: Gesammelte Erinnerungsblätter*. Munich: Süddeutsche Monatshefte.

— (1919). *Im Winter des Lebens: Aus acht Jahrzehnten gesammelte Erinnerungen*. Jena: Diederichs.

Thompson, Emily (2002). *The Soundscape of Modernity: Architectural Acoustics and the Culture of Listening in America, 1900–1933*. Cambridge, MA/London: MIT Press.

Vischer, Friedrich Theodor (1898). *Das Schöne und die Kunst: Zur Einführung in die Ästhetik. Vorträge*. Stuttgart: Cotta.

Wegmann, Peter (1989). "Thoma – Landschaften". Markus Ewel, ed. *Hans Thoma: Lebensbilder*. Exh. cat. Freiburg im Breisgau: Augustinermuseum, 2 October – 3 December 1989. Königstein im Taunus: Langewische. 22–32.

Wellbery, David E. (2003). "Stimmung". Karlheinz Barck et al., eds. *Ästhetische Grundbegriffe: Historisches Wörterbuch in sieben Bänden*. Vol. 5: *Postmoderne – Synästhesie*. Stuttgart: Metzler. 703–733.

Picture Credits

Ill. 1: Eva-Marina Froitzheim (1993). *Hans Thoma (1839–1924): Ein Begleiter durch die Hans-Thoma-Sammlung in der Staatlichen Kunsthalle Karlsruhe*. Karlsruhe: Staatliche Kunsthalle Karlsruhe. 46, cat. nr. 21; Ills. 2, 4, 5: Markus Ewel, ed. (1989). *Hans Thoma: Lebensbilder*. Exh. cat. Freiburg im Breisgau: Augustinermuseum, 2 October – 3 December 1989. Königstein im Taunus: Langewische. 327, cat. nr. 120; 142, cat. nr. 10; 227, cat. nr. 66; Ill. 3: Nils Büttner (2006). *Geschichte der Landschaftsmalerei*. Munich: Hirmer. 347, fig. 184; Ill. 6: Christa von Helmolt (1989). *Hans Thoma: Spiegelbilder*. Stuttgart: Klett-Cotta. 169.

*Illustration 1:
Titanic Belfast, exterior view of
the museum building. Copyright
Titanic Belfast.*

Immersive Exhibition Design
Titanic Belfast and the Concept of Scenography

Matthias Bauer

Located at Queen's Island where the famous ocean liner was built, Titanic Belfast is a museum that combines immersive and non-immersive strategies. The visitor is invited to travel back to the early 20th century and experience the construction and the maiden journey, the catastrophe and the wreck of the ship in a submarine media space. The article discusses different but complementary concepts of scenography. The main argument is concerned with the functional spatiality of layout and display.

1. Titanic Belfast

Museums and exhibitions are made up of galleries that need a design. This design usually goes beyond the basic arrangement of the exhibits in the space and on the walls. Its main purpose is to place the exhibits in a specific context – a context that can remain fairly abstract or, in a concrete configuration, become part of a scenario. Older museums often offered little more than a row of rectangular rooms that seemed like empty containers – obvious descendants of the Renaissance 'Kunstkammer' (cabinets of art and curiosities). With the historical avant-garde in the first third of the 20th century, however, the idea that the design of an exhibition should break away from the existing architecture and create displays visitors can explore and endow with meaning caught on. This could only succeed if the arrangement of objects neither limited visitors to a specific view of things nor patronized them in their perception or assessment in any other way. Nevertheless, visitors' attention had to be awakened, guided, and thereby held, which is why an interesting environment was created. Since the turn of this century, the concept of scenography that resulted from these challenges has been frequently connected to elaborate media installations that often tend to do away with the barrier between visual and pictorial space in favor of an extensive immersion of visitors and viewers. The following observations are based on a specific case, namely the Titanic Belfast museum complex, as it can be used to illustrate several aspects of the topic at hand.

To this end, the first part of my essay will describe a tour through Titanic Belfast (the official name of the museum complex). My intent is to show the extent to which the design of this exhibition relies on an elaborate mix of immersive media installations and a rather contemplative scenography. This part is followed by a brief visualization of some of the central binary oppositions, such as evocation and exemplification, and semiophorology and scenography, that prompt the brief history of museum and exhibition design in the third part. Here, my goal is to trace, as briefly as possible, the recent debate surrounding scenography from the perspective of immersion in order to ultimately arrive at the development of an interpretative and evaluative perspective in the fourth part. In this final part, I attempt to express the true complexity of the phenomena, in particular, their aesthetico-logical dimension.

On March 31, 2012, almost 100 years to the day since the luxury liner *Titanic* set sail on its fateful maiden voyage, a new museum complex was opened in Belfast at the very spot on which the ship was designed and built (see *Illustration 1*). The dock in which the *Titanic* was built still exists today and, together with the former pump house and other buildings of the Harland & Wolff shipyard, constitutes the heart of the no-longer-operational harbor area, in which apartments, offices, and commercial buildings are scheduled to be built.

Before the shipyard that built the Olympic-class ships for the White Star Line – of which the *Titanic* was one – was erected on Queen's Island, this area was home to the largest amusement park in Belfast. The newly opened museum complex indeed bears a resemblance to an amusement park. Be that as it may, the museum uses every trick in the book to teach visitors about the history of the Northern Irish metropolis, the shipyard, and the passenger liners, making it a special experience beyond the ordinary. Titanic Belfast is a heterotopia (see Foucault 1984) composed of various scenographies focused on combining authentic memorial sites, attractive exhibits, and interactive information media. The fact that the creators of the exhibition planned on immersing visitors is made clear in the text used to advertise visits to Thompson Dock – now referred to as "Titanic's Dock" – on the outdoor grounds of the museum. It reads:

> Immerse yourself in history by descending 44ft into the colossal Titanic Dock. Walk the same footsteps that the shipyard men did over 100 years ago. Be inspired by docks towering over cavernous walls that hide the modern world, transporting you back to 1912. […] it's not hard to imagine the atmosphere that

> prevailed at that time. It is only in Titanic's Dock that you grasp the true sense of scale and enormous undertaking involved in creating these ocean-going leviathans. Titanic's Dock and its elegant Pump-House remain the most intact and authentic landmark in the world. An inspiring and thought-provoking experience awaits you. (Titanic Belfast 2012)

Visitors are thus invited to dive into the working world of the early 20th century, let themselves be "inspired" by the location's grandeur and "transport[ed]" to another time, feel the "atmosphere" of the area and, in the light of the "authentic landmark", have a stimulating "experience" that leaves them with a lasting impression. The text begs to be compared with the fulfillment scenario of immersion that Marie-Laure Ryan recognized in the Holodeck on the starship *Enterprise* in the franchise *Star Trek* (since 1966). In her standard work, *Narrative as Virtual Reality*, she writes that

> the scenario of the Holodeck breaks down into the following themes: 1. You enter (*active embodiment*) … 2. into a picture (*spatiality of the display*) … 3. that represents a complete environment (*sensory diversity*). 4. Though the world of the picture is the product of a digital code, you cannot see the computer (*transparency of the medium*). 5. You can manipulate the objects of the virtual world and interact with its inhabitants just as you would in the real world (*dream of a natural language*). 6. You become a character in the virtual world (*alternative embodiment and role-playing*). 7. Out of your interaction with the virtual world arises a story (*simulation as narrative*). 8. Enacting this plot is a relaxing and pleasurable activity (*VR as a form of art*). (2001: 50f.)

Visitors to Titanic Belfast also dive in with their entire bodies (1) into galleries (2) that, for the duration of their stay, become an environment that appeals to all the senses (3). In fact, at one point, even the olfactory universe of a shipyard is simulated. However, in some areas, the creators of the exhibition purposely refrained from making the media devices used invisible or transparent (4). Furthermore, visitors cannot interact with the historical figures they encounter throughout their museum tour (5), although there are several objects that visitors may touch as well as information media that can be used individually. In Titanic Belfast, the role-play that is physically acted out on the Holodeck (6) only takes place in the mind. Nevertheless, several narrative threads that contribute to the concentration of the scenographic discourse – or to visitors' imaginary immersion in the historical chronotope (see Bakhtin 1975/1981) – are constructed and laid out throughout the course of the, in total, nine galleries (7). Finally, over time, the visitor gains an understanding of the exhibition's concept, which is directed toward the creation of an entertaining educational experience through a constant oscillation between impartation and acquisition, immersion and reflection (8).

To this day, the Holodeck remains a fictional setting. As advanced as the developments in electronic and interactive media are, and as refined as the arrangements of these media as 'dispositifs' (cf. Foucault 1978: 119f.) and apparatuses of perception and behavior are, these apparatuses are still measured against the possibilities available only to the characters in the film and television series. The main point of the Holodeck – namely that protagonists in the film and television series can influence the course of historical events that took place outside of the Holodeck – makes this scenario appear, as always, utopian.

At the same time, it is worth comparing the Holodeck to the museum complex in Belfast. The dock, the pump house, the tool shop, and the drawing offices are historical locations visitors can enter, explore, populate, and bring to life with their own imaginations. However, they can alter neither the architectural construction and furnishings, nor the events that took place there in the past. Although these sites were adapted to accommodate visitors, they are still relics of a completed time in the past, sites in a story that one can only imagine. The authenticity of the picture visitors get of the historical circumstances and events is as dependent on visitors' knowledge, feel for the atmosphere, and imagination as it is on the actual characteristics of this location. As I will later explain in further detail, exemplification[1] is a process of referencing that is often used in exhibitions and thereby is expanded upon and strengthened in many instances through the process of evocation. Exemplification is often closely connected with the illustration of a wonder, while evocation is focused on resonance. It was Stephen Greenblatt who recognized "resonance" and "wonder" as being two basic elements of museum and exhibition design:

1 Here, I have borrowed the technical term used by Nelson Goodman, who explains it using the example of a swatch of cloth: it possesses that which it is a sample of; it exhibits and demonstrates that which it is materially suitable for in terms of texture, form, and color. In this sense, historical locations, such as the dock, pump house, tool shop, and drawing offices, exemplify the site and the parameters – in other words, the genius loci – of an activity or work environment that belongs to the past. In doing so, their form and materiality take on an evocative power that, combined with the viewer's imagination, creates the kind of quality of perception that can make a visit to these sites a lasting educational experience (cf. 1968/1976: 52f.).

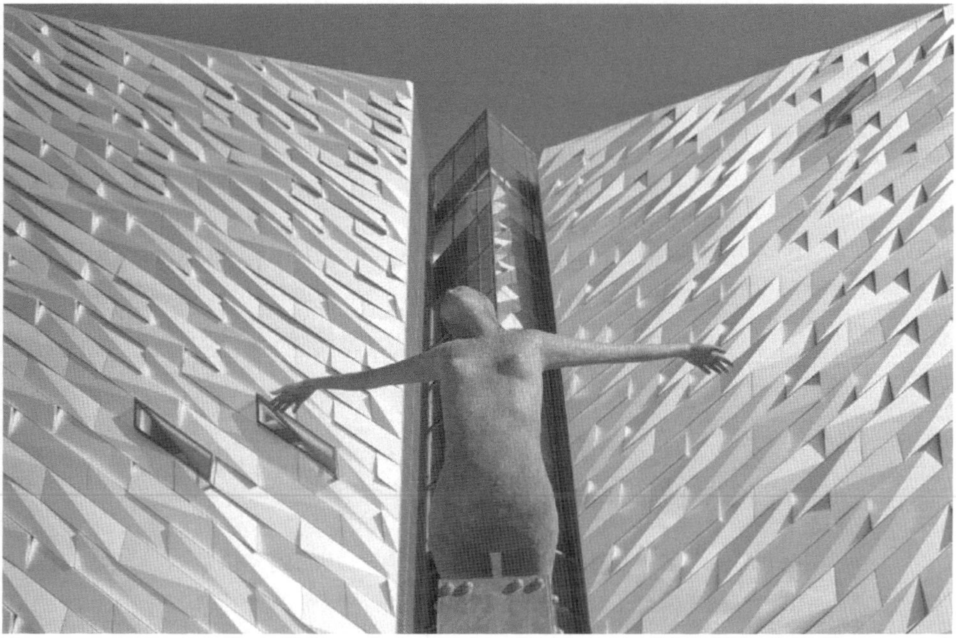

Illustration 2:
Titanic Belfast, exterior view of the museum building.
Copyright Titanic Belfast.

> By "resonance" I mean the power of the displayed object to reach out beyond its formal boundaries to a larger world, to evoke in the viewer the complex, dynamic cultural forces from which it has emerged and for which it may be taken by a viewer to stand. By "wonder" I mean the power of the displayed object to stop the viewer in his or her tracks, to convey an arresting sense of uniqueness, to evoke an exalted attention. (1991: 42)

For Greenblatt, the effect of resonance is exemplified in a particularly impressive way by the Jewish Museum in Prague, primarily a memorial site that is oriented on the ritual of Kaddish, the mourning prayer. As artifacts, the objects displayed there are not particularly significant but serve more as resonators of the voices that have been silenced; they keep the memory of the Jews murdered by the Germans (cf. ibid.: 45f.). Although Greenblatt tries to avoid the implication that resonance has to be bound to destruction and absence, it is this very connection that also seems relevant with regard to Titanic Belfast. At least in certain sections of the museum that deal with the sinking and the aftermath of the ship disaster, it is also about evoking a resonance of silenced voices – an effect that is flanked by the reconstruction of several stories based on factual information. It is certainly no coincidence that these parts of the exhibition are, at first glance, less spectacular than other parts and call for another modality of immersion.

They do not astonish visitors as much as they put them in a (subdued) mood of contemplation and reflection.

Apart from this, the astonishment visitors feel about that which is sensational in this museum, as the advertisement quoted shows, is connected to a feeling of grandeur drawn from being confronted with the gigantic dimensions of the shipyard and the ocean liner, the effort that was put into its construction, and the ever-palpable hubris of humankind. As is widely known, the liner, considered by many of its contemporaries to be unsinkable, was too lightly constructed and moving too fast to be able to withstand the collision with the iceberg without incurring serious damage. The effect of wonder can thus also be gauged based on some of the museum's displays and scenographic elements. The replicas of the first- and second-class cabins, for example, are little cabinets of wonder in terms of décor. However, while in the Renaissance and the Baroque eras wonders were connected to the idea of being owned by a powerful collector, the exhibits in Titanic Belfast almost always go hand in hand with the memory of a loss.

If Greenblatt means that almost every exhibition requires wonder and resonance[2], these elements should not stand separately side by side but should complete and strengthen each other as in Titanic Belfast. Inasmuch as the museum advertises itself by referring to the authenticity and impressiveness of its sites and exhibits and attracts potential visitors with the prospect of a highly immersive experience, it focuses on the suggestion of wonder. To the extent to which it is a memorial site of historical Belfast, the great days gone by of the national shipbuilding industry, and the first catastrophe of the 20th century, it sends visitors through spaces geared toward resonance that tell of a loss rather than of power and wealth. In this context, the dock, pump house, tool shop, and drawing offices virtually serve as exemplification and evocation, as transmitters of atmosphere and history. While this function can be supported and steered by certain measures, ultimately, it rests on the fact that these sites

2 "[…] in fact, almost every exhibition worth viewing has elements of both. I think that the impact of most exhibitions is likely to be enhanced if there is a strong initial appeal to wonder, a wonder that then leads to the desire for resonance, for it is generally easier in our culture to pass from wonder to resonance than from resonance to wonder" (Greenblatt 1991: 54).

are relics of the past and as such exhibit a genesis that did not originally aim at their use as sites and exhibits of the past.

This genesis differentiates them from scenographies and exhibits that are specifically designed to fulfill a museum's intended purpose. These scenographies and exhibits are housed in a newly erected building that, based on its outward appearance alone, is far removed from the architectural language commonly used in the design of office and living spaces. At present, the striking appearance of the building's façade and the structure's appeal are still connected to the fact that this structure stands alone on a flat landscape. One day, however, it will be completely surrounded by closely spaced buildings. Nevertheless, it is sure to remain a focal point in the future. As far as the outer design is concerned, it is probably most accurate to describe Titanic Belfast as a kind of hybrid spatial sculpture (see *Illustration 2*): depending on the visitor's standpoint, it brings to mind the form of an iceberg, the bow of a ship, a crystal, or the emblem of the White Star Line (although the last association can only be seen when one walks around the building or sees a bird's-eye view of its outline). The elegant combination of these evocations corresponds with the topics that unfold throughout the museum's various galleries.

Upon entering the atrium, in which the ticket office, checkroom, gift shop, café, and restaurant are located, the visitor steps into a long, narrow interior with angled walls, the covering of which is reminiscent of the steel plating and rivets that composed the luxury liner's hull[3]. The elevators and escalators that transport visitors to the exhibition spaces also stretch upward (see *Illustration 3*). There are nine galleries with the following themes: Gallery 1: Boomtown Belfast; Gallery 2: The Shipyard Ride; Gallery 3: The Launch of *Titanic*; Gallery 4: Fitting-Out; Gallery 5: Maiden Voyage; Gallery 6: The Sinking; Gallery 7: The Aftermath; Gallery 8: Myths & Reality; Gallery 9: *Titanic* Beneath. At the very beginning of the tour that leads through these nine galleries, visitors are taken back to the emerging industrial city of the 19th century. They become part of the historical setting even before they can take any individual pieces of information from the text panels. Be that as it may,

3 The following description of the atrium's interior design can be read in the souvenir guide: "Stacked like nested deck planes, the arrangement of Titanic Belfast's floor plates mirrors those of the famous liners. Piercing up through the floors, the atrium recalls the awesome size of *Titanic*'s engine room: cathedral-like spaces, four decks in height whose hissing machinery formed the ship's beating heart" (Costecalde/Doherty, eds. 2012: 10).

Illustration 3:
Titanic Belfast, interior view of the atrium. Copyright Titanic Belfast.

they find themselves in the middle of a life-size projection of historical films that show the lively streets of Belfast at the beginning of the 20th century. Between these urban scenes and the viewer, life-size silhouettes – virtually on the threshold between exhibition space and pictorial space – walk across the screen (see *Illustration 4*). In this way, an almost three-dimensional layering of street traffic is created into which the visitors themselves merge. They are integrated into the daily life of the metropolis, become virtual members of a crowd that ultimately passes through the main entrance of the Harland & Wolff shipyard. On the way there, the visitors learn that, from 1851 to 1901, the population of the port city rose from 87,062 to 349,180; that, at that time, Belfast was the world's largest producer and exporter of linen; and that people employed in the expanding shipping industry, mostly as casual laborers with sixty-eight-hour workweeks, were paid very low wages for their hard and dangerous jobs.

By way of the simulated transition to the Harland & Wolff shipyard, visitors arrive at an elevator. This elevator takes them up in a reconstruction of the Arrol Gantry, the frame structure on the shipyard in which the ships were constructed (see *Illustration 5*). From there, they can embark on a journey of discovery through the hull of the *Titanic* still under construction. For this purpose, visitors – like in a dark ride – sit in small black gondolas that do not ride on rails but hang from a conveyor belt. As soon as the ride begins, the gondola is lowered and is subsequently steered toward various dioramas that, in this manner, gradually appear in the visitors' field of vision. Like Jonah looking around in the belly of the whale that swallowed him, visitors go on a 'phantom ride'[4] that is synaesthetically expanded to a highly immersive experience through scents and sounds. The comprehensive 'look' into the conditions under which the *Titanic* was assembled – a hot, crowded space full of deafening noises and foul odors – may be a distillate of sensations, the accuracy of which visitors cannot judge. This caveat, however, hardly diminishes the experiential value of their exploratory trip through the Arrol Gantry. Because the visitor's point of view shifts through the ride, a seamless overlap of the viewing space and the pictorial space is achieved.

4 In film studies, a phantom ride is a kind of tracking shot whose perspective mimics that of someone, for example, seated in front of the engine of a train or in a roller coaster. The result is that the surroundings appear to fly toward and past the viewer, usually at a high speed, as can be seen in the film *The Great Train Robbery* (dir. Edwin S. Porter, USA 1903).

This results not only in the bringing together of the Arrol Gantry and the dramaturgy of a journey of discovery in this complex scenography. Rather, scenography reveals itself to be choreography and seismography as well. Furthermore, the gallery is not simply laid out but, thanks to the clever way the visitors' eyes are directed, divided up into sequences and mini-scenes along the course of the ride in the suspended gondola. Therefore, the coordination of the viewers' eye movements with the movement of the gondola in which they sit serves, first and foremost, to organize the complex scenography in a kind of 'Stationendrama' (station drama). Consequently, it prompts visitors to form a series of conjectural opinions, which, due to the sensorial diversity of their experiences – think, once again, of the Holodeck – contribute considerably to the atmospheric intensification of their museum visit. Furthermore, during the Shipyard Ride, an 'empathic field' ("empathische Feld"; Wulff 2003: 152)[5] is created that gives the scenographic discourse a seismographic quality. The astonishment of visitors, who are shaken around a bit upon entering the underworld of the piecework area, does not end with this physical trembling. Any visitor who, at the sight of the men who had to toil in very confined spaces, does not feel shaken by the working conditions that existed at Harland & Wolff ignores the affective and cognitive point of the scenography and, what is more, misses out on the pleasant feeling of relief that sets in upon exiting the gondola at the transition into the next gallery.

Because the Shipyard Ride exhibits many features that were characteristic of the early cinema of attractions, which counted the phantom ride among its various sensations, it reflects the media world of the early 20th century. At the same time, it connects this reflection with the modality of an immersion that, in the way it is experienced here by visitors, can only be achieved through the use of the technological innovations of the early 21st century. Even though not every visitor will realize this connection to the cinema of attractions, it can be said that, along with the history of the industry, a history of media is also recapitulated in the Arrol Gantry: from the phantom ride to the cut-scenes of computer games, the media spaces of electronic exhibition design, and 3-D virtual realities.

Characteristic of a scenography such as the Shipyard Ride is a strategy of overwhelming that always calls attention to itself, particularly with regard to the complexity of its staging. When this is combined with

5 Unless otherwise indicated, all translations are mine.

the expectations of visitors who want to experience something special and do not want to be disappointed, who expect to get more for their money, and who are always inclined to let themselves be transported to a magical setting in another sphere of experience, a place that is the opposite of their daily environment, the situation is beneficial to both sides: to the paying visitors and to the scenographers, whose efforts have to pay off, first and foremost, financially, but also with regard to what, in the age of 'edutainment', is referred to as a *gain* in knowledge. A museum complex as elaborate as Titanic Belfast can only pay off if visitors who have already explored it advertise it to others by word of mouth and come again themselves. With the Shipyard Ride through the Arrol Gantry, the museum has an attraction that is both exhibition and advertising space: those who have already discovered this scenography will tell others about it, who, in turn, will also want to experience the 'wonder'.

There will, of course, also always be visitors who are irked by strategies of overwhelming and, for various reasons, have reservations about media installations aimed at 'total immersion'. However,

Illustration 4:
Titanic Belfast, exhibition view of the gallery Boomtown Belfast.
Copyright Titanic Belfast.

even in the Arrol Gantry, the museum display does not go to this degree of absorption. It is not until later in the tour that it truly becomes apparent that it was important to the scenographers to frequently allow visitors time to pause and offer phases of contemplation in which their attention is not focused or regulated. One example of this is the contrast between the second and third galleries – a contrast that visitors can hardly overlook when they debouch, so to speak, from the dark of the Arrol Gantry and pass by a glass front that offers a view of Queen's Island. With the original location before their eyes and a little imagination, visitors can automatically envision the theme of the museum's third gallery, showing the launch of the *Titanic*.

Before, visitors were locked up in a small gondola, unable to move; now, they can stroll through an atmosphere as bright as day and collect as much information as they want. Thus, in this section, the creators of the exhibition rely on visitors' personal contributions. They are casually encouraged to imagine what it must have been like when roughly 100,000 people gathered together to see the 271-meter-long colossus of steel glide into the water on May 31, 1911, before it was transferred to the Thompson Dock, where the rest of the construction and the completion of the interior was to take place (see *Illustration 6*). In imagining this scene, visitors have more to draw from than just the information provided in this section of the exhibit. Even before they arrived at this point, the construction plans of the ocean liner were projected on the floor in front of them in such a way that they had to walk on them, thereby gaining a first impression of the ship's dimensions. As visitors realize in the third gallery, the phenomenal Shipyard Ride is embedded in a discourse that allows them to speculatively summarize the dates and facts they have already gathered and bring them into relation with the setting they see before them when they look outside.

Throughout the rest of the tour as well, information, immersion, and imagination are constantly balanced in new ways, and it becomes clear that the exhibition's scenographic concept by no means relies solely on strategies of overwhelming and suspense. The third gallery, for example, is followed by new, milder forms of surprise in the fourth with regard to the interior. Here, what the lodgings were like for the passengers in the first and second classes aboard the *Titanic* is revealed. Similar to the dioramas in cultural/historical museums, the reconstructions of the passenger cabins are arranged in such a way that visitors can look into them from different sides. Their horizontal tier-

Illustration 5:
Titanic Belfast, exhibition view of the gallery The Shipyard Ride.
Copyright Titanic Belfast.

ing is thus always linked to visitors' 'outsideness' – a relationship that is reversed at the end of the passage. Here, visitors enter a 'u'-shaped room in which panorama photographs of the interior of the ship are projected onto the walls. Thanks to the 'plastic transition', these photographs give visitors the impression that they are part of a panning shot of the decks. Furthermore, they suggest to visitors that, with the elevator, they have ascended from down in the engine room, directly over the keel, and all the way up to the bridge of the *Titanic*. Along this vertical axis, they also pass by the imposing grand staircase (see *Illustration 7*), which plays a central role in James Cameron's melodramatic depiction of the first voyage in his film *Titanic* (USA 1997).

A replica of this staircase connects the two highest floors of the museum, on which the rooms for private banquets and other events are located. There one can indulge in the eerily beautiful feeling of dining in this ambience that is a replica of the original rotting on the icy ocean floor in the North Atlantic. The exhibition's course, however, does not lead to these rooms. Rather, the fourth gallery, which focuses on the outfit of the *Titanic*, is followed by a multimedia presentation of an account of the first voyage and the sinking in the fifth and sixth galleries. In the process, several narrative threads that began in the first gallery are continued – stories of individual passengers and crew members who, with the help of photographs and quotations, are given faces and voices. Thanks to these media, the narration is linked to experiential perspectives. Through eyewitness testimonies, the story is made vivid and, in turn, the presentation is grounded in empathy. In the exhibit's brochure, the conative function of the scenography is formulated as directions: "Get to know the crew and passengers; hear their stories, their dreams and learn about their lives on board *Titanic* as they set sail for America on the ship's maiden voyage."

Like the anachronistic and, in reference to a steam liner, inadequate metaphor of 'setting sail', the effect of the fifth and sixth galleries consists mainly in re-transferring media-stimulated affects to a few people stylized as protagonists who attest to the events. Among these people is the film actress Dorothy Gibson. Visitors to the exhibit (or readers of the *Souvenir Guide*) learn that, just a few weeks after the catastrophe, she played a part in *Saved from the Titanic* (dir. Étienne Arnaud, USA 1912), the first feature film to be created about the ship's sinking[6].

The exhibit returns to this and other films, newspaper articles, novels, and conspiracy theories that deal with the disaster in the eighth gallery under the title "Myths & Reality". In the planning process, however, the scenographers had to solve the problem the exhibit was faced with, namely that this subject matter has been adapted for film so many times. The problem is that there are hardly any visitors to Titanic Belfast who do not have at least a few spectacular images from the sinking of the ship 'in their minds' – images that, for the most part, have been drawn exclusively from recent feature-film productions. When viewers of Cameron's version of the story, which not only became hugely popular but also set new benchmarks in production, are sent shooting through the damaged liner's claustrophobically narrow hallways by the flood of water rushing in, they get the feeling that, at any moment, their 'feet could get wet' too. And when, thanks to subjective shots, they gaze almost straight down from the stern of the ship into the abyss at the climax of the suspense, an exhibit that is supposed to recreate the same event is left with the sole choice of either showing the film or surrendering in the face of a visual force that simply cannot be topped.

In Belfast, they found a solution to this problem that – at the very point at which the story of the *Titanic* reaches an emotional peak – relies not on sensual concretion and immersion but on abstraction and contemplation. First, this is accomplished by presenting the physical process of the sinking through animated scenes that openly reveal their mediality. The focus is thus not placed on creating a comprehensive illusion but on the viewer acknowledging the model-like character of the depiction and observing, from a relatively distanced perspective, how quickly the *Titanic* tips forward, its

6 To the extent Dorothy Gibson's appearance in the display was motivated by the scenographers' attempt to tie the story of the sinking of the *Titanic* to narrative voices that evoke an empathetic reaction in visitors, it comes down to a quote of hers from an interview for *Moving Picture World* magazine: "I will never forget the terrible cry that rang out from people who were thrown into the sea and others who were afraid for their loved ones" (qtd. Costecalde/Doherty, eds. 2012: 59).

keel is submerged in water, it breaks apart, and it is swallowed by the black surface of the ocean. Secondly, the animation is abstract because it shows a scene devoid of people and sound. By leaving sound and action out of the film, the creators keep viewers at a distance from what is going on – especially in the way the silent, shadowy animation stands in blatant contrast to the turbulence of events and the panic aboard the *Titanic* as well as to the spectacular images of Hollywood.

In a subtle yet, in their cumulation, effective way, the animated scenes and other scenographies create a mood that is incorporated into the seventh gallery. This gallery is dedicated to the aftermath of the catastrophe and the memory of its victims. By means of many exhibits (models, replicas, historical photographs, and informational text panels) but also with the help of interactive information media that allow visitors to conduct their own research, they can address the direct results of the disaster in detail: the recovery of the survivors and victims' bodies, the spread of the terrible news throughout the world, and the reactions of the families of those on board. Here, too, the scenography reveals a seismographic quality that is not even

Illustration 6:
Titanic Belfast, exhibition view of the gallery The Launch of Titanic.
Copyright Titanic Belfast.

Illustration 7:
Titanic Belfast, exhibition view of the gallery Fitting-Out.
Copyright Titanic Belfast.

exhausted in melodramatic moments. Rather, this quality is tied to the interrogative mode. Visitors are given the opportunity to ask questions and search for answers: how many people died on that night in April? How many survived the disaster? How was the ship able to collide with the iceberg in the first place? And who was responsible for there being so few lifeboats on board?

In light of these and similar questions, the eighth gallery seems like quite a relief. Visitors can relax and take a deep breath as they pass by film posters and other media-based documentations of the *Titanic* catastrophe as well as a vitrine containing, in part, rather strange exhibits. That is, of course, until, once again, they come across anecdotes like the following that take their breath away:

> Morgan Robertson was an American novelist who, in 1898, wrote a short story, *Futility*, in which a very large unsinkable ship called *Titan* (nearly as big as *Titanic*) hits an iceberg on its side and sinks in the Atlantic at high speed, one April night. Only a few passengers and crew survive because there are not enough lifeboats. This story was published fourteen years before *Titanic* sank! (Costecalde/Doherty, eds. 2012: 71)

Robertson's story suggests that there is probably no terrifying event that has not already been played out in someone's mind. It also points to an aspect of scenography that does not play a major role in Titanic Belfast but does wherever scenographies are used prospectively to act out possible risks. This is the case, for example, in flight and ship simulators that are used to train pilots and captains. This anecdote also makes one other aspect clear: immersion has at least as much to do with imaginations as it does with perceptions. This is why the chill that runs down readers' backs when they read something that terrifies them can be such an intense experience. To find oneself entranced in terror is also a modality of immersion that not only occurs in haunted house rides but, above all, in one's imagination, which, at times, can be stimulated with very little effort in terms of media involvement. In the case of the aforementioned short story, this factor certainly plays a role in the way the narrative seems prophetic in hindsight.

In contrast to the prospectively oriented scenographies I have just mentioned, the observatory of the underwater theater, which marks the end of the tour through Titanic Belfast, is just as retrospectively laid out as the other galleries. It is divided into two parts. The discovery of the wreck by Dr. Robert Ballard in 1985, the story behind his expedition, and its results are recapitulated on a large screen. Underneath the grandstand, the multi-level gallery Titanic Beneath is composed of one further media sensation: here, visitors walk on a large glass surface beneath which, once again, the hull of the ship appears – this time, however, from the perspective of a camera that shows an overhead shot of the ship as it moves along its eroded superstructures (see *Illustration 8*). In this way, what viewers see in the final scene of this memorial film, which causes their visit to the museum to play back in their minds, is the eerily beautiful giant shell of a drowned body of steel that floats before their eyes and, in doing so, seems otherworldly. It is precisely in this way, however, that the wreck shows itself for what it truly is: a timeless 46,000-ton coffin that has been ripped in two. In the last glimpse of the *Titanic*, the scenography returns to the origin of the museum with a fantastic media installation focused on resonance (on the resonance of all that which echoes in the minds of the visitors at this point) – on its conception in the spirit of semiophorology.

Illustration 8: Titanic Belfast, exhibition view of the gallery Titanic Beneath. Copyright Titanic Belfast.

2. Semiophorology and Scenography

The origin of the modern museum, as Krzysztof Pomian determined in his study *L'Ordre du temps*, was a collection of objects intended (at least initially) for display only (see 1984; cf. 1990: 8). For this purpose, these objects had either been removed from the economic circuit or were made with this specific purpose in mind. Among the predecessors of this paradoxical practice was the use of objects as offerings and funerary objects (cf. 1990: 11f.). Pomian points out that, among even the earliest examples of funerary objects in human history, one can find priceless replicas and models. This only makes sense if one assumes that what matters here is not the objects' practical value: "[...] the objects were placed in the tombs so that those living in the next world could view them. [...] their function was to be looked at and admired forever" (ibid.: 12).

This presupposes a belief in a world invisible in everyday life that is beyond the living world but in which these objects can be seen. The same prerequisite exists in regard to relics, which are the opposite of funerary objects in that they assure the invisible presence of heroes and saints in this world for the living to look at and admire rather than the dead (cf. ibid.: 16f.). Similar to relics, religious works of art were "go-betweens between those who gazed upon them and the invisible from whence they came" (ibid.: 22). Thereby the numinous sphere of the invisible is multifarious. It can be the realm of myth or the realm of the dead, the sacred world beyond or simply the profane 'beyond' of the past. Whether funerary objects or offerings, relics or religious artworks, things removed from everyday practice or objects made especially for the purpose of representation – "they could not guarantee communication between the two worlds unless they were displayed to the inhabitants of both" (ibid.: 24). In this sense, the wreck that visitors to the Titanic Belfast museum look at is actually a thing from another world: from the realm of the dead and from that biosphere in which humans cannot exist.

Pomian traces the history of the museum and the exhibition back to the Neolithic Age. At that time, a consequential exchange in the relationship between the two areas of the visible and the invisible is said to have taken place. It was then that, for perhaps the first time in human history, objects were created that were (exclusively) intended to serve the mutual permeation of spheres, as representations, and as projections (cf. ibid.: 29f.). "The production effort therefore now had two very different goals, one situated in the visible, the other in the invisible, the aims being to maximize either usefulness or meaning" (ibid.: 30). Pomian calls objects that derive their value from serving exclusively as signs, as intermediaries between presence and absence, between visibility and invisibility, "*semiophores, objects which were of absolutely no use*" (ibid. [emphasis in the original]). Semiophores are 'vessels' charged with meaning and filled with significance – either because they represent a practice that has become obsolete but the memory of which has remained, or because they were created so that, in this perceivable world of the here and now, there would be a material representative of another world that exists beyond sensory perception.

Naturally, the semiophores' task is not left untouched by modern science, which repeatedly pushes the line between the visible and the invisible and redefines the relationship between the real and the imaginary, between the everyday and the fantastic (cf. ibid.: 35f.). It is interesting that semiophores that originally stood for a certain version of the 'other' world still fulfill their function even if people no longer believe in this version or hold another to be determinative. Thus, in museums (as opposed to temples), certain objects of ritual worship represent less the object of worship, which is an 'article of faith', than the culture and community of the subjects integrated through this cult. This applies to the funerary objects of the Pharaohs and the sculptures of Greek gods, to name just two examples. One looks at them in museums not to worship them but because of an interest in the mentality of lost cultures.

Thus, as Pomian establishes, in the case of semiophores, it not only comes down to the fact that, along with a material aspect, they also have a semiotic one. It is also important that they be part of a collection or an exhibition in which they function as display items and signs. It is the context of the presentation that decides in which direction the semiosis will go. Strictly speaking, however, this means that semiophores can only accomplish their purpose within the context of an, at least ideally, existent scenography. Just as religious communities form a mental image of this other world that 'permeates' their everyday reality with the material form of the semiophores, the idea a secular society or another culture (retrospectively) gets of the everyday reality of this religious community is, first and foremost, nothing more than that: an idea.

In this way, one is confronted with an ambiguity inherent to the term 'scenography'. On the one hand, it can mean the concrete, material installation that is presented in a display like a diorama; on the other hand, however, as has been demonstrated by Umberto Eco, it can also refer to the imaginary, condensed version of a story or script (cf. 1979/1984: 20f.) that is associated with a semiophore, such as the script of a myth or a ritualistic activity. When visitors to the Museum of Military History (Heeresgeschichtliches Museum) in Vienna come across the car in which the Austrian heir to the throne was sitting when he was shot and killed in Sarajevo in 1914, they are looking at both: the historical material remnants and the 'film' that plays in their minds (either because they can recall historical photographs, or because, by using their imagination, they develop a collection of images of the sequence of events).

Thus, by no means does one have to pit the two different forms of scenography against one another. On the contrary: the key aspect of scenographic museum and exhibition design lies precisely in the fact that the layout of the exhibits creates a display that allows viewers to play out the scenario they have, more or less, three-dimensionally before them in their minds. Consequently, one can measure the material installations in a museum or in an exhibition by looking at how they construct the relationship between material and conceptual scenography. The Stuttgart designer Johannes Milla makes a similar argument when he states: 'The scenographers' task is to show images and spaces but also to evoke images in people's minds, [...] because the true media space exists in the minds of the viewers'[7]. In its nature as an aggrandized form of scenography, the media space consists, on the one hand, of the showroom that appears when film and video leave the screen and become three-dimensional (cf. Milla 2004: 150). On the other hand, however, it also 'consists' of the ideas that are evoked in this showroom.

Whether it is the media space or, as Milla asserts, the visitor's imagination that presents the 'true' scenography seems to me to be a pointless question that could possibly lead to confusion. As with all scenographic media – in which one must include comics, graphic novels, screenplays, and novels – it is always about creating configurations of symbols that encourage imaginative people to picture, envision, and, in such a way, refresh the dramatic potential of the sequences of events, possible actions, and narrative options that are laid out in a scenario. Which material signs or which media apparatuses are used and how much of the configuration is composed of iconic, indexical, or symbolic signs is different from case to case. The principle that lies in the evocation of vivid mental images always remains the same (although, here, 'vivid' can mean both 'variable' and 'animated' as well as 'not simply flat, but, more or less, three-dimensional').

For this reason, in my opinion, a logical division has to refer back to a formal and gradual difference rather than a substantial one. Evidently, on one side of the spectrum, there are scenographies that rely heavily on exemplification. On the other side, there are scenographies that rely on media in which exemplification is either impossible or does not play a central role.

7 "Die Aufgabe der Szenografen ist Bilder und Räume zu zeigen, aber auch Bilder im Kopf auszulösen, [...] da der wahre Media-Space in den Köpfen der Betrachter stattfindet" (Milla 2004: 152).

In the first category one can undoubtedly include all installations that use remnants and relics or models and replicas that possess exactly those characteristics by means of which they represent a particular scenario. Exemplification is materially bound to the possession of the characteristics that are displayed. Therefore, the preserved Thompson Dock in Belfast (by and large true to the original) belongs in this category, as does the reconstruction of the grand staircase and other similar sites and exhibits.

Because letters and series of letters usually do not possess the characteristics of the objects and events to which they refer, literary texts, in particular, belong in the second category. Naturally there are exceptions to this rule, for example, sound and concrete poems, which focus on synaesthetic sensations or rely on the typeface to 'symbolize' the contours of the object to which they refer. Due to the fact that oral and written discourses, however, do not predominantly tend toward iconic symbol configurations and only use relatively abstract indicators that have to be specified in each situation, their scenographic potential is mainly based on invoking schemas that mediate between term and concept. The power of literature is thus one of evocation rather than of exemplification, for texts only ideally possess that which can be depicted with words.

The same goes for screenplays, but not for comics, graphic novels, or films. This is obvious in the case of films that are shot at original locations. This also applies, however, to the majority of studio lots, which also have to possess at least some of the characteristics that are to be exemplified. Here, one must not only consider naturalistic sets but also those scenographies depicting dream landscapes, such as the one seen in Alfred Hitchcock's *Spellbound* (USA 1945). This is because this landscape exemplifies the protagonist's emotional state. It reveals the traces left by his trauma and simultaneously functions as an objective, physically manifested, and intersubjectively comprehensible correlation of hallucinations under which he suffers. (In the 'talking cure', which the film emulates, these hallucinations, on the other hand, can only be described verbally.)

There is a discrepancy between those scenographies that operate in an exemplificatory manner and those that cannot or should not do so – a discrepancy that is related to the distinction of material and conceptual scenographies but does not have to coincide in all respects. To this one can add a further bifurcation which arises out of the use or non-use of immersive media and media installations. It is thus usually characteristic of media spaces that exemplification takes place virtually within a simulation that 'merely' gives the impression that the scenes and exhibits appear materially to be that which they intend to signify. The reconversion of a wreck that lies on the ocean floor into a brand new ship that glides through the waves is a process shown in Cameron's film. This, however, is not because an actual event was 'filmed' but because a fictional one was staged in the most realistic manner possible using imaging techniques. In contrast to this digital simulation of an irreal metamorphosis, the scenario of shipyard work in the Arrol Gantry through which visitors to Titanic Belfast drift distinguishes itself in that this exhibition space, at least in part, actually exhibits those characteristics that are important in a full-size replica. The costuming of the mannequins corresponds in cut and color to the work clothes worn in that day and age; the scale and lighting conditions, among other things, are also accurate. Although the Shipyard Ride is a simulation and no one can say for sure how authentic the background noises and the metallic smell in the air are, in this case, the scenography is composed of analogous constructions that, in reality, were produced in the 'meatspace' of the physical world.

For Eco, a scenography (or "frame") was "already an inchoative text or a condensed story" (1979/1984: 21). With regard to the film sequence and the Shipyard Ride, one must separate these two characteristics of scenography from one another: the digitally created metamorphosis, thanks to which the *Titanic* appears once again intact, on the film screen is (measured against the possibility of experiencing this process in reality) a virtual text; the scenario of the Arrol Gantry is a condensed story that reincarnates, in a manner of speaking, historical knowledge through analogous constructions. Each form of depiction is immersive in its own way. One should not think that the viewer's body plays no role in the cinematic 'dispositif'. It is not merely a coincidence that visitors' bodies are, for the most part, held still during the Shipyard Ride: in this media installation, as in the case of the apparatus that shows the motion picture, it is assumed that physiological and psychological reactions occur because the images affect the viewers' bodies and 'get under their skin'.

Let us thus assume that the origin of the museum lies in the Neolithic Age, during which the first objects that correspond with Pomian's definition of semiophores were created, but that its actual history began with the collection of wonderful and artistic objects that were worthy of display. This would mean that, with scenography, a concept that confirms the central implicature of semiophorology developed practically by necessity as this practice continued to develop. It consists in the fact that the reference function of the objects that are merely looked at does not become specific until they are placed in a context that virtually composes the horizon of the references. How concretely this context is in turn translated and materialized in viewers' minds is a less important question, the answer to which must not necessarily lead to complex, immersive media installations. It is difficult, however, to imagine an efficient exhibition design that does not attempt to get objects, which are actually silent, to talk. Thus, the implication that objects, in and of themselves, cannot make a point forms the basis of the scenographic discourse. It is, therefore, also no wonder that the speechlessness of things has repeatedly been the point of departure for theoretical considerations of museum work, which constantly faces the choice to present scenographies in material form or let them be realized in visitors' minds.

3. Exhibits, Scenes, and Immersive Media Installations

"The problem with things is that they are dumb. They are not eloquent, as some thinkers in art museums claim. They are dumb. And if by some ventriloquism they seem to speak, they lie" (Crew/Sims 1991: 159). The questionable art of ventriloquism cannot be the solution to the problem raised by Spencer R. Crew and James E. Sims with this observation. It is clear that semiophores can only fulfill their function at the point of intersection between perception, imagination, and memory and that resonance represents a related and important principle of operation of museums. It is, however, equally apparent that, due to reasons of intellectual and scientific integrity, working with interpolations in exhibitions is out of the question. If a scenography wants to expand viewers' horizons beyond their perception of the individual exhibits, there are only two ways it can achieve this without interpolations. One possibility is by arranging several exhibits in such a way that a total picture is created that is super-summative. This, for example, is the discourse formation relied on by painting exhibitions that exemplify an epochal style through an ensemble of representative pieces. The characteristics that these pieces actually embody are, in a way, added together but result in something greater than what can be seen in each piece. The other way to broaden the exhibits' reference radius is to enhance them with information that takes on a scenographic quality when it is translated into sensory data. The sign under the Rococo painting is not yet a scenography. However, if this painting is hung in a contemporary ambience – whether in its original showplace or in a reconstruction – the exhibition space becomes a stage that visitors not only can perceive from a distance but also can set foot on. In a similar way, the information sheet that visitors pick up in order to learn more about an exhibit becomes a scenographic discourse if it contains concise descriptions that enable readers to imagine the mental horizon of the world from which the exhibit originated.

One might be tempted to think of arrangement as a form of syntax. One would have to concede, however, that enhancement also acts syntactically. It is comparable to the embellishment of a statement with adjectives and adverbial periphrases, whereas arrangement strings together verbs and substantives. This stringing together has a tendency to narrate in the same way that enhancement is a kind of furnishing, a way of painting a picture with characteristics and circumstances. Therefore, it seems obvious to see arrangement as a form of telling and enhancement as a form of showing. This differentiation, however, is anything but distinct, since technically it is not nouns and verbs that are being arranged but pieces in an exhibition. For this reason, the basic differentiation should remain between exhibit and scene. The term 'scenography' thus implies that the scene involves a script that can be materially implemented just as well as this task can be left up to the visitors, who, as a rule, can only achieve this using their imaginations[8].

Apart from that, visitors must often be explicitly told which characteristics of an exhibit are to be semiophorologically understood. Conversely, Marcel Duchamp's famous work of art – a urinal as an object of aesthetic observation and as a point of departure for a reflection on what actually constitutes art – is based on the trick of calling on the museum's scenography. Without the script according to which objects found at this location are removed from everyday life and the

8 It is revealing that verbs and substantives are, in fact, scenographic. Dependency grammar assumes that sentences are ruled by action words and, as a result, are always like miniature dramas (cf. Tesnière 1959: 73f.). On the other hand, the example Eco uses to explain his idea of scenography, the word 'supermarket', is a substantive to which various scripts that are all defined with verbs belong: 'shopping', 'paying', 'checking out', etc. (cf. Eco 1979/1984: 21).

sphere of objects of utility and are to be perceived from a purely aesthetic point of view, displaying a urinal would have been rather pointless. (To ensure that the joke would not be misunderstood, the urinal was mounted on the wall upside-down.) As Nelson Goodman determined, in the modern era, one must often transform the question of "What is art?" into "Where is art?" or "When is art?" (1978: 66f.). Essentially, this insight confirms the premise of Pomian's treatment of semiophorology. According to his theory, whether an object is intended for use and can be picked up or can only be viewed as an intermediary of meanings that lie beyond everyday contexts of use depends on the discourse situation.

One can therefore see the function of scenography in the fact that it shifts objects into the context of a narrative and provides them with a 'voice-over' – a narrative voice that inevitably has to come from 'off screen', from outside of the inherently mute things. This is precisely why scenographies, even when they operate in an exemplificatory manner, always involve evocation. This evocation can be sustainably supported through media that enhance the exhibition space. As can be seen in the case of the silent arrangement of exhibits, however, it can also simply arise at the point of intersection between the hodological space of pathways and the train of thought that follows these paths. Both are scenographic acts: evocation through media, which can represent a story and maybe even have a narrative voice, and evocation through the silently implemented narration positioned throughout the room that visitors themselves tap into when they walk through the exhibition and discuss among themselves. Both – the explicit narration as well as the narration implied in the exhibition's layout – require as much understanding of the subject from the scenography as they require sensitivity from visitors. In this context, Crew and Sims emphasize that

> creating a voice for exhibitions is not a straightforward task. Exhibitions have multiple voices – and many of these do not emerge until after the exhibition is in place and the audience comes to view it. However, in the earliest stages the exhibition team must settle on a voice that will run threadlike through the exhibition. Within history exhibitions this voice or point of view often is influenced by research taking place in academic circles. (1991: 163)

Because the discourse that takes place in these circles can often only be understood by insiders, scenographers are often faced with the task of translating the experts' special idiom into a language that is intelligible to everyone. This is not only a question of vocabulary; it is, above all, a question of the frameworks of understanding and interpretative schemata that certain terms invoke. While every story involves such frameworks and schemata, not all frameworks and schemata are suited for an exhibition's aim of conveying information. If one – like Crew and Sims, who have focused predominantly on bringing the past to mind – assumes that the historical event is given primacy and the physical object that remains from this event, which can attest to it and illustrate it, is only of secondary importance (cf. ibid.: 175), then the scenography that is created for this object should, first and foremost, show the historical chronotope. The chronotope, after all, represents the context of the circumstances that allowed for the event to transpire or even caused it to happen. In this regard, the chronotope can be thought of as the habitat of the event and, for that reason, it is no surprise that, like a habitat, it is staged with the use of dioramas or panoramas[9]. These are the devices to which the creators of the Titanic Belfast museum complex adhered. They assume that visitors will want to know what Belfast looked like when the *Titanic* was built, was launched, and set off on its fateful maiden voyage. Visitors can get a better idea of what its sinking must have meant to its contemporaries if they can picture them and the world they lived in.

The comparison of arrangement and enhancement, however, brings yet another function of museum scenography to light that deserves special attention simply because it is often not appreciated enough, even by those who notice it. In this light, Svetlana Alpers correctly determined that a considerable part of museums' effect rests upon the fact that, in principle, they display each object so that it can be viewed like a work of art that amazes, raises questions, and encourages further investigation. (As has already been mentioned, this is the very script of which Duchamp served himself in displaying the urinal). Alpers illustrates the special kind of perception that reigns in museums using the larger-than-life-size model of a crab that impressed her as a child:

9 In this context, the terms 'diorama' and 'panorama' should not be viewed too narrowly. In the first gallery of Titanic Belfast, there are technically no dioramas or panoramas. The tour, composed of life-size film projections, however, functions as a panoramic view of historical Belfast. Similarly, the immersive power of the Shipyard Ride rests on the idea that the viewer is floating through a diorama.

> It was not only the size of the whole but of each of its individual parts. One could see the way it was made. [...] The museum had transformed the crab – had heightened, by isolating, these aspects, had encouraged one to look at it in this way. The museum had made it an object of visual interest. (1991: 25)

Because Alpers places such an emphasis on the transformation that turns the animal model into an object that can be looked at as a work of art, she seems to have missed an aspect that is connected to this, even though it is included in her description: "One could see the way it was made." Due to its isolation (the crab is not displayed as part of a diorama in the midst of its habitat) and due to the enlarged size of its body parts (here, the museum functions as a magnifying glass) one can see how the crab is assembled, the parts of which it is composed, and how these are connected with one another. The animal model is subject not only to the visitors' gaze but also to their analytical reasoning; it is not only treated like an artwork but is also virtually disassembled (diagrammatized). The joke in the display is thus the layout, because, in the words of Schopenhauer, it facilitates an intellectual observation of the 'thing' for the viewer (cf. 1988: 41f.).

Moreover, Alpers realized that the unique character of the perception made possible by the crab model is connected to the fact that, in contrast to a living crab, it is rendered motionless. What is overlooked in a fleeting impression of movement distinctly emerges in a motionless state. From this perspective, in museums, life is treated like a film that one can stop in order to leisurely watch certain recorded moments in as high a definition as possible. Museums thus handle space and time differently; they expose proportions that are too small and too fleeting for people to see by transferring these proportions into a scheme, a diagram, and dissecting them (which, in principle, is the same thing)[10].

Therefore, I believe that the arrangement of the exhibits, particularly when they are used to lay out an educational trail through the exhibition space, as well as the act of revealing how the pieces are arranged (so that, for example, legs and claws come together to make a crab), are already diagrammatical operations. The basic operation of arranging is also always a form of displaying. This displaying (layout), however, is a reading in the sense that, etymologically speaking, the word 'legend' means 'that which is to be read'. This way of 'reading

10 Naturally, this can happen in a variety of ways: two- or three-dimensionally, as a drawing, a model, an analogous construction, or a digital display.

together' begins with collecting, continues in the arrangement of the collected objects into displays in the exhibition, and arrives at its goal in the conjectural understanding of the exhibition in its consolidation into a complex intellectual impression.

In this way, displaying is also always a demonstration and a revelation, a construction and deconstruction of elements and relationships – a 'dis-play' in both senses of the word[11]. The over-dimensional representation of the crab is a staged analysis. It is through this staging that it turns into the aestheticological sensation that fascinates viewers in the first place.

As has already been mentioned, one must differentiate between two variations of the diagrammatical operation. On the one hand, there is the analytical layout of the crab, in other words, the dismantling of the individual display piece, which, in this form, becomes a diagram. On the other hand, there is the layout of the conjecture that operates in a more synthetic manner if it follows the arrangement of the pieces in the exhibition space and uses its scenographic enhancement to construct complex concepts and series of concepts. Thus one could, for example, play out the crab's history by arranging various models representing the different phases of the onto- or phylogenesis throughout the room in such a way that a 'Stationendrama' is created. Each station could then be provided with a fitting ambience, atmospherically condensed, and arranged into a still life. In doing so, the exhibition design takes advantage of the fact that the plot, the plan of a story that is carried out over time, always involves a spatial element. In fact, the origin of the English word 'plot' is a sectioned-off piece of land cultivated for a specific reason, such as a plot of farmland. This etymology refers not only to the culture's natural history but also to Aristotelian Poetics, according to which the term 'myth' has more or less the same reference as the term 'plot' in modern narratology and dramaturgy. Consequently, Crew and Sims also use this term to translate the Greek word:

> [...] another dialectical model exists for the shape of the narrative exhibition: Aristotle's *Poetics*. His elements of the dramatic structure are plot, character, thought, diction, music, and spectacle. Aristotle's list is not arbitrary. This understanding of the human condition is first framed by the event – the performance itself and the story being dramatized, being made present – in the plot, the shape of the relationships changing. Then the agents of the action and its special place of origin are characterized; then, with event and players established, can the au-

11 On the interplay of "lay-out" and "dis-play", cf. Bauer/Ernst 2010: 64–72.

> dience and author intervene with point-of-view, with interpretation. Then comes verbal meaning, the shape of time (music), and the way things look. The visual form – the spectacle – is derived from choices made about the first elements. (1991: 174)

The process of scenographic enhancement described here becomes extremely clear in Titanic Belfast. The base operation is the layout, the plot of the 'dis-play': construction, maiden voyage, and sinking. From this narrative framework, the other acts of sensory concretization, the material furnishing, and the like, begin. The result, as in the case of the Shipyard Ride, can lead to a highly immersive scenography. The fact that the creators of the museum in Belfast consistently relied on an interplay of immersion and contemplation corresponds with the conclusion one can draw from the recent debate about the concept of scenography – a debate in which media-euphoric arguments in favor of upgrading the exhibition's design are faced with media-skeptical arguments in favor of downgrading it.

Szenografie in Ausstellungen und Museen, an edited volume on the scenography in exhibitions and museums (see Kilger, ed. 2004), contains a representative recording of this debate. For one, it makes it clear that, over the last decades, scenography has become the master plot of modern exhibition design. It also indicates, however, how multifaceted and, to a certain extent, controversial the concept is in theory and practice. In the first chapter, for example, Bodo-Michael Baumunk – in a manner very different from that which has been seen in postmodern event culture – exposes the metaphorical character of the concept and the snares associated with it:

> Wherever set designers in theater or film have designed exhibition scenarios, the question of the role the implanted exhibits were actually supposed to play in the piece being performed was always present in the day-to-day design process: that of the actors or merely that of the props. In truth, the staged or scenographically constructed exhibits have less to do with the dynamic of the stage than they do with their frozen form in the shape of the *allegory*.[12]

12 "Wo immer Bühnenbildner oder Filmarchitekten Ausstellungsszenarien entworfen haben, hat in der alltäglichen Entwurfspraxis ständig die Frage im Raum gestanden, welche Rolle eigentlich die implantierten Ausstellungsobjekte im aufgeführten Stück zu spielen hatten: die der Schauspieler, oder nur die der Requisiten. In Wahrheit haben die inszenierten oder szenografierten Ausstellungen weniger mit der Dynamik der Bühne als vielmehr mit ihrer gefrorenen Form in Gestalt der *Allegorie* zu tun." (Baumunk 2004: 14 [emphasis in the original])

This estimate probably applies to scenographies like the diorama, but it certainly does not apply to all media installations that serve to illustrate. Many of them aim at that which Heike Hagebölling calls intermedial or 'interactive dramaturgies' ("interaktive Dramaturgien"; 2004a: 18–29). They are attempts to design exhibitions according to the strategies that have long proven successful in storytelling, on the stage, and in the cinema: a hook is established on which visitors' roaming eyes are caught; it pulls them into stories, the narrative strands of which are educational trails; and, with the use of subplots, it spreads the story out so that 'quasi-interactive environments' ("quasi interaktive Environments"; ibid.: 24) emerge that function as '"multi-user" platforms' ("'Multi-User'-Plattformen"; ibid.). The users determine how long they want to occupy themselves with an installation, when they 'flip to the next channel', and how they navigate through the exhibition.

Navigation is necessary because the interactive and intermedial dramaturgies operate with a network of references, with a complex architecture of knowledge. Above all, in this regard, it goes beyond the linear dimension of myth, past the simple sequence of beginning, middle, and end. If Aristotle still connected myths to the law of consecutivity that left little room for digressions, then interactive dramaturgies rely on excursions that 'let visitors off the hook' and transform exhibitions into grounds of exploration, in which one can and must walk back and forth (recalling the Latin 'discurrere', to wander). At the same time, the dramaturgy of suspense, as Hagebölling emphasizes, lies in the continuity of a culture of memory that has always served itself of all available forms of media: 'In every narrative and communicative act, dramaturgy, above all, aims at impacting the listener and the viewer. Without dramaturgical power, a large part of the traditional body of thought would have probably already been lost.'[13] Gerhard Kilger, on the other hand, has expressed reservations with regard to the 'topography of stimulation' ("Reiztopographie"; 2004: 33):

> Good scenographic concepts are not derived from the exhibition design. It is not new habits of seeing, new designs, or formal structures that offer enough possi-

13 "In jedem erzählerischen und kommunikativen Akt zielt Dramaturgie vor allem auf Wirkung beim Zuhörer und Betrachter. Ohne dramaturgische Kraft wäre wahrscheinlich bereits ein Großteil des traditionellen Gedankenguts verloren gegangen" (Hagebölling 2004b: 179).

> bilities for methods of conveying information but the creation of spaces to be 'used' by visitor traffic.[14]

This sounds pragmatic but it neglects the fact that one of the main points of scenography lies in that it converts the mode of presentation from conveyance to appropriation. The visitor, particularly in the case of interactive dramaturgies, is not thought of as a receiver or reader of information but as a fellow player who enters the stage of intellectual perception with the exhibition – a stage that can only be set with the visitor's own imagination. In other words, the scenographer must approach the situation with the so-called lector in fabula in mind, which means nothing other than that scenography is a "presuppositional machine"[15]. It not only implicitly assumes an active visitor but plans on the fact that he or she needs certain blank spaces in order to be prompted to intellectual activity.

Instead of degrading the visitor to being an 'accomplice' (cf. Gössel 2004: 76) of the scenography, scenographers should use their artistic means and technical media to convey an idea to the visitor; it is then up to the visitor to cultivate it and take it further. In an essay not included in the volume edited by Kilger but in a separate book (see Bohn/Wilharm, eds. 2009), Pamela C. Scorzin arrives at roughly the same concept when she refers to scenographers as arrangers who act as invisible directors, similar to the way good authors stay in the background of the story and understand themselves to be predominantly inspirers and initiators of experiences that are to be had by others. Apart from that, Scorzin also traces scenography back to diagrammatical operations when she considers the creation of relationships the basic task of post-aesthetic scenography, preferably without the authoritarian gesture that leads to the manipulation, forming, and control of how the participant experiences what is presented (cf. Scorzin 2009: 314; see also 2011).

---

14 "Gute szenografische Konzepte leiten sich nicht aus dem Ausstellungsdesign ab. Nicht neue Sehgewohnheiten, neue Formgebungen oder formale Strukturen bieten ausreichende Möglichkeiten für Methoden der Vermittlung, sondern Raumbildungen für ihre 'Benutzung' durch Publikumsverkehr." (Kilger 2004: 33)

15 Umberto Eco uses this metaphor for literary scenography, in which it is implicitly assumed that readers will take on the role intended for them in the text (cf. 1979: 25). For example, readers bridge the gaps in the text using a knowledge of the world and people, their imaginations, and their capacity for empathy (cf. Bibeau/Corin, eds. 1994: 9; Zaczek 1997: 125).

4. Simulation, Immersion, and Absorption

Ultimately, what one can take from the critical examination of the exhibition and museum concept of scenography is that, although it is primarily an immersive strategy, it is also always viewed with skepticism when this strategy threatens to absorb the visitor and diminish the distance that is the prerequisite for every critical reflection of experience.

Immersion can be viewed as a transitory modality of perception that, from the very beginning, has aimed at emerging out of the media space of the scenography. In this case, its function is the same as the one that was already given to the interplay of suspense dramaturgy and the creation of illusion in the traditional forms of theater and literature (see Wolf 2013), that was taken up again and transformed in narrative cinema, and whose main features were already described by Aristotle. Scenography is thus a means of escalating the intensity of experience and sustainability of the creation of ideas at the intersection between perception and imagination, emotion and cognition.

By contrast, if one views immersion as a new quality of perception that has only existed since electronic media have been capable of systematically demarcating the difference between visual space and pictorial space, field of view and performance area, real and virtual (inter-)action, the stage – because it no longer has a forestage – tendentially becomes a Holodeck. Although the utopian potential of this Holodeck has not yet been brought up to date in contemporary museum design, it could appeal to exhibition creators as an aim. Scenographies such as the Arrol Gantry in Titanic Belfast already allow visitors to enter pictorial spaces that envelop them so completely that they collect synaesthetic impressions that are organized in narrative form and temporarily allow visitors to forget that they are only witnessing a production.

If, since the 19th century, a common characteristic of museums and exhibitions, fair attractions such as the panorama, and other media had been the establishment of a practice of "showing and telling" (Bennett 1995: 6), at the turn of the 21st century, this dyad became a triad of showing, telling, and designing. More precisely: designing went through a change of media that alters the structure of reality. If, through traditional art forms and media – to which the museum, according to its origin, belongs – only images of the world were formed in people's minds, the new hybrid media differentiate themselves from this in that they are both imaging and world-creating apparatuses.

Semiophores are objects that one only looks at. They should neither be held nor be used as tools for structuring the world. The only reason they make any sense at all is because they represent a demarcation between the visible and the invisible, whereby this demarcation must constantly be balanced anew with the difference between what is real and what is not real. In principle, however, this demarcation is not subject to negotiation: in the classical museum, the space of human movement and action – at least for visitors – is separate from the space in which the objects that are only meant to be looked at are located. Semiophores evoke ideas and make these ideas a reality but not materially.

Scenographies, on the other hand, are tools of intellectual appropriation that tend to not only evoke ideas but also reify and materialize them. They objectify the invisible world and, in doing so, alter the structure of reality. This is at least true for all of those scenographies that are not merely imaginarily constructed and played out. In 1911, no one took a suspended-cable-car ride through the Harland & Wolff construction hall, no one was able to observe the builders working there the way one can on the Shipyard Ride through the scenography of the Arrol Gantry, and certainly no visitor saw the sinking of the ship in the North Atlantic with their own eyes.

In fact, in the first catastrophe of the 20th century, one can also see the initial spark of a media evolution that culminates in Titanic Belfast's immersive scenographies. As in the genesis of the museum, in its advanced form, it is about establishing an interface between the visible and the invisible. For the precise reason that there are no authentic pictures of the catastrophe, it constantly prompts new attempts at depiction using all available forms of imaging media. The eyewitness testimonies of the survivors are not enough, because they are nothing more than testimonies. It was because of this that even the first newspapers to inform their readers of the disaster were enhanced with illustrations that attempted to depict these eyewitness accounts. The bodies of the recovered victims had only just been buried when the first films were made. The many expeditions undertaken, at first in vain, to locate the wreck and possibly even retrieve it testify to the fact that people cannot accept things disappearing without a trace. As if it were necessary to touch things in order to conceive of their loss, people collect found objects and showpieces, arrange dioramas and exhibitions. These become increasingly comprehensive and immersive through the addition of facts, dates, and details as well as through their arrangement in media spaces that capture all of the senses and, in doing so, people's entire bodies.

Naturally, the development will not stop with the exhibits, installations, and scenographies of Titanic Belfast. Very soon after the museum complex had been opened, the mining entrepreneur and billionaire Clive Palmer announced his plans to build an ocean liner as a replica of the original *Titanic* (see Calligeros 2012). This would constitute 'total immersion': with the reconstruction of the *Titanic*, one could actually graze an iceberg and sink in the middle of the Atlantic exactly 3,000 meters above the spot at which the wreck of the original lies. However, this 'total immersion' would be the end of museums as we know them: a commemorative space dedicated to education from which, so far at least, one can still emerge with their life.

References

Alpers, Svetlana (1991). "The Museum as a Way of Seeing". Karp/Lavine, eds. 25–32.

Bakhtin, Mikhail (1975/1981). "Forms of Time and of the Chronotope in the Novel: Notes toward a Historical Poetics". *The Dialogic Imagination: Four Essays*. Transl. Caryl Emerson, Michael Holquist. Austin, TX: University of Texas Press. 84–258.

Bauer, Matthias, Christoph Ernst (2010). *Diagrammatik: Einführung in ein kultur- und medienwissenschaftliches Forschungsfeld*. Bielefeld: transcript.

Baumunk, Bodo-Michael (2004). "Abschied vom Event". Kilger, ed. 10–17.

Bennett, Tony (1995). *The Birth of the Museum: History, Theory, Politics*. New York, NY/London: Routledge.

Bibeau, Gilles, Ellen Corin, eds. (1994). *Beyond Textuality: Asceticism and Violence in Anthropological Interpretation*. Berlin: de Gruyter.

Bohn, Ralf, Heiner Wilharm, eds. (2009). *Inszenierung und Ereignis: Beiträge zur Theorie und Praxis der Szenografie*. Bielefeld: transcript.

Calligeros, Marissa (2012: online). "Clive Palmer Plans to Build *Titanic* II". *The Sydney Morning Herald*, 30 April. http://www.smh.

com.au/business/clive-palmer-plans-to-build-titanic-ii-20120430-1xtrc.html. [24/06/2014].

Costecalde, Claude, John Paul Doherty, eds. (2012). *Titanic Belfast: Souvenir Guide*. Belfast.

Crew, Spencer R., James E. Sims (1991). "Locating Authenticity: Fragments of a Dialogue". Karp/Lavine, eds. 159–175.

Eco, Umberto (1979). *Lector in fabula: La cooperazione interpretativa nei testi narrativi*. Milan: Bompani.

— (1979/1984). *The Role of the Reader: Explorations in the Semiotics of Texts*. Bloomington, IN: Indiana UP.

Foucault, Michel (1967/1994). "Des espaces autres, Hétérotopies". *Dits et écrits*. Vol. 4. Paris: Gallimard. 752–762.

— (1978). "Ein Spiel um die Psychoanalyse: Gespräch mit Angehörigen des Département de Psychanalyse der Universität Paris VIII in Vincennes". *Dispositive der Macht: Über Sexualität, Wissen und Wahrheit*. Transl. Monika Metzger. Berlin: Merve. 118–176.

— (1984). "Of Other Spaces, Heterotopias". *Architecture, Mouvement, Continuité* 5: 46–49.

Goodman, Nelson (1968/1976). *Languages of Art*. Indianapolis, IN: Bobbs-Merrill.

— (1978). *Ways of Worldmaking*. Indianapolis, IN: Hackett.

Gössel, Peter (2004). "Wahrnehmung und Erfahrung im Museum". Kilger, ed. 68–77.

Greenblatt, Stephen (1991). "Resonance and Wonder". Karp/Lavine, eds. 42–56.

Hagebölling, Heike (2004a). "Interaktive Dramaturgien – mediale Strategien in der Ausstellungs- und Museumsgestaltung: Zur Entwicklung gestalterischer Ansätze in der Ausbildung". Kilger, ed. 18–29.

— (2004b). "Blick zurück in die Zukunft: Zur Geschichte einer Dramaturgie des medialen Raumes". Kilger, ed. 177–189.

Karp, Ivan, Steven D. Lavine, eds. (1991). *Exhibiting Cultures: The Poetics and Politics of Museum Display*. Washington, DC/London: Smithsonian Institution Press.

Kilger, Gerhard, (2004). "Das szenografische Konzept der DASA". Kilger, ed. 30–35.

—, ed. (2004). *Szenografie in Ausstellungen und Museen*. DASA (Bundesanstalt für Arbeitsschutz und Arbeitsmedizin). Essen: Klartext Verlag.

Milla, Johannes (2004). "Media Spaces: Bilder im Raum contra Bilder im Kopf". Kilger, ed. 150–155.

Pomian, Krzysztof (1984). *L'Ordre du temps*. Paris: Editions Gallimard.

— (1987). *Collectionneurs, amateurs et curieux*. Paris: Editions Gallimard.

— (1990). *Collectors and Curiosities: Paris and Venice 1500–1800*. Transl. Elizabeth Wiles-Portier. Cambridge: Polity Press.

Ryan, Marie-Laure (2001). *Narrative as Virtual Reality: Immersion and Interactivity in Literature and Electronic Media*. Baltimore, MD: Johns Hopkins UP.

Schopenhauer, Arthur (1819/1988). *Die Welt als Wille und Vorstellung*. Vol. 1. Ed. Ludger Lütkehaus. Zurich: Haffmans.

— (1958). *The World as Will and Representation*. Vol. 1. Transl. E. F. J. Payne. Indian Hills, CO: The Falcon's Wing Press.

Scorzin, Pamela C. (2009). "Metaszenografie: *The Paradise Institute* von Janet Cardiff & George Bures Miller als inszenatorischer Hyperraum der postästhetizistischen Szenografie". Bohn/Wilharm, eds. 301–314.

— (2011). "Metascenography: On the Metareferential Turn in Scenography". Werner Wolf, ed. *The Metareferential Turn in Contemporary Arts and Media: Forms, Functions, Attempts at Explanation*. Amsterdam/New York, NY: Rodopi. 259–277.

Tesnière, Lucien (1959). *Éléments de syntaxe structurale*. Paris: Klincksieck.

Titanic Belfast (2012: online). "Titanic's Dock". http://www.titanicsdock.com/wp-content/uploads/2011/11/Tourist2012Trifold.pdf. [18/05/2014].

Wolf, Werner (2013). "Aesthetic Illusion". Werner Wolf, Walter Bernhart, Andreas Mahler, eds. *Immersion and Distance: Aesthetic Illusion in Literature and Other Media*. Amsterdam/New York, NY: Rodopi. 1–63.

Wulff, Hans J. (2003). "Empathie als Dimension des Filmverstehens". *montage AV* 12/1: 136–161.

Zaczek, Barbara Maria (1997). *Censored Sentiments: Letters and Censorship in Epistolary Novels and Conduct Material*. Newark, NJ: University of Delaware Press.

Notes on Contributors

Matthias Bauer (matthias.bauer@uni-flensburg.de) is Full Professor of new German literature at the University of Flensburg, Germany. He studied German philology, history, and media studies at the University of Mainz, Germany. His doctoral thesis was concerned with the picaresque novel in Spain, France, England, and Germany. His main fields of research are narratology, film history, semiotics, and modern culture. Among his publications are *Romantheorie und Erzählforschung: Eine Einführung* (2005); *Berlin: Medien- und Kulturgeschichte einer Hauptstadt im 20. Jahrhundert* (2007); *Diagrammatik: Einführung in ein neues medien- und kulturwissenschaftliches Forschungsfeld* (2010, with Christoph Ernst); and *Mythopoetik in Film und Literatur* (2011, ed. with Maren Jäger).

Jörg von Brincken (vonbrincken05@aol.com), born 1969, is Substitute Professor of theater and media at the Department of Theater Studies at the University of Munich, Germany. His field of research includes film aesthetics, film theory, film philosophy, media theory, computer games, porn studies, postdramatic theater, and performance aesthetics. He has published several books and essays on film, theater, and media, including *Tours de Force: Die Ästhetik des Grotesken in der französischen Pantomime des 19. Jahrhunderts* (2006); *Einführung in die moderne Theaterwissenschaft* (2008, with Andreas Englhart); *Fictions/Realities: New Forms and Interactions* (2011, ed. with Ute Gröbel and Irinia Schulzki); and *Emotional Gaming* (2012, ed. with Horst Konietzny). He is currently preparing a publication on Leni Riefenstahl.

Robin Curtis (robin.curtis@uni-duesseldorf.de), born in Toronto, is Professor of theory and practice of audio-visual media at Heinrich Heine University in Düsseldorf, Germany. She has worked as a filmmaker (Nachlass, 1992), curator (e. g.: special program "Out of Time", Oberhausen 2001; Werkleitz Biennale 2002; Goethe Institute Tour "Geschlecht-Konfliktbewältigung", Israel/Palestine 2003), and media scholar. In 2003, she earned her doctorate at the Freie Universität Berlin. Since then she has been Feodor Lynen Fellow of the Alexander von Humboldt Foundation (2008–2011), Adjunct Professor at New York University's Global Academic Center in Berlin (2010–2012), and Research Fellow at the Freie Universität Berlin within the Collaborative Research Center "Cultures of Performativity" (2002–2010). She is also a member of the editorial board of the journal *Pop: Kultur und Kritik*. Her recent publications include the monograph *Conscientious Viscerality: The Autobiographical Stance in German Film and Video* (2006); the special issue on "Immersion", *montage AV*, http://www.montage-av.de/a_2008_2_17.html (2008, ed. with Christiane Voss); and the edited volumes *Einfühlung: Zu Geschichte und Gegenwart eines ästhetischen Konzepts* (2008, ed. with Gertrud Koch); *Deixis und Evidenz* (2008, ed. with Horst Wenzel et al.); *Synästhesie-Effekte: Zur Intermodalität der äisthetischen Wahrnehmung* (2010, ed. with Marc Glöde and Gertrud Koch); *Synchronisierung der Künste* (2013, ed. with Gertrud Koch and Marc Siegel); and *The Autobiographical Turn in Germanophone Documentary and Experimental Film* (2014, ed. with Angelica Fenner).

Burcu Dogramaci (burcu.dogramaci@lmu.de), born 1971 in Ankara, is Professor of 20th-century and contemporary art at the Department of Art History at the University of Munich, Germany. In 2000, she earned her doctorate with a thesis on graphic art in the print media and fashion of the Weimar Republic. In 2007, she completed her habilitation at the University of Hamburg, Germany, with a thesis on the work and influence of German-speaking architects, city planners, and sculptors in Turkey after 1927. She received a research scholarship from the German Research Foundation (DFG) and was awarded the Aby M. Warburg Prize of the City of Hamburg and the Kurt Hartwig Siemers Research Prize by the Hamburg Scientific Foundation. She was also a Senior Researcher in Residence at the Center for Advanced Studies at the University of Munich, Germany. Her research focuses on the areas of 20th-century and contemporary art; exile, transfer of culture, and migration; urbanity and architecture; intermediality in magazines and photobooks; the history and theory of photography; and fashion history and theory.

Thomas Elsaesser is Professor Emeritus at the Department of Media and Culture, University of Amsterdam, Netherlands. From 2006 to 2012 he was Visiting Professor at Yale University and since 2013 has taught part-time at Columbia University, New York. He has authored, edited, and co-edited some twenty volumes on film history, early cinema, film theory, German and European cinema, Hollywood, new media, and installation art. Among his recent books as author are *Film Theory: An Introduction through the Senses* (2010, with Malte Hagener); *The Persistence of Hollywood* (2012); and *German Cinema – Terror and Trauma: Cultural Memory Since 1945* (2013).

Ole W. Fischer (fischer@arch.utah.edu) is an architect, theoretician, historian, and curator. Currently, he is Assistant Professor of the history and theory of architecture at the University of Utah. Previously, he has conducted research and taught at ETH Zurich, Harvard Graduate School of Design, Massachusetts Institute of Technology, and Rhode Island School of Design. He is co-editor of *Precisions: Architecture between Sciences and the Arts* (2008) and *Sehnsucht: A Book of Architectural Longings* (2010). He also contributed to *The Handbook of Architectural Theory* (2012) and wrote *Nietzsches Schatten* (2012).

Gundolf S. Freyermuth (g@freyermuth.com) is Full Professor of media and game studies and a founding director of the Cologne Game Lab, Germany. He also teaches comparative media studies at the international film school cologne (ifs). He has published sixteen books of fiction and non-fiction and more than 500 essays, features, and articles. He has directed documentaries and written scripts for radio plays, feature films, and documentaries. His recent publications include *Games, Game Design, Game Studies: An Introduction* (2015); *New Game Plus: Perspektiven der Game Studies* (2015, ed. with Benjamin Beil and Lisa Gotto); and *Serious Games, Exergames, Exerlearning: Zur Transmedialisierung und Gamification des Wissenstransfers* (2013, ed. with Lisa Gotto and Fabian Wallenfels).

Ursula Anna Frohne (ursula.frohne@uni-koeln.de) is Professor of art history with a focus on 20th- and 21st-century art at the University of Cologne, Germany. From 1995 to 2011 she was a curator at the ZKM | Center for Art and Media in Karlsruhe while teaching at the State Academy for Design in Karlsruhe, Germany. Among other affiliations she has been Visiting Professor at the Department of Modern Culture and Media, Brown University (2001/2002), and Professor of art history at the International University in Bremen, Germany (2002–2006). She has held fellowships from the Getty Research Institute, Los Angeles; The American Council of Learned Societies, New York; and Pembroke Center at Brown University. She chaired a research project dedicated to "Cinematographic Aesthetics in Contemporary Art" (http://kinoaesthetik.uni-koeln.de). In 2014, she was awarded the Leo Spitzer Prize for Arts, Humanities, and Human Sciences by the University of Cologne. Her publications focus on contemporary art and photography, film, video, and installation; political and socioeconomic conditions of art; art's institutional and public spheres; and critical investigations of contemporary visual culture. Her publications include *CTRL [SPACE]: Rhetorics of Surveillance from Bentham to Big Brother* (2002, ed. with Thomas Y. Levin and Peter Weibel); *Kunst und Politik heute?* (2008, ed. with Jutta Held); *Kinematographische Räume: Installationsästhetik in Film und Kunst* (2012, ed. with Lilian Haberer); *Display | Dispositiv: Ästhetische Ordnungen* (forthcoming, ed. with Lilian Haberer and Annette Urban); and *Art 'In-Formation': Communication Aesthetics and Network Structures in Art from the 1960s to the Present* (forthcoming, ed. with Anne Thurmann-Jajes).

Henry Keazor (h.keazor@zegk.uni-heidelberg.de) holds the chair for early modern and contemporary art at the University of Heidelberg, Germany. He studied at the University of Heidelberg and the Sorbonne (Paris IV) and later worked at the universities of Frankfurt am Main, Mainz, and Saarbrücken, Germany. His research covers French and Italian painting of the 16th and 17th centuries, contemporary architecture (with a focus on Jean Nouvel's architectural language) and art forgery. He has published on the relationship between art and media, namely on film and art, *The Simpsons*, and music videos. Among his publications as author and editor are *Hitchcock und die Künste* (2013) and *Der Fall Beltracchi und die Folgen: Interdisziplinäre Fälschungsforschung heute* (2014, ed. with Tina Öcal).

Matthias Krüger (matthias.krueger@kunstgeschichte.uni-muenchen.de) is Guest Professor of art history at the University of Hamburg, Germany. In 2004, he received his doctorate in art history. In the years since, he has worked as a lecturer at the universities of Hamburg, Berne, Bamberg, and Munich. His publications include *Das Relief der Farbe: Pastose Malerei in der französischen Kunstkritik 1850–1890* (2007); *Werkzeuge und Instrumente* (2012, ed. with Philippe Cordez); *Die Biologie der Kreativität: Ein produktionsästhetisches Denkmodell in der Moderne* (2013, ed. with Christine Ott and Ulrich Pfisterer); and *Der Achte Tag: Naturbilder im 21. Jahrhundert* (forthcoming, ed. with Frank Fehrenbach). His research focuses on modern art; color, color theory, and artistic tools; regionalism; and exoticism.

Katja Kwastek (k.kwastek@vu.nl) is Professor of modern and contemporary art at VU University Amsterdam, Netherlands, with a research focus on media art and media aesthetics, (post)digital culture, and the digital humanities. Previously, she taught at the University of Munich, Germany; Rhode Island School of Design, Providence; LBI Media.Art.Research, Linz, Austria; and the Humboldt University of Berlin. Her publications include *Ohne Schnur: Art and Wireless Communication* (2004) and *Aesthetics of Interaction in Digital Art* (2013).

Fabienne Liptay (fabienne.liptay@fiwi.uzh.ch), born 1974, is Professor of film studies at the University of Zurich, Switzerland. She studied film and theater studies as well as English language and literature at the University of Mainz, Germany, where she earned her doctorate in 2002. From 1999 to 2001 she worked as an assistant editor on the TV program *3sat Kulturzeit*. She has been Lecturer at the Department of Film Studies at the University of Mainz (2002–2007) and Assistant Professor at the Department of Art History at the University of Munich (2007–2013). She is co-editor of the quarterly journal *Film-Konzepte* and Visiting Lecturer at the University of Television and Film Munich (HFF). Her research primarily focuses on the theory and aesthetics of film imagery; on audio-visual narrative; and on the interrelations between film and the other arts and media, with a recent focus on the institutional frames of the cinema and the museum.

Karl Prümm, born 1945, is Professor Emeritus of media studies at the University of Marburg, Germany. He studied history and German literature in Marburg and Saarbrücken, Germany, and received his doctorate in 1973 under Ernst Jünger. In 1981, he completed his habilitation under Walter Dirks and Eugen Kogon. Before his appointment to Professor of media studies at the University of Marburg in 1994, he was Adjunct Professor of literary and media studies at the University of Siegen, Germany, and Professor of theater studies (with a focus on film and television) at the Freie Universität Berlin. He is the author of numerous publications on 19th- and 20th-century literary history and on the history, aesthetics, and theory of film, television, and photography. He has also worked as a television critic and has made many contributions to newspapers and television programs.

Martin Warnke (warnke@leuphana.de) is Professor and Director of the Institute for Advanced Study in Media Cultures of Computer Simulation at Leuphana University Lüneburg, Germany. After having studied physics and mathematics at the Freie Universität Berlin and Hamburg University, he graduated in theoretical physics from Hamburg University with a doctoral thesis on suprafluid helium in 1984, then began working at Hochschule Lüneburg, which later became Leuphana University. There he built up the IT infrastructure as CIO, and was also engaged in teaching and research. Since 1990 his scholarly work has cut across the areas of cultural studies, cultural analysis, and computer science. After he acquired his habilitation in 2008, he became a professor at Leuphana University. He is Founding Head of the Institute for Culture and Aesthetics of Digital Media in the Faculty for Humanities and Social Sciences and Vice Dean of Research. Digital media is one of his main subjects and areas of research.

Index of Names

Abel, Alfred 96
Acland, Charles 258
Adams, Ernest 168
Adorno, Theodor W. 169, 302f.
Agamben, Giorgio 219
Agotai, Doris 282–284
Alberti, Leon Battista 180, 183
Allen, Corey 167
Alpers, Svetlana 372, 373
Amenábar, Alejandro 257
Apel, Karl-Otto 264, 269
Arendt, Hannah 303
Argento, Asia 91
Argento, Dario 91–93
Aristotle 29, 374, 376, 378
Arnaud, Étienne 358
Ascott, Roy 187
Atget, Eugène 307
Bach, Johann Sebastian 128
Bachelard, Gaston 25
Bachmann, Stephan 314, 315
Bacon, Francis 205
Balázs, Béla 4, 95, 96, 148, 149, 153, 154, 156, 251, 252, 281, 302
Baldung Grien, Hans 141
Balides, Constance 46, 47, 93
Ballard, Robert 362
Ballhaus, Michael 156
Barenboim, Daniel 314
Barthes, Roland 87, 88, 92, 96, 169
Bathiche, Stevie 167
Baudrillard, Jean 101, 120, 169, 206, 304
Bauman, Zygmunt 1
Baumunk, Bodo-Michael 375
Bay, Michael 47
Bazin, André 142, 161
Benjamin, Walter 101, 169, 301, 303, 306–317
Bennett, Tony 50
Bergson, Henri 131, 311
Beringer, Joseph August 327, 328
Berners-Lee, Timothy 187
Bernhart, Walter 12
Bieger, Laura 88, 216
Bier, Susanne 139, 159
Bigelow, Kathryn 167
Bin Laden, Osama 272
Björk 22, 23
Björk, Staffan 69, 168
Böcklin, Arnold 325
Böhm, Gottfried 289
Böhme, Gernot 180, 316
Böhme, Hartmut 25
Bois, Yve-Alain 291
Bolter, Jay David 101, 102
Bolz, Norbert 233
Bordwell, David 260
Botticelli, Sandro 91
Boudon, Philippe 292
Braun, Christina von 94
Braunfels, Stephan 314
Breton, André 311
Brinckmann, Christine Noll 154
Brock, Bazon 101
Brooks, David 261, 264
Brown, Garrett 155
Brown, Nathaniel 117
Bruegel the Elder, Pieter 91, 92
Brunelleschi, Filippo 141, 179

Bumstead, Henry 101
Burch, Noël 96, 97
Burckhardt, Jacob 180
Butler, Judith 237, 238
Cage, David 188, 189
Cage, John 10
Cameron, James 173, 208, 209, 251, 255, 257, 261–269, 271, 273, 357, 358, 368
Canudo, Ricciotto 285
Carax, Leos 147
Carlson, Marvin 82
Carmack, John, 167
Carus, Carl Gustav 34
Celmins, Vija 26–28
Chandler, Raymond 146
Charcot, Jean-Martin 231, 232
Chatelain, Hélène 99
Chatfield, Tom 174
Chenavard, Antoine-Marie 293
Choisy, Auguste 289–292
Christensen, Jerome 258
Cocteau, Jean 3–6
Connor, J. D. 258
Cook, Peter 306
Cooper, Merian C. 45
Coppola, Francis Ford 265
Cousteau, Jacques 266
Crew, Spencer R. 369, 371, 372, 374
Cronenberg, David 167, 210
Csíkszentmihályi, Mihály 67, 69, 73, 82, 239
D'Almeida, Neville 10
Davidson, Drew 189
Davies, Char 68
Day, Doris 206
de la Huerta, Paz 117
de Meuron, Pierre (see Herzog & de Meuron)
Del Favero, Dennis 192
Deleuze, Gilles 115, 121, 122, 127–129, 131, 133, 262, 265
Democritus 235
Dennett, Daniel C. 270
Der Derian, James 233
Derrida, Jacques 182, 269, 309
Dewey, John 83
Dickmann, Wolfgang 157
Didi-Huberman, Georges 29, 232
Diller + Scofidio 33, 314
Diller, Elizabeth (see Diller + Scofidio)
Dischler, Hermann 337
Disney, Walt 185, 186
Distelmeyer, Jan 263, 265
Ditton, Theresa 216
Doane, Mary Ann 60, 61
Douglas, Mary 7
Dreyer, Carl Theodor 150
Duchamp, Marcel 370, 372
Düffel, John von 25
Eames, Charles 59
Eames, Ray 59
Eberhard, Johann August 90
Eco, Umberto 365, 368, 370, 377
Egger-Lienz, Albin 103
Eichhorn, Maria 32–34
Einstein, Albert 57, 58
Eisenstein, Sergei 284, 289–292
Eliasson, Olafur 10, 33
Elsaesser, Thomas 176, 225
Engels, Friedrich 169
Ermi, Laura 168
Falkenhausen, Susanne von 35
Farocki, Harun 102, 215, 219, 220, 222–225, 227, 230–232, 234, 235, 241, 242
Farrell, Colin 258

Fassbinder, Rainer Werner 211
Felix, Zdenek 29
Fenlon, Pete 190
Ferguson, Graeme 46
Fillion, Odile 289
Fincher, David 257
Fischer-Lichte, Erika 73
Fishburne, Laurence 6
Flammarion, Camille 217
Flavin, Dan 10
Foerster, Heinz von 207
Foucault, Michel 133, 169, 218, 305, 309
Freud, Sigmund 231, 234, 235, 309, 311
Freund, Karl 151
Fried, Michael 302
Friedberg, Anne 166, 181
Gadamer, Hans-Georg 70, 80, 174
Gance, Abel 150
García Linera, Álvaro 262
Gehr, Ernie 104
Gehry, Frank 306, 314
Geissler, Beate 215, 219, 220, 238–242
Gibson, Dorothy 358
Gibson, Mel 258
Gibson, William 195
Glenny, Michael 291
Goethe, Johann Wolfgang von 302
Goffman, Erving 73, 83
Goodman, Nelson 348, 371
Gordon, Douglas 227–232, 241, 242
Gottheim, Larry 55
Gould, Stephen Jay 270
Graf, Dominik 161
Graham, Stephen 240
Grainge, Paul 258
Grau, Oliver 7, 35, 112
Graubner, Gotthard 33
Greenberg, Clement 184, 185, 304
Greenblatt, Stephen 348–350
Griffiths, Alison 48, 56, 57, 112
Grimoin-Sanson, Raoul 145
Groys, Boris 24
Grusin, Richard 101, 102
Guattari, Félix 121, 122, 129, 262
Gunning, Tom 44, 52
Haacke, Hans 31
Haas, Willy 152
Hablik, Wenzel 26
Hadid, Zaha 306, 314
Hagebölling, Heike 376
Hagner, Michael 95
Halbwachs, Maurice 309
Haldemann, Matthias 53, 54
Han, Byung-Chul 218
Hansen, Mark B. N. 83
Hartle, Johan Frederik 218, 219, 230, 240
Hartmann, Britta 256
Haushofer, Karl 332
Haushofer, Max 332
Hegel, Georg Wilhelm Friedrich 169
Heidegger, Martin 303, 315
Helmchen, Rocco 57, 58
Herzog & de Meuron 301, 314
Herzog, Jacques (see Herzog & de Meuron)
Herzogenrath, Wulf 29
Hiepko, Andreas 94
Hilgers, Philipp von 271
Hitchcock, Alfred 87, 93, 94, 98, 99, 101, 265, 367
Hofmann, Werner 185
Holl, Steven 295
Holopainen, Jussi 69, 168
Hopkins, Anthony 258

Horn, Roni 26
Huhtamo, Erkki 113–115, 126, 147, 186
Husserl, Edmund 83
Islinger, Michael 119f.
Jakobson, Roman 256
Jannings, Emil 151
Janz, Rolf-Peter 94
Jauß, Hans Robert 70
Jenkins, Henry 166, 175
Jones, Caitlin 74
Jones, David 172
Jung, Carl Gustav 309
Jünger, Ernst 221
Kämper, Birgit 99
Kandinsky, Wassily 53, 54
Kant, Immanuel 182, 302
Katzenberg, Jeffrey 268
Kay, Alan 187
Kelly, Kevin 176
Kelly, Richard 257
Kieślowski, Krzysztof 147
Kilger, Gerhard 376, 377
Kirby, Lynne 44
Kittler, Friedrich 231, 268
Klein, Melanie 237
Koebner, Thomas 101
Kolhaas, Rem 305
Kondo, Tetsuo 33, 34
Kracauer, Siegfried 47, 52, 53
Kubrick, Stanley 112, 157, 315
Kuert, Beat 295
Lagier, Luc 98
Lane, Anthony 184, 196
Le Corbusier 285, 286, 289–291
Leary, Timothy 167
Ledoux, Jacques 98
Lee, Elan 190
Lelouch, Claude 45, 146f.
Lem, Stanisław 208–210
Lenoir, Tim 268
Lévi-Strauss, Claude 256
Levin, Golan (see Tmema)
Lewontin, Richard C. 270
Licklider, Joseph Carl Robnett 190
Lie Kaas, Nikolaj 160
Lieberman, Zachary (see Tmema)
Lingwood, James 27
Lipps, Theodor 51, 126, 284, 285
Lisberger, Steven 167
Loiperdinger, Martin 44
Lombard, Matthew 216
Loos, Adolf 305
Lowood, Henry 268
Lübbren, Nina 322
Lucas, George 46, 171, 188, 265
Lucretius 222
Lukács, Georg 169
Lumière, Auguste 44, 145, 185, 285
Lumière, Louis 44, 145, 185, 285
Lurf, Johann 102–104
Lynn, Greg 306
MacDonald, Scott 55
Mack, Heinz 30
Magherini, Graziella 91
Magritte, René 305
Mahler, Andreas 12
Malinoski, Bronisław 256
Manovich, Lev 48, 49, 182, 188
Mantle, Anthony Dod 161
Marais, Jean 4, 5
Marker, Chris 97, 99
Marx, Karl 169, 307
Massumi, Brian 131
Maturana, Humberto 207
Mayer, Carl 151
Mäyrä, Frans 168
McDowell, Alex 173

McLuhan, Marshall 169
McTiernan, John 255
Meissner, Franz 328–330, 332, 333, 335
Menzies, William Cameron 5
Mersch, Dieter 113
Métra, Brigitte 295
Meuron, Pierre de (see Herzog & Meuron)
Michaud, Philippe-Alain 242
Mikkelsen, Mads 159
Milla, Johannes 366
Millais, John Everett 23
Montgomery, Robert 146
Moore, Michael 264
Morales, Evo 262, 263, 272
Morris, Robert 31
Motonaga, Sadamasa 31
Mühl, Otto 209
Muller, Lizzie 74
Muratori, Saverio 309
Murnau, Friedrich Wilhelm 96, 139, 151
Murray, Janet 6, 11, 13, 28, 49, 112, 166, 175
Muthesius, Hermann 305
Nadar 145
Négroni, Jean 98
Neuenfels, Benedict 161
Neumann, John von 171, 187
Neveldine, Mark 167
Niblo, Fred 149
Nietzsche, Friedrich 239, 311, 315
Nitsch, Hermann 209
Noé, Gaspar 111–113, 115–118, 120–125, 127–133
Noiret, Philippe 157
Nolan, Christopher 167, 257
Nolde, Emil 26
Norris, Jeff 167
Nouvel, Jean 281, 286–289, 291–295
Novak, Kim 98
Novak, Marcos 1
Novarro, Ramon 149
Obama, Barack 273
Ockman, Joan 281, 285
Odin, Roger 256
Ofak, Ana 271
Oiticica, Hélio 10
Ortega y Gasset, José 182
Pallasmaa, Juhani 295
Palmer, Clive 380
Papenburg, Bettina 7
Paul, Christiane 68
Péréz-Gómez, Alberto 295
Pfisterer, Ulrich 141
Piene, Otto 30
Plato 304
Poe, Edgar Allan 111
Pollet, Jean-Marie 293
Pomian, Krzysztof 363–365, 368, 371
Porter, Edwin S. 353
Propp, Vladimir 256
Pross, Harry 193
Prückner, Tilo 157
Puaux, Françoise 287
Pudovkin, Vsevolod 286
Puyn, Albert 167
Quagliata, Luigi 288
Rasmussen, Steen Eiler 286
Rattenbury, Kester 294
Reeves, Keanu 6
Reimann, Aribert 228
Remes, Justin 56
Renoir, Jean 150
Ribisi, Giovanni 270
Richter, Gerhard 26
Richter, Sonja 160

Riegl, Alois 312, 321–325, 327, 329, 335, 338–340
Rivero, Enrique 3
Robertson, Morgan 362
Robiquet, Pierre 221
Roddenberry, Gene 167
Rokeby, David 79, 80
Rosa, Hartmut 337
Rose, Frank 166, 171
Rossi, Aldo 309
Rusnak, Josef 167
Ruysdael, Jacob van 325
Ryan, Marie-Laure 11, 22, 166, 175, 179, 347
Sadoul, Georges 142
Salen, Katie 68, 69, 167, 168
Salt, Barry 96
Sánchez-Crespo, Daniel 190
Sann, Oliver 215, 219, 220, 238–242
Schanz, Peter 26
Schell, Jesse 189, 196
Schemat, Stefan 71, 73, 79
Schilling, Niklaus 139, 157, 159
Schivelbusch, Wolfgang 43, 44
Schlemmer, Oskar 184
Schmitt, Carl 219, 222
Schopenhauer, Arthur 315
Schweinitz, Jörg 89
Schwitters, Kurt 184
Scofidio, Ricardo (see Diller + Scofidio)
Scorsese, Martin 156, 265
Scorzin, Pamela C. 377
Seeber, Guido 149, 153
Shannon, Claude E. 171, 187
Sharp, Willoughby 21
Shaw, Jeffrey 8, 68
Shyamalan, M. Night 257
Simmel, Georg 7, 182, 324
Simmen, Jeannot 101
Sims, James E. 369, 371, 372, 374
Skladanowsky, Emil 285
Skladanowsky, Max 285
Sloterdijk, Peter 7, 101, 221, 222, 303
Snow, Michael 104
Snyder, Zack 173
Sobchack, Vivian 119, 120, 122
Søborg, Martin 159
Solimini, Angelo G. 90
Souriau, Etienne 96
Spielberg, Steven 176, 190, 259, 265, 268
Spier, Anna 331, 338
Springer, Anton 330
Steen, Paprika 160
Stendhal 91, 92
Stewart, James 99
Stewart, Sean 190
Stindt, Georg Otto 149
Stoermer, Fabian 94
Stoffer, Hellmut 25
Stoichita, Victor I. 3
Stone, Oliver 258
Streuli, Beat 23, 26
Sutherland, Ivan 205, 206, 208, 209, 211
Tarantino, Quentin 256, 266
Tashlin, Frank 206
Tavernier, Bertrand 157
Taylor, Brian 167
Tegmark, Max 57–59
Thoma, Hans 321, 324, 325, 327–335, 337–340
Thon, Jan-Noël 216, 239
Tmema 75, 78
Trier, Lars von 123, 159
Turner, Joseph Mallord William 34
Turrell, James 10, 27–30

Uccello, Paolo 91
Uecker, Günther 30
Valéry, Paul 303
Vertov, Dziga 126, 127, 150
Vidler, Anthony 285
Vinterberg, Thomas 159, 161
Virilio, Paul 101, 268, 287
Vischer, Friedrich Theodor 333
Vogt, Günther 33
Voss, Christiane 24, 146
Wachowski, Andy 6, 167, 208, 209
Wachowski, Lana 6, 167, 208, 209
Wagner, Monika 21
Wagner, Richard 143, 196, 302, 314, 315
Walton, Kendall L. 12
Warburg, Aby 220, 224, 225
Waterhouse, John William 23
Weaver, Sigourney 270
Weber, Max 217
Weibel, Peter 7
Weiner, Andrew Stefan 224
Wellbery, David 322
Welles, Orson 265
Wells, Herbert George 5
Wheeler, Doug 27
Wiener, Oswald 208–210
Wiese, Stephan von 30
Wolf, Werner 12
Wollen, Peter 97
Yoon, Carol Kaesuk 260
Zimmerman, Eric 68, 69, 167, 168
Žižek, Slavoj 261, 264, 269